The Elementary School Teacher

THE

Elementary School Teacher

VOLUME X

SEPTEMBER, 1909—JUNE, 1910

CHICAGO
The University of Chicago Press
1910

Published
September, October, November, December, 1909
January, February, March, April, May, June, 1910

Composed and Printed By
The University of Chicago Press
Chicago, Illinois, U. S. A.

INDEX TO VOLUME X

INDEX TO ARTICLES

* Names marked with an asterisk indicate authors of books reviewed.

* Names marked with an asterisk indicate authors of books reviewed.

INDEX TO AUTHORS

* Names marked with an asterisk indicate authors of books reviewed.

* Names marked with an asterisk indicate authors of books reviewed.

VOLUME X NUMBER I

THE ELEMENTARY SCHOOL TEACHER

SEPTEMBER, 1909

QUALITATIVE ELIMINATION FROM SCHOOL

WALTER FENNO DEARBORN
The University of Chicago

It is considered that one good way to test the efficiency of a school system is to determine what proportion of the pupils who enter school in the early years are finally graduated. Those schools in which a large proportion of pupils remain for eight or twelve years of study are on this basis considered to be superior schools, and those which have a very large percentage of elimination throughout the succeeding grades are similarly judged to be more or less inefficient. A somewhat better criterion than the mere number of graduates would evidently be a determination of what sort of pupils finish school. Whether, or in what proportion, those who might benefit most by school instruction are the ones who actually get it, is a question that school authorities ought undoubtedly to be able to answer. The facts in regard to the first question are known with a fair degree of accuracy in the case of a very few cities in the country. It has, indeed, only recently been recognized that such information in regard to the output of a school system had any particular significance. This is in itself a commentary on the backwardness of educational investigation. The second question has hardly been raised. There is doubtless plenty of opinion on the subject, but it is probably not more accurate than the opinion held a few years ago that practically all pupils in our best city schools finished at least the grammar grades; whereas it is now recognized through recent investigation that certainly not over one-half of them do so.

Similarly, it is probably the current opinion that those who drop out of school are on the whole decidedly inferior students.

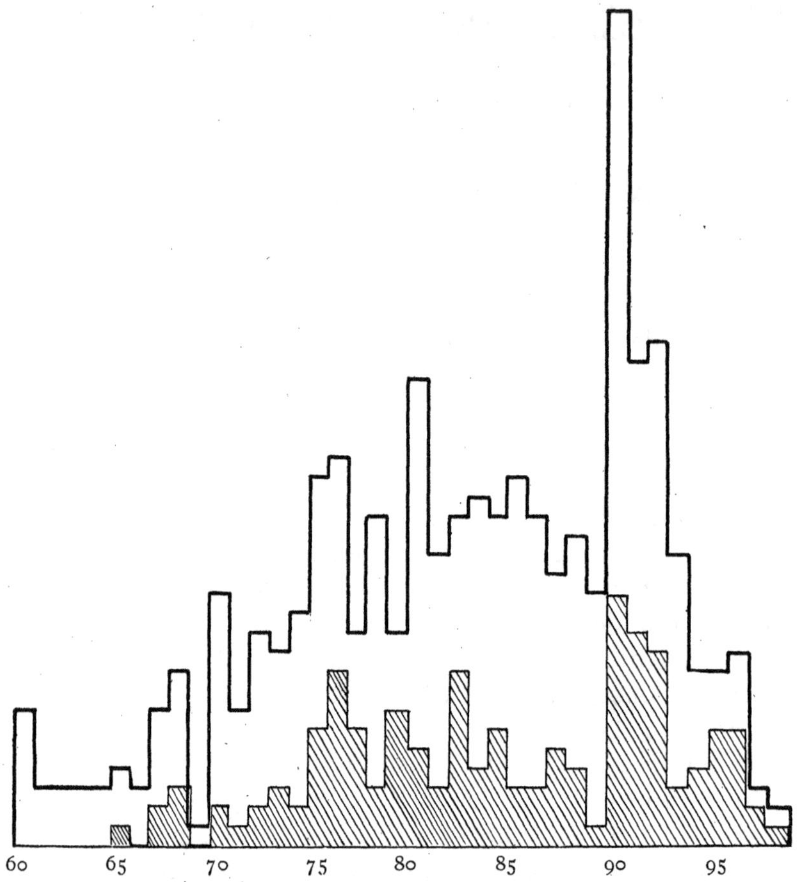

CHART IA.—Standings (or marks) of 486 pupils in the English classes of Grades 3–8 inclusive of City I. Median for total groups =82 per cent. Those in shaded columns entered high school, 146 in number, 91 above and 55 below median.

Whether this is actually so, is a question that is worth answering from merely economic, if not from more general considerations. The object of the present study is largely to call attention to the problem and suggest some satisfactory methods for its investigation. The question may be studied to greatest advantage in smaller cities where there is sufficient acquaintance on the part of the teachers with the causes which take pupils out of school to enable them to follow up the cases; to know, for instance, that leaving school is not merely a transfer to some other public or private school. The problem is of sufficient financial importance alone to the city concerned to make it one that a superintendent

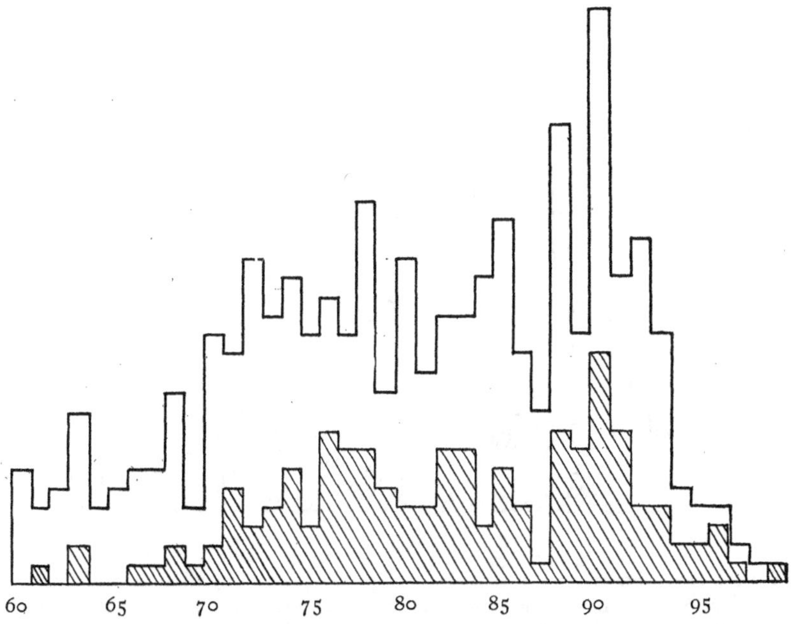

CHART IB.—Standings (or marks) of 445 pupils in classes in arithmetic, Grades 3–8 inclusive, of City I. Median for total group = 81 per cent. Those in shaded columns entered high school, 146 in number, 84 above and 62 below median.

or principal might study to advantage. Detailed information in regard to the facts for a period of several years would also be of considerable general interest and value.

Some results in regard to the quality of the elimination from school in the case of two cities in the state of Wisconsin are presented below, and for the purpose of somewhat more completeness several typical classes have been followed through the state university. Such a study, if carried out with the requisite attention to details—which, it should be added, has not been attempted here—would furnish a survey of an important aspect of an educational system from the primary school through the university. It would determine what sort of raw material goes into the finished product.

In this particular study the school's own judgment of the relative abilities of its pupils, as indicated by the marks or grades assigned them has been accepted as a basis for determining what kind of pupils remain or drop out of school. Whether the school as a selective agency recognizes a sufficiently wide range

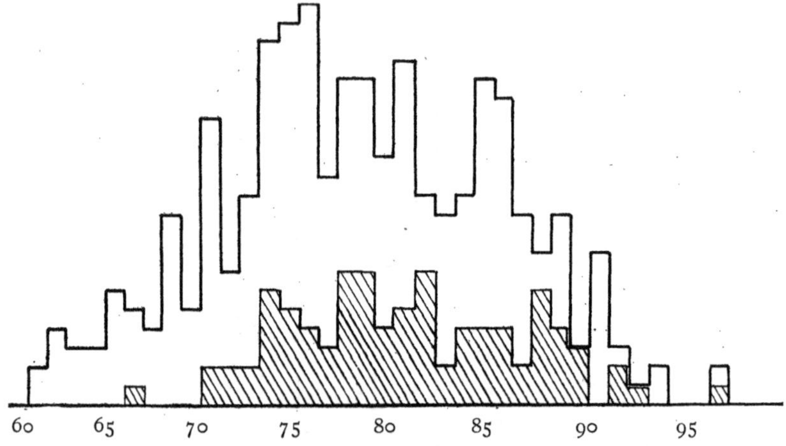

CHART IIA.—Standings (or marks) of 322 pupils in the English classes of Grades 3–8 inclusive of City II. Median for total group = 78 per cent Those in the shaded columns entered high school, 88 in number, 56 above and 32 below median.

of abilities is, for example, a question which is not raised. Accepting the school's own standards, the problem is simply to determine in how far the best pupils are selected for further instruction.

Three groups of pupils have been studied; one group has been followed through the grades of the two cities mentioned above, and a similar group has been traced through the high schools of each city, and finally a group of about five hundred has been followed through the first two years of the state university.

ELIMINATION IN THE GRADES

In the first case, the group chosen was the freshman class of each high school. Their standings in the last six grades of the grammar schools from which they came have been compared with the standings of their former classmates in these schools who did not go to high schools, or at least did not go to the high schools in these cities. This comparison has been made for two typical subjects of study, English and mathematics, for the reason that some form of these studies is found in all the grades. In the accompanying charts for this group (Charts I A and B

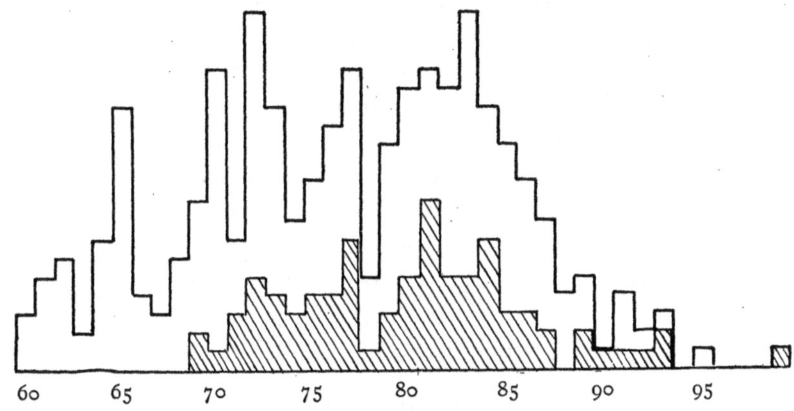

CHART IIB.—Standings (or marks) of 302 pupils in the classes in arithmetic in Grades 3–8 inclusive of City II. Median for total group = 77 per cent. Those in the shaded columns entered high school, 84 in number, 58 above and 26 below median.

and II A and B) the shaded columns show what ranks the school group maintained in the grammar school, the remaining unshaded columns show the ranks of those who did *not* go to high school. The horizontal line at the base of the columns indicates the grades assigned, etc., from 60 to 100, and the height of the corresponding column the number of pupils who attained these grades. In City I for example (see Chart I A) there are in all 486 pupils in English; of these 146 got as far as freshman year in the high school. The *median grade* of the whole group is 82, that is, approximately one half of the whole group secures 82 or a higher grade, and the other half 82 or a lower grade. Of those who entered the high school, eighty-four had thus been in the upper halves of the English classes in the grades and sixty-two in the lower halves. In Arithmetic (see Chart I B), the median grade of the whole group is 81; eighty-four of those who reached the high school stood above this grade in grammar school, and sixty-two of them below it. About 40 per cent. (38 per cent. and *42 per cent.) of those who reached the freshman class of this high school had stood in the lower halves of their classes in English and arithmetic in the grammar school.* In the case of City II (see Chart II, A and B) about one third of the freshman class of the high school had been in the lower halves of their classes in English and arithmetic in the grammar school.

As noted above, some of the pupils undoubtedly moved away to other cities and entered other high schools or attended private academies. This is an error for which no correction has been attempted in this study. Viewing the matter, however, purely from the standpoint of the efficiency of the school system under examination one third of the pupils who were caught in its meshes, so to speak, were of an inferior sort; and the opposite fact is equally true, that over a third of the pupils who slipped through were superior students.

ELIMINATION IN THE HIGH SCHOOL

A method similar to that employed in the study of the grades has been followed in the case of the high schools of these two cities. The accompanying charts have in this case been constructed somewhat differently in that the shaded columns indicate the ranks of those who entered, but did *not* finish the high school course. A study of the charts (see Chart III, A and B) seems to indicate that there is a marked difference in the relative influence of the two subjects under examination—namely, English and mathematics[1]—on the elimination; 27 per cent. of those who dropped out of one school and 28 per cent. of those who dropped out of the other school had been

[1] Physics was included under mathematics in the case of the high school studies.

ranked in the first halves of their classes in English, whereas 38 per cent. and 41 per cent. respectively were in the upper halves of their classes in mathematics. That is, the pupils who dropped

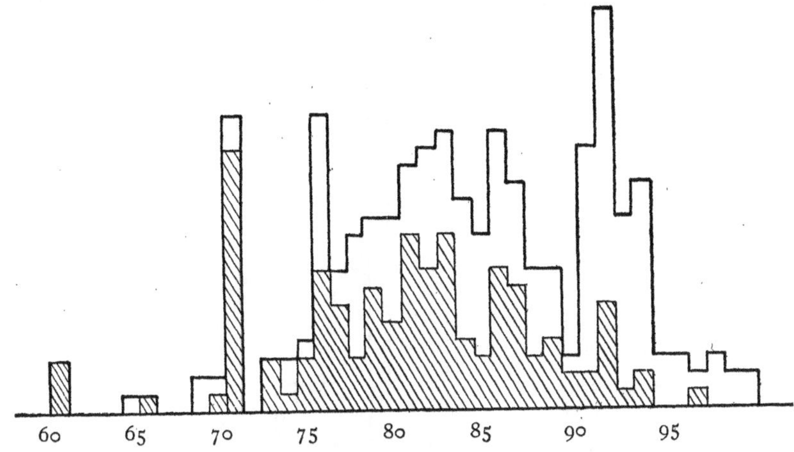

CHART IIIA.—Standings (or marks) of 285 pupils in the English classes of the high school (City I). Median of total group = 85 per cent. *Those in the shaded columns dropped out before the end of the senior year,* the total number eliminated being 129, 36 above and 93 below median.

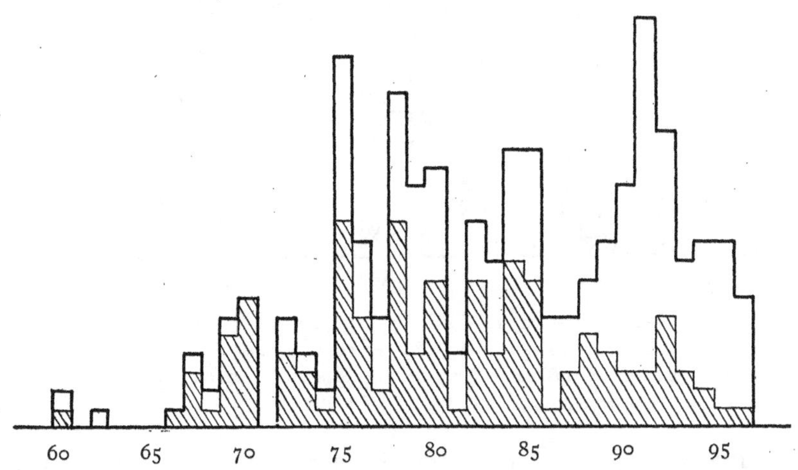

CHART IIIB.—Standing (or marks) of 287 pupils in the classes in mathematics in the high school (City I). Median of total group = 83 per cent. *Those in the shaded columns dropped out before the end of the senior year,* the total number eliminated being 129, 53 above and 76 below median.

out were on the whole better in mathematics than in English. This may be a coincidence, although it occurs in the case of these two schools situated in very different sorts of cities. Taking an average of the standings in these two subjects of study, it appears

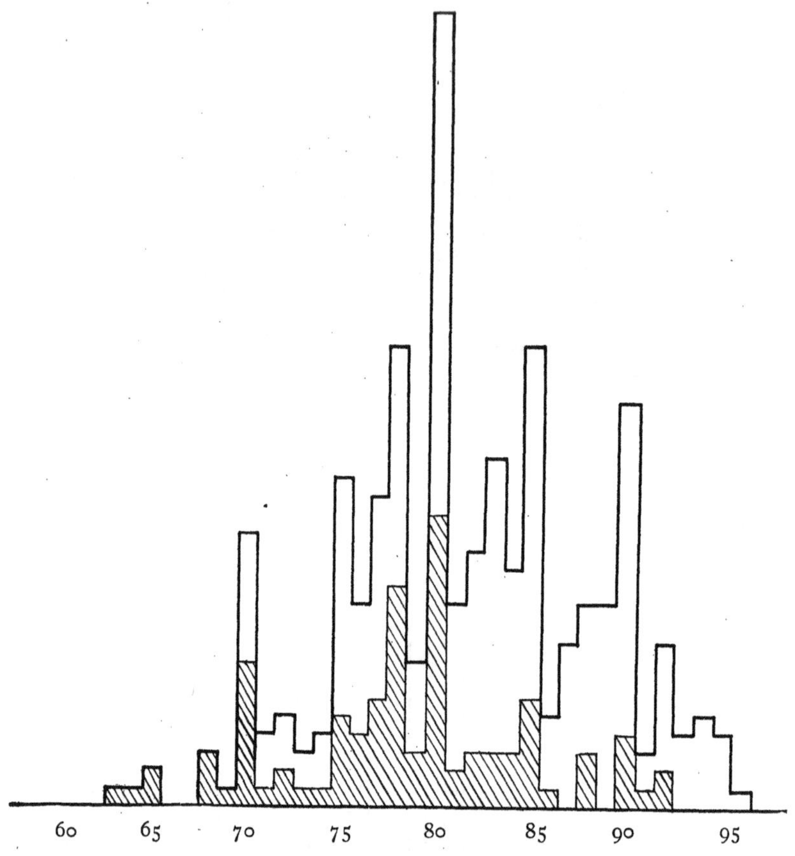

CHART IVA.—Standings (or marks) of 333 pupils in the English classes of the high school (City II). Median of group = 82 per cent. *Those in the shaded columns dropped out before the end of the senior year,* the total number eliminated being 95, 26 above and 69 below median.

that fully one third of those who dropped out during the course of the high school are students who have ranked in the upper halves of their classes while they remained in the high school. It will be recalled that in the last section it was shown that fully a third of the members of this class had been in the lower halves of their classes in grammar school.[2] If now we add to this the fact that a third of the better students of the class dropped out of the high school course, it appears that those who actually finish

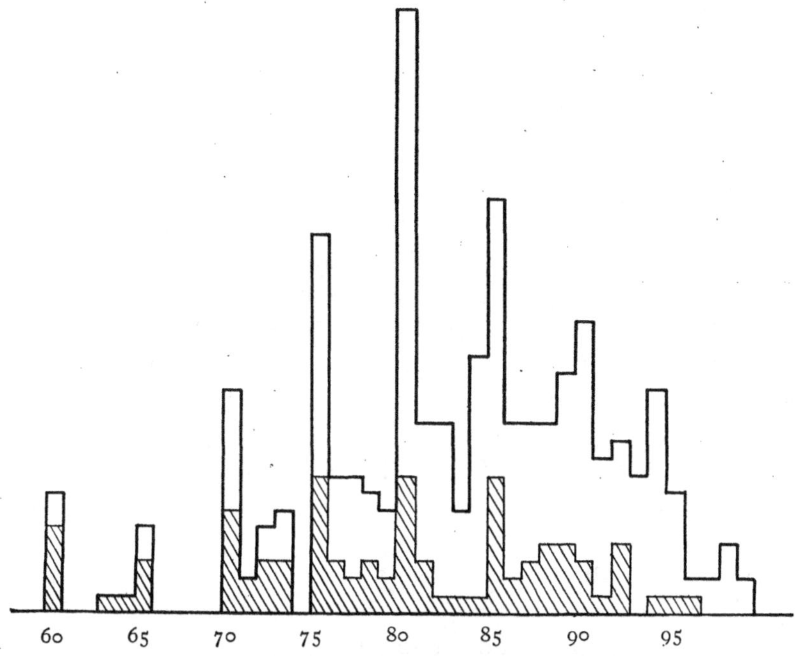

CHART IVB.—Standing (or marks) of 297 pupils in the classes in mathematics in the high school (City II). Median of total groups = 83 per cent. *Those in ths shaded columns dropped out before the end of senior year,* t ?e number eliminated being 88, 34 above and 54 below median.

do not represent a very high order of selection from the pupils who originally started.

It, of course, must be held in mind that the scope of this study and the number of cases involved are not sufficient to warrant any final conclusions on this subject. It should also be remembered that the study began with third grade pupils. The

[2] These two groups, i.e., the third of poor students who enter high school and the third of superior students who drop out are not the same individuals, because there is a definite tendency for pupils to maintain in the high school the same relative rank which they had in the grammar school.

elimination of the earlier grades is undoubtedly very largely based on mental inability, but in the later years it is probable that ability plays a decreasingly less important part.

ELIMINATION FROM THE UNIVERSITY[3]

The group studied in the case of the university entered from eight different high schools, three of them located in the city of Milwaukee, one in Madison, and the remaining four in smaller cities of the state. There were 472 pupils in the group, and they entered the University of Wisconsin during the years 1900 to 1905 inclusive. Their standing as indicated in the accompanying chart has been based on the general averages of all the grades secured by the individual students during freshman year. Out of this group of 472, 93 or 19.7 per cent. left the university during the freshman year, and 43 or 12 per cent. during sophomore year, a total of 136, or 31.7 per cent. of elimination in the two years. In other words, about one third of the group were eliminated in the first two years of college. In this case, however, there is a distinct difference in the quality of the elimination in that only about 12 per cent. were from the upper half of the class.

In order to indicate somewhat more clearly this distribution of pupils in the class, the group has been divided into four quarters, or "quartiles," and the number and percentage of those dropped in each quartile has been indicated in the accompanying table. The first quartile indicates those who ranked in the first quarter of the freshman class on the basis of the general average of the grades secured in the various subjects. The second quartile similarly includes those who stood in the second quarter of the class. As may be seen in the accompanying table, about 50 per cent. of those eliminated were from the lowest quarter of the class, 23 per cent. and 17 per cent. respectively from the third and second quarters of the class, and less than 10 per cent. from the first quarter.

[3] Several paragraphs in this section have been quoted with some modifications from a recent monograph by the writer on "The Relative Standing of Pupils in the High School and in the University," *Bulletin of the University of Wisconsin*, High-School Series, No. 6.

ELIMINATIONS DURING FRESHMAN YEAR
UNIVERSITY OF WISCONSIN

(Total Number in Group, 472; Number in Each Quartile, 118)

		Percentage of Total in Quartile	Percentage of Total Eliminations
First Quartile........	9	7.6	9.7
Second Quartile......	16	13.6	17.2
Third Quartile.......	21	17.8	22.6
Fourth Quartile......	47	39.8	50.5
	93		

ELIMINATIONS DURING SOPHOMORE YEAR
UNIVERSITY OF WISCONSIN

		Percentage of Total in Quartile	Percentage of Total Eliminations
First Quartile........	4	4.5	9.2
Second Quartile......	7	7.9	16.1
Third Quartile.......	10	11.2	23.1
Fourth Quartile......	22	24.4	51.6
	43		

Similar percentages hold of the high school quartiles (based on standing in high school). Only 15 per cent. of those eliminated in freshman year were in the first quarter of their high school classes, whereas 42 per cent. of them were in the lowest quarter of the high school class. The eliminations of the sophomore year are much less dependent on high school standing, and correspond more closely with the university standing.

Rank in high school has, therefore, as is to be expected, a definite relation to the question of elimination in the university. It is evident from these results that a student entering the university from these schools with a rank or general average of 85 or above, for example, is much more likely to continue through freshman year than that one whose high school rank was below 85. In this case there were 244 (56.9 per cent.) of the group who attained this or a higher rank in high school, but 29, or 12 per cent. of them drop out during freshman year, whereas, of the remaining 228, 64 or 27.5 per cent. are eliminated.

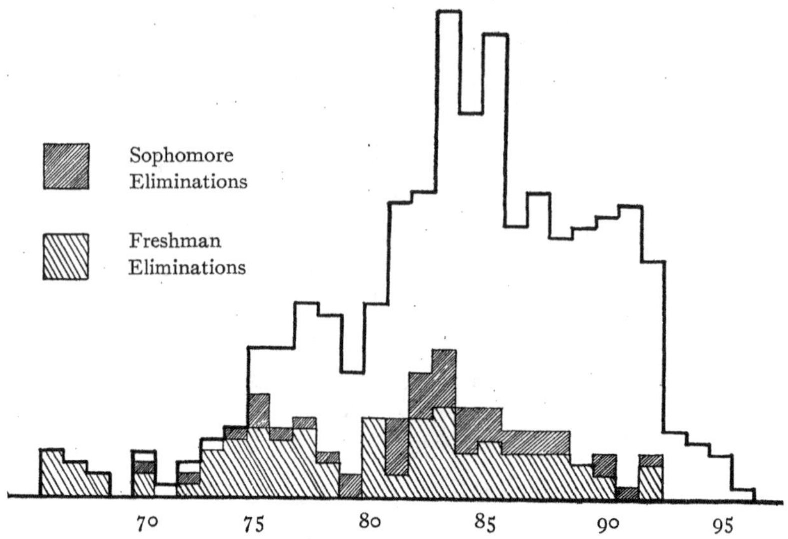

CHART V.—Standings (general averages of all grades) secured by 472 pupils during freshman year at the University of Wisconsin. Those in the shaded columns were eliminated during freshman and sophomore years. (See accompanying table of eliminations.)

The schools or cities from which the pupils come appear also to have some influence in the matter of elimination from the university. The number of cases is rather too small, however, to more than indicate a possible tendency. The largest percentage of elimination is in the case of pupils from Milwaukee, and the smallest from the group of four high schools. The facts are as follows: 40 out of 139, or 29 per cent. of those who entered from the Milwaukee high schools, did not remain in the university after freshman year; in the case of Madison, the figures are, 49 out of 238, or 20.6 per cent. and in the case of the four smaller high schools but 10 out of the 92 who entered, or 11 per cent., were eliminated.

CONCLUSIONS

The somewhat limited data presented above indicate that in the two cities studied fully a third of the very small number of pupils who reached high school had been inferior students in the grades. This group is further reduced by extensive elimination in the high school, and at least one third of those who dropped out were students who ranked in the upper half of their classes in the high school.[1] This goes to show that the pupils prepared for entrance to the university from these schools at least represented at most an average grade of ability; they were certainly not a highly selected group.

Elimination from the university is based more on standards of scholarship than is the case in the high school or grammar school, and is relatively less influenced by other factors.

Rank in high school has a definite relation to the question of elimination in the university, only about 10 per cent. of those who stood in the first quarter of their high school classes dropped out of the university during freshman year, whereas 50 per cent. of those who were in the lowest quarter of their high school classes left the university before the completion of this year.

These conclusions are based on the school's own judgment of the efficiency of its pupils as indicated by the school marks assigned them. It is generally thought at present that the school as an institution does not recognize a sufficiently wide range of abilities. If this is so, we may be justified in concluding that with the exception of the elimination of the first few years of school, the pupils who drop out are as a group very nearly as well qualified for further study as those who remain throughout the course of study in the high school and university.

[1] See footnote to p. 9.

FIELD NOTES IN READING

II. THE READING IMPULSE

MARY E. LAING
Boston, Mass.

The investigation of the reading process made by psychologists in the last ten years gives some valuable insight into its inner aspects and clears up several important questions. First of all it shows us that the reading process involves a very specific eye training.

When we read the eyes move across the line in jerks or short sweeps, pausing with somewhat regular periodicity from point to point to the end of the line. Then they sweep back and "pick up" the next line, repeating the same forward movement of fixating, "springing forward," fixating again, etc., until the end of the line is included in the last fixation when another backward sweep is made. *Seeing takes place at these points of fixation.*

The eyes move with great swiftness between these fixation points. This is shown in the fact that out of the total time in reading from 12/13 to 23/24 is consumed by fixations, leaving only a small fraction of time (from 1/13 to 1/24 of the total time) for the forward movement of the "eye-sweeps."

With a trained reader, all this eye-activity is reflex and rhythmical, the fixation pauses falling with a pretty regular periodicity and automatic ease.[1]

The eye-strain in reading and more especially in learning to read, is much greater than has been supposed. An absolutely new set of eye-movements, very exacting in their nature, must be acquired and reach an automatic perfection.

Small type, fancy lettering, broken lines, lines too long or too short, poor lighting—all these things increase the eye-strain.

[1] Cf. Huey, *The Psychology and Pedagogy of Reading* (Macmillan) and Laing, *Reading, A Manual for Teachers* (D. C. Heath & Co.).

The second great difficulty in learning to read, lies in the reflex mastery of words.

Professor Cattell in making his study of word perception, tested two rather obtuse porters. They required three times as

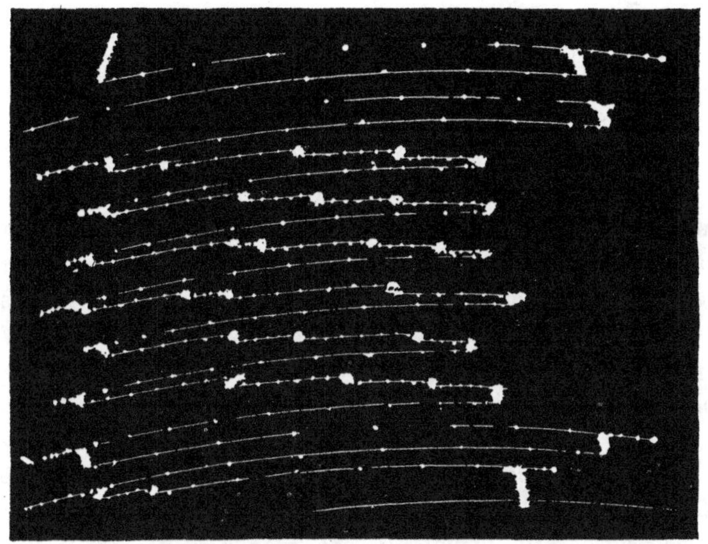

FIG. 1.—SPECIMEN CURVE OF "SPARK" RECORD

This reproduction, cut by a careful engraver upon a block on which the original tracing had been photographed, shows with great accuracy the sort of record from which the times of the eye-movements have been determined. The chief difference between the original and the reproduction is in the breadth of the horizontal lines which are finer in the original. The curve shows the movements of the eye in reading six lines, preceded and followed by two free movements of the eye each way, in which it was swept from one end of the line to the other, the beginning and end alone being fixated. The broad vertical lines and the round blurs in the reading indicate pauses in the eye-movements, the successive sparks knocking the soot away from a considerable space. The small dots standing alone or like beads upon the horizontal lines, show the passage of single sparks, separated from each other by 0.0068 sec. The breaks in the horizontal lines indicate that the writing-point was not at all times in contact with the surface of the paper though near enough for the spark to leap across, as shown by the solitary dots. The tracing shows clearly the fixation pauses in the course of the line, the general tendency to make the "indentation" greater at the right than at the left, and the unbroken sweep of the return from right to left. The cut and description are reproduced by permission from the *American Journal of Psychology,* Vol. XI, from an article written by Professor Edmund Burke Huey.

long as educated people to read a letter or a word.[2] In no art or craft do we expect to develop the trained hand and eye with their acquired co-ordinations and fine, multiple accommodations, except through long and varied practice which draws them into the service of chosen activities. All skill is reflex in character. The acquisition of this reflex power takes time. *The reflex power over words is a skill.*

As we have seen in a former article *meaning or connection is an indispensable element in recognizing words.* Meaning makes the true "attention span" in the reading-process. All else must become automatic. The visual imaging of words is marginal, *meaning is always central, in consciousness.* When it becomes marginal the reading process is crippled and unproductive. This means that we read not wordwise but sentence and paragraph-wise and always meaningwise. *The thought-grasp makes the true reading-impulse.*

This suggests two important facts: *Learning to read is getting control of a new and specific mode of thinking. Word-functioning in reading is bound up in this forward-moving thought-process.* The energy of the reader's mental imagery brings the automatic visualizing of words under its control. This is in harmony with the general psychological law that reflex functions play into and support the higher voluntary activities from which they receive their controlling impulse.

Learning to think through printed words is the third great difficulty in mastering reading. It is reading and everything else is tributary to it. Dr. Zeitler's discovery [3] that the definite fixing of the letters in the word rests in meaning attests this. We *see* the word-form but we recognize it from the thought side of the process.

The greatest contribution to reading made by the psychological laboratory has been to the reading process *per se.* When Professor Cattell discovered that we can grasp twice as many words in a single fixation when they are given in connection, he blazed the way to the most important discovery for reading,

[2] *Brain,* VIII, 299.

[3] Wundt, *Philosophische Studien,* Vol. XVI.

viz., that the perception of meaning dominates word-recognition and makes the essential forward impulse in the reading process.

In all silent reading there is first an automatic perception of word-forms that is marginal in consciousness; accompanying this, there is a grasp of thought or meaning, central in consciousness. The eye runs ahead and the words are imaged; the assimilative process follows a little behind and puts meaning into the word-forms which are now fully perceived.

The process might be illustrated thus:

FIG. 2.—ILLUSTRATING FORWARD MOVEMENT IN SILENT READING

A represents the true attention span or the assimilative process; *B*, the running ahead of the eye in mere visualizing of words.

In reading aloud a new line of activity is added, viz., action of voice and speech with some activity of the ear. In this case vocalization follows a little behind assimilation. *Meaning passes over* into motor expression; we have really joined the assimilative process involved in reading to a process of interpreting meaning. Meaning still dominates and unifies the whole activity both central and motor.

FIG. 3.—ILLUSTRATING FORWARD MOVEMENT IN ORAL READING

A, Central process of assimilation; *B*, Motor-ocular activity; *C*, Vocal accompaniment.

There are several factors that determine the distance between eye and voice in oral reading, as familiarity with content, mastery of words, etc. Dr. Quantz thinks that on an average the eye is 5.4 words ahead of the voice in oral reading.

The thought unit operates in determining the activity of both eye and voice. Dr. Dearborn believes that a new fixation of the eye is made for each unit of perception; the phrase, the clause, the short sentence tend to be units of fixation because they are so grasped by the mind. Professor Scripture [4] believes that the idea or thought determines the "speech-unit." "The fundamental law of speech-melody, is, in my opinion," says Professor Scripture, "that each speech-unit has a convex, that is, rising-falling (or circumflex) melody. This is varied to produce effects of expression."

That meaning fills the mind and dominates the process is further shown by Dr. Dearborn's conclusion that the mind anticipates what is coming so that "while the eye is reading in one line the mind is vaguely conscious of matter lying in succeeding lines. The reading-impulse is distinctly forward-urging. "The attention is ahead and pulling the eye along" and the voice follows—we might add, to tell what the mind perceives.

Unquestionably there has been too much emphasis on oral reading. The thought process is pre-eminently at home in silent reading, where reader and author are "at one." The audience or auditor, which oral reading always supposes, disturbs this relation between reader and book. The thinking process takes on a modified quality in oral reading. It is probable that a vigorous receptive process is always modified when it takes on expressive activity. The receptive activity may still be present but is a *modified form of receptivity*. To make oral reading the dominating thing means that the teacher of reading never helps the child to get down to that intimacy with the book which characterizes the "reader" and which alone makes the best oral reading possible.

But the complexity of the oral process should condemn it as the dominating mode of procedure. If we look at the brain areas active in oral reading we have at least visual center, motor-speech center, auditory center, and association areas for reading. Add to this the complex eye-activity that is present and the result is a process of great complexity. Strike out oral reading and the brain areas active are probably *one-half less*. We have forced children into habits of oral pronunciation by blindly putting an almost impossible burden on them. And even where they have escaped this we have failed to make them

[4] *Experimental Phonetics.*

efficient thinkers with the book—we have defeated the great end of reading by robbing it of its vigorous inner impulse.

There is no doubt that everything that enhances the central process contributes to the reading impulse. *Interest in the thread of the narration or description is the great natural incentive in reading.*

The energy of the reading impulse depends on the wealth of associations which the words in connection call up. But making a reader means much more than this: it means a training in perceiving, thinking, getting connections with mastery. This makes a vivid and truly interesting content possible. In such power lies the discriminating love of the book and of being with the book that marks the real reader.

The study of the rate in reading is most suggestive for an understanding of the process itself. When Dr. J. O. Quantz found[5] that his rapid readers remembered more of the original thought, that the character of their reproduction was better both with reference to expression and logical content—when he found in other words that his rapid readers were his best readers he brought forward another proof showing that the *dynamic of reading lies in the assimilative process.*

Thought is incredibly quick. Swiftly the mind uses its ideas in grasping a relation, forming a logical sequence, getting a completed image or picture. On the language side we begin with a sentence, read paragraph after paragraph, chapter after chapter, and at last we have the book. On the mental side we grasp thought after thought, until the import of a minor whole is grasped and this simply becomes a significant relation to be joined to the next unity so that a larger whole may be grasped. Reading is a process of *cumulative thinking.*

On the whole the practice in the best primary schools is in striking harmony with the results of laboratory study.

Reading is made a process of thought-getting. Word drills and phonic analysis are separated from the work in reading proper. There is an effort made to so thoroughly master the

[5] *Problems in the Psychology of Reading.*

word that its recognition may become subservient to the needs of a reader. Short sentences, or words that stand for the sentence, are introduced at once and the child *reads* these. And all the while the child is helped to form intelligent mental imagery. In short, from the beginning, mental process is made the controlling factor.

But the reading activity is a larger thing than the wisest of us have suspected. Not in one year, nor in three, can it be mastered. To learn to read well is to learn to think vigorously and efficiently in not one field of literature, but several. The beginning may be made in the primary grades but if the work is accomplished by the school the upper grades must continue and greatly enlarge on the work already begun. *Training in reading as a process of thinking calls for expert work in higher grades.*

Beginning reading has been pretty thoroughly mastered in the last twenty-five years. The work of reading above the earliest grade has been little investigated. Psychological research points to reading as a complex mental process that it would require continuous training to master. The child who leaves the primary has some power in simple narrative reading, and little else. He must learn to grasp more complex narration. He must learn to grasp and enjoy description, argument, and the more logical forms of thought.

He should be tested by exercises in rate reading—always making grasp of content the test. There should be varied tests for content, irrespective of rate, as, for instance, tests in getting the central thought or main import of the paragraph, or chapter; tests in grasping the logical sequence or of seizing on to important details in narration or description, and tests of mental imagery.

We can in no wise teach reading well without giving at the same time a most valuable training that will react into all other school studies. The efficient reader will not only supplement his work in history, literature, nature-study, etc., by getting into the best books that are tributary to these, but he will bring to all his other activities a mental discipline which he has acquired by being *trained to read.*

III. THE CHILD AND THE BOOK

The present outlook in reading points definitely to the three great difficulties of the process: (1) definite eye-training accompanied by a complex and strenuous demand on the physical side of attention; (2) mastery of a vocabulary of printed words carried to a point that means ease of function in reading proper; (3) the mastery of a new mode of thinking which necessitates the exercise of attention under a new and strenuous form.

The process of imagery, of grasping sequences and connections and seizing on the import of literary wholes—stories, poems, descriptions—requires a high degree of mental alertness continuously exercised. The disciplinary value of reading as a means of augmenting mental power is probably much greater than most of us have supposed. It is one of the greatest disciplines of the school.

The impulse to read goes along with the power to read. It is almost certain that this power cannot be developed apart from a growing taste for some definite worth-while form of literature. As this reading power slowly develops in the child the great world of books begins to open, now in one aspect, now in another. That, out of the past, which has won survival through its intrinsic worth to the race: that, out of contemporary thought, which is vigorous, vitally worthful, and which suits the particular individual demand, it is now possible to begin to make a part of the child's inner experience.

The disciplinary value of reading is only matched by its enormous practical worth. To make a reader is to make a disciplined thinker. To make a reader is to educate. The outcome of this growing life with books ought to result in enabling the child gradually to get out of the past the best it has to give to him and it ought ultimately to put and keep him in touch with the currents of vital present-day movement. Reading more than any school study except history (which reading in this broad sense includes) should educate for citizenship. The reader only is fit to be a citizen.

The very great difficulties in mastering reading mean that from the beginning it must be strongly, and sustainedly *motived.* The *source* of this motive power must always *lie inside the process itself.* From the beginning the individual must find in reading a means for self-realization. This means that the content of reading must continually augment the inner life in such wise as to react helpfully into everyday experience. *The source of motive power in reading is the child's interest and this rests directly and surely in the content of reading and in nothing else.*

This makes the book itself an indispensable agent in making a reader. Given an intelligent and sympathetic teacher and the right things to read, and the rest follows.

This brings us to a great question: What does a child *want* to read? What *ought* he to read?

There is pretty strong evidence that the child's native tastes are strong and pure. The study of children's favorite books show that the appearance of an appetite for vitiating books comes rather late and arises out of wrong conditions rather than a native bent.

In making a study of the favorite books of 3,000 Boston children from the fourth to the ninth grades inclusive, the writer found that the trashy book appeared increasingly in upper grades and that girls more than boys were addicted to reading worthless books. When adolescence is reached, the boy is usually keenly interested in the activities and make-up of the world, distant and near. The girls' interests take on a stronger social-aesthetic character. The reading of the poet begins now if ever and the the drama and romance now make a strong appeal. The trashy stories read by girls may well arise from the fact that, the poets aside, the books well adapted to the needs of the adolescent girl are all too few. Meanwhile the boy reads too many books that take him into distant places away from his own life. It is safe to affirm that a truly worth-while book will always react helpfully into everyday life.

The school reader is responsible for two great things: (1)

It must develop *motive power* by awakening the child's interest; (2) it must keep this interest growing until it develops into a settled habit.

How do present-day reading-books meet this demand?

The reading-book has been under a process of rapid development for the last twenty-five years or more. Advance in the last ten years has been very marked. The number of reading-books that have appeared during this time is past belief.

In the Boston Public Library the writer ran over the very imperfect collection of reading-books—a collection made incidentally with no effort to be representative. In this collection the number of readers and sets of readers issued since 1890 reaches the astonishing number of forty-four, and this is far below the true figure since a great number of book-series are not represented there. Twenty-two of these series were issued between 1896 and 1898. Unfortunately a new set of readers does not necessarily mean an advance, although some of them show a distinct forward movement.

The making of the supplementary reader began fully thirty years ago. An idea prominent in the making of some of these early supplementary readers seemed to be to give the child *more of the same thing*. Such books were simply made up of "selections." But this has rapidly changed and the supplementary reader today in its choice and organization of matter is vitally adapted to the child's needs. It represents continuity of subject-matter, and is calculated to awaken a sustained interest. One has only to glance through such books as *In Field and Pasture* and *Hunting and Fishing* in Dutton's "World at Work Series," or read the books of Elizabeth Dopp on prehistoric man to realize that the supplementary reader is rapidly becoming the work of art that it should be.

The present-day supplementary reader is made by an expert. Perhaps in some cases it requires an expert to use it successfully. Miss Dopp's readers, giving progressively the story of prehistoric man in his slow upward climb toward civilization, are a markworthy illustration of this. A thoughtful student of ethnology cannot fail to see the enormous social-ethical value of these books and the great service they should render to the child's social-industrial education. In the hands of a teacher who gets meaning and beauty from the finished products of a developed civilization only, who has developed no sympathy for the humble beginnings of life, these books cannot be effectively used. But in this case the teacher and not the book is at fault.

During these last twenty-five years the regular reading series has improved markedly in at least three directions—in the choice and arrangement of content; in illustration and press-work; in the consideration of the reading-problem, especially at the beginning. Early pages have, however, been too much overloaded with "suggestions to teachers." The latest series improve on this by publishing a small suggestively written manual for the teacher, or by putting suggestions directly to the children, or by inserting remarks to teachers at the end of the book. When the child opens his book he should not find first of all something intended for another.

The presence of a manual in the book-series shows that the bookmaker is studying the whole situation of teaching reading—a very desirable indication which promises increasingly good things.

It would seem as if the book-illustration had well-nigh reached perfection—perhaps it has been overdone. There are indications in some of the series that have appeared in the last ten years, that the illustration has been made a means of selling the book. Especially is this true of the primer and first reader. Very shallow content has been "made to pass" because of the attractive pictures. Books must be first chosen for content, nevertheless illustrations are important adjuncts because of their relation to mental imagery.

Our study of mental imagery has hardly begun. We do not yet know to what extent the illustration helps the mental imagery of the reader or to what extent it may hinder it. Not many of us have ever been consciously helped in imaging Longfellow or Shakespeare or Eliot by the illustration. This, however, constitutes no argument. In reading of other lands, of natural history, etc., we have certainly been greatly helped by truthful pictures. Where the content has new facts for us and the appeal is to correct interpretation, the illustration that truthfully and suggestively pictures those facts is an enormous help. When the appeal is directly to the imagination as it is in very much of literature, the illustration may hinder, and merely suggestive illustrations rather than elaborate pictures are probably most valuable in such cases. But always the illustration must be subservient to the text: it is valuable in proportion as it vitally enhances the text. The danger in an art literature-series is of course that the content will be made up to "carry the pictures."

The essential *value of any book-series lies in its content.* A content to be valuable must be vitally *good for the individual who reads it.*

In selecting a content for the child's book, literature *good for* him is the aim of our quest. That which is good, and for which the child naturally and rightly has an appetite should be our standard.

The best books today have most of them been commendably successful in gathering classic gems, myths, stories, and folktales for children. The *modification* of this material has often been unpardonably poor. A classic is a classic because it has a content of enduring value which is embodied in a highly suitable form. "Adapting the classic" calls first of all for a *preservation of content.* The plot gives the large lines which embody the meaning. For this reason it is doubtful wisdom to change the plot. To illustrate: The story of "Little Red Riding Hood" appears in many book-series. In a majority of cases the effect of the adventure on Little Red Riding Hood herself is left out. According to an author like Grimm she is made to see that she has escaped a greater danger brought on because she *disobeyed her mother at the suggestion of the wolf and left the path:* the moral of the story is developed in the last line where the child says: "As long as I live I will never go out of the path when my mother tells me not to." The "modifier" of a child's classic so little sensitive to plot-significance as to leave this out has no right to "make over" stories for the education of children. But the writer in the majority of cases borrows a "made over" and simply inserts a few "attractive" changes more, to show that it is "his version."

Bookmakers should acquaint themselves with the original forms of classic literature. Bookbuyers should be assured that when a classic story is empty of meaning it has been garbled in content and is no longer a classic. If its empty form is dramatic it has been simply degraded into the field of sensational literature by the irresponsible bookmaker. A single classic so degraded should condemn a book: it is unfit for the child.

The *form of the classic should not be made commonplace.* This has been done *ad nauseam.* The "enlarging on" a condensed myth or folk-tale by the addition of poorly adapted details has been responsible for much abuse of the classic. The condensed form is not an objection. Writers of children's books should not be "space-fillers." The child's own story is brief, condensed, pointed: the stories that he seizes on with most interest are so; the stories best suited to memory are so.

The lack of continuity of thought, in fact the lack of any thought at all, spoils primers and first readers. This lack still mars the books fresh from the press. When an intelligent child could not possibly tell what he has read, it is safe to conclude that he has read nothing.

What adult could read a page from a child's primer or first reader after the fashion of "I see the cat;" "The cat sees me;" and tell an hour afterward what he has read. In our attempt to give the child graded first books we have simply given him word-lists disguised in the form of silly sentences that are falsely called "stories" in the reading-hour.

The content of the book must lie inside and not outside the child's power of interpretation. It must be within the reach of his own vital experience. Too often the writer is ignorant of the children for whom he is writing.

Apparently most makers of children's readers have been well saturated with country sights and sounds. The vital, vigorous imagery which grows up from ever-recurring daily life inevitably develops certain modes of reaction, certain powers of "looking at things," certain deep-lying "familiarities." The city-bred child who has seen the country by scraps or not at all has little indeed to help him out in his knowledge of the barnyard, the meadow, the farmer, many of the domestic animals, nearly all the birds, etc. His imagery of these must often be of the same type as for the "fairy," the "dwarf," the "goblin." This is bad teaching. The reason of course lies in the fact that one set of objects belongs to the world of perception and correct interpretation while the other belongs exclusively to the world of fancy. The lack of an adequate experience compels the child to image them through an act of pure fancy if he does it at all. Instead of the cow he has the milk-cart, instead of the orchard the fruit-vender, instead of the song birds the English sparrow. His domestic animals are the horse which he knows "at a distance," the occasional cat or dog, and the more occasional squirrel, rabbit, or guinea-pig. He is a child who does not as a rule "play on the grass," or listen to brook or bird, or pick or cultivate flowers and plants.

The difficulty with the elementary-school reader, from the standpoint of the city child, is that it *assumes* that he has had these experiences. That careful introduction into a different world that characterizes the best supplementary books is left out.

Meanwhile the city child has a rich social experience that helps him to get at many aspects of social-industrial life, the world over, quickly and appreciatively. He greatly needs insights into life and work that will help him to look on his own world more intelligently and therefore with more real interest and sympathy. His book should give him these insights by helping him to significant aspects of his own world.

The classical content of our best series is, as a rule, excellent; the social-industrial content, poor and limited, especially for the city child.

We are still waiting for a standard reader that will enable the child in New York, Boston, Chicago, St. Louis to get hold of his own daily life more vigorously and intelligently through the attractive mediation of his early reading-book. For after all the "bent" comes early and the fatal habit of living in two worlds must be avoided. The ideal that does not react into the present is inevitably helping us to find the present a dreary place out of which we escape into the world of dreams.

There is every reason to believe that the next quarter-century will witness the direction of energy toward the work of reading *all along the line,* with the sole purpose of making reading contribute directly to individual power. If we succeed, and we shall succeed, the "yellow literature" that is corrupting our children will be banished. The adolescent will drop the "silly" book with disgust because he has already "elected" another sort. The school, in making him an efficient reader, will have erected defenses in his own character; for to make a reader is to help most effectively in training mind and in forming character.

THE SCHOOL EXERCISE WRITTEN AT HOME

ANNETTE SAWYER MANNY

The following translation from Paul Keller's story, *The Son of Hagar,* taken from *Der Säcmann* of March, 1909, illustrates a type of work which is happily becoming less common in our American schools. Yet it would not be difficult to find in almost any city or town, compositions written, after careful "developing lessons," which show no more initiative than little Peter displays.

Those of us who have attempted to co-operate in the home work are perfectly familiar with the child's attitude. "You were not in school to hear what the teacher said, so how can you know about it?"

Though the story is of course an exaggeration, yet it opens up many lines of thought.

Little Peter had written an exercise upon the subject, "The Joys and Sorrows of Winter." Every boy in the German Empire writes upon this subject in the month of December.

Peter was very proud of his accomplishment and took the composition to his friend, old Gottlieb Peuker, who was sitting smoking in his little room in the house behind the residence of the Hartmanns.

Gottlieb put on his spectacles and examined the composition book. "Pretty good, all but the disgraceful penmanship," he read aloud.

"O, Father Gottlieb, that is the criticism upon the one before, 'Life a Journey.'"

"That is a beautiful theme," said Gottlieb, not without sarcasm. "It is not exactly new. I have heard it sixty times in the annual school sermon. Well, I realize that. Really you have not written well."

"Give me the book, Father Gottlieb; I rather read it aloud to you."

He seated himself on the table, coughed three times, and began:

"The Joys and Sorrows of Winter.—The winter is an evil time."

"No, no," said Gottlieb, "the harvest is much worse."

"The teacher said so," replied Peter in self-defense, and continued his reading. "The winter is an evil time. It begins the twenty-first of December."

"But why is it so bad in the winter to begin on the twenty-first of December?" inquired Gottlieb.

Peter looked at him in disgust. "Because it begins on the twenty-first of December and it is bad—do let me read! 'The rabbits and deer freeze in the fields and the fox goes forth in search of prey.'"

"Peter," interjected Gottlieb, "have you ever seen a frozen hare? No? I have seen two in my lifetime and many more live ones. And have you ever seen a fox seeking its prey? No? Nor I either. We have no foxes about here."

"Well, there are in other places; let me read. 'The snow is over the top of the house and a poor old woman is looking for wood in the forest.'"

"What kind of a poor old woman?"

"Why, just a poor old woman."

"What if she should get stuck in the snow that is deep as a house? She better not run the risk."

"Father Gottlieb, you are ——— but do let me read! 'The poor people are shivering in their rooms and have nothing to eat.'"

"The poor people won't survive long then. It is good that you and I are rich folks. We are not shivering and we have something to eat."

"Gottlieb, if you are so ——— I don't wish to read anything more."

"Why, I cannot help it if we are rich. No, no, go on; probably we are coming to the joys of winter now."

"No, there is one more sorrow. 'When icicles hang from the roof they fall upon the heads of careless children.'"

He paused here, expecting another reproof, but Gottlieb nodded assent as much as to say, "Yes, yes, those icicles are a national torment."

"The winter has its joys, too. Children skate."

"Ah! Do you go skating now?"

"No, I have no skates. But the others do. Let me read. 'And many coast merrily on their sleds. The snow is like a shroud,' No, that won't do for a joy. That goes better with a sorrow. I will cross out 'shroud' and write 'bridal robe' above it. It is all the same. 'Good St. Nicholas brings presents and most beautiful of all is the Christmas time. The end.'"

"Yes, yes," said Gottlieb. "Last year you received nothing. But you can write it. It is a beautiful composition. I am going to write one different from that."

"You?" said Peter in astonishment. "How can you write one when you didn't hear what was said in school?"

"I will try it. I will pretend I am little Peter and have a composition to write."

Perhaps half an hour passed; then Gottlieb said, "Now I will read my exercise aloud to you.

"'THE JOYS AND SORROWS OF WINTER: A COMPOSITION BY LITTLE PETER.— The winter is not very pleasant because I rather go barefoot than to wear the heavy wooden shoes. With wooden shoes one cannot run well. In winter my father works in the factory but my mother can earn but little, so we have meat only on Sundays, and there is never any sausage. In summer our food is better. Otherwise there is not much suffering in Teichau. Only old Mrs. Pätzolder has a hard time because she is a letter-carrier and Wilke Bauer always gets chilblains. Then I am always sulky because I have neither sled nor skates. If I had not spent the mark and a half that I saved for a scarf, I might have bought some skates and that would have been a joy of winter. Winter has its joys, however. I don't get up until half-past seven. That suits me. And I pelt all the girls and boys with snow. That suits me, too. The grocer is glad because he can sell so much petroleum. My old friend, Gottlieb Peuker, is happy also because he has nothing to do and can smoke his pipe all day long. Everybody is warm, even those in the poorhouse. The dog is happy, lying by the fireside. The field rejoices because it is not being plowed or harrowed or mown. But one cannot see the gladness of the field, he can only think about it. At Christmas time we have no school and that makes us happiest of all.'

"Finished," said Gottlieb. "Well, what do you think of my composition?"

Peter stared at him. In his astonishment, he had made no protest. Now he gathered himself together. "You did not sit erect," he said; "Give it to me."

Gottlieb passed him the paper.

As Peter read he uttered cries of amazement, mingled with delight. Seizing the pen he began to mark mistakes. "Thirty-five commas omitted," he said. "Unsatisfactory, careless, stay after school and rewrite. You must be punished."

Gottlieb smiled with some embarrassment. "That is not all," he said; "turn the paper over."

Peter turned the page and read: "It is a very great deal of fun in the winter to have old Gottlieb write a composition and make so many mistakes that one nearly dies of laughing. And then it is a great joy of winter to have Gottlieb buy me a pair of skates for Christmas and make me a little sled."

Peter leaped with joy and, seizing the paper, rushed from the room. Soon he returned and, with an embarrassed expression, peeped in at the door. "Say, Gottlieb, you are not angry because I spoke of the thirty-five mistakes?"

"No, no, little Peter, you didn't count in those on the second page."

A COURSE IN FORM STUDY

CHARLES H. JUDD
The University of Chicago

It is commonly assumed that recognition of the form and position of objects will develop in children without special instruction on the part of the teacher. No place has been provided in the ordinary school programme for the purpose of training such types of recognition. If one refers to the spatial characteristics of objects as a subject of special study, he is likely to be referred to geometry as an advanced science and as appropriately placed late in the high school course of study. The idea that one may definitely study spatial characteristics in the early grades must be established by some argument and such argument will always encounter the inertia of tradition.

In the effort to show the unreasonableness of the present tradition, one may first review certain salient historical facts. If one considers the development of mathematical science in European history, he finds that the great emphasis was at first on geometry. If this means anything, it shows that the early Greeks, who developed the science long before they had any definite notions of algebra or many of the higher forms of mathematics, were dealing with a problem that naturally suggested itself to those who were beginning the study of the world about them. The early Greeks worked out a kind of experimental geometry. They learned the properties of angles and of the various plane figures by actual contact with these figures and through the effort to fit them to each other. In this way they developed a body of geometrical knowledge which was very complete. It was mature because it had been long studied. At this point came the historical event which made the study of space appear to be a very complicated and advanced form of knowledge. Euclid at the University of Alexandria was acquainted not only with geometry, but also with the forms of

Aristotelian logic, a highly organized system of formal reasoning. Euclid used his twofold knowledge to work out a type of logical geometry which has been the subject utilized in European and American institutions of learning ever since the Alexandrian period.

In a way it was a great misfortune that geometry should thus be elevated to the position of an advanced subject. Later educators made the mistake of assuming that its highly logical form was due to the inherent complexity of the subject itself and they made no effort to take up the study of space in lower schools because of this apparent complexity of the science. Geometry, however, is not necessarily connected with the logical form in which we ordinarily think of it. Instead of defining a triangle in a strictly logical or syllogistic way as Euclid did, it is quite possible to become acquainted with the general characteristics of this figure in a practical way as the Greeks had done long before the time of Euclid. Indeed, it cannot be too vigorously pointed out that geometry was one of the first and most primitive sciences.

What has been the result of substituting the Euclidian type of geometry for the natural type? Most people go through life with no ability to deal with form and distance. The only angle which is recognized with any degree of precision by the ordinary individual is the right angle in which the lines are vertical and horizontal. Even this very simple angle is not clearly recognized if it is placed in such a position that its sides are oblique. When it comes to the more complicated shapes, the ordinary observer not only has no training in the recognition of these forms, but he definitely turns away from them. A person who goes about every day and pays no attention to the forms of the trees which he passes and the shapes and positions of the other objects of his environment except to avoid them, is cultivating a habit of seeing the objects of his environment only to the extent necessary to escape contact with them. Such a habit of neglecting objects is none the less a definite habit because it is negative in its results. The habit of neglecting the form of objects is often furthered by a subtle training received in learning to read in such a way as to avoid detailed observation of words. We often train children to see only the outlined characteristics of the words at which they glance. They are thus trained to read rapidly, but are unable to spell.

There is still another tendency of elementary education which contributes to the neglect of form. Whenever there is any reference in this earliest school course to spatial matters, that reference is in terms of abstract tables in which the various metric units are described in words rather than through actual contact with objects. In this way we make space an abstract matter from the beginning of our work. We prepare the way for a later geometry which shall be nothing but a description of spatial characteristics and not an appreciation of them. Anyone can test this statement by asking a group of adults to define what they mean by fifteen inches or any other spatial unit. It will be found that the ordinary observer's knowledge of fifteen inches is very precise so far as its verbal description is concerned, and so far as its arithmetical relation to other spatial quantities is concerned, but very vague in concrete reference to the actual space itself. Gross errors will be found if we try to get comparative estimates from a group of individuals of the length of lines or the area of figures.

In a general way it is universally recognized that the ability to recognize form can be developed by practice. A suggestive experiment which can easily be worked out by those who are interested in the problem of mental development or the special problem of development of the power to recognize space, is to draw a series of simple lines which constitute a figure that can easily be reproduced by anyone who observes it. Cover such a figure as this with some sort of a shield and when all is in readiness expose it for a period of five seconds and after covering it up require the observer to reproduce it as best he can. After he has attempted to make a reproduction allow him to make a second observation of five seconds and make a second drawing. A series of such drawings will show in a very instructive way that the recognition of a simple figure consists in a series of analyses. The different parts of the figure will be seen with different degrees of clearness in the successive observations until finally the whole figure is recognized. Such a series of experiments as this is to be compared with the experiences of a child who is for the first time confronted by any object. He sees its different parts at the outset in a vague general way, and it is only through some analysis of these parts that he gets a clear notion of the size and arrangement of the different portions of the figure. If there is no strong motive for carrying out the study of the figure in detail, the child will go away with only a vague general notion, and this general notion will not be adequate if at any later time he is put to a severe test in the recognition of the object.

The same general principle applies to such observations as children are called upon to make when they are taught to observe words. Here again there must be at some time in the child's experience a systematic analysis of the different parts of the word. In the absence of such analysis he may acquire a habit of looking at the word as a whole which will interfere seriously with the later requirements that he see the word with sufficient precision to reproduce it when he tries to spell it or when he tries to distinguish it from some similar word.

Up to this time the discussion has aimed to make clear the necessity for explicit attention to matters of form in the elementary schools. The question which now arises is the question of the method of giving such training. Certain general exercises can readily be suggested. The reproduction of lines of a given length and the careful comparison of different lines would furnish a good starting point for a series of form study lessons. After comparing lines, a comparison of surfaces could be taken up, beginning first of all with simple surfaces drawn on the blackboard or a sheet of paper, and leading ultimately to a comparison of surfaces of familiar objects surrounding the child. Speer's work with blocks as a means of training in the estimation of ratios showed very conclusively that children can learn to make accurate comparisons of cubical contents and this would furnish a third type of exercises to add to the exercises of estimation of length of lines and the sizes of surfaces.

These exercises in estimation of size could be followed by a study of angles. Children should be taught to recognize various angles such as an angle of 45°, of 15°, and intermediate angles. These angles should become familiar in various positions, as when one side is horizontal, when one side is oblique, and so on. Children should also learn something with regard to the addition of angles to each other so that they can easily estimate the total of two or three given angles. Following this work with plane angles, a number of exercises could be introduced in solid angles and in the rotation of figures. For example, children can very readily be taught to imagine the result of three or four successive rotations of a line through various planes of space. Let a line be rotated 10° to the right, 15° backward, 30° to the left, and 5° forward, and imagine the final position of the line when it starts from any given position.

Such estimation of spatial relations as this can readily be associated with training in the recognition and appreciation of symmetry in shape and well-balanced distribution of figures.

One may indulge at this point in a digression from the discussion of practical exercises in space perceptions to call attention to the fact that the work of drawing in the schools is relatively unproductive because it is not based on general training in the minute recognition of space relations. Most people are unable to draw because they do not see the forms of objects about them with any degree of precision. Training of the type described above will improve the attention for space relations in such a way as to lead to a closer examination of all objects, with the result that these few formal lessons in the recognition of certain typical space relations will serve as a basis for a self-education of a much more general type. Children who recognize forms readily will see more in a landscape or more in a printed word which is presented to them than will children who have no such training.

Thus far the suggestions with regard to training have dealt altogether with visual space. Undoubtedly much of our recognition of distance depends upon experiences which arise from actual muscular movements over the space recognized. That we are in general vague in the estimation of such traversed spaces is due to the fact that we depend for the most part on vision even when the experience of traversing the space is present. When vision is cut out, as for example when one shuts his eyes, the ability to estimate distances through which one walks appears as very little developed. Children can be readily trained to recognize distances with great precision if they are given practice in closing their eyes and moving about from one fixed point to another.

Again, there is usually great weakness in localization of sounds. Our ears are not constructed as advantageously as are those of animals for the recognition of space relations through sound, but here again improvement will follow upon training. Sounds can be produced in different positions with reference to the observer's head and he will learn very soon how to utilize the sound sensations for the more definite localization of these various positions.

Tactual space can also be cultivated to a very high degree. It is a well known fact that the blind man utilizes his sense of touch to gain many of the types of information which the normal individual gathers through his sense of vision. It has been repeatedly shown by scientific experiments that the sensitivity of the blind man is no greater than that of the normal individual. That is, his skin does not respond more intensely to external stimulations. What the blind man has gained through experience is an increased ability to utilize his sensations. When he places his hand upon an object the sensations mean more to him because he has been training in the use of his hands for purposes of recognizing form and distance. All of the experiments which were described for vision can be repeated for touch and they have the advantage not merely of training the individual so that he recognizes objects which he handles with his hands, but they also serve to train in the general recognition of form, so that he will be interested in shapes and distances wherever he comes in contact with them.

Another type of form study has been suggested in the experiments above described. The rapid reproduction of space relations seen for a very brief time is one of the very best ways of training children. The recognition of a map can be greatly facilitated by exhibiting a map for a very short time and then covering it up and asking for a drawing of the map. Such exercises as these have been described as flash reading and flash writing. What is gained in these various cases is immediate and precise recognition of form, under conditions which keep the attention of the children at a maximum intensity.

After such general exercises as these which have been described, the work may be turned directly into constructive geometry. The division of a line into parts by the projection of a line of known dimensions, the dissecting of an angle into different parts, the development of various surface relations, are all problems which can be taken up in the fourth and fifth grades. In the upper grades this can be made to take a form closely related to conventional geometry. This approach to conventional geometry will not necessitate the introduction of logical forms at the early stage of school work, but will furnish one of the very best means of introducing the children later to those forms of reasoning which can then be utilized chiefly as means of training in precision and coherency of thought; the study of geometry will not end, if thus introduced, in purely verbal descriptions of matters which the pupil learns in an abstract way. Teachers of geometry frequently find that the pupils who come to them in the advanced years of the high school are unable to solve the problems of geometry chiefly because they have no spatial imagination. Some of our recent textbooks have attempted to cure these common defects in imagination by presenting models of the figures which are to be utilized in the geometrical demonstration. What is needed as a foundation for more advanced geometrical study is form study of a very concrete type.

The concrete form study which would thus prepare the way for geometry would also serve other ends as has been pointed out in the foregoing discussions. Nature study would profit; spelling would improve, map study would become easy. Furthermore, such training would exercise an influence on the whole life of the individual. By way of contrast with the ordinary individual untrained in the recognition of space relations, a child who had taken a course such as that described would be prepared to deal with such a problem as fitting a dress or assembling a machine. Space is the most fundamental fact of our environment. The reason we have neglected it in school work is that it is taken for granted as if it were perfectly recognized in everyone's experience. That this assumption is unwarranted, that we should study it as one of the most essential lessons of our elementary school, is the contention of this paper.

EDITORIAL NOTES

Editorial Announcement

The *Elementary School Teacher* will participate in the enlargement of the School of Education. The school and its publications aim to serve two purposes; the first is to show how practical classroom work can be organized, and the second is to subject all methods and results to careful scientific study. In carrying out the first of these functions the *Elementary School Teacher* will continue to publish articles of a practical type presenting accounts of methods and directing teachers to materials available for classroom use. During the coming year Professor Sargent, who has taken charge of all the work in Manual Training and Art in the School of Education after long and successful experience in these lines in Massachusetts, will write a series of monthly articles on art and constructive work in the grades. These articles will set forth a course of work for each grade for each month and will be sufficiently detailed to be made the basis of regular classroom work. The first of the articles will appear in October. Professor Caldwell who is in general charge of the science work in the School of Education will present in a series of articles a course in nature study. This will include the fundamental elements of botany, zoölogy, physics, and chemistry. It will, in short, present a plan for teaching elementary science at a level where subdivision into separate sciences is not desirable. Professor Davis, of Miami University, will present a series of articles on the teaching of agriculture. The materials for such teaching are now very abundant and can be had for the asking. Professor Davis' articles will direct teachers to these materials. The articles will also summarize the various lines of agricultural education now organized throughout the United States. The first article will appear in November. Other series of articles are in preparation and will be announced later.

The second purpose of the School of Education, that of reducing elementary school work to a subject of scientific study, will be expressed in articles of the type which Professor Dearborn contributes to this number. The classroom teacher is likely to look upon such scientific studies as foreign to his or her personal interests and obligations. It is the creed of this journal and the institution back of it that the efficient class teacher must attack the problem of teaching in a sound and scientifically justifiable way. One may chance upon good methods of teaching without the pains of scientific study, but one can never hope to be consistently safe and successful until he works out the problem of education systematically and with the best means of investigation which can be devised. There will be, it may be safely assumed, a strong tendency on the part of many teachers to leave uncut the pages of the scientific articles. This will be a mistake and we believe that time will justify our contention that such studies contribute an element to education which is indispensable.

In announcing these policies it is fitting that a word be said with regard to the apparent change in editorial management. The names which should properly be printed in the editorial staff are now so numerous that it has seemed wise to omit the mention of all and indicate the active co-operation of the whole faculty in this journal. Fortunately Professor Mead and Professor Tufts continue in such close organic relation to the school and its publications that nothing will be lost of their efficient and highly appreciated services by the change in the form of announcing their relations to the work. A full announcement of the faculty of the school is given on the page following the table of contents.

A Woman as City Superintendent

The city of Chicago is the first of the large cities of the country to elect a woman to the office of superintendent of schools. There are some who are doubtful as to the ability of a woman to carry on the functions of this exacting office. The physical strain is great and the conventional requirements of business life, it is said, will make it difficult for a woman to meet all of those with whom the office of public school superintendent must deal. To those who are interested in an impersonal way in the strictly scientific testing of these objections to a woman superintendent, it will be a matter of satisfaction that the experiment is being undertaken under the most favorable conditions. Mrs. Ella Flagg Young who was elected to the Chicago superintendency in the closing days of July is perfectly familiar with the needs of the system of which she takes charge. She is recognized by common consent as the best qualified educational authority in the system; and she has the high respect and good will of the teachers, officials, and members of the Board of Education.

There are, however, others than the strictly impersonal observers who look with satisfaction on this move. Mrs. Young has long stood for education as a vital form of social activity not to be confused with city politics. She has been a fearless advocate of needed reform. She is a practical teacher who has so formulated her experiences as to be in the best sense a master of theory. Those who are interested in making education a profession see in her selection to this position a sign of gratifying advance.

Finally, Mrs. Young carries with her into office the warmest personal sympathy of all who have labored with her as colleagues.

The editors of this journal take the keenest delight in seeing one whom they have never ceased to regard as an intimate coworker elevated to a position where the broadest application can be given to principles which have been matters of common advocacy and devotion.

The experiment of putting a trained woman, amply qualified, into a most important administrative position in the public schools is well launched. We need indulge in no prophecies; it is appropriate however to express the present feeling which is shared by all, the feeling of complete confidence in the favorable issue of the experiment.

NOTES AND NEWS

"Instruction in the Fine and Manual Arts in the United States" is the subject of *Bulletin* 1909, No. 6, of the United States Bureau of Education. It is a statistical monograph prefaced by a statement of the aim of instruction in these subjects. The attitude of the federal government, of the several states, and of municipalities whose population is four thousand or over is indicated by institutions for education in the fine and industrial arts and appropriations therefor.

A joint committee on school organization representing the New York Teachers' Association and the Brooklyn Teachers' Association is carrying on an investigation to ascertain the various practices in common use with regard to the promotion of pupils. A card has been prepared which enumerates the different plans now being tried, and asks for a statement on the part of the teachers of experience and principals and superintendents of their judgment regarding the various special plans enumerated. The card is reproduced below. It is suggestive as a list of current experiments in this difficult problem and it also furnishes teachers an opportunity to contribute to a report which should be of interest in contributing to a final solution of the problem. Anyone willing to contribute should send answers to Mr. Charles S. Hartwell, 234 Willoughby Ave., Brooklyn, N. Y.

Are you trying or have you tried any of the following plans of school organization? Do you recommend any of these plans as superior to the "common plan" of school organization? (1) Cambridge plan: Bright pupils may be transferred to shorter course; slow pupils to longer course; (2) Elizabeth plan: Opportunities are provided for frequent promotion; (3) Pueblo plan: Each individual child progresses as fast as he can and is promoted at any time; (4) Batavia plan: Two teachers are employed to teach one large class; (5) Departmental Teaching: Seventh and eighth years taught similarly to the high-school method; (6) Group teaching: Class is divided into two or more groups for study and recitation; (7) Preacademic school: Seventh and eighth years organized as a separate school; (8) Extension classes: Short commercial or industrial courses used to supplement elementary course; (9) Special classes of over-age or foreign-born children; (10) Ungraded classes: Classes organized for defectives or for incorrigibles; (11) Promotion by points: A proposition to advance pupils by subject and not by grades; (12) Chicago plan: Teachers can promote entire class as soon as grade work has been completed; (13) North Denver plan: Bright pupils help other pupils; (14) Are you trying any other plan than those named above? If so, describe on other side; (15) How long is your school term? . . . . mos.; (16) How long is your elementary course of study? . . . . yrs.; (17) How long is your high-school course of study? . . . . yrs.; (18) How long is your daily school session or sessions? . . . . hrs.; (19) Do you believe it is feasible to place each child in that grade or subject in which he may "work up to his fullest capacity"? (20) Should pupils repeat work in which they have satisfactorily "passed"?

BOOK REVIEWS

Teaching to Read. By James S. Hughes. New York: A. S. Barnes & Co., 1909. Pp. 124. $0.50.

Inspector Hughes, of Toronto, is known to many teachers of the United States as a lecturer on the philosophy of education. He is one of the most active of American exponents of the Froebelian doctrines of initiative, self-activity, self-expression, etc. It is instructive to find such a person describing methods of teaching the oldest and most formal of the traditional elementary school subjects.

The author's main contentions are: (1) that the teaching of reading has failed in the past because reading aloud has been emphasized instead of silent reading; (2) that reading should be taught primarily to develop the power of getting thought accurately, comprehensively, and rapidly from visible language; and (3) that by pursuing the methods advocated in this book good reading may be taught in much less time than is ordinarily consumed. Schools "have wasted the time of the child, and generally dwarfed his powers by tiresome and discouraging attempts to train him to read aloud before he has been trained to read."

Reading is analyzed into word recognition, silent reading, and oral reading. "Silent reading at sight, the results of which are to be reported to the teacher and the class, should be a specific department of the training in reading." In oral reading "it would be profitable for the rest of the class to write or draw or do manual training work with cardboard or raffia or other available materials, while each pupil is reading." "If children were trained to read well without being asked to read aloud till they were fourteen or fifteen years of age it would be a great advantage in many ways."

Objection is made to memorizing word forms. "If possible the same word should never be seen twice by the pupil while he is gaining the power of word recognition. The recognition of each word should be achieved by the child at first by a conscious process of uniting the powers and sounds of letters in new combinations."

Objective methods of word recognition are criticized. "An object should never be used to suggest the name of a visible word. Reading is not a means of obtaining thought from objects. Reading is not a method of learning a new language, but of recognizing the child's own language in a new form."

Phonic methods are argued for at length. Word and sentence methods and all analytic methods are rejected.

About one third of the book is devoted to a description of the method approved by the author for learning the sound elements, and associating the visual symbols with them. This part is largely a description of devices. The author suggests the provision of more reading material by collecting clippings, anecdotes, etc., pasting these on cardboard, and giving each child a different one to read.

Such books as this, dealing in a philosophical, psychological, and yet practical way with the dominant formal studies of the curriculum are needed by many teachers. Some may take exception to such special points as the rejection of objective and analytic methods of teaching reading. But when we consider such a condition as is indicated by the fact that a majority of the students entering normal schools know no other method of teaching reading than the alphabet method, it is clear that many need to have their eyes opened by just such readable books as this. The rather exaggerated form of statement common to Froebelian writers will probably find an adequate corrective in the conservatism of such formal teachers.

S. C. PARKER

"Riverside Educational Monographs." Edited by HENRY SUZZALLO, of Columbia University. Boston: Houghton, Mifflin & Co., 35 cents each net, postpaid.

Education. An essay and other selections by EMERSON. Pp. 76.

The Meaning of Infancy and the Part Played by Infancy in the Evolution of Man. By FISKE. Pp. 46.

This is an important series which reminds one of the excellent little books published for educational purposes in Europe at little expense. A dozen numbers are announced and it is hoped that there will be sufficient demand for these to justify the extension of the list. The announcement gives six books in general educational theory, two in administration and supervision of schools and four in methods of teaching. In the first group are the two that have already appeared and numbers by President Eliot, Professor Dewey, Commissioner Brown, and the editor. In the other groups Professor Hanus's title is "Continuation Schools;" Professor Cubberly will treat of "Changing Conceptions of Education;" Professor Farrington of "Types of Teaching;" Dr. Earhart of "Teaching Children to Study." The two remaining numbers will be Professor Palmer's "Self-Cultivation in English," and "Ethical and Moral Instruction in Schools."

It will be seen that even this preliminary venture offers a wide range of material appealing to various interests. It is probable that the numbers by Emerson, Fiske, and Dewey will have the widest circulation as the subject-matter contained in these has been used by many teachers who will welcome it in this more convenient form.

The Emerson selections include the essay on "Education," "Culture in Education" from "Culture" in *The Conduct of Life,* "Education for Power" from "Power" in the same volume, and concludes with half a dozen pages on "The Training of Manual Work" from *Man the Reformer.* The Fiske material is from *Excursions of an Evolutionist* and *A Century of Science.*

The editor's introduction to the Fiske number briefly and definitely places the material chosen in its setting in the scientific and democratic movement. The Emerson introduction seems less adequate, but after all none is really needed.

This series is only one of a number of evidences of the new policy of this firm with reference to furnishing a broader range of educational publications, and we have reason to be grateful to those who are responsible for it.

FRANK A. MANNY

KALAMAZOO, MICH.

BOOKS RECEIVED

T. Y. CROWELL & CO., NEW YORK

Self-Cultivation in English. By GEORGE HERBERT PALMER. Pp. 32.

Das Rothkäppchen. A play in five scenes, by MATHILDE REICHENBACH. Cloth. Pp. 27. $0.25.

Easy German Stories. By HEDWIG LEVI. Edited by MRS. LUISE DELP. Cloth Pp. 100. $0.40.

Deutsche Gedichte zum auswendiglernen. Selected and edited by W P. CHALMERS. Cloth. Pp. 138. $0.40.

First Lessons in French. By P. BANDERET AND PH. REINHARD. Adapted for Common School Use by GRACE SANDWITH. Cloth. Pp. 182. $0.50.

GINN & CO., BOSTON

The McCloskey Primer. By MARGARET ORVIS McCLOSKEY. Illustrated by CHARLES COPELAND. Cloth. Pp. 160. $0.30.

Public-School Penmanship. A Handbook for Teachers. By ALBERT W. CLARK. Cloth. Pp. 161. $0.75.

Emergencies. Book Two, "Gulick Hygiene Series." By CHARLOTTE VETTER GULICK. Cloth. Illustrated. Pp. 173. $0.40.

HENRY ALTEMUS CO., PHILADELPHIA

We Have With Us Tonight. What Happens at that Great American Institution, the Banquet. By SAMUEL G. BLYTHE. Decorated Boards. Pp. 92. $0.50.

THE MACMILLAN COMPANY, NEW YORK

Irving's Tales of a Traveller. Edited by JENNIE F. CHASE. Pocket Edition. Cloth. Pp. 270. $0.25.

Primer. "Language Reader Series." By FRANKLIN T. BAKER, GEORGE R. CARPENTER AND JULIE T. DULON. Illustrated by RUTH S. CLEMENTS. Cloth. Pp. 23. $0.25.

The Elements of Hygiene. For Schools. Compiled by ISABEL McISAAC. Cloth. Illustrated. Pp. 172. $0.60.

MOFFAT, YARD & CO., NEW YORK

The Romance of American Expansion. By H. ADDINGTON BRUCE. Cloth. Illustrated. Pp. 246. $1.75.

OXFORD UNIVERSITY PRESS, NEW YORK

The Elementary Geography. A First Physiography. Vol. I of "The Oxford Geographies." By F. D. HERBERTSON. Cloth. Illustrated. Pp. 79.

SILVER, BURDETT & CO., NEW YORK

The Progressive Road to Reading, Books One and Two. By GEORGINE BURCHILL, WILLIAM L. ETTINGER, AND EDGAR DUBS SHIMER. Cloth. Illustrated. Book One, 128 pp.; Book Two, 160 pp.

CURRENT EDUCATIONAL LITERATURE IN THE PERIODICALS [1]

IRENE WARREN
Librarian, School of Education, University of Chicago

ALLPORT, FRANK. A plea for the systematic annual and universal examination of school children's eyes and ears. Psycholog. Clinic. 3:67–71. (15 My. '09.)

Are the college entrance requirements excessive? Educa. 29 (My. '09): WILLIAM ORR, The point of view of the preparatory school, 551–61; ALEXANDER MEIKLEJOHN, The college point of view, 561–67; WILSON FARRAND, The reasonable solution, 567–16.

AYRES, LEONARD P. The effect of physical defects on school progress. Psycholog. Clinic. 3:71–78. (15 My. '09.)

BEAN, C. HOMER. Starvation and mental development. Psycholog. Clinic. 3:78–86. (15 My. '09.)

BICKNELL, PERCY F. A life of scientific research. Dial. 46:322–24. (16 My. '09.)

BROOKS, STRATTON D. The relations of the university to the secondary school. Educa. 29:576–85. (My. '09.)

CARTER, MARION HAMILTON. The conservation of the defective child. McClures Mag. 33:160–72. (June '09.)

COBURN, F. W. Old-age annuities. Journ of Educa. 69:513–15. (13 My. '09.)

DELABARRE, EDMUND BURKE. Formal discipline and the doctrine of common elements. Educa. 29:585–601. (My. '09.)

ELIOT, CHARLES W. Ideal American teacher. Journ. of Educa. 69:485–86. (6 My. '09.)

EMERSON, HENRY P. English secondary schools. Amer. Educa. 11:395–98. (My. 09.)

FLEXNER, ABRAHAM. The problem of college pedagogy. Atlan. 103:838–44. (June '09.)

FOUCHER, LAURE CLAIRE. Story telling in public libraries. Story Hour. 1:10–14. (My. '09.)

GREEN, J. A. Experimental psychology and education. III. Individual differences in children. Sch. World. 11:172–74. (My. '09.)

[1] Abbreviations.—Amer. Educa., American Education; Atlan., Atlantic Monthly; Educa., Education; Harp. W., Harpers Weekly; Ind. Educa., Indian Education; Journ. of Educa., Journal of Education; Lib. Journ., Library Journal; Pop. Sci. Mo., Popular Science Monthly; Psycholog. Clinic, Psychological Clinic; Sch. World, School World; Tech. World Mag., Technical World Magazine.

GREENWOOD, J. M. Disregard for law. Journ. of Educa. 69:511–13. (13 My. '09.)

HEETER, S. L. Medical inspection in the Saint Paul schools. Psycholog. Clinic. 3:61–67. (15 My. '09.)

HENDERSON, ERNEST N. Formal discipline from the standpoint of analytic and experimental psychology. Educa. 29:601–14. (My. '09.)

HERBERT, CLARA W. Establishing relations between the children's library and other civic agencies. Lib. Journ. 34:195–97. (My. '09.)

HICKS, FREDERICK C. The public library in political theory and in practice. Lib. Journ. 34:197–200. (My. '09.)

HORNE, HERMAN H. The practical influence of the new views of formal discipline. Educa. 29:614–24. (My. '09.)

HUNT, CAROLINE L. The century of the child. Dial. 46:325–27. (16 My. '09.)

JOGARAO, C. H. V. An examination of the new method of teaching foreign languages. Ind. Educa. 7:401–5. (Ap. '09.)

JURADO, RAMON. Prehistoric home for new university. Tech. World. Mag. 11:368–75. (June '09.)

(The) library situation in Chicago. Lib. Journ. 34:215, 216. (My. '09.)

OLSEN, J. W. Library work among the children of Minnesota. Harp. W. 53:24, 25. (15 My. '09.)

PITKIN, W. B. Training college teachers. Pop. Sci. Mo. 74:588–96. (June '09.)

Plato and educational co-ordination. Ind. Educa. 7:396–401. (Ap. '09.)

PRESSLAND, A. J. The reorganization of secondary education in Switzerland. Sch. World. 11:166–70. (My. '09.)

(The) public school and the home. By the editor. Craftsman. 16:284–91. (June '09.)

ROWAN, JOSEPHINE MORRIS. Reading rooms and libraries for the blind. Lib. Journ. 34:221, 222. (My. '09.)

SABIN, HENRY. Concerning examinations. Journ. of Educa. 69:489, 490. (6 My. '09.)

SADLER, M. E. Education in England. Ind. Educa. 7:388–96. (Ap. '09.)

SAYERS, W. C. BERWICK. Co-operation between school and library. Journ. of Educa. (Lond.) 40:351–53. (1 My. '09.)

STEVENS, EDWARD L. Prophylaxis in the practice of the school superintendent. Amer. Educa. 11:401–4. (My. '09.)

WALKER, SYDNEY F. Fire appliances for use in schools. Sch. World. 11:163–66. (My. '09.)

WINSHIP, ALBERT E. Tory argument of high schools answered. Journ. of Educa. 69:487, 488. (6 My. '09.)

WREN, P. Physical education without apparatus—III. Ind. Educa. 7:405, 406. (Ap. '09.)

VOLUME X NUMBER 2

THE ELEMENTARY SCHOOL TEACHER

OCTOBER, 1909

THE FINE AND INDUSTRIAL ARTS IN ELEMENTARY SCHOOLS

WALTER SARGENT
The University of Chicago

This article presents some considerations on the place of fine and industrial arts in elementary schools. It is the first of a series in which the work of each grade will be discussed in detail.

The fine and industrial arts are steadily securing recognition as important elements in public education, and as factors necessary to industrial supremacy. In elementary schools only rudiments of these arts can be taught, such as the beginnings of freehand drawing, simple forms of constructive work, and problems in design as related to common things. Careful work in these lines, however, is the best preparation for advanced study, and is also of definite practical value even if instruction ends in the elementary schools.

The different phases of fine and industrial art in public schools may be grouped under the following heads: (1) representation which gives pupils experience with the graphic language used in fine and constructive art; (2) construction which gives acquaintance with the methods employed in crafts and industries and trains that judgment which comes from carrying out the processes by which raw materials are converted into predetermined products; and (3) design which trains the discrimination necessary to choose what is in good taste and to enjoy what is excellent in fine and industrial art.

These phases of manual expression are not separated by sharply defined limits. It is impossible to construct an object without exercising judgment in design, or to design an object satisfactorily without some knowledge of construction and some ability in representation. The school activities continually call for simultaneous work along all three of these lines. In order to insure definite progress, however, it seems necessary to supplement general work in manual expression by special study, which will emphasize particular phases of representation, construction, and design for a period of time, and thus deal with each more thoroughly than is possible when that topic appears incidentally with others. For example, while the material for the larger part of the special study of drawing may be found in the other school subjects, it still remains true that drawing has a content of its own. To obtain the full value of this, some work is occasionally necessary, which does not relate immediately to the description of other school subjects.

The valuable results evident from these three phases of manual expression are as follows: Representation develops ability to image form clearly. If one asks children to draw from memory a supposedly familiar shape, such as the map of the country they are considering in geography, he will probably be surprised at the vague ideas of form which are discovered. If he shows the children the map for a moment, and then, removing it, asks them to draw again, and repeats this a few times, allowing no drawing while the map is in sight, he will again be surprised at the sort of attention given to the map during the brief period, which follows one attempt to draw it, and precedes another effort to reproduce it better. This attention differs greatly from that which is unaccompanied by any necessity of reproducing from memory what has been seen. The image is defined, clarified, and made comparatively permanent.

Children trained to express themselves by drawing, learn to think in terms of form. Drawing from objects requires a selection of the essential features. Out of the bewildering complexity of details which nature presents, one must learn to recognize those which are significant, which if reproduced will represent the object. Such discrimination trains a quality of observation which is likely to remain undeveloped unless awakened by drawing.

Drawing is more completely a convention than is generally supposed. An oriental or an occidental draws each in the way he thinks will represent the form best, yet the results differ remarkably. Each is expressing himself in his own graphic dialect. The appreciation of another people's method of drawing is akin to an appreciation of another language in the revelations it gives of different ways of seeing and thinking. Drawing, as it exists at present, is an evolution. Its vocabulary has been added to by each generation. One imagines that he is expressing himself in terms suggested directly by the object, but this is only partly true. Therefore, drawing an object means translating the aspect of it into terms which demand careful selection.

In addition to these general educational values, elementary representation is of direct industrial, scientific, and aesthetic importance.

To the man engaged in constructive work, drawing offers a means of endless experimentation. Workers in metal or wood, when discussing a mechanical or constructive problem can often present its different possibilities and define the results almost as well by the use of the pencil as by manipulating the actual material. Constructive sketching is also a great stimulus of invention. The more finished working drawings, afford a means of recording all necessary data, regarding form and construction.

A manufacturer thus refers to the value of ability to sketch and draw:

> I wish to emphasize the importance of industrial drawing for the mass of trade workers in these lines of manufacturing where the artistic or aesthetic sense is not supposed to hold a prominent place. For example, in the line of machine building the art of drawing has a very important relation to our industrial future. To this particular class of mechanics drawing has a broad field of usefulness: first, because it is a valuable means of expression. The mechanic who is able to express himself by a rapidly made drawing is inspired thereby to more and better thought. Second, because it opens up for him especially a broad field for experimentation and choice.

When by a sketch the manufacturer or the mechanic can place before himself and others many ways of doing a thing, he at once makes comparisons, and immediately chooses what he deems the best, the fittest, or the most beautiful. He hits the mark after such a comparison, because with his sketches he has tried many schemes and compared them.

Experimentation, comparison, and choice mark the way of advancement. But life is too short to try many experiments, unless the methods of trying them are very simple. To build things of wood and stone and metal in order to test them, and to prove which one is best and fittest, requires too much waste of time and material. But the realm of experimentation that is possible with a pencil is wonderful and fascinating; it is almost as unlimited as is thought itself.

I have asked myself from whence comes this fascination as we find it in the shops; and I think it is because through the art of drawing, by delineating and by designing, the mechanic himself becomes a creator of things. He not only learns to see things emanating from others clearly, but, behold, he finds he can express his own ideas to himself and to others, and above all he recognizes that they are his own evolution.

For mechanics of all grades and ranks the habit of sketching and drawing becomes a great developing force. For a mechanic drawing becomes the avenue out of himself into the universe. He is not only learning about other people and other things as we do in the study of history and geography, but he is revealing himself to himself and to others, and the things revealed are new—new to him and new to the world. This to him is the inspiring quality of his work.[1]

In scientific studies, drawing quickens observation and furnishes a means of making accurate records.

Representation is also the language of the fine arts of painting and sculpture. The regular work in drawing in elementary schools, involving, as it does, continued use of lines, light and dark, and color, is giving children constant practice in expressing their ideas and observations by means of the same vocabulary which the artist himself employs. These attempts to use, even though crudely, the terms by which art is expressed, are necessary to that kind of artistic appreciation which yields the fullest pleasure.

Instructors in drawing must choose between a course planned for the few in every school who have what is commonly called

[1] From an address by Mr. Milton P. Higgins, president of the Norton Emery Wheel Co., Worcester, Mass., printed in the sixty-eighth *Annual Report* of the Massachusetts State Board of Educaton, 1904.

"talent," and a course planned for the majority of the children, within easy reach of those of no special ability. While any public-school system should ultimately take account of special talent and encourage it, yet in the elementary grades, such work should be planned as will justify itself on general grounds and be valuable for all, whatever their future occupations are to be. The plan of these articles is based upon the second policy, and the work outlined is such as can be taught by the regular grade teacher and well done by as large a proportion of the children as can accomplish the work given in other subjects.

In order to carry out such a plan it is necessary to teach drawing in the most direct and simple way possible, testing all methods by the resulting increase in ability to draw on the part of the majority of the children. A lack of such increase in the many, should be interpreted as a fault of the method rather than of the children. Results have already shown that the majority of children can learn to draw sufficiently well for purposes of ordinary practical expression with pencil or brush, and can be led to appreciate what is in good taste, as readily and generally as they can progress in other studies of the school curriculum. Special talent is no more a factor to be reckoned with in elementary drawing than in elementary language or mathematics.

Constructive work makes possible a proper balance of motor and intellectual activities which is to the advantage of both. School authorities sometimes discuss the question as to whether any time in the burdened school curriculum can be spared for occupations involving muscular activity, and presume to settle the matter by official action. The nature of children has already settled that question in the affirmative. Muscular activity will be an important part of any school programme. The only jurisdiction which the authorities have in the matter is in deciding whether these activities shall hinder or help school work, whether they shall appear as mischief-making or manual arts.

Elementary woodwork gives familiarity with common tools, processes, and materials, and develops a comprehension which every householder should possess of problems of ordinary constructive work. It brings the invigoration of dealing with the unvarying, impartial laws of matter and being compelled to face the obvious fitness or unfitness of visible results. It awakens the healthy pleasure of shaping material to a predetermined form by patience, foresight, and skill.

Constructive work is not only an essential element in general education, valuable alike to the scholar and the artisan, but is also a means of awakening industrial interests and promoting industrial efficiency. The fact that about two-thirds of the school population leave at the end of the eighth grade and go to work should be considered in its full significance by teachers of the manual arts. These children are too young to enter skilled industries. A few rise through any circumstances, but the majority drift from one to another unskilled occupation taking whatever pays best. They spend two important years in employments which present no industrial interests and offer no vocational outlook.

A teacher of manual training who explores industrial life for educational suggestions will often find forms of work-teaching which awaken interest in effective ways of doing things and bring discontent with unskilled work and foster a desire for thorough industrial training.

The study of design in elementary schools should aim first to develop good taste regarding the things which make up the environment of everyday life.

The power to discern between the merely pretty with attractiveness which is superficial and transitory, and that which is permanently and universally beautiful, gives capacity for an enjoyment the possibilities of which are unlimited.

Among the problems in design especially appropriate for public schools are school and home surroundings, the artistic possibilities of the community and of local industries and crafts.

Every home is an example of good or bad taste. Whatever develops aesthetic judgment raises the standard of living. The general appearance of written school work, arrangement of plants and flowers, framing and hanging of pictures, choice of wall papers, rugs, furniture, etc., are among the opportunities for that sense of fitness which is artistic taste.

Unless the problems of design relate to familiar surroundings, pupils are likely to consider the term "artistic" as one which applies only to unusual things, whereas it does not describe the class to which an object belongs, but means that the object, because of its adequacy, and the refinement of its essential parts and proportions, and the grace and fitness of its decoration, if it possesses any, is unusually excellent of its kind. A kitchen chair or utensil may be artistic and thus a source of continual pleasure as truly as may a vase or a picture.

By collections of photographs or other representations children should be interested in ways in which towns and cities are solving the problems of public structures. They should see pictures of the best designs for bridges, water fronts, public buildings and private houses of all classes, park furnishings, sculpture, fountains, and other things which may contribute to beauty in modern communities.

Schools should give some acquaintance with noted examples of drawing, painting, and sculpture. Abundant material is at hand in the shape of photographs, illustrations, and the best of modern color prints.

The main question, however, is not how many pictures can be brought within the child's range of vision, but on how many can his imagination be awakened to lay hold. In the days when pictures were fewer, a child would often pore for a long time over some poor print till his imagination wandered far into its perspective and lived with its characters. Such a print grew to be so full of suggestion that in later years the grown man hesitated to throw it away even after he had come to see its artistic worthlessness. Even the wayward cracks in the walls of old bare schoolrooms became interesting to the imaginations of children who pictured scenes among them as one sees constellations in the stars.

When imagination can be set at play under the stimulus and direction of a good picture, feelings may be awakened that later may develop into aesthetic enjoyment.

Many small pictures distract the attention of the pupils. Two or three excellent pictures in a classroom, appropriately chosen and carefully hung, usually have a finer influence and give more enduring memories than a large number scattered about the walls.

The fine and industrial arts are taught in schools because of their close relation and definite value to the life and work of people at large. During the past few years there has been steady improvement in the quality of instruction and an excellent foundation for further progress has been laid.

We are confronted, however, with the somewhat surprising fact that in many cities and towns people who as children have spent eight years in the elementary schools and four years in high school, and have studied drawing and constructive work during most of the time, are unable to use drawing at all freely or correctly. They find that their public-school course has added little to their natural ability to choose things in good taste in dress and home furnishings, and this course has increased but slightly their appreciation of works of art. In industrial fields, employers say that boys come to them after a study of constructive work and working drawing taken in grammar schools and high schools, exhibiting a lack of ability to read plans and blue prints. College professors remark that students from these same schools have no skill in delineation of form and cannot make accurate graphic records of observations. Even those who have attended normal schools and have become teachers often confess that they cannot draw and hesitate to use the blackboard for purposes of illustration. These facts justify a careful consideration of the purpose and scope of these subjects in elementary schools, and of the most effective methods of accomplishing the aims in view.

One reason for the tardiness with which these conditions are disappearing is that the problems for manual expression have too often been artificial. Two influences will contribute toward more effective teaching: (1) Supervisors of manual arts who are students of the aim and spirit of the school curriculum as a whole. To such a supervisor the general teachers' meetings held by the superintendent will be as valuable to him as to the grade teachers. He will gather hints from superintendent, from teachers, from the children in their work and play and home life, and from the local industries and the needs of those engaged in them; and from the natural and architectural features of the town. These will modify his work, which will aim to present what the arts have to offer in promoting industry and making life more enjoyable. (2) Grade teachers who make use of manual expression in school work. In promoting drawing for instance, the most effective influence is the example of a teacher who is accustomed to draw on the board before the children. Compared with the effect of this, methods and courses without such example are of secondary importance. We must look to the normal schools for training which will lead teachers to use the arts in this way. The place of the arts in school is realized by the teacher who found them necessary and helpful to his own general work and standing in the normal school. Teachers thus trained cease to regard as specialties such beginnings of the arts as are appropriate to elementary schools. The study of these becomes a simple and natural training in one of the fundamental requisites of civilization.

MEASUREMENT OF GROWTH AND EFFICIENCY IN ARITHMETIC

S. A. COURTIS
Home and Day School, Detroit

The following pages describe in some detail the efforts of the writer to establish a standard from which to measure the success or failure of a reorganization of the mathematics courses in his charge, and to trace the development of ability in arithmetic from the primary grades through the high school. Such tests, repeated at frequent intervals, would, it seems to the writer, make standardization of yearly work possible, would show exactly the place, manner, and amount of development of any particular ability, and would give a rational basis for the estimation of the influence exerted by any method, material, or teacher.

The direct inspiration of the experiment was No. 19, of the *Teacher's College Series, Contributions to Education,* published by Columbia University and entitled, "Arithmetical Abilities; Some Factors Determining Them," by Dr. C. W. Stone. For the benefit of those who are not familiar with that publication, a brief summary of one or two of the essential points is given.

Dr. Stone visited and personally gave, under conditions as nearly identical as possible, two tests, one in fundamentals and one in reasoning, to 3,000 sixth-grade children in 26 school systems in 6 different states from Indiana to New York. The tests are given in full on pp. 61 and 64 although the method of scoring there found is not that used by Dr. Stone. Dr. Stone made a careful examination of the course of study, time allowance, character of supervision, etc., of each school, but with these we shall not be concerned. The scores made by the different schools show that, taking the efficiency of the school making the highest score in fundamentals as 100 per cent., the efficiency represented by the median score was 76 per cent., that of the lowest score 45 per cent. In reasoning the results were even worse, the median score representing an efficiency of 60 per cent., the lowest score an efficiency of 39 per cent. In other words, for most schools the work that is now done in four years could be accomplished in three for fundamentals, and two and a half for reasoning, if more efficient methods were adopted. If the time element is considered, the results are much worse; for the percentage of the school time given to arithmetic was found to vary from 7 to 23 per cent., and high ability appeared more commonly with the small rather than with the great expenditure of time. It was not possible to say what are efficient methods; for there was wide variation even among schools using essentially the same method and the same general course of study.

Moved by the laudable ambition of finding the place of the school with which he is connected among the 26 school systems, the writer undertook to give Dr. Stone's tests to the sixth grade. A little consideration made it evident that parts of the tests were within the abilities of third-grade children, while the length of the tests would provide work to keep even the seniors busy during the whole of the allotted time. Here then was a means of testing the development of the arithmetical abilities throughout the school, and with the consent and co-operation of the principal, Dr. Stone's tests were given under as nearly identical conditions as possible to every grade in the school from the third to the thirteenth, or last year in the high school, inclusive. The tests thus became a measure, not only of the ability gained during the eight years of arithmetic, but also of what happens to that ability as the child undergoes the training of her high-school mathematics and science. Before considering the test itself, however, the reader needs to know something of the school and of the conditions under which the ability tested was gained.

The school in question is a private school for girls. The total enrolment last year (1908–9) was 317, making the average number of girls in a grade 23. Any class is sectioned as soon as its membership rises above twelve, and further provision is made, through a system of "interviews" for a careful, yet legitimate, assistance of the weaker members. The method of instruction is thus distinctly "individualistic." Girls are received in the kindergarten, carried through eight grades in the elementary school, five in the high school, and are then admitted to the leading colleges without examination. Approximately half the girls take the college course. This past year, for instance, there were 24 graduates of the school enrolled in Vassar College alone.

The instruction in arithmetic, as in other subjects, has during the last ten years undergone radical changes. Complaints of lack of ability in arithmetic shown in the laboratory work in science has lead to correlation between the two subjects, and the gradual adoption of laboratory methods in arithmetic itself, while many laboratory exercises and methods are making their way into the algebra and geometry classes of the high school. Two years ago the two subjects, science and mathematics, were made one department, under the control of one head, and a strict, objective laboratory system of instruction adopted throughout. It will be noted that the past few years have been a transition period and the conditions of teaching have been unsettled. The changes may be described as an adoption of the cyclic-objective method in place of the topic-drill method. At the present time grades 1–4 have had a fair amount of laboratory training, grades 5–7 a small amount for one year, grade 8 a large amount for one year, grades 9 and 10 a less amount for a year, and grades 11, 12, 13 none except through their science work. Part of grade 13, however, reviewed algebra and geometry during the year, following the general plan of the new method, but with few laboratory exercises.

The general method of giving the tests was that followed by Dr. Stone. The examples were typewritten and the paper fastened to a sheet of blank paper by means of a clip so that the typewriting was on the inside. These papers were distributed in the assembly rooms of the school, the whole of each division of the school being tested at one time. The girls were told to write their names and grades on the blank sheet, but not to look at the examples until given a signal. It was explained that the purpose was to test the ability of the whole school in arithmetic, not the individual, but that each must do her best for the honor of her class. Then the signal was given and at the end of the allotted time, twelve minutes for fundamentals, fifteen for reasoning, another signal was given and the papers collected. The tests were given on successive days at about the middle of the morning near the close of the year. The children did not know the tests were to be given, nor how much time they were to have.

The test in fundamentals and the score in points for each example (see below) was as follows:

ARITHMETIC TEST

Work as many of these problems as you have time for: work them in order as numbered.

		SCORE IN POINTS
1. Add:	2375 4052 6354 260 5041 1543	19 additions.
2. Multiply 3265 by 20.		2 additions, 5 multiplications.
3. Divide 3328 by 64.		2 additions, 3 subtractions, 4 multiplications, 2 divisions.
4. Add:	596 428 94 755 302 645 984 897	20 additions.
5. Multiply 768 by 604.		7 additions, 7 multiplications.
6. Divide 1918962 by 543.		6 additions, 10 subtractions, 12 multiplications, 4 divisions.
7. Add:	4695 872 7948 7499 6786 567 858 9447	28 additions.
8. Multiply 976 by 87.		8 additions, 6 multiplications.

9. Divide 2782542 by 679.	6 additions, 7 subtractions, 9 multiplications, 4 divisions.
10. Multiply 5489 by 9876.	28 additions, 16 multiplications.
11. Divide 5099941 by 749.	6 additions, 7 subtractions, 9 multiplications, 4 divisions.
12. Multiply 876 by 79.	9 additions, 6 multiplications.
13. Divide 62693256 by 859.	10 additions, 13 subtractions, 15 multiplications, 5 divisions.
14. Multiply 96879 by 896.	28 additions, 15 multiplications.

It will be noticed that the ability tested is that involved in the handling of abstract numbers in addition, multiplication, division, and (incidentally in division) subtraction. Speed and accuracy in such work are certainly fundamental in all mathematics, and whatever else the course in arithmetic may give, it must produce such ability. Criticism of the test itself will be made later.

The papers were scored in two different ways. By the first method, called hereafter "by examples," each example attempted gave a count of one. When the correct answer was obtained the example was scored as one right. If the answer was wrong for any reason it was not scored in the second count. For instance an example copied wrong but worked correctly was counted one attempted, but not one right, as was also example 6, worked correctly but marked example 4. A record was kept by name and grade of the examples attempted (Attempts), and the examples right (Rights). The individual scores were analyzed into examples in addition, multiplication, and division. Here a record was made, for each example wrong, of the character of the mistake, whether in addition, subtraction, multiplication, division, or copying or carrying. The total for each grade was found from the individual records.

The second method of scoring was "by points." It grew out of a desire to analyze the papers and mistakes on a basis of mental effort involved, but proved rather unwieldy and unsatisfactory. It was found that no two persons would use quite the same judgment in analyzing a paper, and that it was difficult for even a single individual to follow a consistent system. The scores and the results are given, however, as with a suitable test, such a system of scoring would be of value. In the main, the results obtained even in this test are believed to be correct within two or three percentages, all the scoring being done finally by one person. For several grades the scores were marked separately by two individuals and the results compared. For all the grades the different points scored made a certain checking of the results necessary and this also contributed to the general accuracy.

In detail the scores by points as given were determined as follows:

The first example given above was

Add:

$$\begin{array}{r} 2375 \\ 4052 \\ 6354 \\ 260 \\ 5041 \\ 1543 \\ \hline \end{array}$$

In solving this example the child in the third grade goes through four additions for the first column; $3+1=4$; $4+4=8$; $8+2=10$; $10+5=15$: six additions for the second column; 1 (carried) $+4=5$; $5+4=9$; $9+6=15$; $15+5=20$; $20+5=25$; $25+7=32$: four for the third column, and five for the last column, a total of 19. If the answer to example 1 were given as 19,685 (correct answer, 19,625), the child was given a score of 19 points in addition attempted, 13 points (the total 19, less the additions in the second column, 6), right. In multiplication and division the attempt was made to separate the incidental additions and subtractions from the multiplications and divisions. For instance, in example 3,

$$\begin{array}{r} 64)3328(52 \\ 320 \\ \hline 128 \\ 128 \\ \hline \end{array}$$

the steps are $33\div6=5$, one point in division; $5\times4=20$, one point in multiplication; $5\times6=30$, one point in multiplication, $30+2$ (carried)$=32$, one point in *addition;* 0 from $2=2$, one point in *subtraction:* 2 from $3=1$, one point in subtraction, and so on, the total score for a correct answer being, as given, 2 additions, 3 subtractions, 4 multiplications, 2 divisions. In some respects the scores were arbitrary assignments of value, as when the recognition of 128 as equal to 128 was counted as one point in subtraction, but in all such cases the same scores were used throughout and affected all alike. In most cases it was comparatively easy to form an opinion as to whether a mistake was in the actual multiplying and dividing or in the carrying. For instance, when 5×543 was given as 2,615, the multiplication $5\times5=25$ was counted as correct and the mistake that of carrying 1 in place of 2 from the previous 21. This was counted as a mistake in addition. If 6×768 was given as 5,208, the four from the previous 40 was probably carried correctly and the mistake one of multiplication, 6×7 being called 48. In other cases the character of the mistake was not so plain and the classification a mere guess. Most mistakes in multiplication, however, seem to consist in the substitution of one part of the multiplication table for another. This and other similar experiences formed a basis from which judgments could be made. After all the papers had been scored as above, they were gone over a second time and the attempt was made to separate mistakes in carrying and copying from all others. These were called mistakes due to faulty attention (A).

As to whether it is worth while, or not, to give the time needed for such careful scrutiny of each result, there will undoubtedly be two opinions. The writer wished to know, however, whether the children performed the different operations with equal ease, and in case of failure, to what the failure was due. It is manifestly useless to drill children on the multiplication tables for instance, if failure in multiplication is due to inability to carry, and it is equally useless to attempt elaborate examples in multiplication and division if the fundamental combinations are imperfectly mastered. The writer personally considers his time well spent, but the results must speak for themselves.

The test for reasoning, and scores by points, was as follows:

ARITHMETIC TEST

Solve as many of the following problems as you have time for; work them in order as numbered.

1. If you buy two tablets at 7 cents each and a book for 65 cents, how much change should you receive from a two-dollar bill?

SCORE

2—[(2×7)+65]. One point each for addition, subtraction, and multiplication.

2. John sold 4 *Saturday Evening Posts* at 5 cents each. He kept ½ the money and with the other half he bought Sunday papers at 2 cents each. How many did he buy?

SCORE

4+5=20. 20÷2=10. 10÷2=5. One point for multiplication and two for division.

3. If James had 4 times as much money as George, he would have $16. How much money has George?

SCORE

16÷4=4. One point for division.

4. How many pencils can you buy for 50 cents at the rate of 2 for 5 cents?

SCORE

50÷5=10. 10×2=20. One point for multiplication, one for division.

5. The uniforms for a baseball nine cost $2.50 each. The shoes cost $2 a pair. What was the total cost of the uniforms and shoes for the nine?

SCORE

(9×2.50)+(9×2). One point for addition, two for multiplication.

6. In the schools of a certain city there are 2,200 pupils; ½ are in the primary grades, ¼ in the grammar grades, ⅛ in the high school, and the rest in the night school. How many pupils are there in the night school?

SCORE

2,200÷2=1,100. 2,200÷4=550. 2,200÷8=275. (1,100+550+275)=1,925. 2,200—1,925=275. One point for addition, one for subtraction, three for division.

7. If 3½ tons of coal cost $21, what will 5½ tons cost?

SCORE

5.5(21÷3.5). One point for multiplication, one for division.

8. A newsdealer bought some magazines for $1. He sold them for $1.20, gaining 5 cents on each magazine. How many magazines were there?

SCORE

1.20—1=.20 20÷5=4. One point for subtraction, one for division.

9. A girl spent ⅛ of her money for carefare, and three times as much for clothes. Half of what she had left was 80 cents. How much money did she have at first?

SCORE

1/8+3/8=4/8. 1—4/8=4/8. 4/8÷2=1/4. 80×4=3.20. One point each for addition, subtraction, division, and two for multiplication.

10. Two girls receive $2.10 for making button-holes. One makes 42, the other 28. How shall they divide the money?

SCORE

42+28=70. 2.10÷70=.03. .03×42. .03×28. One point each for addition and division, two for multiplication.

11. Mr. Brown paid 1/3 the cost of a building; Mr. Johnson paid 1/2 the cost. Mr. Johnson received $500 more annual rent than Mr. Brown. How much did each receive?

SCORE

1/2—1/3=1/6. 500×2. 500×3. One point for subtraction, two for multiplication.

12. A freight train left Albany for New York at 6 o'clock. An express left on the same track at 8 o'clock. It went at the rate of 40 miles an hour. At what time of day will it overtake the freight train if the freight train stops after it has gone 56 miles?

SCORE

56÷40=1.4. .4×60=24. 8+1:24=9:24. One point each for addition, multiplication, and division.

This test was scored in the same two ways as the test on fundamentals, by examples, and by points. It will be noted from the scores given that a point stands for a single operation, a three-step problem counting three points. Individual and grade records were kept as before, each score being analyzed in the same way. Mistakes in the work were grouped in several classes. Using 8 cents instead of 7 cents in problem 1 was called a mistake in attention (A); adding the difference of 65 and 14 to 2.00 was called a total failure to comprehend the meaning of the example (T); using 1 block at 7 cents instead of 2 was called a mistake due to incomplete reading or appreciation of the English of the example—a mistake in attention (A)—such mistakes were not made by those who re-read the problem for the purpose of checking their work; problems correctly planned but containing mistakes in the work were said to be wrong because of mistakes in fundamentals (F).

Besides these general records, a special record was kept of the number of examples in which there was an attempt to use either algebra or proportion. Approximately 100 girls were in possession of enough algebraic skill to have enabled them to use simple equations had they cared to do so, although the fact that the paper was marked "Arithmetic Test" would have influenced many against the use of algebra. The neatness of the papers in both tests was also recorded in a rough way, two grades of neatness only being recognized—neat and untidy. Each paper was scored twice, however, and the doubtful ones near the dividing line gone over a third time. A paper was judged neat when its examples were arranged in a clear orderly fashion, properly numbered, and were without serious blots or untidy marks and figures. A record was kept, also, of the perfect papers.

Before leaving the subject of scoring, it might be well to say again that many of the judgments upon which the scores were based were quite arbitrary in their nature, but that as nearly as possible the scoring was uniform throughout. In scoring by points allowance was made for individual variation by making up new scores of the same character where the individual had worked the problem in a longer or shorter way. That is, the scores by points represent scores upon the work that each individual put upon her paper, while the scores by examples show

TABLE I. PART 1

TOTAL GRADE SCORES

Actual results

"F" refers to fundamentals; "R" to reasoning

Grade	No. in Grade		Fundamentals				Reasoning			
			Examples		Points		Examples		Points	
	F	R	At	Rt	At	Rt	At	Rt	At	Rt
3	12	12	23	3	441	237	41	20	97	71
4	16	16	67	40	1005	891	81	57	203	175
5	22	22	130	81	2266	2080	186	94	538	383
6	13	12	82	57	1585	1463	112	48	323	202
7	23	22	160	120	3062	2889	189	123	555	455
8	21	21	181	131	3634	3344	204	150	580	507
9	18	18	136	108	2566	2474	178	129	518	439
10	21	21	189	139	3719	3566	217	167	632	559
11	23	25	177	144	3305	3155	255	218	768	710
12	33	29	264	203	5136	4840	279	223	828	740
13	16	19	147	122	3090	2998	198	160	599	531
	218	217	total number taking tests.							

TABLE I. PART 2

TOTAL GRADE SCORES

Scores used for comparison of grade achievements. Computed on basis of uniform grades of 25 members each

" F " refers to fundamentals; " R " to reasoning

Grade	Multiplier		Fundamentals				Reasoning			
			Examples		Points		Examples		Points	
	F	R	At	Rt	At	Rt	At	Rt	At	Rt
3	2.08	2.08	48	6	917	493	85	42	202	148
4	1.56	1.56	103	62	1567	1390	126	89	317	273
5	1.14	1.14	148	93	2583	2371	212	107	613	437
6	1.93	2.08	158	110	3059	2824	233	100	672	420
7	1.09	1.14	174	131	3338	3149	215	140	633	519
8	1.19	1.19	216	159	4324	3979	243	178	690	603
9	1.39	1.39	189	150	3566	3439	247	179	720	610
10	1.19	1.14	225	165	4426	4243	247	190	720	637
11	1.09	1.00	193	157	3602	3439	255	218	768	710
12	.76	.86	201	155	3903	3678	240	192	712	636
13	1.56	1.32	231	191	4820	4677	260	211	791	700

how nearly the individual came to perfection. In each a mistake counted, but by points a careless inverting of two figures would deduct a single point, while by examples the paper lost the whole score for the example. Both scores should be considered in estimating the ability of a grade.

The results of the tests are given in the accompanying tables and graphs.

It is obviously unfair to compare the achievements of a grade with 33 members with that of a grade containing but 12 members. Accordingly these results have been equalized by computing what they would have been if the grade membership in each case had been 25.

Graphically the results in Part 2 may be represented as shown in Plots 1 and 2.

The interpretation of the curves obtained is difficult in the absence of standards with which to compare the results. It must be remembered throughout this discussion that the inferences and conclusions made are from a single measurement only and are therefore tentative except as the writer is able to bring additional evidence to bear from his knowledge of the classes and conditions. It will need the tests of several years to eliminate differences due to variation in ability and class spirit alone. The factors determining ability are so many and their individual effects so little known that the results of the present test will

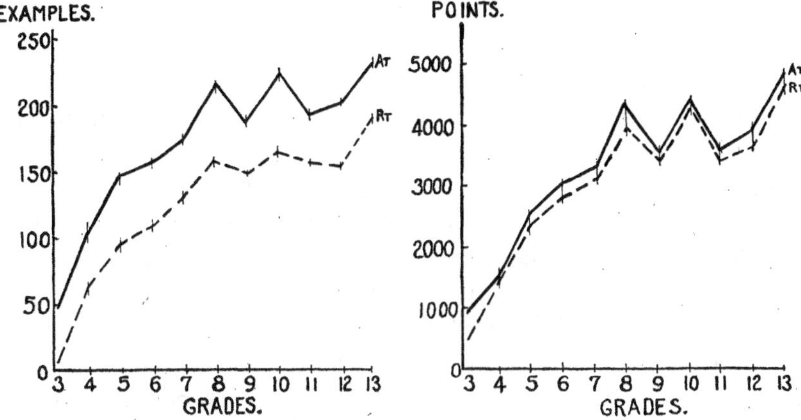

PLOT 1.—Grade abilities in fundamentals as shown by scores in examples and points, Table I, Part 2.

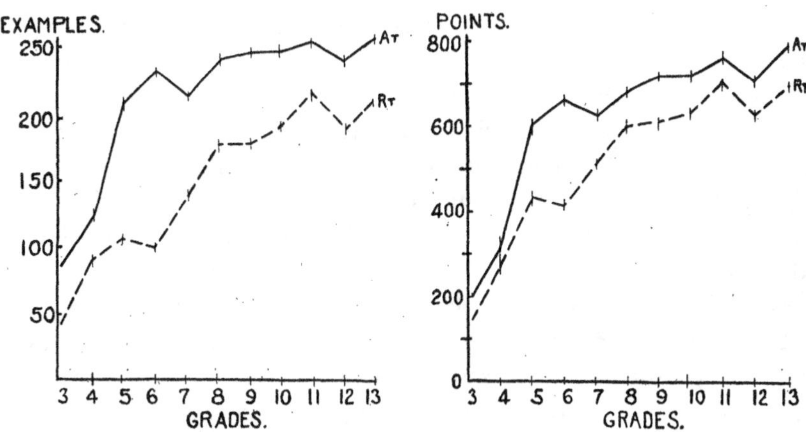

PLOT 2.—Grade abilities in reasoning as shown by scores in examples and points, Table I, Part 2.

furnish at best merely a working hypothesis for the planning of the next year's work, which hypothesis must stand or fall by the results of next year's tests.

Certain facts, however, seem to the writer to stand out plainly. The test in fundamentals appears to have been more difficult than that in reasoning. The latter, in attempts at least, rises to a maximum earlier. Criticism of the test on reasoning will be made later. In the general development of ability there seems to be a rapid and quite uniform rise during the grammar grades and a slight but steady rise during the high-school period. Grade variations in ability make the meaning of the changes in the curve in the upper grades doubtful. It may be that grades 8 and 10 are of exceptional ability and the other grades represent the normal results. On the other hand, and this supposition seems the more probable from experience in teaching the various classes, it may be that grades 6, 7, 9, 11, and 12 are poor classes, and the true standard curve should follow the crests instead of the troughs of the present curves. Grades 6 and 9 are notoriously poor, grade six because of a peculiar history and grade nine because of poor ideals of work. The real test of the effect of high-school mathematics will come as the results of a good class, as the eighth grade, are successively known through the upper grades. It is to be remembered also that a change of system has been taking place, and that grades 11, 12, and 13 may mark the highest achievements under the old régime. For the present it is a pleasure to know that the eighth grade, which has been given a large amount of the new training, is at least not below the standard of any class except the seniors, and it may not be out of place to call attention to the fact that if high-school mathematics does add to ability in arithmetic, the present eighth grade ought to set a new senior record by the time it has finished its course.

It is to be noted that the curves of ability by examples and by points are of the same general character, differing mainly in the degree of accuracy shown. Such differences are due to the character of the mistakes as explained under the discussion of scoring. Hereafter, plots will show either one set of scores or the other unless there is marked difference between them.

The inaccuracy of grades 5 and 6 in the reasoning test needs explanation. These two grades work with fractions and attempted every example containing the fractional idea. It can be seen from the test, however, that some of the problems dealt with the principles of partition, about which these classes have learned nothing. Nevertheless, that the sixth grade should succeed in solving less problems than the fifth grade shows the necessity for special and vigorous training if the class as a whole is ever to come up to the standards of the other classes. Yet here again who can say that the factors which have contributed to this result may not operate at a later period to give increased ability?

In comparing the curves for fundamentals with those for reasoning, it will be noted that some classes are high in both, or low in both, while others are high in one and low in the other. This corresponds to classroom experience. The child that can reason well but is poor in abstract work usually passes with the child that is perfect in abstract work and poor in reasoning. This suggests that the truest measure of the abilities of the grades would be a combination score from both tests. It is manifestly unfair to combine 4,820 points in fundamentals with 791 points in reasoning, the achievements of the thirteenth-grade class. Accordingly, in Table II, the scores of Table I, Part 2, have been

TABLE II

PART 1. Comparison scores of Table I, Part 2, adjusted to equality of achievement in fundamentals and reasoning. Thirteenth-grade attempts in both tests called 250 in examples, and 5,000 in points. Other scores given proportionate values.

PART 2. Total achievements of the grades. Sum of F and R scores Part 1 for each grade.

Grade	Fundamentals				Reasoning				Total Scores			
	Examples		Points		Examples		Points		Examples		Points	
	At	Rt	At	Rt	At	Rt	At	Rt	At	Rt	At	Rt
3	51	6	952	508	82	40	1277	934	133	46	2229	1442
4	111	67	1628	1443	121	85	2003	1726	232	152	3631	3169
5	160	101	2682	2482	204	103	3874	2761	364	204	6556	5223
6	171	119	3177	2930	224	96	4248	2654	395	215	7425	5584
7	188	142	3463	3267	207	136	4000	3280	395	278	7463	6547
8	234	172	4487	4131	233	171	4361	3811	467	343	8848	7942
9	205	162	3703	3568	237	172	4550	3855	443	334	8253	7423
10	244	179	4593	4403	237	182	4550	4025	471	361	9143	8428
11	209	170	3739	3568	245	209	4854	4487	454	379	8593	8055
12	217	168	4051	3819	230	184	4500	4019	447	352	8551	7838
13	250	207	5000	4856	250	203	5000	4424	500	410	10000	9280

equalized by calling the thirteenth-grade achievements in both fundamentals and reasoning an arbitrary equal value and recomputing the other scores to correspond. The values chosen were

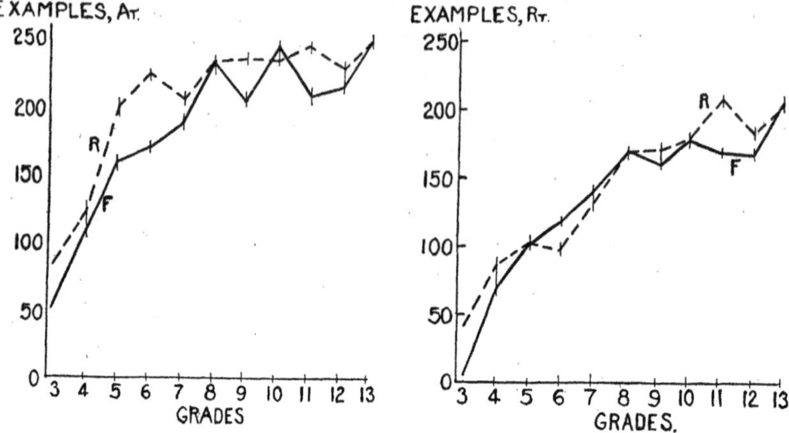

PLOT 3.—Comparison of achievements in fundamentals and reasoning by examples. Scores recomputed and equalized on a basis of 250 for the 13th grade attempts. Full lines show fundamentals; dotted lines show reasoning.

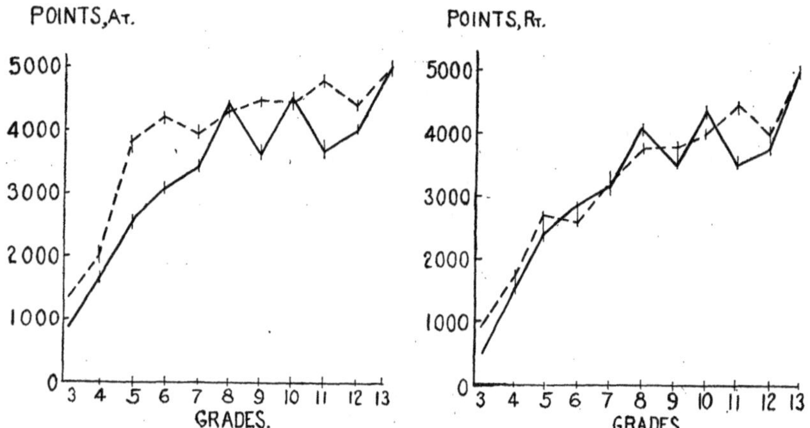

PLOT 4.—Comparison of achievements in fundamentals and reasoning by points. Score recomputed and equalized on the basis of 5,000 for 13th grade attempts. Full lines show fundamentals; dotted lines show reasoning.

250 for examples, and 5,000 for points. Plots 3 and 4 show the relations between the equalized scores graphically. The combined scores are also given and are shown graphically in Plot 5.

Plots 3 and 4 make very plain the different types of ability. Grade 12 is seen to be comparatively poor in both tests, grades 9 and 11 good in one and poor in the other, grade 8 good in both. It is certainly a significant fact that grades 5, 8, 10, and 13, taken as representing the normal abilities, should have equal ability in the two tests.

The characteristics of the different grades and the general trend of the development is at once apparent from the curves

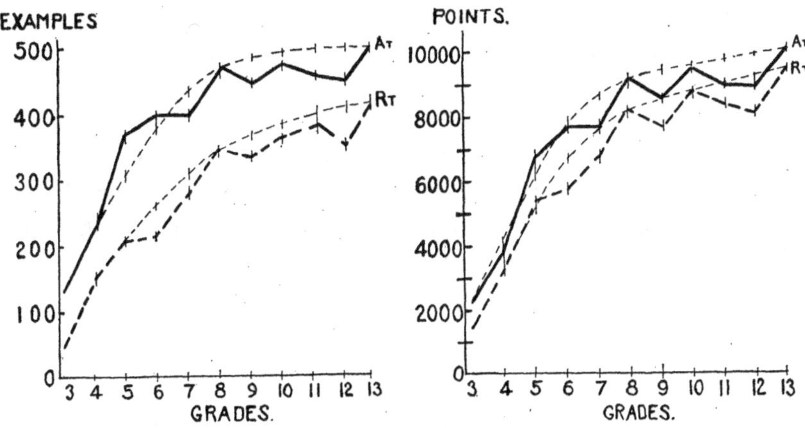

PLOT 5.—Total ability as shown by combination of equalized scores. Light dotted curves show probable normal product of present conditions.

obtained from the combination scores, Plot 5. It will be noted that grades 5, 6, and 12 are inaccurate; grades 7, 9, and 11 somewhat below normal in ability. The combination scores have evidently made less the marked variations in ability present in the scores for either test alone. The meaning of this is not apparent to the writer. It has been a puzzling fact of his teaching experience that ability to reason and ability to be exact in abstract work seldom go together. He is inclined to believe that there is a psychological principle at work, which, if known, would solve more riddles than one in educational procedure. Whatever the explanation, statistical proof of the fact is given here.

On Plot 5 are drawn in light dotted lines the curves that will be taken as representing the normal product of the training given in the school at present (1909). These will serve as standards from which to judge of the effects in changes and methods in the years to come. There are slight differences in form between the curves by examples and those by points, but the most noticeable feature of the plot is the change in accuracy. Accuracy gradually decreases through the grammar grades and increases through the high-school grades at about the same rate. If this result is confirmed by future tests, there is an important lesson here. If inaccuracy in grades 7, 8, and 9, is due to some natural cause outside of arithmetic proper, to insist on accuracy or to spend much time in working for it may be not only wasteful, but harmful. These curves not only furnish a standard of accuracy for the different grades but a measure of the effect of accuracy as well. For instance, in the thirteenth grade, being able to perform correctly 93 out of a hundred operations (as 3×4, 8–5), means an efficiency of 83 per cent. in working examples like those in the test.

[*To be continued*]

OUR INHERITED PRACTICE IN ELEMENTARY SCHOOLS

S. CHESTER PARKER
The University of Chicago

Many who are interested in the training of elementary teachers are questioning the value of the history of education. Could not the time be spent to better advantage on a more direct study of present educational practice? The critics of the history of education may admit that doubtless any serious consideration of education by students helps them somewhat in their thinking. They will contend, however, that too much rumination about theories as theories, with no occasion for application, develops habits of pure speculation which not only waste time, but often interfere with efficiency. When this speculation concerns itself with situations and thought, hundreds or thousands of years removed, there is little chance of its functioning in the actual work of the young teacher.

Without attempting to argue the matter out with these critics, we may fall back on the simple consideration that the history of education will continue for some time to form a part of most normal-school courses. As long as this is the case, it is important to put into the instruction such content as will be most likely to modify the everyday thinking and practice of the students. Looked at from this standpoint, the material ordinarily found in the histories of education may be roughly classified as follows in the order of increasing value:

1. The history of philosophy masquerading as the history of education. The substitution of this material for education results from the fact that courses in education have often developed in higher institutions in departments of philosophy, and the speculations of philosophers about education have been most accessible for treatment. Material of this sort is almost meaningless even to many graduate students; it is certainly incomprehensible to the

great majority of normal-school students, and its connection with practice is very remote.

2. Biographical accounts of the more concrete writers on education, such as Montaigne, Ascham, Locke, and Rousseau. Quick's *Educational Reformers* is the best example of this type of history of education. Such material as that presented by Quick is so simple that normal-school students understand it. Much of it belongs rather to the history of literature than to the history of education. It serves the purpose of introducing students to a consideration of many educational questions in an unsystematized form, as, for example, through Montaigne's discussion of the futility of memorizing. These writers are, however, generally studied without adequate historical setting. The student does not realize the social and educational situation which confronted them nor does he appreciate the effects of their works on future practice.

3. Summaries of the more obvious aspects of education in various parts of the world beginning with China 2,000 years before Christ and coming down to the present century in America. Often all of this is contained in small volumes of about 300 pages. The worthlessness of such skeleton outlines of historical development has long been admitted in history courses which have for their sole aim information and culture. As material which may function in modifying a teacher's attitude and practice, a cursory outline is even more worthless. Changes in education are relatively meaningless to the student of such a text, because the social situation from which these changes arise and which they in turn modify, is not presented.

4. Type studies of limited periods, with their social and economic and material setting. One of the best examples of this kind of history of education is the account of Renaissance education given by Professor Woodward, of England. The classical humanistic education is filled with meaning for the student as he realizes that it was a necessary consequence of the life of the castles and city states of northern Italy. Such a study continued down to the present time should furnish a valuable perspective for those interested in practical problems of high-school cur-

ricula. An appreciation of our inherited practices in high schools thus gained from an examination of the historical setting of such schools may become a strong factor in rationalizing a teacher's attitude toward high-school problems.

This fourth kind of treatment of the history of education, namely, type studies of limited periods, showing the social, economic, and material conditions of the period, is possible in normal schools for elementary teachers. Some material for such a course is now available and a few chapters will be presented in this and subsequent papers. The period of central interest will be the time from the American Revolution to the present day. To understand the conditions of educational practice about 1775 it will be necessary to devote the remainder of this first paper to a brief consideration of the period just prior to the Revolution.

In the New England colonies a bookish elementary education originated from the demand that everyone read the Bible.

Most teachers are familiar with the life and character of the New England Puritans. Their educational practice followed logically from their mode of life. Let us review a few of their characteristics, important from this standpoint.

In the first place the Puritans were religious reformers, a part of the Protestant Reformation. Theoretically, they believed in the principle that an individual's religion was a matter between himself and God, and that a study of the Bible was the way to religious truth. They had rejected the authority of the church of Rome and the dogmas that had developed in the Middle Ages. They desired to "purify" the English church even further and reject prayers read from a book, the surplice, and all other religious forms. As Fischer expresses it, "They wanted to reduce Christianity to its most primitive form of four bare walls and the literal words of the Bible."[1] They came to America to establish a condition of religious life in accordance with these ideals. To be sure, they soon developed canons of religious orthodoxy almost as narrow and bigoted as any that had been held during the Middle Ages, and that were utterly inconsistent with the freedom of conscience which the Reformation advocated. But reli-

[1] S. A. Fischer, *Men, Women, and Manners in Colonial Times,* Vol. I, p. 125.

gion continued to be their chief interest, and the Bible the central object of study. As Elson says, "The state was founded on religion and religion was its life. The entire political, social, and industrial fabric was built on religion."[2]

The intense interest in the Bible and the prominent place it occupied in their intellectual and religious life is most significant. The same condition existed in Puritan England and is described by Green in these words:

> England became the people of a book and that book was the Bible. It was as yet the one English book that was familiar to every Englishman; it was read at churches and read at home, and everywhere its words, as it fell on ears which custom had not deadened, kindled a startling enthusiasm. The popularity of the Bible was owing to other causes besides that of religion. The whole prose literature of England, save the forgotten tracts of Wyclif, has grown up since the translation of the Scriptures by Tyndale [1525] and Coverdale [1538]. So far as the nation at large was concerned, no history, no romance, hardly any poetry, save the little-known verse of Chaucer, existed in the English tongue when the Bible was ordered to be set up in churches. Sunday after Sunday, day after day, the crowds that gathered around Bonner's Bible in the nave of St. Paul's, or the family group that hung on the words of the Geneva Bible in the devotional exercises at home, were leavened with a new literature. The power of the book over the mass of Englishmen showed itself in a thousand superficial ways, and in none more conspicuously than in the influence it exerted on ordinary speech. It formed, we must repeat, the whole literature that was practically accessible to ordinary Englishmen.[3]

Such was the intellectual life of the New England Puritans. It was intense and vigorous in its way. This is shown by the attendance on sermons, Sunday morning and afternoon, note-taking at such sermons, long theological discussions. But it lacked many of the interests considered important at the present day. There was no popular interest in science, no appreciation of secular literature, no art, no drama, no forms of higher amusements. The natural impulses were considered evil, and a moody introspection of one's sins a virtue.

On the practical side, the New England settlers were small farmers, fishermen, shipbuilders, sailors, and merchants. There

[2] Elson, *History of the United States,* p. 128.

[3] Green, *Short History of the English People,* chap. viii.

was little manufacturing, most necessary articles being made in the home. The farmer was generally his own mechanic, and the women made a variety of products. G. Stanley Hall has enumerated about sixty trades that were represented in the activities of a New England farm.

The importance of keeping in mind the industrial activities of the household, and neighborhood in a study of colonial education has been emphasized particularly by Dr. Dewey in his *School and Society*.

> The household was practically the center in which were carried on, or about which were clustered, all the typical forms of industrial occupation. The clothing worn was for the most part not only made in the house, but the members of the household were generally familiar with the shearing of the sheep, the carding and spinning of the wool and the plying of the loom. Instead of pressing a button and flooding the house with electric light, the whole process of getting illumination stood revealed in its toilsome length, from the killing of the animal and the trying of the fat, to the making of wicks and dipping of candles. The supply of flour, of lumber, of foods, of building materials, of household furniture, even of metal-ware, of nails, hinges, hammers, etc., was in the immediate neighborhood, in shops which were constantly open to inspection and often centers of neighborhood congregation.[4]

These were the activities and interests for which education had to prepare. Let us see what provision was made for them in elementary schools. The well-known preamble to the law passed by the Massachusetts General Court in 1647 is the clearest expression of the religious basis of this education. The same preamble is copied in the Connecticut law of 1650, the phraseology being slightly improved.

> It being one chief project of that old deluder, Satan, to keep men from a knowledge of the Scriptures, as in former times, keeping them in an unknown tongue, so in these latter times, by persuading them from the use of tongues, so that at least, the true sense and meaning of the original might be clouded by false glosses of saint-seeming deceivers; and that learning may not be buried in the grave of our fore-fathers [the court decreed that whenever a township increased to fifty householders they should employ someone] to teach all such children as shall resort to him, to write and read.

[4] P. 22.

An earlier Massachusetts ordinance of the year 1642 had required parents and masters of children to train the latter "to read and understand the principles of religion and the capital laws of the country." The Connecticut law of 1650 made the same requirement, with additional religious training as follows, "That all masters of families, do, once a week, at least, catechize their children and servants in the grounds and principles of religion."

The work of elementary education is definitely stated in these laws. It is to be writing and reading, a knowledge of the principles of religion and the capital laws, and the learning of the catechism.

The chief work of the school came to be the teaching of the two formal subjects, writing and reading. There is no mention of spelling, arithmetic, composition, drawing, singing, object-study, physiology, nature-study, geography, history, secular literature, or manual training. For the purpose of rural New England Puritan life even writing was of minor importance. Reading was the all-important subject. Our first systems of American elementary schools were fundamentally reading schools for religious purposes.

Such was the training given in elementary school. But there was another kind of training of importance provided in the same laws, but not given in the schools. It was training in industrial activities. As stated in the Connecticut law of 1650 the requirement reads:

> that all parents and masters do breed and bring up their children and apprentices in some honest lawful labor, or employment, either in husbandry or some other trade profitable for themselves and the commonwealth, if they will not nor cannot train them up in learning, to fit them for higher employments, and if any of the selectmen, after admonition by them given to such masters of families, shall find them still negligent of their duty, ... the said selectmen, with the help of two magistrates, shall take such children or apprentices from them, and place them with some masters for years, boys until they come to be twenty-one, and girls to eighteen years of age complete.

The Massachusetts law of 1642, the Pennsylvania law of 1683, and other colonial laws made similar provisions.

Thus we find compulsory industrial education provided for

very early, in fact at the same time as schools for teaching to read. This training for a trade, together with the many things learned in the home, and the narrow interests and austere life of the New Englanders, enable us to understand why such narrow and specialized instruction was left to the elementary school. It is essential that the student keep in mind the industrial training formerly received outside the school, in order to appreciate recent developments in elementary education.

Elementary education of the early type continued with little change to the Revolution. Reading and writing were fundamental; spelling and arithmetic were added.

Little change occurred in the instruction offered in the American elementary schools from their establishment to the time of the Revolutionary War. They remained primarily reading-and-writing schools, with one or two other subjects for older children. This is evident from the account given by Noah Webster of the schools in which he had been educated. I quote his statement because it presents very definitely and concretely what is shown by other accounts to have been the common practice. Spelling and arithmetic had been added to the work of the elementary schools, otherwise there was little change. Webster's account is as follows:

> When I was young, the books used were, chiefly or wholly, Dilworth's *Spelling Books,* the Psalter, Testament, and Bible. No geography was studied before the publication of Dr. Morse's small books on that subject, about the year 1786 or 1787. No history was read, as far as my knowledge extends, for there was no abridged history of the United States. Except the books above mentioned, no book for reading was used before the publication of the third part of my *Institute,* in 1785. In some of the early editions of that book, I introduced short notices of the geography and history of the United States, and these led to more enlarged descriptions of the country. In 1788 at the request of Dr. Morse, I wrote an account of the transactions in the United States, after the Revolution; which account fills nearly twenty pages in the first volume of his octavo editions.
>
> Before the Revolution, and for some years after, no slates were used in the common schools: all writing and the operations in arithmetic were on paper. The teacher wrote the copies and gave the sums in arithmetic;

few or none of the pupils having any books as a guide. Such was the condition of the schools in which I received my early education.

The introduction of my *Spelling Book,* first published in 1783, produced a great change in the department of spelling.

No English grammar was generally taught in common schools when I was young, except that in Dilworth, and that to no good purpose. In short the instruction in schools was very imperfect.[5]

A concrete picture of the work of elementary schools in Boston at the beginning of the nineteenth century, may be found in the reminiscences of Henry K. Oliver, who attended them. He went to three grades of school, first the A B C school, second the reading school, and then the Latin grammar school. We are not concerned with the latter which was to prepare for college, but will follow his career in the elementary school.

A B C SCHOOL

In the year 1805, or thereabouts, being then something under five years of age, I was consigned to the care of one Mr. Hayslop, who, with his wife and widowed daughter, kept school in an old building. By him I was taught my A, B, C, D, E, F, G, my a, b, ab's and my e, b, eb's, after the old, old way—praised because ancestral—the old gentleman holding an old book in his old hand and pointing, with an old pin, to the old letters on the old page, and making each of us chicks repeat their several names till we could tell them at sight, though we did not know what it was all for. We must have been a bright set, excellent of memory, for with this excellent old method, and with the excellent old books of the old times, and the excellent old teacher, and our own excellent young wits, we were not more than four or five weeks in acquiring complete knowledge of the twenty-six arbitrary marks constituting the English alphabet. To be sure, I learned the names, family and Christian, of all my fellow-scholars, and they were quite a host, in a week; but that was, as it were, naturally—by instinct, as Falstaff knew the true prince—while to learn the letters must only be done after the good old fashion of the ancestral teaching, the teachers of those days holding faithfully to the first line of Pope's couplet:

> Be not the first by whom the new is tried,

And wholly ignoring the second:

> Nor yet the last to lay the old aside.

DAME SCHOOL OR READING SCHOOL

From this school I was removed to another, Madam Tileston's, in Hanover, below Salem Street, of the same general character, where I was

[5] Barnard, *American Journal of Education,* Vol. XXVI, p. 196.

taught elementary reading and spelling, after the same ancestral fashion—that is, I received about twenty minutes of instruction each half day and as school was kept three hundred and sixty minutes daily, I had the privilege of forty minutes' worth of teaching, and three hundred and twenty minutes' worth of sitting still (if I could), which I could not—playing, whispering, and general waste of time, though occasionally a picture-book relieved the dreary monotony.

My nervous temperament, dislike of confinement at busy nothingness, want of affection for books—slates then we had none—love of mischief, and general habit of fidgetiness, often entitled me to Madam Tileston's customary punishment of sundry sharp taps on the head, with the middle finger of her right hand; said finger being armed, for its own defense, with a large and rough steel thimble.

Both of these teachers taught as well as they knew how—and as well as the times in which they lived and worked permitted them to know. Nobody taught any better so far as I have learned. Nor was there anything like the philosophy of teaching known or thought of, so far as I can judge on retrospection, by any teacher into whose hands I fell.

There were no schools systematically graded; there were no blackboards; there were no globes, nor ordinary apparatus in schools I attended. I never saw a full-sized map, nor illustrative picture of any sort suspended against the school wall.[6]

There was no object-teaching; in fact, there was no teaching at all, in the modern sense of the word. The master's time was all consumed with hearing lessons, making pens, setting copies, and keeping order.

The account given of New England education from its origin to the Revolutionary War has shown the following general points: (1) that elementary schools were established primarily to teach children to read the Bible and other religious literature; (2) that compulsory industrial training was provided for by law; (3) that little change had taken place up to the Revolution, the main purpose of the schools continuing to be the teaching of children to read and write.

This development of elementary education in America is paralleled by similar developments in many of the countries of Europe, particularly those in which the spirit of the Protestant Reformation was strongest. In some of the Catholic countries, the Catholic Reformation (or so-called Counter Reformation),

[6] Barnard, *American Journal of Education,* Vol. XXVI, p. 209.

resulted in a similar general establishment of schools in which children were trained in reading and writing, and in a knowledge of religious texts. Most notable among the Catholic schools were those maintained by the Brethren of the Christian Schools, particularly in France. The schools of this order (which was founded in 1684) were superior to practically all other schools of that period in two respects. They were taught by teachers who had been trained in the normal schools maintained by the brethren, and they used the method of simultaneous or class instruction, instead of the method of individual instruction which was almost universally used. England was most backward in providing elementary education, almost no provision being made until the nineteenth century.

The accounts ordinarily given of elementary education during this period describe at length the development in Germany in connection with the Lutheran Reformation. In order to show that the educational development in this case was similar to that which I have described in the case of the Puritan Reformers in New England, I shall give a summary statement of the German situation.

A very close parallel to the New England laws requiring schooling in reading and writing, and the learning of a trade outside of school, is found in this statement by Luther: "My opinion is that we must send the boys to school one or two hours a day, and have them learn a trade at home for the rest of the time. It is desirable that these two occupations march side by side." It will be remembered that Luther prepared a very careful translation of the Bible into German and wrote two catechisms as a further aid to individuals in arriving at religious truth. Paulsen says, "Instruction in reading and catechism, which were to pave the way for the general use of the Scripture and assist in its interpretation, was the root-stock from which has grown up the Protestant elementary school."[7]

The religious motive continued to dominate the German elementary schools to the nineteenth century. The curriculum as represented in the Prussian regulations of 1763 provided only

[7] *German Education*, p. 75.

for reading, writing, religious instruction, singing and a little arithmetic and some "general information about God, the world, and mankind."[8]

The German elementary teachers were men either incapacitated for other employment, or teaching to supplement their scanty earnings at some other trade. Describing these Paulsen says:

> As late as 1738, the Prussian country schoolmasters were granted the tailoring monopoly within their respective villages for the improvement of their economical position. Some reading and writing, with the addition, at most, of a little arithmetic, was, of course, all that such men could manage; method of any kind was out of the question. It is not surprising, therefore, that, in many cases, the instruction never went beyond the first rudiments. Even in schools of a little higher standing, especially where the attendance was irregular, many children never achieved anything beyond a little reading and knowing a few things by heart. [For many] the instruction was never anything else but a torture, protracted through years, from saying the alphabet and formation of syllables to the deciphering of complete words, without any real success in the end, while writing was nothing but a rough and wearisome tracing of the letters, the net result of all the toil being the gabbling of the Catechism and a few Bible texts and hymns, learnt by heart over and over again.[9]

Such is the history of modern elementary-school practice, from its beginning in the sixteenth century to the end of the eighteenth. There was very little change in content, and practically no change in methods of instruction, during a period of one hundred and fifty years in America, and two hundred and fifty years in Germany. Contrast this with the remarkable change that has taken place during the last hundred years, a change in the whole conception of elementary education, its purpose, its content, and its method. The changes in this one century, are far more significant for teachers than all the development in elementary education in the previous history of the world. They were initiated by Rousseau and established in practice by Pestalozzi and his followers. The history of this practice will be traced in subsequent papers.

[8] *Ibid.*, p. 139. [9] *Ibid.*, p. 141.

SUGGESTIONS FOR GROWTH OF BULBOUS PLANTS IN SCHOOLROOMS AND SCHOOL GARDENS

OTIS W. CALDWELL
The University of Chicago

The bulbous plants that are best for schoolroom,[1] home, and school garden or lawn uses are tulips, hyacinth, narcissus, crocus, gladiolus, freesia, and amaryllis. Many others may be added to this list by persons experienced in growing plants. There are several varieties of each of the kinds named as, single and double tulips, single and double hyacinths, varieties in color, etc. For work with children it is usually best to use the less specialized and more common forms, since success in growing them is more probable and they are no less interesting, attractive, and instructive.

Any dependable seed salesman can supply these bulbs or they may be ordered direct from one of the large supply houses as Vaughn's Seed Store, Chicago, Ill., or Peter Henderson & Co., New York City, N. Y. Prices will vary with the kind of bulb, also with the particular variety desired. The usual range in price is suggested in connection with the discussion of each kind of bulb. Suggestions for planting are based upon the climate and seasons of the Chicago region.

All of the plants here mentioned thrive best in good loamy soil. If manure is used it should be thoroughly decayed and the soil should be thoroughly mixed. It is best to use soil that has been enriched some time prior to the time of planting in order that no undecayed organic matter may be present. Plant no bruised or defective bulbs since they may become a source of infection of others.

Planting for indoor flowering may be done in earthen pots or in wooden boxes. Care must be taken to secure adequate drain-

[1] These preliminary directions are inserted in advance of the general series of articles on nature-study so that teachers who wish to follow the suggestions of the articles may have suitable material at hand.

age. In general, planting in pots should be done at the same time as in outdoor beds, namely about four or five weeks before the first freezing of the ground is expected, though successful indoor planting may be done at a later period. In all cases after bulbs are properly placed in pots or boxes, water well and place in cold frames, in pits in the ground, or in a dark, cool basement room. Keep moist but not wet by an occasional watering. In this way roots grow from the bulbs and become well established before leaves develop and good strong plants may thus be secured. From the cold frames or basement room the pots may be taken to the schoolroom at any time after six weeks or more, and with proper care good flowering plants should soon be secured. During chilly nights partial or complete protection against low temperature may be secured by covering the plants with heavy paper cones made from newspapers.

1. *Tulip, hyacinth, narcissus, and freesia.*—These bulbs are the most widely used for school garden and indoor work. They cost from ten cents to seventy cents and more per dozen. The above directions cover most of the points necessary for proper growing. In beds or in pots the bulbs should be planted with the tops three inches from the surface. In beds best results are secured by planting so that each bulb is allowed at least eight or nine square inches of earth. In pots closer planting is usual, as two or three bulbs in a six-inch pot. Narcissus may be grown in a dish of water with a few stones to serve as supports for the roots.

2. *Crocus.*—Cost, about fifty cents per hundred. This plant is for outdoor planting but often flowers well indoors. Excellent results may be secured by scattering the corms (bulbs) about in the lawn, since they flower early in the spring and appear to best advantage when they come up in irregular distribution. The use of several colors increases their attractiveness. Plant in early November. By use of a stick an inch in diameter make a hole in the sod about three inches deep. Insert the corm with its root end downward and press soil so that it is close upon the bulb. The corms need no further attention and if undisturbed will flower for several years. For indoor growth plant six or eight

bulbs in a four-inch pot in good black soil. Plant so that the tops of the bulbs are 2½ to 3 inches below the surface, and care for them as suggested in preliminary directions.

3. *Gladiolus.*—Cost, thirty to sixty cents per dozen. These plants are useful for outdoor planting and should be planted in the spring so soon as all freezing is past. Since they grow to a height of two to four feet they appear best, and are best protected from winds, if planted along a fence or wall. A bed a few inches wide should be prepared and the bulbs planted in a row with the tops about three inches from the surface of the soil. The corms should be three inches apart in the row. In the spring the soil should be carefully tilled.

4. *Amaryllis.*—Since these plants cost from twenty-five cents to one dollar and more each they are not recommended for general use, but one or two kept by a room of pupils will prove of value. From November to February or March the pots containing the bulbs should be set in a dark cool place since this is the normal dormant period of the plant. By care the plants may be kept from year to year increasing in vigor and flowering qualities.

EDITORIAL NOTES

The Science of Education

The educational world has been waiting for some scientific man or other to supply the necessary facts on which to base the "new education." Sometimes it is the psychologist who has seemed to be the most promising source of this much-dreamed-of reform. With an eagerness almost pathetic, teachers have rushed to the various psychologies and have read them in the hope of finding there the solutions of their school problems. The reaction has often been as violent as the first enthusiasm. The psychologies do not solve school problems and the teachers discovering this have complained bitterly against the writers of books on psychology. Sometimes the biologist has been consulted. If we could only find out how nature brings up young animals, if we could only know the formula of evolution by which animal life has been raised from the lower to the higher forms, then surely we should have an answer to our questions of school reform. But here again the teacher is confronted by the result that the school must be different from the playground and that the problems of social heredity differ from the problems of physical heredity. The biologist cannot solve with his formulas the problem of the schools.

The trouble in all these efforts to borrow a science of education is that the field of educational activity is a special field and requires special research. Educators cannot evade the problem by going to specialists in other fields. There must be a direct attack upon the problems of education by students of education. If we wish to teach spelling well why should we wait until the psychologist in the midst of his various discussions drops a few remarks here and there which will be applicable to our problem? Why should we not rather organize a direct investigation of spelling? If oral reading is a problem, why not take it up? We may go to the biologist and the psychologist and the sociologist and the student of all the related sciences for suggestions, but we can never deal with these problems until we take them up as distinct problems worthy of the energies of well-trained students.

Why has there been such delay in the development of a science of education? Because educators have been such busy folk dealing with the problems of classroom management and schoolroom organization. Curiously enough the leaders in practical education have been taken by their duties farther and farther away from the problems of educational research. The principal or superintendent chosen because of his ability as a teacher has been set doing clerical work and solving financial problems rather than studying education. The high school specialist, and above all the college professor, absorbed in their special lines of study, have never had time to consider themselves and their activities as suitable subjects for investigation. We are all disposed to think of everything except our own activities as suitable matters for scientific examination. The world examined scientifically the remote objects of nature before developing a science of physiology or sociology or psychology. And so the educator has been a close student of everything except his own activities as an educator.

It is time for a concerted movement in the direction of a special science of education. The time has come in our institutions of scientific research when there is a career for the student of educational problems. The time has come when teachers are sufficiently critical so that they can begin to appreciate genuine scientific discussions. Let us mark this new era as the era of a definite and distinct science of education which is to supersede all unsystematic borrowings from related sciences and all helpless waiting for someone else to do the task so obviously at hand for those interested in education.

NOTES AND NEWS

An account of educational conditions and school problems in the Panama Canal Zone, taken from the *Canal Record*, gives not only an interesting account of the peculiar problems that the cosmopolitan life of the zone presents, but it is interesting as throwing what might be called an exaggerated light upon many centers of population in our larger cities. There are school centers in Chicago and New York which present practically the same problems. For this reason the report is given in some detail.

In the work now in progress of grading the schools of the Canal Zone, three great obstacles are encountered: (1) the difficulty of harmonizing the points of view of people coming from hundreds of different places; (2) the absence and tardiness; (3) the constant changing of places of residence.

It is probable that, in its extent at least, the first of these problems is unique in education. In the Canal Zone schools for white children the 722 pupils represent over 500 different schools, and a score or more distinct educational systems. Thirty-six states, two territories, and the District of Columbia have representatives among the pupils, and the teachers themselves represent sixteen different states. Not only are the systems of the various states different, but in only a few of the states is there a thoroughly uniform system of education, so that each city or town has some distinct features in its school system.

Twenty-one different nationalities other than American are represented by pupils in the schools for white children, and practically every one of the alien children began school work under a system differing in some respects from that in which each of the others began.

It is not only in reconciling differences in methods of teaching that difficulty is experienced. Indeed the more elemental difficulty is that the attitude of children, parents, and teachers is fixed by conditions in the particular locality from which they come. A local coloring suffuses their thought and action. The teachers themselves are the product of local conditions, and no matter how advanced their professional training may be their work reflects their school education and professional experience. More than the teachers, the parents and children show a natural local pride in the schools of their home community, and this is occasionally reflected in their attitude toward the school system of the zone.

One phase of this local coloring is the conviction of teachers, parents, and children that the grading of the schools with which they are familiar should be the standard. To adopt their ideas would mean several hundred different standards. It is seldom that two schools can be found in the states in which the grading is exactly the same. In one school a certain grade will carry the student farther than it will in another, and if there is a general similarity of grading it will yet be found that in the extent to which some studies are pursued there is a difference. There is no harm in this where the community schools take children from the primary grade through the high school, for there the change in the personnel of the student body is slight, and there is no conflict of grades. But in the zone schools each pupil has been started on a different scheme, each parent has his own confirmed idea of how a school should be graded and conducted, and each teacher has a similar difficulty in overcoming his local coloring.

The burden of readjusting himself and the pupil and reconciling the parents falls on the teacher. How well the Canal Zone teachers have overcome these difficulties may be judged from the fact that the work of grading is making good progress.

The constant changing of parents from one part of the zone to another is a condition that makes grading difficult, and will continue to do so until one standard has been thoroughly established. A school for white children at Gatun began the year last September with twenty-one pupils and by accretions from other parts of the zone this number has been increased to forty-six. In one of the schools for colored children there have been fifty changes in the past six months. This changing unsettles the children who are transferred and the school to which they go. It also adds to the absences.

The one great cause of absence in the schools for white children is the six weeks' vacation granted to "gold" employees engaged in the states. Practically every white child in the zone comes from a family which spends six weeks of the year away from Panama. A great majority of these are away from the Isthmus during six weeks of the school year, for it is not possible or desirable to let all employees have their vacation in the summer months. This condition in the schools for white children has led to the appointment of two teachers who, when not substituting, spend their time in the schools along the line of the canal giving special instruction to pupils who have missed school part of the year.

Among the colored children absence and tardiness are chronic and under present conditions are practically incurable, although efforts to lessen the absence and tardiness are not spared. A constant change of residence, indifference on the part of parents and children, the large number of pupils to each teacher, and the legal restrictions on the punishment of truants and sluggards are the more important obstacles in the way of curing absence and tardiness.

The following letter written by Commissioner Brown to *Science* is quoted in full in order to show the progress which is being made by the Bureau of Education.

The Bureau of Education at Washington, which has occupied for thirty-seven of the forty-two years of its existence the rented building at the corner of Eighth and G streets, northwest, was removed in July to the second floor of the old Post-office Department building between Seventh and Eighth and E and F streets, with storage and mailing rooms in the basement. Its new quarters are more commodious and much more comfortable than the old. This is the first time in the history of the bureau that it has been quartered in a government building.

A measure of reorganization in the staff of the bureau was made during the month of July. Mr. Lewis A. Kalbach, who has been connected with the bureau for twenty-two years and has served during the past three years as clerk to the Commissioner in addition to his duties as specialist in land grant college statistics, has been appointed chief clerk of the bureau. He has been succeeded as specialist in land grant college statistics by Professor James E. McClintock, of the University of Maine, whose principal work will have to do with the relations of the federal government with the land grant colleges of agriculture and mechanic arts. The former chief clerk, Mr. Lovick Pierce, continues his connection with the bureau as chief of the correspondence division. Dr. Harlan Updegraff, who has served as chief of the Alaska division during the past two years, has been appointed collector and compiler of statistics, succeeding Mr. W. Dawson Johnston, who has been made librarian of Columbia University. Dr. Updegraff's principal duties will have to do with the relations of the bureau with the chief school officers of the several states and cities of the country. It is expected that he will serve as an advisor in matters affecting school administration.

Mr. William T. Lopp, who has served as district superintendent of schools in Alaska, has been appointed superintendent of education of natives of Alaska and will have direct charge, under the supervision of the commissioner of education, of education and the reindeer industry among the Alaskan natives. He will divide his time between Alaska and Washington and will have charge of the Alaska division of the bureau.

Some time will be taken in closing up the special work upon which Dr. Updegraff and Mr. Lopp are now engaged, in the Alaska service, and it is expected that they will not enter their new duties before November or December.

Arrangements have been made by the Bureau of Education and the Bureau of the Census for the collection by special census agents of financial statistics of the school systems of the larger cities. The statistical form used by the Census Office will be furnished shortly by the Bureau of Education to a number of these cities that cannot be reached this year by the census agents. This form is the outcome of a conference between the two offices concerned. It is still in an experimental stage, but its use by the Census Office and the Bureau of Education is expected to develop any defects or weaknesses in it, and lead to the adoption of a form that will meet the conditions existing in the various cities of the country.

Another forward step has been taken as regards the prompt issuance of the *Annual Report of the Commissioner of Education.* On certain conditions, which can undoubtedly be met, the public printer has agreed to furnish bound copies of Volume I of the *Annual Report* for 1909 on December 1 of this year, and Volume II on March 1 of the year 1910. In view of this arrangement, it may now be confidently expected that the first volume, containing general surveys, directories, etc., will be in the hands of readers before the convening of those educational associations which meet during the holiday season; and the second volume, containing the statistical tables, will be received prior to the Easter vacation meetings.

BOOK REVIEWS

Laggards in Our Schools: A Study of Retardation and Elimination in City School Systems. By LEONARD P. AYRES, A.M. New York: Charities Publication, 1909. Pp. 120.

This is the second volume which has appeared as a result of the Backward Children Investigation conducted by the Russell Sage Foundation under the general direction of Dr. Luther H. Gulick, a preliminary report of the work having been published under the title of *Medical Inspection of Schools* by Dr. Gulick and Mr. Ayres. Several of the chapters of this book have appeared as articles in the *Psychological Clinic* and elsewhere, and a report of the study in as far as it related to the New York City schools has been incorporated in the annual report of Superintendent Maxwell for 1908.

The book, although very clearly written, is not a merely popular discussion of the subject as the wording of the title might lead one to suspect, but gives evidence of careful research, of keen analysis of the material presented, and of much insight into statistical procedure.

The most significant of the general results as summarized by Dr. Gulick in an introductory statement are:

"(1) That the most important causes of retardation of school children can be removed;

"(2) That the old-fashioned virtues of regularity of attendance and faithfulness are major elements of success;

"(3) That some cities are already accomplishing excellent results by measures that can be adopted by all;

"(4) That relatively few children are so defective as to prevent success in school or in life."

The class of pupils made the particular object of study are the so-called "retarded" pupils. A special meaning is attached to this word. Children "who are older than they should be for the grade they are in are considered 'retarded.'" The term, therefore, covers both "those who are over-age on account of slow progress and those who have progressed normally but entered school late." As used, the word does not, therefore, necessarily denote a pathological condition, but simply the school status. A justification for this use of the term is given in chap. iv.

From a study of the data from 31 cities, it is concluded that "approximately one-third of all of the children in our city schools are above the normal age for their grades—they are retarded." There is a very considerable variation between the various cities and even between the schools of the same city (New York City). One city showed but 7.5 per cent. of retardation, while at the other extreme one city is cited as showing 75.8 of retardation. Differences of over 25 per cent. were found in different schools in New York City. A careful analysis of the effects of the factors of population, retardation, and elimination on the number of pupils in the succeeding grades is made in chap. iii, and on the basis of the method there established a comparison and criticism is made in chap. vi of the "Elimination Study of the Bureau of Education." The results presented differ from the latter study in presenting evidence to show first that "the general tendency of our schools is to hold practically all of the pupils to the sixth grade," and, in the second place, that about one-half of the pupils who enter school finish the seven or more grades. The earlier study argued that this proportion was about one-third, and that extensive elimination began with the third grade or earlier.

Some of the more detailed results of general interest are as follows:

"It is safe to count on 10 per cent. of the children leaving on reaching the age of thirteen, 40 per cent. by the time they are fourteen, 50 per cent. of the remainder at fifteen, and again 50 per cent. of the remainder at the age of sixteen."

The same fact stated in terms of the grade reached is that "the general tendency of city school systems is to keep all of the children to the fifth grade, to drop half of them by the time the eighth grade is reached and to carry one in ten to the fourth year of the high school."

"According to the New York investigation, among each one hundred retarded pupils thirty are retarded because of late entrance; thirteen because of late entrance and slow progress; and fifty-seven because of slow progress.

"The courses of study of our city school systems are adjusted to the power of the brighter pupils. They are beyond the powers of the average pupils and far beyond those of the slower ones."

"The average pupil cannot complete the work of eight grades in eight years. So far as can be ascertained, in no city does the average child regularly succeed in doing each year's work in one year. The average child in the average city school system progresses through the grades at the rate of eight grades in ten years."

There is little or no relation between foreign birth or parentage and retardation in school; "ignorance of the English language does not constitute a serious handicap."

Physical defects have, as has been well established, an important bearing on the progress of school children. Especially is it true that there are more dull children suffering from enlarged glands, defective breathing, and adenoids than there are of bright children.

Irregular attendance is an important cause of retardation and is very prevalent. "Such figures as are available indicate that in our cities less than three-fourths of the children continue in attendance as much as three-fourths of the year."

The factor of sex is also important, and very instructive results are presented in this connection. Retardation among boys in elementary schools is shown to be 13 per cent. more prevalent than among girls. The conclusions drawn seem warranted by the data presented that "our schools as they exist are better fitted to the needs and natures of the girl than of the boy pupils."

The age of the pupil is a further important element in retardation and elimination. The age of starting to school is not, however, the controlling factor, but the retention of pupils at the upper ages.

"The reason why retention at the upper ages and not age at starting is the controlling factor in securing a large percentage of survivors is that our school courses are too difficult to be completed in eight years by the average child who starts at the age of five, six, or seven, and our systems of grading are too inflexible to permit the more mature child to make up the handicap he is under through late start."

The children who start late to school are apt to progress more rapidly than those who start early, but most of the former never graduate. "Those who start early are the ones most likely to finish."

Remedial measures and means for increasing the efficiency of schools in the matters of the advance and progress of pupils are discussed in concluding chapters.

The results of the study, as outlined above, are very evidently of much importance in the general administration of our public schools, and should lead to further studies at first hand by school superintendents and by grade teachers in their own school systems.

WALTER F. DEARBORN

THE UNIVERSITY OF CHICAGO

BOOKS RECEIVED

B. D. BERRY & COMPANY, CHICAGO

Berry's Writing Books. Books I, II, III, IV, V, and VI. Paper covers. Illustrated.

Teaching Writing, Part II. Material and method for teaching *Berry's Writing Books.* Paper cover.

T. Y. CROWELL & COMPANY, NEW YORK

Exercises in French Conversation and Composition. With Notes and Vocabulary. By GUSTAV HEIN. Cloth. Pp. 120. $0.40.

Dornröschen: Ein Märchenspiel in vier Scenen. With Songs and Music. By EMMA FISHER. Cloth. Pp. 31. $0.25.

One Thousand Common French Words. Selected and Arranged by R. DE BLANCHAUD. Cloth. Pp. 32. $0.25.

When America Won Liberty, Patriots and Royalists. By TUDOR JENKS. Cloth. Illustrated. Pp. 280. $1.25.

D. C. HEATH & COMPANY, BOSTON

Finger Play Reader ("The Davis-Julien Readers"), Parts I and II. By JOHN W. DAVIS AND FANNY JULIEN. Cloth. Illustrated. Part I, 134 pp.; Part II, 134 pp. $0.35, ea.

PERSONALLY PUBLISHED

Ophthalmic Neuro-Myology: A Study of the Normal and Abnormal Actions of the Ocular Muscles from the Brain Side of the Question. By G. C. SAVAGE, M.D. Cloth. Illustrated. Pp. 210. (Published by the author. Printed by Keelin-Williams Printing Co., Nashville, Tenn.)

HOUGHTON, MIFFLIN COMPANY

Social Development and Education. By M. V. O'SHEA. Cloth. Pp. 550. $2.00.

CURRENT EDUCATIONAL LITERATURE IN THE PERIODICALS[1]

IRENE WARREN
Librarian, School of Education, the University of Chicago

ADAMS, EMMA L. The social opportunity of the public library. Pub. Lib. 14: 247–49. (Jl. '09.)

BATCHELDER, ERNEST A. London municipal arts and crafts schools. Craftsman. 16:641–44. (S. '09.)

BOBBITT, JOHN FRANKLIN. The growth of Philippine children. Pedagog. Sem. 16:137–68. (Je. '09.)

BOYER, JACQUES. The disinfection of school books. Sci. Amer. 101:60, 61. (24 Jl. '09.)

BRUCE, G. L. The staffing of elementary schools. Circular 709. Educa. Rec. 17:751–64. (Je. '09.)

CHAMBERLAIN, ALEXANDER F. Activities of children among primitive peoples. I. Pedagog. Sem. 16:252–55. (Je. '09.)

CHANCELLOR, WILLIAM E. Just teachers. Journ. of Educa. 69:687. (24 Je. '09.)

CHARLES, FRED. The scholarship scheme of the London County Council. Sch. World. 11:287–89. (Ag. '09.)

(A) children's pageant. Liv. Age. 44:49–52. (3 Jl. '09.)

COLBY, CHARLES W. The library and education. Lib. Journ. 34:340–45. (Ag. '09.)

Commemoration of the fourth centenary of St. Paul's School. Sch. World. 11:281–83. (Ag. '09.)

Compulsory continuation schools. Educa. T. 62:305–6. (Ag. '09.)

COOLEY, MRS. ALICE W. Story-telling and the teaching of literature. Story Hour. 1:3–8. (Je. '09.)

CURTIS, ELNORA WHITMAN. Out-door schools. Pedagog. Sem. 16:169–94. (Je. '09.)

[1] Abbreviations: Atlan., Atlantic Monthly; Craftsman, The Craftsman; Educa. Rec., Educational Record; Educa. T., Educational Times; Engin. N., Engineering News; Harp. W., Harper's Weekly; Journ. of Educa., Journal of Education; Lib. Journ., Library Journal; Liv. Age, Living Age; Nat. Study R., Nature-Study Review; Out., Outlook; Pedagog. Sem., Pedagogical Seminary; Pop. Sci. Mo., Popular Science Monthly; Pub. Lib., Public Libraries; Relig. Educa., Religious Education; Sch. World, School World; Sci. Amer., Scientific American; Scrib. M., Scribner's Magazine; South. Educa. R., Southern Educational Review; Story Hour, The Story Hour; Teach. Coll. Rec., Teacher's College Record.

DANIELS, JOSEPH F. The need of manual training in the development of our nation. Craftsman. 16:650–55. (S. '09.)

DIACK, WALTER T. Development in religious education in the Y. M. C. A. Relig. Educa. 4:277–80. (Ag. '09.)

DILLARD, JAMES H. Negro rural schools. South. Educa. R. 6:303–8. (Fe.–Mr. '09.)

DILLON, CHARLES. The university as an aid to commerce: how the industrial fellowships in the University of Kansas are serving the practical needs of man. Harp. W. 53:12, 13. (7 Ag. '09.)

DOWNEY, JUNE E. The variational factor in handwriting. Pop. Sci. Mo. 75:147–56. (Ag. '09.)

EDMISTON, HOMER. A classical education in America. Atlan. 104:260–73. (Ag. '09.)

Equipment for teaching of domestic science. Teach. Coll. Rec. 10:1–96. (My. '09.)

FLETCHER, W. I. To make libraries more effective. Lib. Journ. 34:354–55. (Ag. '09.)

GALPIN, FREDERICK T. The normal religion of a boy. Relig. Educa. 4:271–76. (Ag. '09.)

GATES, HERBERT WRIGHT. Classified material for graded Sunday schools. Relig. Educa. 4:281–92. (Ag. '09.)

GEISTWEIT, WILLIAM H. Present needs in young people's work. Relig. Educa. 4:262–67. (Ag. '09.)

GIBSON, C. B. Recent tendencies toward industrial education in Europe and America. South. Educa. R. 6:275–84. (Fe.–Mr. '09.)

GREEN, J. A. Experimental psychology and education. IV. Sch. World. 11:206–8. (Je. '09.)

HARRISON, ELIZABETH. The religious training of children. Relig. Educa. 4:256–60. (Ag. '09.)

HATCH, L. A. Why many fail in teaching nature-study. Nat. Study R. 1:97–100. (My. '09.)

HATTON, A. P. The status and emoluments of army schoolmasters and schoolmistresses. Sch. World. 11:203–5. (Je. '09.)

HYDE, WILLIAM DEWITT. Personality and college professors. Out. 92:931–37. (21 Ag. '09.)

Inspection in Penguinland. A recension of certain MSS relating to education. Sch. World. 11:201–3. (Je. '09.)

JENNINGS, J. T. Municipal civil service in libraries. Pub. Lib. 14:250–54. (Jl. '09.)

JOHNSTON, CHARLES. A Chinese girl student's view of America. Harp. W. 53:15. (24 Jl. '09.)

———. A college of ideals: an impression of Bryn Mawr. Harp. W. 53:16, 17. (7 Ag. '09.)

———. The trouble with our universities. Harp. W. 53:27. (21 Ag. '09.)

JONES, T. J. Relation of the state to the education of the negro. South. Educa. R. 6:309–13. (Fe.–Mr. '09.)

JORDAN, DAVID STARR. Jane Lathrop Stanford. A eulogy. Pop. Sci. Mo. 75:157–73. (Ag. '09.)

JUDSON, HARRY PRATT. Religious co-operation. Relig. Educa. 4:249–52. (Ag. '09.)

KAYLOR, M. A. Feelings, thought, and conduct of children toward animal pets. Pedagog. Sem. 16:205–39. (Je. '09.)

LISHMAN, R. The wastage of pupils in municipal secondary schools. Sch. World. 11:285, 86. (Ag. '06.)

MACKAYE, PERCY. American pageants and their promise. Scrib. M. 56: 28–34. (Jl. '09.)

MCLENNAN, WILLIAM E. Courses of study for young people. Relig. Educa. 4:267–71. (Ag. '09.)

MEAD, H. R. The value of the study of reference books. Pub. Lib. 14: 158, 159. (Jl. '09.)

MESERVE, C. F. Results of attempts at the higher education of the negro of the South. South. Educa. R. 6:285–93. (Fe.–Mr. '09.)

MIALL, L. C. Ready-made lessons in nature-study. Nat. Study R. 1: 101–4. (My. '05.)

MILLER, G. A. The future of mathematics. Pop. Sci. Mo. 75:117–23. (Ag. '09.)

MORRISON, H. C. Federation of New England educational associations. Journ. of Educa. 70:87–89. (22 Jl. '09.)

MOTT, MAJ. T. BENTLEY. The new army school of horsemanship. Scrib. M. 56:63–73. (Jl. '09.)

MUTCH, W. J. The biblical preparation of the Sunday-school teacher. Relig. Educa. 4:260–62. (Ag. '09.)

NORTHROP, ALICE R. Flower shows in city schools. Nat. Study R. 1: 104–9. (My. '05.)

PHILLIPS, J. H. The essential requirements of negro education. South. Educa. R. 6:294–302. (Fe.–Mr. '09.)

Physical education in all schools. Sch. World. 11:211, 212. (Je. '09.)

PICKERING, EDWARD C. The future of astronomy. Pop. Sci. Mo. 75: 105–16. (Ag. '09.)

RANCK, SAMUEL H. Municipal legislative reference libraries: should they be established and maintained as a part of the public library of a city or as an independent department or organization. Lib. Journ. 34: 345–50. (Ag. '09.)

RICHARDS, S. A. International Congress on Modern Language Teaching. Sch. World. 11:210. (Je. '09.)

SALMON, PRINCIPAL. The early grants for education. Educa. Rec. 17: 765–72. (Je. '09.)

SAWTELL, W. W. Athletics in mixed secondary schools. Sch. World. 11: 289–91. (Ag. '09.)

SCUDDER, MYRON T. Play days for country schools. Out. 92:1031–38. (28 Ag. '09.)

Secondary education in industrial centres. Sch. World. 11:283–85. (Ag. '09.)

SERCOMBE, PARKER H. The evils of American school systems. Craftsman. 16:603–11. (S. '09.)

SMITH, JESSE M. The Rensselaer Polytechnic Institute and the development of engineering education. Engin. N. 62:185, 186. (19 Ag. '09.)

SMITH, P. A. Some phases of the play of Japanese boys and men. Pedagog. Sem. 16:256–67. (Je. '09.)

Some Old-Fashioned Children's Books. Liv. Age. 43:754–60. (19 Je. '09.)

STEVENS, D. H. What college students read. Out. 92:651, 652. (18 Jl. '09.)

STEWART, GEORGE B. The Sunday school as an educational force in social duty. Relig. Educa. 4:253–56. (Ag. '09.)

WADE, HERBERT T. A museum to illustrate the development of mathematics. Sci. Amer. 101:10, 15, 17, 19. (3 Jl. '09.)

WATTERSON, ADA. Guide to periodical literature, September, 1904, to April, 1905. Nat. Study R. 1:136–40. (My. '05.)

WIGGAM, AUGUSTA. A contribution to the data of dream psychology. Pedagog. Sem. 16:240–51. (Je. '09.)

WILLEY, DAY ALLEN. An American forestry school. Sci. Amer. 101: 113, 114. (14 Ag. '09.)

WILLIAMS, TOM A. How inebriety might be prevented by early education. Pedagog. Sem. 16:195–204. (Je. '09.)

WINSHIP, A. E. From absurd to beautiful books. Journ. of Educa. 69: 681–86. (24 Je. '09.)

(The) year in education. Out. 92:675–80. (24 Jl. '09.)

VOLUME X NUMBER 3

THE ELEMENTARY SCHOOL TEACHER

NOVEMBER, 1909

AGRICULTURAL EDUCATION[1]

THE UNITED STATES DEPARTMENT OF AGRICULTURE

BENJAMIN MARSHALL DAVIS
Miami University

Historically the movement for agricultural education in the United States dates back to 1785 when associations for the promotion of agriculture began to be formed. A few years later, in 1792, mainly in response to the agitation of these associations, colleges undertook to provide for instruction in agriculture, first Columbia, and then Harvard and Yale.

It was not, however, until 1862 that the real movement for scientific agriculture had its beginning. Congress of this year authorized the establishment of a department of agriculture (1, p. 57),[2] and also passed the Morrill Act giving to each state a grant of land with which to establish a state college of agriculture and mechanic arts (1, pp. 62–64). The Hatch Act of 1887 provided for agricultural experiment stations in each state and territory (1, pp. 64–66), and during the following year the Office of Experiment Stations was created as a separate bureau of the Department to serve as the official head of all the agricultural experiment stations.

On July 1, 1862, the United States Department of Agriculture was organized. Its growth as expressed in terms of

[1] This is the first of a series of articles on elementary and secondary agricultural education in America, and the various agencies concerned in its promotion.

[2] These references in parentheses refer to the annotated bibliography at the end of the article.

people employed and total expenditures may be seen by comparing 29, the number employed the first year with 17,819, the number employed in 1908, and $63,704.21 expended the first year with $13,628,696 expended in 1908. For the last twenty years Congress has provided liberally for the maintenance of the Department. It has been estimated that nearly $100,000,000 has been spent during this time for agricultural research and education, for the most part through the Department. This vast expenditure, of course, would never have been made had it not been justified by results as measured in dollars and cents. In 1908 the agricultural products of our country amounted to $7,778,000,000. The value of the corn crop alone amounted to $1,615,000,000. It may be readily seen that a very slight increase in yield per acre would aggregate many times the running expenses of all the institutions engaged in promoting agriculture. The work of the Department has made possible not only a slight increase but in nearly all kinds of production a very large increase (1, pp. 44–46).

The aim of the Department has been twofold: first, scientific, developing a scientific knowledge of every phase of agriculture; second, educational, conveying this knowledge to all the people. In both these aspects of its work the Department has been closely allied with the land-grant agricultural colleges. Indeed, the Department and the agricultural experiment stations in different states and territories, organized chiefly as departments of land-grant colleges, stand at the head of our system of agricultural research and education.

Since 1889 the Association of American Agricultural Colleges and Experiment Stations has been holding annual meetings. Members of the Department take prominent part in these meetings, and the proceedings are published through the Office of Experiment Stations. The director of this office is chairman and the specialist in agricultural education is secretary. The educational policy of agricultural colleges, such as terms of admission, courses of study, matters of administration, etc., is determined largely by a standing committee of this association known as the "committee on instruction in agriculture." For several years agricultural instruction of collegiate grade has been well organized and on a good working basis. Recently the efforts of this committee have been directed to a consideration of instruction of secondary grade. A course of study has been worked out in considerable detail to serve as a model for schools contemplating such instruction (2, 3). Some attention has also been given to work in elementary schools (4, 16).

The Department is organized into eleven scientific bureaus as follows: weather, animal industry, plant industry, forest service, chemistry, soils, entomology, biological survey, statistics, experimental stations, and public roads. All of these are doing much to encourage and help agricultural education throughout the country. In a general way they reach the people through publications, a great many of which are distributed free (5, 7) while others are for sale at a nominal price (6, 7). Those for free distribution are as a rule written in a popular style, free from technical terms, and are easily understood by the average reader. The series known as "Farmers' Bulletins" contains contributions from all the bureaus and there is scarcely any phase of agriculture that has not received attention. These bulletins are especially useful to elementary and secondary schools giving instruction in agriculture.[3] Many of them dealing with such subjects as birds, insects, tree planting, school gardening, and plant propagation, would be useful in any elementary or high school.

Besides general contributions to agricultural education made by all the bureaus of the Department, certain bureaus are taking an active part in public education.

The weather bureau from its central office at Washington and through its officials at various stations throughout the country is doing much to encourage the study of meteorology.

[3] The following are suggested for school libraries; for titles see (5): Nos. 22, 24, 28, 32, 34, 35, 42, 44, 47, 49, 51, 52, 54, 55, 59, 61, 62, 63, 64, 66, 74, 77, 80, 81, 85, 86, 91, 99, 101, 104, 106, 112, 113, 121, 126, 127, 128, 131, 134, 142, 154, 155, 157, 165, 166, 170, 172, 173, 177, 181, 182, 185, 187, 188, 192, 194, 195, 196, 98, 199, 200, 201, 203, 205, 213, 218, 220, 228, 229, 235, 236, 241, 242, 245, 248, 253, 254, 266, 270, 272, 282, 283, 285, 287, 289, 293, 295, 297, 298, 303, 306, 313, 315, 324, 327, 336, 339, 340, 346.

During the school year a million or more children of the public schools make weather observations and study the daily weather maps and forecasts. From its earliest days the Weather Bureau has co-operated to some extent in public-school work, and during the past ten years this co-operation has been widely extended. The public schools and the Weather Bureau have a mutual interest in the matter. The school authorities have found in the study of the weather with the assistance of the Weather Bureau a means of satisfying part of the requirements of modern methods of study; and the Weather Bureau is able through the school gradually to dispell popular superstitions and fallacious beliefs that have hampered its work . . . . and to enable both the commercial and the agricultural world to make more intelligent and more complete use of the forecasts, special warnings, weather maps, and climatological publications (8. p. 267).

About 15 per cent. of the daily issue of weather maps is used in the public schools. Lectures are given by officials of the Weather Bureau at teachers' institutes and elsewhere. The policy of this bureau has been to assist the public schools in every way possible as far as general duties to the public will permit.

The Forest Service is reaching the schools through its publications, lantern slides, and other illustrative material concerning the conservation of the forests of our country. The Forest Service believes that "the public school should treat forestry as one of the important economic and public questions in the life of the world" (9, p. 6), and that forestry should have a prominent place in our education. "Below the secondary school forestry should form part of nature-study, arithmetic, and general geography; in the high school, of United States history, civics, physical geography, commercial geography, botany, agriculture, and wood working" (9, p. 7). One of the recent efforts of the Forest Service to co-operate with the public schools is through phenological studies of our native forest trees. On request the Forest Service will send to any school a set of blanks on which to record observations on such matters as general character of country, situation of trees, character of season, date of swelling of buds, of bursting of buds, of beginning of leafing out, of general leafing out, of blossoming, of change of color in foliage, etc. (dates of fifteen special observations in all).

These blanks are accompanied by a circular giving complete directions for study of trees and making records. This work is of great value not only in encouraging pupils to make a close acquaintance with trees, but also in the reaction that must come to them in feeling that they are materially assisting the government in its work. Similar phenological studies of common flowering plants, have been carried on very successfully for a number of years by the public-school children of Canada under the direction of the Botanical Club of Canada.

The Bureau of Plant Industry has been especially active in promoting the movement for school gardens. At Washington, under direct supervision of the Bureau, experiments in school gardening have been carried on for several years. A part of the government grounds with a green house has been devoted to this work. The Bureau sends to schools throughout the country special packages of vegetable and flower seeds accompanied by circulars containing directions for planting and care of school gardens (10, 11). The Bureau also furnishes sets of

one hundred samples of seeds of economic and wild plants put up in glass vials, labeled with Latin and common names and arranged in an herbarium tray for reference purposes. The seeds and the work of preparation are furnished by this office free of charge, but it is necessary for those desiring sets to supply the tray and vials used. These can be obtained at a cost of $1.50 from Messrs. Mackall Bros., 9th and H Streets, N. E., of this city [Washington, D. C.] to whom remittances should be made direct with the request that the material be forwarded to this office. At the same time kindly notify us that such remittance has been made.[4]

The following is a good summary of the educational work of the Office of Experiment Stations:

While the other bureaus of this Department are doing valuable educational work along the lines of research in which they are engaged the Office of Experiment Stations is the general agency of the Department for the promotion of agricultural education throughout the United States and is constantly enlarging the scope and extent of this branch of its work. The educational work of this Office is now organized into two branches, one dealing with agricultural colleges and schools and the other with farmers' institutes and other forms of extension work in agriculture. The

[4] From circular letter: "Seed Laboratory," Bureau of Plant Industry, United States Department of Agriculture.

work of the Office relating to agricultural colleges and schools includes four general classes: (1) The collection and publication of information regarding the progress of agricultural education at home and abroad; (2) studies of different grades of American and foreign schools in which agriculture is taught; (3) work in co-operation with the Association of Agricultural Colleges and Experiment Stations and other important associations dealing with educational matters; and (4) the giving aid to agricultural colleges and local school authorities along the lines of agricultural education. This work is in charge of Mr. D. J. Crosby, as specialist in agricultural education.

This branch of the Office conducts a department of agricultural education in the Experiment Station Record (13), prepares and publishes statistics, courses of study, circulars of information, and other literature relating to agricultural education, aids state and local school authorities in organizing agricultural courses in schools and colleges and in securing competent teachers, takes part in important agricultural conventions and conferences, aids teachers in securing suitable agricultural literature for their work, and, in short, acts as a clearing-house for agricultural education in this country (12, pp. 7, 8).

The work of the Office dealing with farmers' institutes and extension work is in charge of Professor John Hamilton, farmers' institute specialist. Although all the work undertaken by this branch of the Office has to do with agricultural education as presented to adults, it also reaches the public schools indirectly through correspondence with persons interested in agricultural education, by distributing agricultural literature, by preparing and editing bulletins, illustrated lectures and courses of study for movable schools of agriculture. In the movable schools of agriculture a course is offered for country school teachers including nature-study teaching, school gardens and grounds, and school architecture and sanitation (14, p. 6).

The attitude and interest of the Department toward unifying our educational system, in so far as it concerns agriculture and country life, into a complete system extending from the elementary schools, through the secondary schools, into the colleges and graduate schools has been well expressed by Assistant Secretary Willet M. Hayes in a recent address (15, pp. 4, 5). He says:

A movement is well begun to organize better, as a part of our great American school system, the secondary schools as to meet especially the needs of country life. This movement contemplates that, below and leading to our more than 60 state colleges of agriculture already established, we shall have 300 to 400 agricultural finishing schools—practically one in each country congressional district of ten or more counties, either separate or as a strong department of an existing institution. . . .

But vastly more important is the larger movement to establish a system of consolidated rural and village schools, and of courses in agriculture in town and city schools so near the homes of farm youth that something of instruction in agriculture, in home economics, and in social and civil affairs, as well as in the accepted subjects of a so-called general education, shall be taught to all the boys and girls of the farm. To meet this first need the consolidated rural school in the open country and the consolidation of rural schols about the villages and cities is rising rapidly into prominence along with the vocational high school; and many city and non-public schools of secondary and higher grade are seeking to add agricultural instruction to their courses of study. . . .

It is conceded that the large and important task of supplying trained teachers for approximately 30,000 consolidated rural schools in our rich rural communities, for thousands of town and city schools, for 100,000 small rural schools in isolated and sparsely settled communities, for 300 or 400 large agricultural high schools, for 150 state normal schools, and for 60 state colleges of agriculture may be taken up in a practical way and solved in one or two decades. The demand and organization for training teachers going forward together will meet with only the usual pioneering difficulties.

BIBLIOGRAPHY

The following annotated references have been referred to by number on the preceding pages. Directions are given for obtaining these and other publications of the Department. The titles with summary of contents of all publications of the Office of Experiment Stations on agricultural education, corrected to Oct. 1, 1908, are in reference (16).

1. *Historical Sketch of the U. S. Department of Agriculture: Its Objects and Present Organization.* Charles H. Greathouse, Division of Publications, Bul. 3, second revision (1907), pp. 97.

   The first part (pp. 5–57) deals with early government aids to agriculture, agricultural division of patent office, organization of the independent department, the department raised to first rank, buildings, bureaus, divisions and offices. The second part gives an account of legislation and a tabulation of expenditures.

2. *Secondary Courses in Agriculture* (seventh report of the Committee on Instruction in Agriculture), Office of Experiment Stations, Cir. 49, pp. 10.

   A number of high-school courses are given with suggested changes adapting them to the introduction of agriculture.

3. *A Secondary Course in Agronomy* (eleventh report of the Committee on Instruction in Agriculture), Office of Experiment Stations, Cir. 77, pp. 43.

This report contains a syllabus of agronomy, instructions to teachers and 113 lectures, recitations, demonstrations, and laboratory exercises on various phases of agronomy. The plan is a good one to work to, but is somewhat in advance of, or too advanced for, the average high school.

4. *The Teaching of Agriculture in the Rural Common Schools* (ninth report of the Committee on Instruction in Agriculture), Office of Experiment Stations, Cir. 60, pp. 20.

This report discussed the development of industrial training in the common schools and gives an outline of work in nature-study, and elementary agriculture for such schools.

5. Publications for free distribution (revised annually), Division of Publications, Cir. 2 (1908), pp. 76.

This list of publications and copies of all publications which it mentions will be sent free on application to the Secretary of Agriculture, Washington, D. C.

6. Publications for sale (revised annually), Division of Publications, Cir. 3 (1908), pp. 99.

This list may be obtained in the same way as (5) but applications for publications mentioned in this list must be addressed to the Superintendent of Documents, Government Printing Office, Washington, D. C. Only coin or currency should be sent, as stamps are not accepted.

7. Monthly list of publications, Division of Publications, Monthly Circular, pp. 4.

This circular will be sent regularly to all who apply for it. Address, Secretary of Agriculture, Washington, D. C. The list contains titles of all new publications, including reprints and revisions, of the Department.

8. *The Weather Bureau and the Public Schools.* JOHN R. WEEKS; reprint from *Yearbook of Department of Agriculture for 1907*, pp. 267–76.

This reprint contains a discussion of methods of teaching, an outline by grades of meteorology for the elementary schools of the state of New York, the purpose and value of meteorology in school work, weather map and other aids to teachers, home-made apparatus, lantern slides.

9. *Forestry in the Public Schools.* HUGO A. WINKENWERDER, Forest Service, Cir. 130 (1907), pp. 20.

This circular suggests how various school subjects may be correlated with forestry and gives an outline for such correlation with each subject. It also contains a very complete classified list of references.

10. *The School Garden.* L. C. CORBETT, Bureau of Plant Industry, Special Cir. (1905), pp. 6.

Brief plans are given for a school garden. Six common vegetables and six common flowering plants are described with cultural directions.

11. *The School Garden.* L. C. CORBETT, Farmers' Bul. 218 (1905), pp. 40.

This bulletin discusses value of garden work, type of plants for garden, laboratory exercises, studies of soil, plants, roots, stems, leaves, cuttings, budding, window boxes, and decoration of school yard.

12. *The American System of Agricultural Education.* A. C. TRUE AND D. J. CROSBY, Office of Experiment Stations, Cir. 83 (1909), pp. 27.

Agricultural education in America is discussed briefly as follows: Departments of original research and graduate study in agriculture; agricultural colleges; secondary schools of agriculture; elementary schools; schools for negroes and Indians. Under elementary instruction the work in different parts of the country includes, (1) nature-study with plants, farm crops, domestic animals, and soils; (2) school garden work, including improvement of school grounds; (3) lecture courses and institutes for rural school children; (4) organization of clubs among school children.

13. *Experiment Station Record.* E. W. ALLEN, editor, Office of Experiment Stations.

The *Record* contains numerous abstracts of publications of the agricultural experiment stations and kindred institutions in this and other countries; articles and editorials on topics of special interest in agricultural science by American and foreign experts. One department is devoted entirely to reviews of publications on agricultural education. With the beginning of the current volume (XXI) this serial will be issued in two volumes a year of six numbers each. Subscription, one dollar per volume, payable in advance to the Superintendent of Documents, Government Printing Office, Washington, D. C.

14. *Form of Organization for Movable Schools of Agriculture.* JOHN HAMILTON, Office of Experiment Stations, Cir. 79 (1908), pp. 8.

A plan is proposed to organize movable schools of agriculture for farmers over nineteen years of age and for teachers in rural schools. A course is to extend over three or four seasons. The purpose is to equip several persons in each community "so that they will be able to improve in their locality the branch of agriculture which the school represents."

15. *Education for Country Life.* WILLET M. HAYES, Office of Experiment Stations, Cir. 84 (1909), pp. 40.

This is a reprint of an address given before the Minnesota Educational Association, January 2, 1908. It contains a general discussion of agricultural education, followed by plans for organization of schools for country life, county system of consolidated rural schools, or the farm school, the agricultural high school, and financing consolidated rural schools in Minnesota.

16. List of publications of the Office of Experiment Stations on agricultural education, Office of Experiment Stations, Cir. Oct. 27, 1908, pp. 13.

This comprises 136 publications: 24 circulars, 65 bulletins, 25 separates, 9 lectures, 3 documents. All phases of agricultural education from elementary to graduate instruction are represented. The following are some of the publications relating to elementary schools: Separates, *Boys' Agricultural Clubs, Illustrative Material in Teaching Agriculture in Rural Schools, Training Courses for Teachers of Agriculture;* Bulletins: 160, *School Gardens,* 186, *Exercises in Elementary Agriculture—Plant Production,* 195, *Simple Exercises Illustrating Some Applications of Chemistry to Agriculture;* Circular 52, *Books and Bulletins on Nature-Study, School Gardening, and Elementary Agriculture.*

FINE AND INDUSTRIAL ART IN ELEMENTARY SCHOOLS. GRADE I

WALTER SARGENT
The University of Chicago

An effective plan of teaching the fine and industrial arts in elementary schools must consider not only the topics to be presented but also the age when each phase can be assimilated with greatest economy of effort and prove of highest value. Often things which come first in a logically arranged course based on a series of exercises which continually increase in difficulty can be taught to small children only at great expense of time and effort. A few years later these same things can be apprehended with great ease and the principles involved be put to immediate practical application. On the other hand, ways of working that seem from an adult standpoint to lead less directly to the desired result, or even away from it, but ways in which children persist, often prove to be the best foundation for efficiency. Careful observation is necessary in order to discern among children's peculiar ways of working what are faults to be overcome and what are hints of the best method of procedure.

Many courses in the arts lay strong emphasis on the importance of developing originality during the first two or three years in school. In order to avoid any opportunity for imitation, teachers are often advised not to draw for the children or furnish them with examples of design which they may follow, lest they copy and thus fall into the use of conventions. In constructive work this precaution against allowing children to shape their work after a given pattern is not so strongly urged. In representation and design, however, this attempt to safeguard individuality by eliminating suggestive examples during the first few years is so common, that any discussion of the course for the first school year must consider the proper scope for the originality of small children and the question whether, at an age when children are making progress in other lines mainly by imitation that stimulus is not also the most important factor in advance in the arts.

Many of the opinions brought forward in favor of leaving very young children to take their first steps in drawing from objects, without that help which consists in showing them how by drawing for and with them lose force when full significance is given to the frequently repeated statement that drawing is a language. Its symbols are the result of evolution, the embodiment of observations of generations. Unless one is familiar with the drawing of various peoples in different centuries, he is likely to accept the graphic methods with which he is familiar as matters of course and to regard them as the only reasonable way of representing objects, a way which the object itself will suggest to small children.

The nature of graphic language and that of speech are not identical but are more alike than appears at first thought. To teach a child by example how to draw a few things so he may know the way in which others do it, is to give him a developed medium for expressing his own ideas, which is a more potent impetus to individuality than can come when he is compelled to find his own symbols for expression. Those which he invents or which are suggested to him by the objects he is drawing, if left without enrichment from other sources seldom develop beyond a meager set of crude conventions which he repeats over and again. He is not brought early into contact with those graphic interpretations which the race has worked out.

There would appear to be abundant and appropriate scope for the exercise of early original activity in employing an accepted and rich medium of expression in an original way. In any line the surest path to one's own originality is often through familiarity with the good ways of several other personalities.

In the teaching of design also, a subject which should exert a direct influence in developing good taste, a strong plea is made in many courses in the arts for fostering originality on the part of primary children by protecting them from opportunities for imitation. This article, however, does not hesitate to recommend familiarity with well-selected examples of design, and opportunity to imitate them as a direct influence in developing originality, and as the best introduction to the study and practice of design. It is probably true that familiarity with and discrimination of what is excellent is a much more valuable asset than ability to produce what did not exist before if it is not good enough to be in itself a reason why it should exist at all.

FIG. 1

For example, if a child in the first year in school is to make his first design, and it is to be a Christmas souvenir, consisting of a star pasted on a card and a greeting written or printed underneath (Fig. 1), the problem may be made one of original and unaided arrangement, or of following the suggestion and example of the teacher as he makes and thus leads the child by imitation to make an arrangement which is excellent in the consistent relation of its spaces and the beauty of its proportions.

In the first case the child may produce something original in the sense that it is a chance concoction of shapes that never happened before. Such a result, however, is not necessarily a design because it is original. Good design is not the chance output of an uninformed mind. It implies a clear understanding of the function, the form and the materials of the object, so that the result may be an adequate and graceful fulfilment of its purpose. It implies also a sensitiveness to fine proportions and good spacing in order that the object may be a source of pleasure to the eye.

Ability to produce good designs unaided is not often within the power of immature minds. Children who with no example or suggestion, have made an original arrangement generally like it because it is their own production. A commonplace result is fixed in their minds and influences their next attempts.

The beauty of the Christmas souvenir just referred to depends largely on the spacing of the parts. The relations of spaces which are "good" are so because they give pleasure to a discerning eye. This pleasure appears to be dependent upon spacing which results in consistently related measures. It is not an individual whim or passing preference, but depends upon conditions which may be defined, although allowing within their limits abundant play for individuality, in conforming to these conditions in an original manner.

Final appreciation is better developed and originality is enabled the sooner to exercise itself if children are acquainted with good types from the first, and are not left to fix in mind the impressions of their own chance productions, so difficult to dislodge. Because these types are conventions is not necessarily a reason for avoiding them. They are results people have arrived at by long experimentation. The most rapid progress in original design comes by furnishing original minds with the best that has been done in order that they may start from that vantage point.

Under any circumstances of instruction, originality in design will be evident in only a few persons. For one who makes designs, a hundred must select and use those produced by others. Therefore it is of great importance that standards of excellence be established, and that children produce their first designs under the stimulus of excellent examples. This emphasis of the value of imitation as a means of developing ability to represent and of awakening and guiding ideas of design should not be interpreted as a recommendation that children be left to copy finished results, but that they be allowed to work with and imitate the methods of a skilful instructor.

The following work in representation, construction, and design is recommended as appropriate for children during the first year in school.

Representation.—This should consist in the drawing of things of interest to the children, with much encouragement and little criticism from the teacher.

The first interest children show in using a pencil seems to be awakened by the pleasure of making marks with it, regardless of any significance in the marks themselves. They will cover one sheet of paper after another with meaningless scrawls and apparently be delighted by the fact that movements of the pencil over the paper leave visible marks in their path. This period has been termed the "scribble stage."

By degrees the marks take on significance. Interest in representing things is added to interest in mere scribbling. When children enter school they are usually just emerging from the scribbling stage and are beginning the use of forms somewhat as hieroglyphics in a sort of picture writing.

At this time children show little interest in representing a particular object placed before them. Passy thus describes the attitude of a primary child toward a model given him to draw:

> He does not hesitate but seizes his pencil and draws rapidly in an automatic manner. It is impossible to make him look at his model with any attention. If any one commands him to look at it, he hurriedly casts upon it a distracted and disdainful glance and continues without concerning himself with that which he sees. The moment he has finished he shows it to you with a triumphant air.[1]

At first children are interested in depicting by crude symbols the ideas which things suggest, rather than the correct appearance of the things themselves. They draw what they know about objects, rather than what their eyes see at any given moment.

[1] Quoted by Frederick Burk in "The Genetic vs. the Logical Order in Drawing," *Pedagogical Seminary* (1902), p. 296.

For example, they will show both ends of a house in the same drawing, and will sketch not only the exterior, but, if allowed time, will add the furniture and people inside, as if the walls were transparent (Figs. 2 and 3). They are very ready to draw pictures representing their games and home occupations, street

FIG. 2

scenes, and any incidents or objects with which they are familiar, or which make vivid impressions upon their minds. The drawings thus made are crude, and often meaningless to an adult, but not to the child who made them. He has a reason for every mark.

The temptation sometimes arises to substitute for such apparently complex topics a logically progressive arrangement of type forms and geometric figure. In reality, however, a bird's nest is simpler for a child to draw than a hemisphere, and a locomotive than a cylinder. Wise teachers frankly accept this stage of crude drawing as a period which has its own value, and which should be given free exercise while it lasts. The nature of its value should be clearly understood. It consists primarily in the formation of a habit of ready graphic expression of ideas, to which can later be added training in correct delineation.

FIG. 3

Ability to record observations correctly can be developed subsequently with much less expenditure of time and effort, but facility of graphic expression comes most readily during these early years, and is difficult to obtain later. During the first year or two of school life, the acquisition in drawing which is of greatest advantage to the next stage of the work is this facility which a child gains by drawing in his own way with encouragement and example, but little criticism by the teacher. He needs continual use of this primitive picture language in describing things associated with home, out-of-door, and school life. Thus, expression by drawing becomes a habit before the age of self-consciousness and hesitation is reached. Illustrative drawing, as it develops, has a double value. It cultivates both the imagination and the power of expression. Imagination is founded on memory. To represent by lines an image existing in the mind is to force that image to its utmost clearness, thus strengthening, as few other exercises can, the power to visualize.

Construction work.—The first steps in construction should be made with easily manipulated material. The problems should be such that complicated planning and prolonged processes of construction are unnecessary. Results should be quickly evident from the effects.

The sand table offers great possibilities for constructive work. The sand is readily shaped to represent various configurations of land and on these, with easily shaped materials, different locations and occupations may be represented.

Modeling in clay or other plastic material is an occupation which commands strong and long-sustained interest. Both hands are required to shape the responsive material into the desired form, and every touch makes an evident modification.

The work in modeling may well parallel that in drawing. When the hands have shaped forms so they are complete in their three dimensions, the next step of representing three dimensions in terms of only two is more easily taken. Modeling has not been so universally adopted as its value would seem to justify, largely on account of the difficulty of caring for the materials. It is, however, one of the most important modes of manual expression in primary grades.

Cutting pictures and other given shapes from paper gives valuable training in using a common implement to shape material to a predetermined form. It develops control over a tool and at the same time clarifies spatial images and is an important part of manual work in primary grades. Practice in paper cutting of pictures and given forms results in marked progress in ability to control the hand so as to follow an outline. The effect upon the power to image form clearly is seen in added vigor in drawing with pencil and also in representing objects in silhouette by free-hand paper cutting (Fig. 4 and 5).

Accuracy in measurement should not be expected from small children but first steps in handling a rule may be taken by using it as a means of drawing a straight line between two points.

Toward the end of the year some simple measurements which do not involve fractions of inches may be undertaken with profit.

Building with blocks is a type of constructive work which is of great value for small children. By matching the blocks together and selecting those which fit they learn to estimate form with some degree of precision. By placing one block upon another so the structure stands firmly, they gain a sense of horizontal and vertical relations.

FIG. 4

Design.—Two lines of work in design should begin in the lower grades and be evident throughout the course: first the designing of things to serve a particular and useful purpose; second, practice in the repeated drawing and spacing of units and shapes in order to gain facility in estimating space relations and to develop an appreciation of rhythmic intervals in spacing.

The first, involves consideration of the purpose of the object and how it may fulfil this most adequately, and judgment as to the finest proportions and most appropriate ornamentation. This phase appears incidentally in Grade I, in such simple designs as Thanksgiving souvenirs, Christmas cards, valentines, etc. The teacher should work out with the children designs which are simple and yet excellent, and thus accustom them to examples of good arrangement which will influence the choice of the children when later they plan their own designs.

The second may consist of exercises in which the children repeat a simple unit at intervals approximately equal, but without previous measurement, so as to form a border. The units should be drawn in concert to rhythmic time which at first is counted by the teacher as in music, or indicated upon the piano.

FIG. 5

This practice in repeating a series of forms to a corresponding movement of time gives a sense of rhythm which is not developed by drawing borders in which the spacing of the units is indicated either by dictated points or with the aid of measurements before the units are drawn (Fig. 6).

Exercises with these simple borders are the first steps toward more complicated work in upper grades, such as surface designs, bilateral forms, and balanced designs of abstract shapes, or conventionalized flower forms produced with a few pencil or brush strokes.

In this practice, as in penmanship, beautiful form and style are gained, not by pausing over one unit to perfect it, but by repeating the shape till the hand has mastered it and can use it with facility.

During the first year in school children should become familiar with the colors most easily recognized, such as red, orange, yellow, green, blue, and violet. This may be done by placing before the children a fairly large sample of one after another of these colors, and having them collect objects of a similar color. In bits of cloth and paper, and in flowers and leaves, the color under consideration will be discovered and its sensation perceived more clearly than by chance observation. The use of colored crayons and water colors for drawing is an important means of training recognition and discrimination of color.

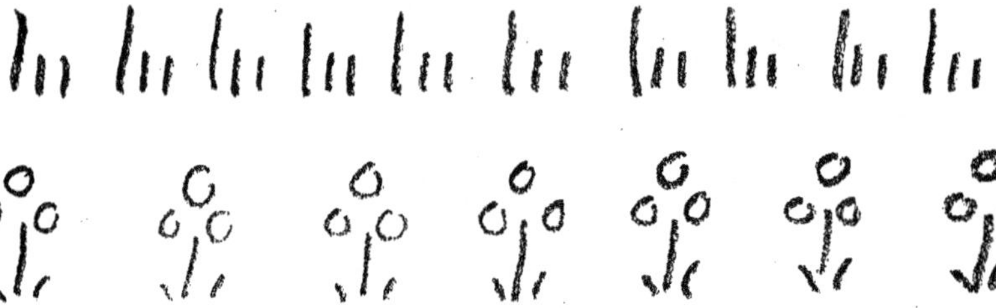

FIG. 6

A reasonable standard of accomplishment has been reached, if at the end of the first year in school the children have developed a habit of expressing their ideas with pencil so that drawing seems to them a matter of course, if they have gained ability to handle simple material such as paper, clay, sand, and blocks so that such materials assume desired shapes, and if they have gained some ideas of good spacing and arrangement under guidance of the teacher, and have begun to enjoy the rhythmic spacing of forms and to discover the general distinctions of color.

That their graphic expressions during this first year are crude and their constructions inaccurate when judged by adult ideas, and that their standards of good design are gained from their instructors, are not causes for apprehension.

The primary instructor who draws with and for the children and who constructs objects with them is furnishing the most potent stimulus and inspiration for progress toward individual ability. Compared with the effect of this, methods and courses without such example are of secondary value.

FROEBELIAN LITERATURE IN KINDERGARTEN TRAINING

NINA C. VANDEWALKER
Milwaukee State Normal School

The kindergarten has been a slow growth. Its underlying theory was the result of many influences; its technique the product of years of thought. Because it was conceived before an adequate study of the child's development had been made, however, the reorganization both of its theory and practice was inevitable. Had the larger knowledge of later years been brought to bear upon the kindergarten before its procedure had assumed fixed forms, however, less reorganization would have been necessary. The inadequate knowledge upon which the kindergarten was originally based is one reason for the reconstruction that is now in progress; the fact that its procedure developed apart from the movement which has given general education its present basis is another. Some of the defects in kindergarten procedure today grow out of methods adopted by kindergarten training schools during the early years. Since these methods have not yet been fully outgrown the reconstruction of the kindergarten involves a reconstruction in kindergarten training as well.

The incorporation of the kindergarten into the school system was the goal of kindergarten effort even in the early years of the movement; that such incorporation would involve a co-ordination of kindergarten theory and practice with the theory and practice of the school was but vaguely realized, if realized at all. The kindergarten leaders therefore took little note of general education until they were compelled to do so at a later period by the incorporation of the kindergarten into the school. The procedure of the kindergarten was therefore built up without reference to educational procedure beyond the kindergarten, and methods of training were evolved in which those employed in the training of other teachers received little recognition. The difficulties in the kindergarten situation today are in no small degree the result of these facts.

The fact that the organization and methods of the training school tended in some respects in the direction of weakness rather than of strength did not become apparent until the adoption of the kindergarten by the school became general. When kindergartners and grade teachers came to work side by side, it became evident that the kindergartner outranked the grade teacher on some points but that she fell below in others. Her strength was found to lie in her sympathetic attitude toward children, her enthusiasm for the kindergarten and the doctrines it represents, and her fine womanliness; her weakness in the early days, lay in her lack of adequate scholarship, her blind following of precedent in method, and her ignorance of, and indifference to, general education. An inquiry into the causes of these weaknesses showed them to be in large measure the result of the methods adopted in kindergarten training schools.

A teacher may adopt one of two attitudes in the work of instruction—the dogmatic or the inquiring. If the first is adopted he will present knowledge to his students for their acceptance; if the second, he will seek to have them acquire it for themselves. The first attitude in the teacher makes the student depend upon authority; the second leads him to do independent thinking. The tendency to follow authority only, on the part of any group of people, indicates that the teaching has been dogmatic in character; the ability on the part of another to do independent thinking indicates that the teaching received has been characterized by the spirit of inquiry. The fact that kindergartners are so generally followers instead of thinkers is circumstantial evidence that in the past at least, dogmatic methods have been the rule in kindergarten training schools. To call attention to this aspect of the methods adopted by kindergarten training teachers is the purpose of this paper.

The kindergarten training course doubtless raised many questions while in process of evolution—questions of subject-matter as well as of method. Its organization as compared with the organization of a normal-school course is of interest, but those who wish information upon it are referred to the article entitled "The Curriculum and Methods of the Kindergarten Training School," in the *Kindergarten Review,* Vol. XIII, p. 642. This paper must confine itself to one phase of training school work—the methods of teaching the kindergarten subjects. Since the study of these subjects calls for the reading of Froebel's most important contributions to educational literature, the discussion of the first will imply a discussion of the second likewise.

The making of a kindergartner calls for instruction in several different lines, but the most important phrase of kindergarten training is the kindergarten instruction proper. As customarily given this instruction falls into several lines. Upon entering the course in the average training school, the student is assigned to practice-teaching during the morning, and is scheduled for several lines of work in the afternoon, reciting in each subject once or twice a week. Among these lines of work is a course in the kindergarten gifts, another in the occupations, still another in the mother plays, and usually one also in games. In each course frequent reference is made to the work of the other, but on the whole the several subjects are independent, and not phases of an organic whole. Since the students are wholly unfamiliar with all of these, and with the books used as textbooks—Froebel's *Pedagogics of the Kindergarten* and *Education by Development* in connection with the gifts and occupations, and the *Mother-Play Book* in connection with the mother plays, the instruction must of necessity be more or less dogmatic in character.

Such an organization of work doubtless seems right and justifiable to those responsible for it, and they would perhaps be surprised to learn that many educational experts regard it as violating the fundamental principles of educational procedure in several respects. The gifts, occupations, and games, are means to an end—the child's development. Unless that development receives the primary emphasis, and the means are studied with constant reference to that development, the student's conception of both end and means will be a wrong one. The fact that the kindergarten instrumentalities are studied first, or that the study of these is placed on the same level with the study of the child, gives an erroneous impression and places the emphasis where it does not belong. Such an organization of work would alone account for the undue exaltation of the kindergarten material which most kindergartners show.

The organization in question is further at fault in the fact that it begins, not with the student's fund of observation and experience, but with the unknown and the unfamiliar. When students begin with their own experiences and proceed by natural processes to the unknown they learn to think for themselves in the process; when they begin with something wholly new they can only accept. Kindergarten students know that the instrumentalities presented to them have value, though they may as yet be unable to see that value themselves. What can they do but take them on faith? When the methods employed in giving kindergarten instruction are considered, it is not surprising that independent thinking on the part of kindergartners should be the exception rather than the rule.

A course so organized is open to criticism on several other grounds. The kindergartner is said to lack interest in general education. How can she acquire such interest when Froebel alone is studied and the literature of general education is ignored and even avoided? She is said to lack scholarship. So large a part of her time is devoted to practice-teaching that the formation of scholarly habits is out of the question. When students are scheduled for half a dozen subjects, in each of which they recite but once or twice a week, thorough work is impossible. Because of the amount of practice-teaching required there is no time for the academic broadening that every student needs. That practice-teaching in the senior year would be of a much higher order if the junior year were devoted to the right kind of study does not yet seem to have occurred to kindergarten training teachers, although normal schools have long recognized that fact. The sins of the kindergartner may be many but the responsibility for a large proportion must be laid at the door of the training school.

Fortunately for the kindergarten cause, however, all kindergarten training is not organized upon the plan described. In a few institutions at least, a course has been adopted which is not open to the criticism in question. In this the correlating center of the whole is a study of the child's development, which continues throughout the junior year, and to which all the other phases of the work are related. The instruction in the kindergarten instrumentalities, which forms another course, is organized into one whole, the foundation of which is a study of the child's play and play material. This also continues throughout the year. The practice-teaching is postponed until the senior year because those in authority consider it unpedagogical to assign students to teaching before they have gained a knowledge of the aims of education, and of the means by which these aims are to be realized. The course includes several academic subjects that the students' scholarship may be strengthened.

A description of the different courses as such is not called for by this paper. As an aid to clearness of comprehension it may be said, however, that in the child-study course mentioned, important phases of the child's development are taken up, on the basis of observation, reading, and class discussion, and that the mother plays are studied in this setting. For a fuller discussion of such a course the reader is referred to an article by the writer, entitled "The Place of the Mother Play in the Training of Kindergartners," in the *Kindergarten Review,* Vol. XVIII, p. 6. The methods of beginning the course in the kindergarten instrumentalities is given in some detail since it illustrates points that will be more fully discussed.

The aim in this course is to lead students from the foundation which their own observation and experience furnishes to a gradual comprehension of the doctrines that underlie kindergarten procedure, and which are embodied in the Froebelian literature. The teacher begins therefore, by turning the student's attention to the games, play, and play material of their own childhood, leading them to consider the various forms of play, and the interests that underlie them. She will direct their attention also to the organized games, both as to form and content, and to the play material used at different ages. She may have them collect available nature material and use it for play purposes as children would, or as their own greater ingenuity directs.

This reminiscent study should be accompanied by the observation of children's play wherever opportunity may offer. From this and their own recollections they may be led to the discovery of several of the principles that underlie kindergarten procedure.

From such a beginning the students can be led to the reading and discussion of the more important theories of play, the views of Froebel included. This in turn may be made the foundation for a more thorough study of the child's play from infancy up—before the kindergarten period, during that period, and after it. The basis for such study must of necessity be the observation of children, and the reading of the literature of child-study bearing upon the topic. With such a foundation the organized play of the kindergarten will assume a significance that it could not otherwise have. The work up to this point should be considered as the foundation for the study of the kindergarten instrumentalities as a whole. Should it seem desirable to study the games independently from this point on, it can be done without danger of separating them in the student's mind from their relation to the child's development.

The games as such form but one phase of the child's play, however. Of equal importance is the play that requires material. In the study of the child's play at different ages, already mentioned, many references will doubtless have been made to the child's use of material for play purposes. This phase of play should now be considered more fully, as before, on the basis of observation and reading. Children's play with balls and blocks in the nursery should be made the basis for the later study of the kindergarten gifts, and the nursery use of clay, sand, paper, pencils, and other materials the basis for a detailed study of the occupations. On such a foundation alone can the instruction in the gifts or occupations be considered pedagogical. When the students have grasped the necessary difference between play with material that retains its form, and that which is changed in the play process, the work may differentiate into a study of the gifts on the one hand, and of the occupations on the other. The methods of procedure with these, on the basis of the new views, have been so well indicated in the preceding papers of this series that a further discussion is unnecessary.

The two modes of organizing kindergarten instruction here presented, and the two kinds of method indicated show two different attitudes among kindergarten training teachers, the dogmatic and the inquiring. These attitudes, with the methods that result from them, produce kindergartners of very different types. The training teachers who embody the first attitude exalt Froebel and the kindergarten. Because of this the emphasis in their instruction is placed upon the study of the kindergarten instrumentalities instead of upon the study of the child. The literature that pertains to these instrumentalities—"Pedagogics of the Kindergarten," and "Education by Development"—is presented as authority to be accepted without question. The study of the child is made upon the basis of Froebel only, and the literature that deals with the child's development—the *Mother-Play Book,* is presented in the same spirit. To make the student see through Froebel's eyes instead of through her own is, consciously or unconsciously, the purpose of the work. It is the acceptance of Froebel's views that is sought for in the student, rather than the power of independent thinking.

The training teachers of the second type emphasize the study of the child instead of the study of the kindergarten instrumentalities. They regard these instrumentalities as the best series yet devised for the development of the child by means of his play activities but are unwilling to accept them as ultimate and final. Instead of presenting the gifts and occupations as a series to be accepted, therefore, the teachers of this type aim to give students such an insight into the principles that underlie children's play that they will be able to use the Froebelian materials or any others to further the child's development. In the study of the child they aim to present Froebel's views of its development, but not in such a manner as to compel their acceptance, until by a comparison with other views the student's own judgment has been satisfied. The attitude which they wish to cultivate toward Froebelian literature as toward any other, therefore, is the attitude of inquiry. It is needless to say that this attitude is in harmony with the spirit of modern education.

It may be asked whether the kindergarten would ever have attained its present status in American education if the inquiring instead of the positive attitude had been assumed at the beginning. It is doubtless true that the advocacy of a theory or an institution is needed for the inauguration of a movement, and there is little doubt that the dogmatic presentation of Froebel's views during the early years was a needed service to American education. Such presentation may continue too long, however, and thereby endanger the existence and progress of the movement it seeks to further. Any institution tends to assume fixed forms. If the underlying thought of that institution is sufficiently vital, these forms will give way at intervals because of growth from within. If the forms which represent it at a given period do not thus give way, the forms will remain but will lack life and substance. The forms which the kindergarten has assumed no longer represent current conceptions of that institution. The dogmatic presentation of Froebel's views at the present time is an attempt, therefore, to maintain a form which is no longer instinct with life. The acquainting of the American people with the views of Froebel was a great service but the present needs a different one.

The literature of American education has been materially enriched by the contributions of Froebel. Although many influences have combined to give that literature its present value, one of its most vital elements would have been lacking if at any time the contribution of Froebel had been eliminated. The influence of that contribution has deepened with the passing years, and there are at present few phases of educational effort in which it has not been felt. The presentation of Froebel's theories to American educators is largely the work of the kindergarten training teachers. In performing this important service, have they rendered the course of education the whole service which they should have rendered?

In acquainting the public with the literature of Froebel the training schools could hardly have labored more faithfully. It is estimated that more than twenty-five thousand young women have taken a kindergarten training course since the kindergarten has become a part of American life. All of these have therefore a first-hand acquaintance with Froebel's masterpieces. The mothers' clubs organized under training school auspices have added to the numbers of those who have studied Froebel more or less thoroughly. The additional number of those who have become familiar with Froebel's views as a result of the efforts of kindergarten graduates cannot be estimated. The majority of these have accepted Froebel's views with little question. It is because of their loyalty to, and their enthusiasm for, the Froebelian doctrines that the kindergarten movement has attained its present momentum.

Such a service challenges admiration, yet one cannot help asking what the effect would have been if Froebel had been taught less dogmatically. What would have been the effect upon the kindergarten and upon the application of Froebel's doctrines to general education if training teachers had emphasized the development of the child more and the technique by which that development is effected less; if the technique of the kindergarten had been studied as a phase of the problem of education by activity instead of something ultimate and final; and if the kindergarten games had been regarded as an initial attempt to show the significance and value of play for education and life, instead of a closed series to which no profane hand should dare to add and from which none should subtract? To know Froebel aright is to know the education of the present and to be able to forecast that of the future. In the *Education of Man,* written over eighty years ago, Froebel struck the keynote of current educational thought—that of education by development; in the *Mother-Play Book,* published seventeen years later he showed how the development a child has already attained can be made the basis for the more formal educational process; and in his *Pedagogics* he indicated a method by which the child's activities may be utilized for educational purposes. The lines of educational effort then inaugurated are now in the process of organization, not for the kindergarten alone but for general education. The kindergartner claims for Froebel the credit of inaugurating such lines of educational effort as child-study and education by activity, but she is unwilling to recognize value in any phases of such effort that are not carried out on strictly Froebelian lines. Many kindergartners are not only out of sympathy, therefore, with the great movements that are shaping American education, but have assumed an attitude of antagonism toward these and toward the literature that embodies them. Such an attitude must eventually bring disaster to the kindergarten, and retard the application of Froebel's doctrines to other lines of educational effort. The educational world at one time needed the presentation of Froebel's doctrines. A different service is needed at present—the reinterpretation of these doctrines from the standpoint of modern scholarship. It would have been appropriate for the kindergarten training teachers to lead in this service also, but in their desire to maintain the forms which the Froebelian doctrines have assumed, the majority have failed to perceive the new problems that have arisen. Because of this, the leadership in kindergarten thought is fast passing from the kindergarten training school to the university. The lines along which Froebelian influence will be exerted in general education have already been pointed out by university men, and such men are giving effective service in the reconstruction of kindergarten theory and practice. In the new educational era that has begun the doctrines of Froebel will receive greater emphasis than they have in the past. If these doctrines are to exert their fullest influence, however, there must be co-operation instead of antagonism between the forces that value such influence. The methods that have produced weakness in kindergarten instruction must be discarded and the attitudes and methods adopted that will make for strength and union with other educational forces. The literature of Froebel has proved a great stimulus to educational thought, but that stimulus is by no means exhausted. When it is approached in the spirit of modern thought its true value will become apparent.

NATURAL HISTORY IN THE GRADES

OTIS W. CALDWELL

In a series of short articles it is my purpose to outline the natural-history materials that are suggested for each of the grades in the elementary school. This discussion presumes that work with nature may be so arranged as to have sequence in order of interest and difficulty of study. It presumes also that in each grade the training and information involved in the study of the materials of the preceding grade may be depended upon as the basis for succeeding work. It is recognized that in different localities there is greater variation in the materials for this work than in arithmetic or the languages, and that substitutions of other materials must often be made. In arranging these substitutions, however, selection should be so made that the new materials will serve similar interests, cultivate similar relative acquaintance on the part of the children, and have similar informational value. That any object in nature will suffice for the natural-history work of a given grade is no more and no less true than that any topic in arithmetic is quite as good as any other for use in this grade. A somewhat closely related body of knowledge organized upon a broad underlying educational purpose is essential to giving any subject a position of dignity in the school curriculum. Nature-study has by no means reached this dignified position of organization, but it is toward this end that its advocates are working.

In the grades three dominant attitudes of mind toward nature are noticeable. The younger children in grades one and two and sometimes in grade three appear to be interested primarily in finding out what and where things are and what is being done. This is chiefly an orientation attitude, one of development of speaking acquaintance with nature. Consequently during this period a relatively large number of things in the local environment may be studied, but not studied in detail.

In the intermediate grades the attitude of orientation and general acquaintance is not lost but added to it is a larger and more definite interest in knowing how and why things happen; this leads to a somewhat more intensive study of a smaller number of things, a study of causes, processes, and results, and of the relation of natural objects and processes to the needs of men. In the upper grades, seventh and eighth, and sometimes the sixth, the preceding interests are still present but there is an added interest in the use of nature and nature's forces in the industries and also in what may be called elementary science.

FIRST GRADE

In extending acquaintance with nature, obviously the work should begin with those things that are most closely related to the life and experiences of the home and school. These materials have been classified under the heads of (1) Animal Life, (2) Plant Life, (3) Garden Work, (4) Earth Materials, (5) Climatology.

1. *Animal life.*—Under animal life are included the horse, dog, cow, sheep, pigs, chickens, rabbits, squirrels, pigeons, doves, robin, English sparrow, crow, blue-jay, flicker, turtles, toads, fish, fly, mosquito, butterfly, and angle worm. Obviously acquaintance with several of these things will have been secured before the children come to the first grade, but they should be included in the outline lest some may not know them. Sometimes certain animals such as the cow and sheep, will not be observable, while at other times these will be so well known that others may more profitably be substituted for them. Out of the entire list will be found those that will make up an adequate amount of animal work for the first grade regardless of the differing degrees of acquaintanceship that pupils already have. The point to be made perfectly clear is that at the end of this grade the children should know the things included in the outline and have considerable general knowledge of their habits. Many of them in connection with casual observations will know something of animals such as the polar and black bear, deer, and buffalo; and descriptions, pictures, and true stories concerning

these animals will prove valuable. Local animals, however, are the ones upon which the regular work should be based.

In the schoolroom aquaria some of the smaller water animals may be grown and used for daily observation. In a box covered by wire or mosquito netting toads may be kept. During all favorable weather the box should be kept out of doors in a cool shady place. Hodge's *Nature-Study and Life* contains an excellent discussion of work with the toad. If suitable places for such work may be had some of the larger animals should be kept by the children, as a pair of rabbits, and hen and chickens. A well-trained dog may be made extremely valuable for a few days in the schoolroom, and horses are so abundant that more or less intermittent observations upon them are possible. Animals that the children have as pets in their homes may often be secured for school use.

2. *Plant life.*—Materials suggested for study are such vegetables as beets, potatoes, radish, lettuce, asparagus, cabbage, rhubarb, parsley, cauliflower; such fruits as apples, oranges, lemons, bananas, melons, pumpkins, pineapples, berries; such house plants as geranium, nasturtium, ferns, mosses, palms; such trees, shrubs, and herbs as the oak, elm, maple, lilac, dandelion, plantain; and finally a few bulbous plants such as tulip and narcissus.

3. *Garden work.*—Window boxes in which are grown several of the plants mentioned above are valuable. By constructing the window boxes in such a way that they may stand within a galvanized iron pan proper watering and drainage may be had; plants may be germinated and grown, and seed matured inside the room. Decorative plants should be used almost exclusively in these boxes, and their habits and the care requisite to proper growth should be made points of special study.

Outdoor gardens should consist of one vegetable and one flower garden for the grade. In the window boxes decorative plants, as geranium and nasturtium, may be prepared for later planting out of doors; also many vegetables may be started in small boxes or pots for transplanting thus giving profitable indoor work and an earlier result in the outdoor garden. One-inch pots in which each child plants a few radish or lettuce seeds give plants which may readily be transplanted as suggested below. In the outdoor gardens children of this grade can do little cultivation except such as is done by weeding and by use of small single-hand tools.

Names and characteristics of the common garden plants should be learned and some knowledge should be secured of proper ways of planting and caring for each. Beets, radish, and lettuce suggested for the grade's group garden furnish types of plants that the children must grow from seed which they should plant at the time when outdoor garden work may be begun. If planted too deep the young plants will not live to reach the surface, and if too shallow excessive dryness, heat or cold may injure them. Radish and lettuce seed should be planted at a depth of one-half inch from the surface and beet seed at a depth of one inch. The rows of radish and lettuce should be six inches apart with fifteen to twenty seeds to the foot, while beet rows should be one foot apart and the number of seed per foot should be ten or twelve. It will be well to plant in a box or pot in the schoolroom a week or two before beginning the outdoor garden work a few of each kind of seeds to be used in order that the pupils may learn the characteristic appearance of the different kinds of seedlings before they appear in the gardens. This helps to distinguish the desired plants from the weed seedlings that are certain to develop.

Cabbage, cauliflower, and tomato furnish types of vegetables that need to be started in the schoolroom early enough so that plants three or four inches in height above the ground may be had for transplanting, when the weather is suitable for outdoor planting. In transplanting care must be taken first to remove the plants without injuring the roots, which can be done by moistening the soil, then carefully lifting the plants by use of a dull knife or the fingers. Secondly, in resetting each plant there should be made an opening in the soil amply large enough to allow the roots to be spread out in their normal position. Upon the well-spread roots, sprinkle a half-inch of fine soil and then water carefully so that the soil is well settled about the roots, thus in a measure reproducing the relations that previously existed between the soil and the roots. After watering fill in soil about the plant until the opening is filled. The plant is then ready to begin work in its new location. It should be remembered, however, that these plants are not yet able by means of their recently disturbed roots to secure a large supply of water, and should excessive drying of the leaves occur the demand upon the roots for water would be greater than could be met, hence the necessity, in case of hot, dry weather, of covering the plants for a day or two by use of old newspapers or of inverted earthen pots.

The potato offers still another method of starting plants, and at least one or two hills should be planted so that the pupils may observe the cutting out, planting, and development of the "eye" or bud from which the new plants are propogated. Direction for the growth and care of nearly all the garden vegetables may be found in French's *A Book of Vegetables,* published by the Macmillan Company at a cost of $1.75. Suggestions concerning work with bulbous plants may be found in the October *Elementary School Teacher,* pp. 86–88.

4. *Earth materials.*—The names, and general characteristics of rock, clay, sand, and loam may properly constitute earth work in this grade. If the garden work precedes this study much general data will have been secured, and that may now be used as the basis for the beginning discussion. Rocks of all available kinds should be collected. At the outset simply ask that different kinds of rocks be brought to the schoolroom, after which there will doubtless develop many lines of difference, as those of color, form, size, hardness, and composition. If the stones are not fairly clean they should be washed so that their true appearance may be had. Have the pupils classify the stones according to color, then examine to see if they can determine different structures between stones of different colors, and between stones of the same colors. To enable pupils to observe composition, freshly broken faces of stones are best. Compare the hardness of the different stones and arrange them in a series of decreasing hardness. Compare the hardness and the weight. Measure the larger

pieces of stone that are fairly regular in form and weigh carefully. Determine whether hardest stones are heaviest. By the above and other similar methods of study there should be developed clear general ideas about at least several kinds of rocks such as quartz, limestone, sandstone, and shale. Various kinds of crystal stones are likely to be found; also some stones containing fossil remains will prove of great interest and will demand simple explanations.

After having studied stones, work may be done with gravel, sand, clay, and loam, first by noting general appearances, then by studying the texture of each and making comparisons. Gravel soils when sifted first with a coarse sieve then with a fine one prove instructive by demonstrating the gradations in breaking of the rock particles. From such gravel soils composed of different sized stones, sand and sometimes loam may be secured. If some disintegrating sandstone can be secured, it will, when studied together with coarse and fine sand, make the connection between stones and sand. Clay is but very finely divided particles of sand together with relatively small quantities of material resulting from the decay of animal and plant bodies. Pupils may determine its texture and rigidity as compared with other soils. Sandy loam should be sifted to discover the sand and remains of plant and animal decay that compose it. In this grade little or no attempt should be made to study the water-holding, ore-carrying power of soils, but in connection with window boxes and garden work the kinds of soils in which plants thrive best should be noted. Valuable suggestions for this study may be had in a pamphlet entitled *How to Read a Pebble,* by F. L. Charles, University of Illinois, Urbana, Ill. This pamphlet may be secured from the author, postpaid, for twenty-five cents.

5. *Climatology.*—The length of day and night; the position of sun, moon, and stars; clouds, dew, rain, snow, frost, ice, steam; air currents, wind, carrying power of wind, storms. A simple weather record kept upon the board or upon a chart for a few weeks will serve as the basis for the study of the weather, and will stimulate observation while the pupils are on their way to and from school. A chart blank with spaces for a month's

record may be made to include the days of the week, the number of days in the month and the weather record for an entire month. To furnish the data for making this record, the children must observe accurately, read the thermometer carefully, and report in terms that are definite. Determination of quantity of precipitation should not be expected in this grade.

	Monday	Tuesday	Wednesday	Thursday	Friday
Date					
Length of day { Sunrise / Sunset					
Temperature { At opening of school / At noon / At close of school					
Character of the day. Include the time of each observation, cover points as cloudy, clear, rainy, variable, frost, dew, snow					
Wind. Its direction, constancy, strength, stormy					
Moon. Time of rising, its size, and changes					

The accompanying plan for keeping records, while extremely simple, provides for things that first-grade pupils may determine. In doing the work involved in keeping this record, training will be given in accurate observation as in reading the thermometer, in noting the kind of day, in securing from the daily paper the time of sunrise and sunset. In deciding just how to express observations of phenomena training will be given in choice of accurate and adequately descriptive words.

If a month's records are kept in this way interesting comparisons are then possible. Some of the questions suggesting these comparisons are: How many partially or wholly rainy days were there in the month? How many cloudy days? How many entirely clear days? What variations in temperature have there been in any single day? Is there a regularity in daily temperature variations? Is the whole day warmer or colder at the close of the month than at the beginning? Are cloudy days the coldest days?

Although the materials suggested herein are arranged under five headings, it does not follow that one group is to be finished before another is begun, nor that groups should be studied in the order given. In actual practice it has not been found possible nor desirable to study materials as classified into separate groups. Availability of materials, seasonal changes, previous experiences of the pupils, and individual preferences of the teacher help to determine the order of consideration of topics. It is hoped that at a later date there may be published a more detailed suggestion of the order of topics in making up the year's course. In all the work of this grade as well as in the immediately succeeding grades the natural history and different forms of work in expression run closely together. Well-made sentences and sketches in description of the things observed are invaluable to proper observation and interpretation, and the pupils should understand that they must see and know things well enough to enable them to express to others what they see and know.

OUR INHERITED PRACTICE IN ELEMENTARY SCHOOLS

S. CHESTER PARKER
The University of Chicago

II. THE DANCING-MASTER EDUCATION OF THE EIGHTEENTH CENTURY

This is the second of a series of articles which describe the development of modern practices in elementary education. The previous paper presented the religious conception of education which dominated the American and European elementary schools down to the nineteenth century. More progress was made in the development of elementary-school practice during the nineteenth century, than during all previous centuries. The nineteenth-century movement was inspired by Rousseau, whose educational treatise the *Emile* was published in 1762.

At the time that Rousseau wrote, the people of Europe were divided into three distinct classes or castes: (1) At the bottom were the laborers and peasants, in various stages of degradation, varying from the serfs of Russia and eastern Europe to the free but overtaxed peasants of France. (2) The middle class was composed of manufacturers, shop-keepers, lawyers, physicians, actors, professors. During the eighteenth century this class steadily increased in power and importance, largely as a result of their economic influence. (3) The highest class, from the standpoint of power, was composed of the nobility, the king and his court, and the higher clergy.

When the members of the lowest class received any education, it was the crudest of the type described in the previous paper. The aim of such education was religious and it provided a very limited schooling under incompetent teachers who were often lame soldiers, shoemakers, tailors, etc. The result of several years of study by a pupil was a knowledge of the catechism and a little ability to read in stumbling fashion.

The elementary education of the middle classes was of the same general type, but usually more effective owing to the larger and better organized schools to be found in the cities. The apprenticeship system provided industrial training for the boys of the artisan class; those intended for professional careers entered Latin schools very early, usually about the age of nine, and from these schools they proceeded to the university.

The education of the children of the nobility during the eighteenth century was determined by the conditions of court life and might be characterized as the dancing-master education. It aimed to make the child completely fit for the drawing-room life of the period.

Rousseau was most concerned in criticizing this type of education which prevailed among the nobility and the *élite* of the middle class. In the accounts ordinarily given of Rousseau attention is called to the degraded position of the peasants, to their poverty and sufferings. It is true that the misfortunes of the poor and oppressed most concerned Rousseau in his political writings, but it is not primarily for a reform of the education of the peasantry or the lower middle class that he is contending in the *Emile*. As a matter of fact, he heartily favors the free development which the peasant children enjoyed, and the trade apprenticeship which was provided for middle-class children. Moreover, he says definitely that he is not concerned with such children.

> The poor man has no need of an education, for his condition in life forces one upon him, and he could receive no other. On the contrary, the education which the rich man receives from his station is the one which befits him the least, both with respect to himself and to society. Moreover, the education of nature ought to make a man fit for all the conditions of human life. Now, it is less reasonable to educate a poor man for becoming rich, than to educate a rich man for becoming poor; for, in proportion to the number of these two classes, there are more men who are ruined than there are who rise from poverty to wealth. Let us, therefore, choose our pupil from among the wealthy, for we shall at least be sure of having given one more man to society, while a poor man may make a man of himself.[1]

[1] Rousseau, *Emile* (Appleton), p. 20.

To be sure, the training provided in the common schools was as defective from the standpoint of Rousseau's general principles as was the dancing-master education, and his criticisms apply as well to the former. But one cannot help feeling as he reads the *Emile,* that it was the education of wealthy youths that Rousseau had principally in mind as he wrote.

The point, then, that I desire to make is this. To really appreciate the revolutionary character of Rousseau's ideas, to grasp the true historical significance of his suggestions, it is necessary to have a clear notion of the kind of education which he desired to reform. This was the education which prevailed among the privileged and wealthy classes of France in the middle of the eighteenth century. Therefore, a part of this paper will be devoted to giving a picture of the life of these people and the dancing-master education which prevailed among them.

One other preliminary statement will help in getting the point of view which will enable us to appreciate Rousseau's historical significance. It is this statement which we find in the preface of the *Emile* and which seems to me to be just as significant as the opening sentence of the first chapter which is so commonly quoted.

> We do not know childhood. Acting on the false ideas we have of it, the farther we go the farther we wander from the right path. Those who are wisest are attached to what is important for men to know, without considering what children are able to comprehend. They are always looking for the man in the child, without thinking of what he was before he became a man. This is the study upon which I am most intent, to the end that, though my method may be chimerical and false, profit may always be derived from my observations. I may have a very poor conception of what ought to be done, but I think I have a correct view of the subject on which we are to operate. Begin, then, by studying your pupils more thoroughly, for it is very certain that you do not know them. Now, if you read this book of mine with this purpose in view, I do not believe that it will be without profit to you.[2]

Thus we see that a knowledge of the attitude toward children which prevailed in the eighteenth century is fundamental in understanding Rousseau.

[2] *Ibid.*, p. xlii.

As an introduction, then, I shall describe certain of the activities of the French aristocracy, the nature of family life, the treatment of children, the dancing-master education, and show further that the same ideas and practices prevailed among some of the wealthy people of the American colonies.

The members of the court of the French king originally served him as a bodyguard and exercised other military functions. They were a body of efficient people concerned with practical affairs of state and war. By the eighteenth century these conditions had materially changed. In theory the king was supreme, absolute in control. As a matter of fact, the business of administering state affairs had become so vast that only a very intelligent and energetic king could keep track of it. Under an incompetent ruler the administration and control were really in the hands of some faction of the nobility or courtiers. The dominant "ring" conducted affairs for its own profit. The only way to secure preferment was to make one's way personally at court.

> It was the court that controlled most appointments, for no king could know all applicants personally and intimately. The stream of honor and emolument from the royal fountain-head was diverted, by the ministers and courtiers, into their own channels.[3]

The court became a great body of idlers, each individual feeling the necessity of being constantly present to look after his own interests.

These courtiers were governed in their actions toward one another by an elaborate system of rules of etiquette. Most of these were antiquated customs which had originally served a useful purpose, but did so no longer. As Lowell says,

> They had been devised to prevent confusion and regulate the approach of courtiers to the king. As all honors and emoluments came from the royal pleasure, people were sure to crowd about the monarch, and to jostle each other with unmannerly and dangerous haste, unless they were strictly held in check. Everyone, therefore, must have his place definitely assigned to him.[4]

Thus there developed a most involved body of artificial rules and customs which governed social intercourse. Brilliant de-

[3] Lowell, *Eve of the French Revolution*, p. 13.

[4] *Ibid.*, p. 18.

scriptions of this "drawing-room" life are to be found in Taine's *Ancient Régime.* I shall summarize some of these and quote others. The points to be considered are the idleness, extravagance, barrenness and artificiality, separate life of husband and wife, formal relation of child and parent, the dancing-master education.

The idleness has already been referred to. Most of the nobility were owners of vast country estates. Yet

the nobility in France had no more idea of practicing agriculture, and making it a subject of conversation, than any other object the most remote from their habits and pursuits. . . . . Through tradition, fashion, and deliberately, they are, and wish only to be, people of society; their sole concern is to talk and to hunt.[5]

The chief occupation of a well-qualified master of a house is to amuse himself and to amuse his guests.

As is the general so is his staff: the grandees imitate their monarch. Like some costly colossal effigy in marble erected in the center of France, and of which reduced copies are scattered by thousands throughout the provinces, thus royal life repeats itself, in minor proportions, even among the remotest gentry. The object is to make a parade and to receive; to make a figure and pass away time in good society.[6]

The second characteristic of this aristocratic society was its extravagance. The attitude of contempt for money is thus expressed by Taine:

What kind of a seignior is he who studies the price of things? And how can the exquisite be reached if one grudges money? Money, accordingly, must flow and flow on until exhausted, through structures, furnitures, toilets, hospitality, gallantry, and pleasures. The extreme of profusion must accompany the height of gallantry, the man of the world being so much the more important according to his contempt for money.[7]

A third characteristic was the lack of home life, the separation in interests of husband and wife.

In a drawing-room, the woman to whom a man pays the least attention is his wife, and the same with her. Hence, at a time like this, when people live for society and in society, there is no place for conjugal intimacy.[8]

[5] Taine, *The Ancient Régime* (Holt, 1896), p. 49.

[6] *Ibid.*, p. 113. [7] *Ibid.*, p. 130. [8] *Ibid.*, p. 131.

Husband and wife often maintained separate households and greeted each other in the same formal way as they greeted strangers.

"Here at Paris," writes Mme. d'O——, "I am no longer my own mistress. I scarcely have time to talk with my husband and to answer my letters. I do not know what women do that are accustomed to lead this life; they certainly have no families to look after, nor children to educate."

The formal and unnatural relations which existed between husband and wife, were paralleled by similar relations between child and parent. Children addressed their parents as they would strangers, no expression of affection being permitted. Often children scarcely saw their parents, and when they did the attitude of the children was usually that of deferential timidity. "M. de Tallyrand stated that he never slept under the same roof with his father and mother." Says another man of the period, "Like all the children of my age and station, I was dressed in the handsomest clothes to go out, and naked and dying in the house." Girls, for the most part, were placed in convents.

The spirit of education is everywhere the same; that is to say, in the eyes of the parents there is but one intelligible and rational existence, that of society, even for children, and the attentions bestowed on these are solely with a view to introduce them into it or to prepare them for it.[9]

Barrenness and artificiality are the dominant characteristics of this life.

In the first place all naturalness is excluded from it: everything is arranged and adjusted—decoration, dress, attitude, tone of voice, words, ideas and even sentiments. "A genuine sentiment is so rare," said M. de V——, "that, when I leave Versailles, I sometimes stand still in the street to see a dog gnaw a bone."[10]

There was then [said George Sand, who was educated in that style] a certain way of walking, of sitting down, of saluting, of picking up a glove, of holding a fork, of tendering any article, in fine, a complete mimicry, which children had to be taught at a very early age in order that habit might become a second nature, and this conventionality formed so important an item in the life of men and women in aristocratic circles that the actors of the present day, with all their study, are scarcely able to give us an idea of it.[11]

[9] Taine, *The Ancient Régime* (Holt, 1896), p. 136.

[10] *Ibid.*, p. 157.

[11] *Ibid.*

Any departure from this studied behavior resulted in the individual being considered uncultured and uncouth, " a specimen" or "a simpleton." All natural forms of emotional expression were considered bad form. Apparent indifference in all situations was the ideal, all spontaneity and initiative were stamped out. Mr. Taine gives the following incident as an illustration. A young lady having obtained through family influence a pension for Marcel, a famous dancing-master, ran to his house to present him with the patent. Marcel received it but immediately dashed it on the floor, saying, "Mademoiselle, did I teach you to offer an object in that manner? Pick up that paper and hand it to me as you ought to." She picked up the patent and presented it to him in the proper manner, whereupon Marcel said, "That's very well, mademoiselle, I accept it although your elbow was not quite sufficiently rounded, and I thank you."

The dancing-master was the most important factor in the whole educational situation. His function was to make little children into young ladies and gentlemen as expeditiously as possible. In Monroe's *History of Education* is printed a fashion plate of the eighteenth century showing two children as miniatures of two adults who are represented in the same picture. The same condition is pictured in words by Taine as follows:

Even in the last years of the ancient régime [down to 1783] little boys have their hair powdered, "a pomatumed chignon (bourse), ringlets, and curls;" they wear the sword, the chapeau under the arm, a frill, and a coat with gilded cuffs; they kiss young ladies' hands with the air of little dandies. A lass of six years is bound up in a whalebone waist; her large hoop-petticoat supports a skirt covered with wreaths; she wears on her head a skilful combination of false curls, puffs, and knots, fastened with pins, and crowned with plumes, and so high that frequently "the chin is half way down to her feet;" sometimes they put rouge on her face. *She is a miniature lady and she knows it;* she is fully up to her part, without effort or inconvenience, by force of habit; the unique, the perpetual instruction she gets is on her deportment: it may be said with truth that *the fulcrum of education in this country is the dancing-master.* They could get along with him without any others; without him the others were of no use. For, without him, how could people go through easily, suitably, and gracefully the thousand and one actions of daily life, walking, sitting down, standing up, offering the arm, using the fan, listening and smiling, before eyes so experienced and before such a refined public? *This is to be the great thing for them when they become men and women, and for this reason it is the thing of chief importance for them as children.*[12]

This was the kind of life and education that Rousseau had before him when he wrote the *Emile;* a life in which everything that was spontaneous, emotional, natural, childlike, was eliminated in favor of indifference, artificiality, and polite formality.

Not only did these ideals prevail among the nobility proper, but they played a large part in the life of the wealthy members of the middle class and even descended to shoemakers and other artisans.

These ideals and practices were most highly developed at the French court, but they were copied in all the courts of Europe. Taine says,

Paris is the schoolhouse of Europe, a school of urbanity to which the youth of Russia, Germany, and England resort to become civilized. Lord Chesterfield in his letters never tires of reminding his son of this and of urging him into these drawing rooms, which will remove "his Cambridge rust."[13]

Even in the American colonies, among people of quality, the same ideals and practices in the training of little children were quite common. Much evidence of this is given in Alice M. Earle's *Child Life in Colonial Days* which is the best and most concrete history of educational practice in the American colonies that I have seen.

In the physical development of little girls, delicacy of figure and whiteness of complexion were considered ideal by many mothers. "Little Dolly Payne, afterward Dolly Madison, wore long gloves, a linen mask, and had a sunbonnet sewed on her head every morning by her devoted mother." Very light high-heeled shoes were worn, making exercise impossible. Sometimes little girls five years old were bound up in stays "made of heavy strips of board and steel, tightly wrought with heavy buckram or canvas into an iron frame like an instrument of torture." [14]

[12] Taine, *The Ancient Régime* (Holt, 1896), p. 137. Italics not in the original.

[13] *Ibid.,* p. 139.

[14] Earle, *Child Life in Colonial Days,* p. 57.

It was fashionable to dress the hair of little children just the same as that of adults. Little boys five to seven years of age had their heads shaven and wore wigs. A little girl had her hair dressed over a high roll, which was so heavy and hot that it made her head "itch & ache & burn like anything." She described her first experience with it as follows:

When it first came home, Aunt put it on & my new cap on it; she then took up her apron & measured me, & from the roots of my hair on my forehead to the top of my notions, I measured about an inch longer than I did downwards from the roots of my hair to the end of my chin.[15]

The conception of the child as a miniature adult which prevailed in the eighteenth century in America appears in the portraits of children painted at that time. Nearly all of them are characterized by apparent maturity in dress, expression, and gesture. Either children were so trained and dressed that they actually did appear like miniature adults, or the artist's conception of the child as an adult prevented him from seeing the real child. A picture of a girl of fourteen might very easily be mistaken for a woman of thirty. A boy standing beside his father seems different only in size. Speaking of two of these portraits which were being returned from the Boston Museum of Art a gentleman wrote, "I shall miss the little grown-ups—were there no children in those days?" Portraits painted after the American Revolution "show the definite changes in dress which set in with other Republican institutions. At this date there began to be worn a special dress for both boys and girls." [16]

Digressing somewhat from the treatment of children in polite society as if they were adults, and from a special discussion of the education of wealthy children, there is another phase of the general failure to understand children that should be mentioned. I refer to the lack of stories and other suitable literature written especially for children. In this connection Locke said, "The only books I know of fit for children are Aesop's *Fables* and *Reynard the Fox*." Earle says there seem to have been no books especially intended for the delight of children either in England or the American colonies. Three books, how-

[15] *Ibid.*, p. 59.

[16] *Ibid.*, p. 61.

ever, which were written for adults for religious or other social purposes, soon became regular story-books for children. These were *Pilgrim's Progress* published in 1688, *Robinson Crusoe* in 1714, and *Gulliver's Travels* in 1726. About 1750, however, an extensive trade in English story-books written for children was begun by an English bookseller named John Newberry. We shall find a very definite connection between this lack of children's books and the reform movement of Rousseau and his followers.

Although the drawing-room ideal and dancing-master practice played a much smaller part in the American education than it did in French, there was little more consideration for the child or realization of his needs. Earle summarizes the position of children in colonial days in these words:

> The child of colonial days was emphatically "to be seen, not to be heard"—nor was he even to be very much in evidence to the eye. He was of as little importance in domestic, social, or ethical relations as his childish successor is of great importance today: it was deemed neither courteous, decorous, nor wise to make him appear of value or note in his own eyes or in the eyes of his seniors. Hence there was none of that exhaustive study of the motives, thoughts, and acts of a child which is now rife.[17]

The strongest influence in stimulating Europe to study the child's capacities, attitudes, and reactions as a basis for a reform of the practices and methods of elementary education was Rousseau's *Emile.*

[17] Earle, *Child Life in Colonial Days,* Foreword, p. vii.

EDITORIAL NOTES

Teachers' meetings are often conducted in such a way as to contribute little or nothing to the improvement of school work.

Teachers' Meetings

The common mode of procedure in organizing these meetings is to import one or more speakers who address the association for an hour or less in general terms on some subject which is remote from the immediate work and interests of most of the audience. The conscientious teacher who tries to get something to carry away from this kind of a meeting usually has to be satisfied with what is vaguely described as the inspiration of the occasion. The less faithful teacher comes to regard the meeting as worth while chiefly because of its social accessories. The case is still worse when the organizers of the meeting try to escape the difficulties and tedium of the situation by the importation of cheap humor or shallow sentiment. It is time for a readjustment of the whole theory and practice of teachers' meetings.

Possibilities of Committee Work

All one needs to remember in working out this readjustment is the familiar maxim that development in moral and intellectual life comes only through self-activity. No teachers' gathering can be successful which fails to present a genuine opportunity for self-activity on the part of the members of the gathering. Why should teachers be doomed to listen forever to general discussions by imported speakers when they might work out through committees their important local problems? Let a committee be organized to draw up a detailed course of study for the section of country covered by the association. Let the teachers compare statistics regarding the elimination of children in their various schools. Let someone show his or her drawing work, or constructive work. It may be that these results will be less perfect than those described by imported speakers, but they will be so directly related to the local situation that they will be immensely more valuable in furnishing others in the assembly with material. Let the teachers describe to each other the methods which they employ in securing the co-operation of their respective communities. Let the problem of securing library material be discussed. Let the money which is lavishly spent for organization of an ephemeral sort be spent in preparing a circulating collection of commercial specimens to supplement geography. Let a plan for interchange of visits be organized so that each school shall present its best work for neighborly inspection.

In short the meeting of teachers should serve the ends of organized educational co-operation. There is no group of teachers unacquainted with difficulties which need first-hand co-operative attack. A gathering of teachers which contributes nothing but theory and sentiment and entertainment to the local educational situation is a failure and ought to be recognized as a failure.

Editorial Announcement

The editors of the *Elementary School Teacher* call the attention of their readers to the enlargement of this journal in the last issue and in the present number. Last month four pages were added. This month there are eight pages more than the standard former edition. The material at hand calls for further enlargement and this will be made as fast as possible. We have confidence that systematic material, such as is being presented, has its place in the education of today. We look forward to the future of this journal with the expectation that it will develop to the point where it can offer at least twice the present amount of material each month and contribute its large share to the demonstration that educational practice can be put on a sound scientific basis.

Lack of space makes it necessary to postpone until December the second part of the paper by Mr. Courtis. Two new series of articles are introduced this month. Hereafter papers in two of the four current series will appear each month and the remainder of the issue will be devoted to miscellaneous articles.

BOOK REVIEWS

Graded Games and Rhythmic Exercises for Primary Schools. By MARION B. NEWTON. New York: A. S. Barnes. Pp. 110. $1.00.

Physical exercise for all children is a comparatively new idea. For a long time boys have been regarded as requiring plenty of exercise, and they have had gymnasiums and regulated athletic sport; most likely because they insisted on having it. But it is only recently, that we have shown our conviction that boys and girls, little children as well as big ones, have a right to room and time for organized and directed physical activity. This conviction has expressed itself by putting opportunities for exercise into the public as well as the private schools, by endeavoring to regulate the exercise according to the age and interests of the children, and by the preparation of courses and manuals of exercises, chiefly for children from the fourth or fifth grade up, where most of our experience has been gained.

It is a new experience, and a most welcome one, to find in Miss Newton's book of *Graded Games and Exercises* a course for little children, from the first to the fourth grades. There is nothing, I think, in print as yet of just this kind. Miss Stoneroad published a book of rhythmic exercises for young children and Miss Fanny Johnson and others have given us suggestive work in other lines. Miss Newton's book endeavors to present a fairly complete list of games, exercises, marches, and plays, based on sound physical principles which will be of great help in the schoolroom and do much to give consistency and value to the work in the schools.

There is a tendency to too great repetition in some lines; there is advance and variety in the repetition, but the new phases it emphasizes are social and intellectual rather than physical. In the third and fourth grades, especially, some of the very active and heavier type of folk games might have been given, and if it were possible, in the earlier grades, simple climbing, stretching plays would be of value.

But the list as given is very good and any group of children would be fortunate who for four years had had the fun and physical benefit of these plans.

The book is well printed, in clear type and with attractive spacing, the pictures are interesting, the directions simple and practical. Miss Harris has supplied a wise and earnest preface.

ALICE O'GRADY

CHICAGO NORMAL SCHOOL

The Wonderful House that Jack Has. By C. N. MILLARD, Supervisor of Grammar Grades, Buffalo Public Schools. New York: Macmillan. 8vo. Pp. 359. $0.50 net.

There has been a great need of textbooks of physiology which would be suitable for school use. Most of them have been too technical, and have given undue prominence to anatomical description, whereas the chief emphasis with children should be placed on a discussion of hygienic habits of living; the physiological processes and the anatomical structures should be described very simply and with a definite bearing on their hygiene.

This book takes the hygienic point of view, and deals with the subject in a simple, conversational manner, with little use of technical terms but with scientific knowledge. It is a valuable contribution to this field of instruction. As the name implies the body is regarded as a house, built up and warmed by food, ventilated through the lungs, cleaned inside and out by water, and supplied with a set of windows—the senses—that must be kept bright and clean. The value of right habits is clearly shown, and "much is made of the fact that more fun, better looks, and increased power to do usually accompany improved health."

Under "Building Materials" are discussed food stuffs, their production and the intelligent care which is needed to insure their freshness and cleanliness, the values of different kinds of food, digestion and hygienic habits of eating. In this connection is a chapter on beverages, including an excellent section on alcohol, consistently and strongly treated without being overemphasized. Breathing habits, the function of respiration, exercise, and the necessity and problem of ventilation are next taken up with their obvious relations. Under the suggestive heading, "The Adulteration of Air," the use of tobacco is given a short chapter. Then follow chapters on drinking-water and its protection from contamination, sleep, the essentials concerning clothing, and the care of the teeth, ears, and eyes, contagions, and emergencies.

Suggestions for experiment are made and many convincing stories are told in illustration of the subject-matter, as for instance the vivid story of Dr. Hodge's dogs, Nig, Bum, Topsy, and Tipsy and their relation to the alcohol habit. But a good teacher would find it to her advantage to use both experiment and illustration to a greater degree than is done in the book.

It is doubtful whether the pathological side of human function should be discussed with a child. His attention should be directed to normal action and how to attain it. Therefore I should say that the section on the symptoms of pulmonary tuberculosis should be omitted in elementary-school work. On the other hand this information is something that every adult should have.

The chapter on "Emergencies" is a very valuable one. There is good reason for children to be acquainted with simple methods of affording "first aid" in the common accidents which are likely to happen to them or their playmates. Prompt action in the right direction while the doctor is being sent for may save much suffering.

J. A. Norris

BOOKS RECEIVED

AMERICAN BOOK COMPANY

The Human Body and Health, an Intermediate Text-Book of Essential Physiology, Applied Hygiene, and Practical Sanitation for Schools. By Alvin Davison. Illustrated. Cloth. Pp. 223. $0.50.

Foundations of German. By C. F. Kayser and F. Monteser. Cloth. Pp. 224. $0.80.

Selections from Byron, Wordsworth, Shelley, Keats, and Browning. Edited by CHARLES TOWNSEND COPELAND AND HENRY MILNER RIDEOUT. Cloth. Pp. 311. $0.40.

Le Comte de Monte-Cristo. Par ALEXANDRE DUMAS. Edited, with Notes, Exercises, and Vocabulary, by C. FONTAINE. Pp. 208. $0.40.

RAND, McNALLY & CO.

The Story of Chaucer's Canterbury Pilgrims. Retold for Children. By KATHERINE LEE BATES. Illustrated by ANGUS MACDONALL. Cloth. Pp. 316.

A Primary History: Stories of Heroism. By WILLIAM H. MACE. Illustrated by HOMER W. COLBY. Portraits by JACQUES REICH AND P. R. AUDIBERT. Cloth. Pp. 396.

Napoleon the Little Corsican. "Little Lives of Great Men" Series. By ESSE V. HATHAWAY. Illustrated by LOUIS BRAUNHOLD. Pp. 162.

THE MACMILLAN COMPANY

Elements of Agriculture. By G. F. WARREN. Illustrated. Cloth. Pp. 434. $1.10.

The Trinummus of Plautus. With Introduction and Notes by H. R. FAIRCLOUGH. Cloth. Pp. 118. $0.60.

HOUGHTON, MIFFLIN & CO.

The Book of Fables and Folk Stories. By HORACE E. SCUDDER. Illustrated. Cloth. Pp. 179.

HARPER & BROTHERS

Boy Life: Stories and Readings Selected from the Works of William Dean Howells. Arranged by PERCIVAL CHUBB. Illustrated. Cloth. Pp. 190. $0.50.

LAIRD & LEE

Laird & Lee's Webster's New Standard Dictionary of the English Language. Compiled by E. T. ROE. Pp. 750. $0.75.

LITTLE, BROWN AND CO.

Little People Everywhere: Ume San in Japan, Kathleen in Ireland, Rafael in Italy, Manuel in Mexico. 4 vols. By ETTA BLAISDELL McDONALD AND JULIA DALRYMPLE. Illustrated. Cloth. Pp. 118 each. $0.60 each.

THE MANUAL ARTS PRESS, PEORIA, ILL.

The Construction and Flying of Kites. By CHARLES M. MILLER. Pp. 34.

Coping Saw Work. By BEN W. JOHNSON. Pp. 23.

TEACHERS COLLEGE, COLUMBIA UNIVERSITY

Later Roman Education in Ausonius, Capella, and the Theodosian Code. With Translations and Commentary by PERCIVAL R. COLE.

The Indians of Manhattan Island and Vicinity: A Guide to the Special Exhibition of Natural History. EDMUND OTIS HOVEY, editor. Prepared for the Hudson-Fulton Celebration Commission by the Museum. Pp. 60.

CURRENT EDUCATIONAL LITERATURE IN THE PERIODICALS[1]

IRENE WARREN
Librarian, School of Education, The University of Chicago

ABBOTT, ALDEN H. The non-urban high school in Massachusetts and New York. Educa. R. 38:244–60. (O. '09.)

ASHLEY, M. L. The physiological and the logical. Educa. Bi-mo. 4: 35–46. (O. '09.)

AUSTIN, ISABELLA. What the school needs from the library. Lib. Journ. 34: 395–98. (S. '09.)

BENNETT, CHARLES A. Visiting manual-training schools in Europe. Man. Train. Mag. 11:1–26. (O. '09.)

BOONE, CHESHIRE LOWTON. A course of study in manual training. VII. Man. Train. Mag. 11:46–58. (O. '09.)

BULLOCK, AMASA ARCHIBALD. Observations concerning government higher schools in West China. School R. 17:467–75. (S. '09.)

BUTLER, NICHOLAS MURRAY. The call to citizenship. Educa. R. 38: 288–98. (O. '09.)

CALL, ARTHUR DEERIN. Some problems common to high and grammar school. Educa. 30:1–14. (S. '09.)

CASTLE, WILLIAM R., JR. The college and the freshman. Atlan. 104: 547–57. (O. '09.)

CHAMBERLAIN, JAMES F. Report of the committee on secondary school geography. Journ. of Geog. 8:1–9. (S. '09.)

CHAMBERS, WILL GRANT. Modern psychology and music study. Educa. Bi-mo. 4:28–34. (O. '09.)

CHANCELLOR, WILLIAM ESTABROOK. The desirable superintendency. Journ. of Educa. (Bost.). 70:311, 312. (30 S. '09.)

CLARKE, JOHN E. Solving problems. Educa. 30:25–27. (S. '09.)

COLTON, HAROLD SELLERS. Peale's Museum. Pop. Sci. Mo. 75:221–38. (S. '09.)

[1] Abbreviations.—Atlan., Atlantic Monthly; Atlan. Educa. Journ., Atlantic Educational Journal; Dial, The Dial; Educa., Education; Educa. Bi-mo., Educational Bi-monthly; Educa. R., Educational Review; Educa. T., Educational Times; El. School T., Elementary School Teacher; Harp. W., Harper's Weekly; Journ. of Educa. (Bost.), Journal of Education, Boston; Journ. of Educa. (Lond.), Journal of Education, London; Journ. of Geog., Journal of Geography; Lib. Journ., Library Journal; Man. Train. Mag., Manual Training Magazine; Pop. Educa., Popular Educator; Pop. Sci. Mo., Popular Science Monthly; Pub. Lib., Public Libraries; School R., School Review.

COLWELL, LEWIS W. Education as the evolution of conduct. Educa. Bi-mo. 4:47–53. (O. '09.)

COOLEY, E. G. The adjustment of the school system to the changed conditions of the twentieth century. Educa. Bi-mo. 4:1–11. (O. '09.)

DEARBORN, WALTER F. Qualitative elimination from school. El. School T. 10:1–14. (S. '09.)

DOOLEY, WILLIAM H. Practical education for industrial workers. Educa. R. 38:261–72. (O. '09.)

DREVER, JAMES. The professional education and training of teachers. Journ. of Educa. (Lond.). 41:599–602, 604, 606. (S. '09.)

DUCKWORTH, J. The development of initiation. Educa. T. 62:378–80. (S. '09.)

ELLIOTT, EDWARD C. Educational advancement and the new federalism. Educa. R. 38:217–25. (O. '09.)

ELMENDORF, MRS. THERESA W. The things that matter. Pub. Lib. 14: 281–89. (O. '09.)

FAVILL, HENRY BAIRD. Should the public school be the bulwark of public health? Educa. Bi-mo. 4:12–27. (O. '09.)

GARDNER, EVELYN E. Dramatization as a factor in education. Pop. Educa. 27:57–59. (O. '09.)

GAUSS, CHRISTIAN. Popular education in literature. Lib. Journ. 34:391–94. (S. '09.)

GIDEON, A. The phonetic method in teaching modern languages. School R. 17:476–89. (S. '09.)

GILLETTE, JOHN M. Reconstruction of history for teaching purposes. School R. 17:548–57. (O. '09.)

HAAS, JOHN A. W. The church and the college. Educa. R. 38:273–81. (O. '09.)

HANEY, JAMES PARTON. The national society for the promotion of industrial education. Man. Train. Mag. 11:27–35. (O. '09.)

INGLIS, WILLIAM. Venerable Trinity School. Harp. W. 53:25. (2 O. '09.)

JUDD, CHARLES H. A course in form study. El. School T. 10:32–39. (S. '09.)

———. An introduction to experimental pedagogy. Educa. Bi-mo. 4:54–59. (O. '09.)

LEACH, ARTHUR F. Colet and St. Paul's School, a joinder of issue. Journ. of Educa. (Lond.). 41:609–12. (S. '09.)

LULL, HERBERT G. The six-years high school. Educa. 30:15–24. (S. '09.)

MANNY, FRANK A. Discussion: a problem for the Religious Education Association. School R. 17:502. (S. '09.)

———. Middlemen in education. Atlan. Educa. Journ. 5:5, 21. (O. '09.)

MAY, MAUDE G. A new method in infant education. Journ. of Educa. (Lond.) (Sup.). 41:645–47. (S. '09.)

MOORE, CHARLES LEONARD. On teaching literature. Dial. 47:221–23. (1 O. '09.)

MORTENSON, PETER A. The Chicago parental school. Educa. Bi-mo. 4: 64–67. (O. '09.)

MUNRO, WILLIAM BENNETT. The inauguration at Harvard. Harp. W. 53: 10. (9 O. '09.)

MUNROE, JAMES P. A suggested introductory course in English literature. School R. 17:542–47. (O. '09.)

MÜNSTERBERG, HUGO. The standing of scholarship in America. Atlan. 104:453–60. (O. '09.)

New librarian for Chicago Public Library. Pub. Lib. 14:295. (O. '09.)

O'SHEA, M. V. Everyday problems in teaching: gaining the respect of pupils. Pop. Educa. 27:5, 6. (S. '09.)

———. Everyday problems in teaching: on securing attention. Pop. Educa. 27:59, 60. (O. '09.)

PARDUE, H. AVIS. An experience with a subnormal boy. Educa. Bi-mo. 4: 73–75. (O. '09.)

PARLIN, C. C. High-school courses of study. School R. 17:490–94. (S. '09.)

PEABODY, ENDICOTT. The aims, duties, and opportunities of the head-master of an endowed secondary school. School R. 17:521–28. (O. '09.)

RAMALEY, FRANCIS. The educational significance of Minot's theory of age and growth. Educa. R. 38:282–87. (O. '09.)

RICHARDSON, MYRON W. Making a high-school programme. School R. 17:449–66. (S. '09.)

ROUSSEAU, VICTOR. A school for souls. Harp. W. 53:25–31. (9 O. '09.)

SCOTT, JAMES BROWN. The classics and modern life. School R. 17: 498–501. (S. '09.)

SKINNER, M. M. Some practical hints for teaching students how to read German. School R. 17:529–41. (O. '09.)

STAHL, FRANK W. Some phases of the delinquent boy problem. Educa. Bi-mo. 4:60–63. (O. '09.)

WENLEY, R. M. The elective system and the Scottish universities. Educa. R. 38:224–43. (O. '09.)

WILLIAMS, HARVEY R. Professional loyalty. Educa. 30:29–35. (S. '09.)

WILLIAMS, S. HORACE. The educative value of manual training. Man. Train. Mag. 11:36–44. (O. '09.)

WRIGHT, C. T., AND FREMONT, JOHN C. The laboratories for physical geography in two California high schools. Journ. of Geog. 8:10–14. (S. '09.)

VOLUME X NUMBER 4

THE ELEMENTARY SCHOOL TEACHER

DECEMBER, 1909

NATURAL HISTORY IN THE GRADES

OTIS W. CALDWELL
The University of Chicago

II. SECOND GRADE

For a brief statement of the general plan of organizing the work in natural history for the grades the reader is referred to the November *Elementary School Teacher*. In each article of this series, in addition to outlining the materials to be used in the grade under discussion, some of those materials will be selected for a more detailed treatment in order that the method of work may be indicated. In the last article, the garden work, earth materials, and climatology were selected for detailed suggestions and the directions there given should be kept in mind in following up the work in those subjects in succeeding grades, though later further details will be given. In the Second-Grade outline, after the statement of topics to be included, the work in animal life is discussed more at length.

It must be kept in mind that the "what" and "why" attitude of the First Grade still is dominant in this grade, but work that is somewhat more prolonged and a little more investigative in character may well be undertaken. The First-Grade acquaintances in nature should be reviewed, and used as the starting-point, and subsequently used for constant reference. Indeed all First-Grade topics should at some time be used again in the Second Grade, else they will be forgotten. Repetition is essential, but this repetition now comes in connection with and as the basis of new work. The following materials are used in this grade:

1. *Animal life.*—A pair of rabbits, or a pair of nesting pigeons or doves; life cycle of the toad; blue-bird, red-headed woodpecker, grackle, junco, yellow warbler, gulls, the passing of wild ducks and geese, birds that remain through the winter, nesting habits of robin and English sparrow; dragon-fly, honey-bee, bumble-bee, wasp and nest, ants and nest, and the community life and activities of insects; caterpillar, cocoon, and adult butterfly or moth; grow in the room any common butterfly or moth through its life cycle, or a silkworm and moth in case such is available.

2. *Plant life.*—Plants of the farm such as corn, wheat, oats, millet, rice, and the materials derived from these that are used by man and his domesticated animals; sunflower, wild aster, goldenrod, cat-tails, water lily, plantain, thistle, evening-primrose, ash, cottonwood, hickory, black walnut, pine; seeds of several kinds of common plants; the fruits of wild plants, such as grapes, cherries, Indian currant, and nuts.

3. *Garden work.*—Window boxes containing house plants and a box or bed of bulbs some of which are different from those grown in the First Grade. Indoor gardening should be carried on throughout the year. In the outdoor garden the children of this grade should have one group garden or a few group gardens each in charge of a smaller group of pupils. Children of this grade should do their own planting and cultivation. The plants used should include some of those grown by First-Grade pupils but also some additional ones. The addition of a few of the less common plants as gourds and peanuts add interest. If three or four group gardens are used, interest is increased by having one group grow house plants—geranium, nasturtium, Coleus—another, radish, lettuce, and beets, another, pumpkins, another gourds, and another peanuts. Records of the garden work should constantly be made in written work and in sketches.

4. *Earth materials.*—Action of waves upon stones and sand, weight of stones as compared with water and wood studied by weighing and by displacement, and their properties such as hardness, color, and composition. Each child should be encouraged to make a collection of stones of different kinds.

5. *Physical and meteorological materials.*—In connection with the study of earth materials are included elementary experiments and observations upon physical and meteorological phenomena associated with changes in the condition of materials. These include a study of water, steam, fog, clouds, dew, rain, snow, frost, hail, ice, air, and air currents. The plan for study of climatology in the preceding year may again be used advantageously in this connection, but the work should be based upon schoolroom experiments in evaporation, boiling, and condensation, and upon careful observations of out-of-door phenomena.

In addition to acquaintanceship with all the animals included under "animal life," and some knowledge of their homes and habits there is made a careful study of the more conspicuous features of three life cycles—that of a dove or pigeon, of a moth or butterfly, and of the toad. As will appear in discussions of the outline for succeeding grades, there is arranged a series of life cycles of increasing complexity, so that there may be developed in a logical and natural way an understanding of the significance of the life round from one generation to another. To this end a pair of tame birds as pigeons or doves may be kept within the room and observed through all the nest building processes. We have had several pigeon nests built while under constant observation by children, and with never-ending interest on the part of all who observed the process. Indeed, old and young students find something new in the habits of each pair of these birds as they build their nests. Immediately following the completion of the nest, sometimes before, there appear the eggs, first one, then the second, and the period of incubation has begun. Questions such as the following help to give the study definiteness and also to insure that important points will not be omitted. Such questions do not remove opportunity for spontaneity in observation. In answering these questions the children should place on the board or upon a special pigeon-nest-calendar the dates and times of day on which various events are observed. Accurate records have great value in such work. Did incubation begin before the second egg was laid? How many days were used in building the nest? How many until egg laying was finished? How many were consumed in incubation before the first young were hatched? Did both young birds hatch on the same day?

During the period of incubation there are also many things to be observed, as: Does one parent do all the sitting? If not, do they divide the time equally? Do they behave in the same way? Does one parent ever feed the other? Do they "handle" their eggs in any way? Do they repair their nest while sitting? Do they make the same sounds while sitting as before? Do they eat as before? How do they behave when the young birds begin to hatch? How do the young birds get out of the shells of the eggs? What is the appearance of the old shell? How do the parents feed the young birds? Do both parents feed them? When do the first feathers appear? When do the young birds first stand up? How do they act? When do they leave the nest? While studying these and similar questions records should constantly be kept on the chart, by means of simply written stories, by numerous sketches, and sometimes by modeling in clay.

Not infrequently a robin or other common bird may nest upon a window ledge or so close to the schoolroom that it may be studied, though rarely would its nest enable pupils to observe closely enough to answer many of the above questions. (For suggestions upon the study of a robin's nest see an article by Jessie R. Mann in *The Nature Study Review,* Vol. IV, No. 9, pp. 265–71.)

Another life-cycle study used in this grade is that of the moth or butterfly. This is best studied by use of one of the larger moths as the Cecropia whose caterpillar stage often may be found in the autumn after the opening of school. The feeding habits of this caterpillar are so ravenous that children are stimulated to extreme interest in observing it, and in attending to its needs. The caterpillars may readily be removed from the plants upon which they are feeding (often the willow) and carried to the schoolroom. A supply of leaves of the kind that were being used as food should also be taken, though these must be replenished daily in order that fresh food may be had.

Various kinds of cages may be used. A pasteboard box with holes punched in the cover and sides is sometimes used, this having the disadvantage of darkness and difficulty of maintaining cleanliness. A small wooden box with wire or cloth netting over the top makes a better cage, but better than either of these is one constructed by use of a lamp chimney. Over the top of a large lamp chimney (the larger the better) tie a piece of netting, this being for ventilation. In a glass dish or earthen pot put one and a half or two inches of sand or porous soil. Upon the sand place the lower end of the lamp chimney. The sand or loose soil will absorb the moisture of the excretions from the caterpillar and by being renewed every two or three days enables the children to keep the cage attractive.

When placing the caterpillars within this cage put in a few twigs bearing the kind of leaves which are known to serve as food, inserting the base of the twigs into a small bottle or dish of water. Several kinds of willow leaves serve well as food for the Cecropia caterpillar. In connection with feeding these insects, interesting experiments may be made to determine the quantity of food eaten in a given length of time. Count and weigh the leaves put into the cage in one day. Also weigh the caterpillar in the morning before putting in the fresh leaves, and by weighing the caterpillar and the leaves that are left see how the weight of food eaten by it in one day compares with its own weight. A liberal supply of leaves should be put into the cage since the caterpillar eats almost constantly during the day. Does it eat at night?

Immediately before the period of cocoon spinning the caterpillar is likely to be rather sluggish. Constant watch should be made for the beginning of spinning, since it is a sight of extreme interest and instructiveness. From the appearance of the first threads of silk until the cocoon is complete may sometimes be a surprisingly short time—an hour or two—or it may be prolonged throughout a day. The pupils should see as much as possible of this process, and the gradual disappearance of the caterpillar within his cocoon, else the future developments will be unrelated to things already seen. Indeed to many grown-ups the performance of the apparent impossibility of development of the large, highly decorated and striking form of the adult moth from the caterpillar or from the apparently dead cocoon and contents (chrysalis) is a never-ending surprise. It is one of the wonders of nature's truths, no less wonderful than many improvised and truthless stories of nature.

The cocoons should be placed where they may remain undisturbed until the moth emerges. Especially must there be no handling of the cocoon during the first stages of the emergence of the moth, since at such a time it may very easily be killed. Should both male and female moths be secured it is possible to keep them in a cage—a cage at least a foot or more in inside dimensions—to secure the eggs. If these may be placed upon proper kinds of leaves the young caterpillars may be secured and observed through the earlier stages of their development.

A third life-cycle study suggested for this grade is that of the toad. In the first grade the toad was studied in so far as its ways of living and habits in general could be observed. The acquaintance thus developed is used in early spring in the Second Grade as the beginning point at the time when frog's eggs begin to appear in ponds and along banks of streams. Collect these eggs (the toad's eggs are in strings, the frog's in clumps or masses) and place in an aquarium in the schoolroom. The water in the aquarium must be shallow or aeration must be had by blowing air into the water several times per day. If abundant plant material is growing in the aquarium sufficient oxygen will be produced, and also sufficient slime to nourish the hatching tadpoles for a time. If not too many are placed in one aquarium (25 to 40 tadpoles may be kept in a dish one foot in diameter) they will be able to get sufficient food from slime and small plants that should be secured from ponds or streams and placed in the aquarium at intervals of two or three days. Careful observation should be made concerning the development, movement, and feeding habits and these should be recorded in written work, stories, and drawings. One pupil has prepared a clay model life-history series of the toad which illustrates admirably the changes that occur throughout the entire development. Excellent suggestions and directions for the carrying-on of work with the toad may be found in a pamphlet by S. H. Gage, *Teachers' Leaflets,* No. 9, College of Agriculture, Ithaca, N. Y., and in pp. 274–94 in Hodge's *Nature Study and Life.*

AGRICULTURAL EDUCATION

UNITED STATES BUREAU OF EDUCATION. STATE DEPARTMENTS OF EDUCATION. STATE LEGISLATION

BENJAMIN MARSHALL DAVIS
Miami University

UNITED STATES BUREAU OF EDUCATION

Agricultural education receives the attention of the Bureau of Education in several ways. These may conveniently be grouped under three heads: publications, land-grant colleges, and legislation.

Having little administrative authority except that relating to land-grant colleges the Bureau has confined its efforts mainly to its publications and correspondence. "No other educational office of the world has done so extensive literary work as this office," is the fine tribute paid by the Royal Prussian Commission of 1904 in its report to the Prussian Parliament. The Bureau's publications consist of annual reports, special reports, circulars of information, and bulletins.

The policy of the bureau toward agricultural education recently expressed by the commissioner applies especially to its publications:

> It can do its best I think as a co-ordinating influence. It can bring to the notice of less favored institutions information concerning the experience of more advanced institutions. It can call attention from time to time to the relation of agricultural education to general education. It can survey the educational field and possibly point out dangers to be averted or weak places to be strengthened. It can, finally, discover things that need doing and are not attended to by any other agency, and can see that some part of such lack is supplied. So much as this I hope the Bureau of Education may be able to do for agricultural education. And so much as this, I may say, it will undertake to do as far as its resources will permit (18, p. 53).

The Bureau has done much already in two ways: one by bringing to American educators the work of foreign countries, and the other by reviewing the work being done in various parts of this country. Of the former the most important are the accounts of agricultural education in Austria, Belgium, Canada, France, Germany, Great Britain, and Prussia. One of these publications on school gardens, deserves special mention (19). It contains a very complete historical account of school gardens and has been extensively quoted in the school-garden literature of this country. Of the reviews of work in our own country two are noteworthy. One written at the beginning of the movement for instruction in elementary agriculture is made up chiefly of reprints of leaflets from Purdue and Cornell Universities (20). The other, appearing in 1907, gives an account of the present status of agricultural education throughout the world (21).

The first Morrill Act of 1862, the second Morrill Act of 1890, and the Nelson Act of 1907 providing for government aid to agricultural and mechanical colleges are administered by the Department of the Interior (17, p. 31).

The annual payments under the acts of 1890 and 1907, are made on certifications of the Secretary of the Interior, which are based upon the proper expenditure of preceding appropriations. All of these reports required to be made by the act are collected and passed upon by the Commissioner of Education, upon whose recommendation is based the action of the secretary (17, p. 32).

While the duties of the Commissioner of Education in his relation to land-grant colleges consist chiefly in gathering statistics and making reports to the Secretary of the Interior he has opportunities for making suggestions and recommendations of importance to agricultural education. For example, in his letter of April 17, 1907, to the presidents and boards of control of state colleges of agriculture and mechanic arts he calls attention to a provision of the act of 1907 "providing for courses for special preparation of instructors for teaching the elements of agriculture and mechanic arts" and adds, "With the increasing number of secondary schools of agriculture and of industrial and trade schools, there will arise a considerable demand for specially prepared teachers to give instruction in special branches of study" (22, p. 870). In his report of 1908 to the Secretary of the Interior he gives an account of the action of several institutions taking advantage of this provision (23, pp. 740, 741).

On July 1, 1909, the Bureau appointed a specialist in land-grant college statistics who is expected also to pay attention to the general subject of agricultural education and to be able to furnish information and advice concerning that subject.

The Commissioner of Education holds an important advisory position with reference to any proposed national legislation concerning education, particularly agricultural education. During the sixtieth session of Congress several bills were introduced providing for national aid to education in agriculture and other industrial subjects. Of these the most important were the Burkett bill (S. 3,392) providing for "the advancement of instruction in agriculture, manual training, and home economics in the state normal schools of the United States," and the Davis bill (H. R. 534) providing in a similar way for national aid to agricultural and industrial education in the secondary schools only. The latter was finally revised (H. R. 18,204) so as to include the provisions of the Burkett bill (S. 3,392).

The Davis bill provides for annual appropriation of "ten cents per capita of the population of each state and territory and the District of Columbia" for aid to maintain instruction in agriculture and home economics in agriculture schools of secondary grade, and an appropriation of one cent per capita to maintain similar instruction in state and territorial normal schools (24, pp 85–87).

The large amount of money concerned, and the establishment of separate schools not already a part of our national system of education called for careful study and deliberation. The Bureau of Education was freely consulted in the matter. No one had a clearer insight into the far-reaching influence of the bill, a clearer understanding of its importance upon the economic and educational welfare of the nation, or a greater appreciation of the principles involved in such legislation, than the Commissioner of Education. In a letter dated September 26, 1907, to Mr. Davis he says:

> One strong argument in favor of such national aid, when extended to special forms of education which are in special need of encouragement, may be drawn from the workings of the appropriation for support of land-grant

colleges, contained in the second Morrill Act of August 30, 1890. The recent effect of the national appropriations under that act has been to stimulate greatly the support of the land-grant colleges by the states in which they are situated.

He calls attention to a provision of the measure giving administrative authority over the appropriations therein provided to the Department of Agriculture, whereas "appropriations which are primarily for agriculture are now administered by the Department of Agriculture, and these which are primarily for education (land-grant colleges) are administered by the Bureau of Education."

I think [he says] as matters now stand this is a good working division, particularly as the relations between the Bureau of Education and the Office of Experiment Stations of the Department of Agriculture are very close and cordial. Educational interests are becoming so strongly unified throughout this country, and in fact in foreign lands, that the present tendency points to unifying of government activities of a purely educational sort, or of predominantly educational sort, under the Office of Education. Another reason for bringing the activities provided in your bill under the Bureau of Education is that they deal not only with agricultural high schools but with high schools of mechanic arts in cities as well. In institutions of both classes, while industrial ends are sought and industrial means employed, the main purpose, as I understand it, is educational.

It seems to me worth considering, also, the question whether it is advisable that rural schools, to which the bill relates, should in all cases be designated as agricultural high schools. There is still a good deal of difference of opinion as to whether high-school work in agriculture may be done to best advantage in general high schools which are properly equipped on the agricultural side, or in agricultural high schools which pay incidental attention to studies other than agriculture. It is likely, in fact, that we shall have institutions of both types for many years to come, and that both of them will do good and efficient work in the promotion of agricultural education. For this reason it seems to me doubtful whether it is wise to limit the distribution of the fund by using the distinctive designation of agricultural high school.

In a letter to Senator Proctor, dated March 4, 1908, the whole matter of national aid as proposed by the Burkett bill and by the Davis bill is carefully reviewed. The entire letter should be read in order to form a just conclusion of the Commissioner's position. After citing the difficulties arising from our complex industrial situation, both urban and rural, he recognizes the probable need of federal aid in the following words:

For all these reasons (referring to our industrial situation) the problem of a better education of an industrial type, in both country and city, has steadily become more acute. It is extremely doubtful whether these growing needs can be met in the near future in the majority of the states, unless the encouragement of federal appropriations be added to the efforts of the states and of local communities.

While approving the measure in principle he urges "that any forward step which the national government may take in the encouragement of public education should be carefully weighed, and given its proper place in a well-digested general policy." Furthermore, the conditions in several states are widely different, and any bill should be framed with a full knowledge of these differing conditions in order that it may be made sufficiently flexible to accomplish the best results in all parts of the country. In order "to make possible for Congress to act on bills like S. 3,392 with full knowledge of the situation and needs of the country" he recommends that a commission be appointed to make a thorough investigation of the question and "report to Congress on or before January 1, 1910."[1]

Neither the Davis bill nor the Commissioner's recommendation became a law. The bill was an indication of the interest of the country at large in extending agricultural education into the elementary and secondary schools. The attitude of the Bureau of Education was one of accord with the general principles on which the measure was based, but at the same time one of caution, recognizing that national appropriation to agricultural education, when given, should be of the greatest possible service.

STATE DEPARTMENTS OF EDUCATION AND STATE LEGISLATION

Each state or territory has at the head of its school system a central office. This office is administered in most states by a state superintendent or state commissioner of education, and in

[1] For permission to quote from letters to Congressman Davis and Senator Proctor, and for other assistance in getting material for this paper, the writer is indebted to Commissioner Elmer Ellsworth Brown. A portion of his letter to Senator Proctor appears in the Commissioner's *Report* of 1908.

some states, as in Connecticut, Delaware, Rhode Island, and Massachusetts, by a state board of education through its secretary or commissioner (25).

These state offices vary in details and plan of organization, and somewhat in authority over educational matters, but are alike in essential respects. But however efficient the departmental organizations, the personality and aggressiveness of those in charge count for much in the influence that these offices exert in the educational welfare of their respective states.

It is especially true that the introduction of a new subject of instruction like agriculture may be greatly hindered or promoted by the attitude taken by the state office. If favorable, the subject may be recommended for legislation, it may be put in the course of study, a textbook may be adopted, through personal influence on local boards it may be introduced in certain sections of the state, interest may be aroused by making it a reading-circle subject, special publications may be issued to help teachers who wish to teach the subject, by promoting interest through clubs or other organizations. The main facts concerning the efforts of all the states and territories in the promotion of agricultural education in the elementary and secondary schools through their central offices of education and by legislation are indicated in the following tabulation.

In Delaware and Nevada interest in agricultural education has not seemed to warrant any attention from their state departments of education. Kentucky, although an agricultural state, has apparently shown much less interest in agricultural education than have other southern states. This may be readily explained by the fact that until 1908 the public-school system was organized under the old district plan. The schools were practically controlled by about 25,000 school trustees, 5,000 of whom could neither read nor write. The action of the legislature of 1908 has changed the whole aspect of the Kentucky educational situation, and already remarkable progress has been made toward the improvement of her public schools.

A glance at the tabulation shows that the southern states have been more active (at least recently) in the promotion of agricultural education than the northern states. This activity is a part of the general educational movement extending throughout the South. Educational campaigns have recently been conducted in several of these states and have done much to increase interest in all educational matters.

The earliest legislation concerning introduction of agriculture into elementary schools was the Nixon law of New York in 1897 (20, 1610–14). It provided for the extension of agriculture into the public schools under the direction of the Agricultural College of Cornell University. It was carried out by means of visits to schools and lectures before teachers' institutes, and by means of teachers' and pupils' leaflets for use in rural schools. The Cornell leaflets not only stimulated much interest in elementary agriculture and nature-study in the state of New York but in other states as well. Similar publications have since been issued by agricultural colleges of several other states.

Requiring the teaching of elementary agriculture by law has not met with unqualified success. In some states where it is supposed to be in force little attention is paid to it on account of lack of qualified teachers. The establishment of state secondary schools of agriculture and provision for state aid to high schools teaching agriculture is probably the most important recent legislation concerning agricultural education. The latter form of state aid seems to be growing in favor.[2]

Courses of study vary much in their treatment of agriculture as a school subject. The newness of the subject is usually recognized by special directions and suggestions for teaching. These are generally given in a state school manual or handbook for teachers. In some states they are in separate publications. In New York, for example, suggestions are outlined in syllabi, one for elementary schools and one for high schools. In other states bulletins on certain phases of the subject are issued, as in Michigan.

Perhaps the most significant fact showing the widespread general interest in agricultural education in elementary and sec-

[2] The subject of agricultural secondary schools will be taken up in detail in a later paper of this series.

ATTITUDE OF STATES TOWARD AGRICULTURAL EDUCATION IN ELEMENTARY AND SECONDARY SCHOOLS

LEGISLATION AND STATE DEPARTMENTS OF EDUCATION

States	Required by Law	When Passed	Agr. High Schools	Teachers' Examination	Text-book	Course of Study	Reading Circle	Special Aid	Recommendations	Addenda	Addenda
Alabama	Yes	1903	9 Districts each $4500 per year	Yes	Yes	Yes	......	....	To be given in H. S. receiving state aid	$2,000 state aid to H. S., but each must have 5 acres of land	
Arizona	....	....	....	....	......	....	......	....	Favorable	Probably be taken up by next legislature	
Arkansas	Yes	1909	4, $160,000 appropriated, 1909	After 1910	......	....	......	Organization of boys' corn clubs	Favorable	....	....
California	Agricultural nature-study	1907	2, 1903 and 1907	....	By counties	Optional	......	Bulletins	Urges school gardens and agr. clubs	....	....
Colorado	....	....	....	....	......	....	Yes, 1908	....	School gardens	State supt. favors legislation	....
Connecticut	....	....	....	....	......	....	......	Directions for teaching agr., 1903, '06, '07, '08	By educational commission, 1907	....	....
Delaware	....	....	....	....	......	....	......	....	....	....	....
Florida	Yes	1909	....	Yes	Yes, 1909	8 grade	......	....	Favorable	$65,000 for state aid to H. S., 1907, course of study to include agr.	....
Georgia	Yes	1903	11 District H. S. $77,000 1906	Yes	Yes, 1908	4–7 grades	......	Educational campaign; Cirs. to co. supts.	Favorable	Legislature of 1907 recommended to Congress that Davis bill be passed	....
Idaho	....	....	....	....	Yes, 1907	7–8 grades School gardens	......	Teachers' manual	Favorable	....	....

Illinois	…	…	…	…	…	8 grade	Yes, 1908	Special buls. Mo. press bul. State manual	Favorable	…	…
Indiana	…	…	…	…	…	7–8 grades	Yes, 1909	Buls. Manual	Favorable	…	…
Iowa	…	…	…	…	…	…	…	…	Favorable	Appropriation for extension work in agr. including teaching, 1907	Bill to require agr. ed. in all accredited colleges nearly passed in 1907
Kansas	…	…	…	Recommended to legislature by commission of 1908	Yes	8 grade H. S.	…	Manual	Favorable	…	…
Kentucky	…	…	…	…	…	…	…	Educational campaign	Favorable	…	…
Louisiana	Yes	1898	10, 1909	…	…	H. S. correlated with other sciences	…	Organization of agr. H. S.	Favorable	…	…
Maine	Forestry	1903	…	Yes	…	H. S.	…	…	Favorable	One-half expense for agr. teaching by incorporated academies to be paid by state, 1909	…
Maryland	Yes, at discretion of State Board	1904	…	…	…	7 grade	Yes, 1902 1908	Teachers' Yearbook	Favorable	…	…
Massachusetts	…	…	$10,000 annually to Smith Agr. School, 1906	…	…	…	…	Special buls. for teachers	Favorable	$5,000 appropriated for training teachers in agr. college, 1907	Industrial commission appointed, 1906

ATTITUDE OF STATES TOWARD AGRICULTURAL EDUCATION—*Continued*

State	Required by Law	When Passed	Agr. High Schools	Teachers' Examination	Text-book	Course of Study	Reading Circle	Special Aid	Recommendations	Addenda	Addenda
Michigan	....	....	County, 1907; 1 organized	....	......	....	......	Sp. buls. for teachers Field work by Asst. supt.	Favorable	In 48 county normal schools agr. is required to be taught	....
Minnesota	....	....	County, 1905	....	......	7–8 grades	......	Buls. for teachers	Favorable	State aid to 10 H. S. giving instruction in agr. $2,500 each	Special appropriation of $4,000 to promote agr. instruction in rural schools, 1901; county training schools give courses in agr.
Mississippi	Yes	....	County, 1908; $1,000 each	Yes	Yes	6 grade H. S.	......	Organization of co. agr. H. S. Buls.	Favorable	....	....
Missouri	....	....	....	Yes; 1899	Yes	7–8 grades H. S.	......	Sp. buls. Teachers' manual	State aid to H. S. teaching agr.	....	....
Montana	....	....	....	....	Yes	5–8 grades	......	....	Favorable	....	....
Nebraska	....	....	....	Yes	Yes	8 grade H. S.	......	Boys' clubs Field work by asst. supt. Teachers' manual	20 agr. H. S. recommended	....	County normal schools and junior (summer) normal schools give courses in agr.
Nevada	....	....	....	....	......	....	......	....	....	....	....
New Hampshire	In approved H. S.	1906	....	For H. S. certificate	......	H. S.	......	Teachers' manual	Favorable	....	....

New Jersey	...	...	...	...	...	Sch. gardens	...	Summer school at Cape May, 1909	Favorable	Recommended by Industrial Commission of 1908	...
New Mexico	...	...	...	...	Yes	8 grade	...	Teachers' manual	Favorable	...	...
New York	...	...	3 special, 1908	Teachers in training schools	...	8 grade H. S.	...	Syllabus for elementary and H. S.	Favorable	Nixon law of 1897 provided for agr. extension including public schools	...
North Carolina	Yes	1901	...	Yes	Yes	7–8 grades H. S.	...	Field work	Favorable	...	...
North Dakota	...	...	1, 1905; to include forestry after 1907	...	...	7–8 grades H. S.	Yes, 1909	...	Favorable	...	...
Ohio	...	...	...	...	...	7–8 grades	Yes	...	Industrial Commission to be appointed by legislature of 1910	...	...
Oklahoma	Yes	1908	2 supreme court districts, 1908; county, 1901	Yes	Yes	7–8 grades H. S.	...	Sp. buls. Teachers' manual	Appointment of supt. of public-school agriculture	...	...
Oregon	Yes	1905	...	...	Yes	7–8 grades H. S.	...	Teachers' manual	Provision be made for deputy county supt. of public-school agr.	...	...
Pennsylvania	...	...	...	...	...	...	...	Agr. in 3 summer schools for teachers	Establishment of 300 tp. H. S. with agr. taught in each	...	...
Rhode Island	...	...	...	...	...	...	...	...	Favorable	...	...
South Carolina	Yes	...	...	...	Yes	8 grade	...	Educational campaign	Establishment of agr. H. S.	...	...

ATTITUDE OF STATES TOWARD AGRICULTURAL EDUCATION—*Continued*

State	Required by Law	When Passed	Agr. High School	Teachers' Examination	Text-Book	Course of Study	Reading Circle	Special Aid	Recommendations	Addenda	Addenda
South Dakota	...	...	...	...	...	8 grade H. S. elective	...	Meetings with school officers	Favorable	...	...
Tennessee	In H. S.	1907	...	...	Yes	H. S.	...	H. S. inspector	Favorable	...	...
Texas	Yes	1907	...	Yes	Yes	8 grade H. S.	...	Teachers' manual	Favorable	...	...
Utah	...	...	...	Yes Nature-study	...	In grades as nature-study	...	...	Favorable	Last legislature passed resolutions favoring Burkett-Polland bill	...
Vermont	...	...	...	...	...	Optional but recommended	...	Buls.	Favorable	...	...
Virginia	...	...	...	Choice of one of physical geography, physics, or agr.	...	...	...	Organization of 10 H. S. to teach agr.	Favorable	State aid of $2,000 each to 10 H. S. teaching agr.	
Washington	...	...	...	Nature-study	Yes 1908	8 grade	Yes, 1907	...	Favorable	...	...
West Virginia	Yes	1908	...	Yes	...	7–8 grades H. S.	Yes, 1908	Teachers' manual; special attention at teachers' institutes	Favorable	...	...
Wisconsin	Yes	1905	4 county, 1901; amended to increase to 8, 1908	Yes		7–8 grades H. S.	...	Teachers' manual organization of county H. S.	Favorable	County training schools give instruction in agr.	
Wyoming	...	...	...	...	...	Optional	...	...	Favorable	...	...
Totals (48 states)	Yes 18, including optional and forestry No. 30		13 states 52 schools*	19 including nature-study	17	34 including optional	Yes, 8	33, probably others	46		

*Agricultural secondary schools connected with agricultural colleges are not included in tabulation; although receiving state aid they are under control of state agricultural colleges. The first was established in 1888 in Minnesota. Similar schools are now connected with agricultural colleges of over thirty states.

ondary schools is the attitude of the administrative officers of the various state departments of education. Special mention of the subject is made in nearly all of the latest annual or biennial reports from these offices. In some reports considerable space is given to discussions of industrial education with particular reference to agriculture.

Finally, if any interpretation is to be made of the attitude of state departments of education toward agricultural education it must be remembered that these offices represent the people, and that any policy or action taken is in a certain sense an expression of public opinion.

NOTE.—The writer wishes to express his appreciation of the cordial responses which he has received from his inquiries addressed to all the state and territorial departments of education.

BIBLIOGRAPHY

The facts of the text dealing with legislation and state departments of education have been obtained from reports, school laws, courses of study, and other state educational publications, and from personal correspondence with the departments. As about two hundred publications have been consulted it will be impossible to give more than this general reference to these sources.

17. *The Work of the Bureau of Education.* U. S. Bureau of Education. Report of Commissioner (1907), pp. 1–36.

A short historical account is given, followed by purpose, publications, organization, agricultural and mechanical colleges, and appendix containing laws relating to Bureau, descriptions of facilities for research, education in Alaska, and statistics of maintenance of Bureau.

18. *Development of Agricultural Education.* ELMER ELLSWORTH BROWN, U. S. Department of Agriculture. Office of Experiment Stations, Bulletin 196 (1907), pp. 49–54.

An address given on the occasion of the fiftieth anniversary of the founding of Michigan Agricultural College. The Commissioner discusses the relation agricultural education bears to general education.

19. *School Gardens.* E. GANG, U. S. Bureau of Education. Report of Commissioner (1898–99), pp. 1067–84.

This is one of the best short accounts, especially from historical standpoint, published. "*Contents:* Historical review; sites and arrangement of school gardens; different sections of school gardens; management; instruction in school gardens; educational and economic significance of school gardens."

20. *Methods of Instruction in Agriculture.* U. S. Bureau of Education. Report of Commissioner (1897–98), pp. 1575–1616.

This chapter contains reprints of several Cornell University and Purdue University leaflets, and a report of the work at Cornell University under the Nixon law of 1897.

21. *Agricultural Education, Including Nature-Study and School Gardens.* JAMES RALPH JEWELL, U. S. Bureau of Education. Bulletin 2 (1907, revised 1909), pp. 148.

The subject is discussed under six heads: Nature-Study, School Gardens, Elementary Agricultural Education, Agricultural Education, Practical Advantages of Agricultural Education. There is also a bibliography of 134 titles, and appendices on nature observations in schools of Nova Scotia, and on the Irish system of agricultural education.

22. *Agricultural and Mechanical Colleges.* U. S. Bureau of Education. Report of Commissioner (1907), pp. 869–924.

The first part of this chapter is devoted to general statements including summary of legislation; the second part is statistical.

23. *Agricultural and Mechanical Colleges. Ibid.* (1908), pp. 737–69.

24. *Industrial Education. Ibid.* (1908), pp. 84–89.

The full text of the Davis bill (H. R. 18,204) is given.

25. *Digest of School Laws. Ibid.* (1904), pp. 249–518.

A condensed account of organization of all state departments of education is given and a summary of school laws from time of organization of each state department to 1904.

26. *State School Systems.* EDWARD C. ELLIOTT. U. S. Bureau of Education, Bulletin No. 3, 1906.

This contains legislation and judicial decisions relating to public education from October 1, 1904, to October 1, 1906.

27. *Idem.* Bulletin No. 7, 1908.

This contains legislation and judicial decisions relating to public education from October 1, 1906, to October 1, 1908.

MEASUREMENT OF GROWTH AND EFFICIENCY IN ARITHMETIC (*Continued*)

S. A. COURTIS
Home and Day School, Detroit

Taking up now the analysis of the tests, Table III gives the grade scores in the four operations. They have been recomputed from the actual results on a basis of uniform grade membership and equalized on the basis of equal thirteenth-grade attempts in each operation. The scores for fundamentals are by examples. The scores by points show no fundamental differences. The scores for subtraction, which occurs incidentally in division, have the same general relations as those for division and are not given. The scores in reasoning are by points. It is to be remembered, however, that a point in reasoning was one step of a problem, really a simple example by itself. The results are given graphically in Plots 6 and 7.

TABLE III

GRADE SCORES IN THE FOUR OPERATIONS

Recomputed on basis of uniform grade membership and equalized on basis of equal thirteenth-grade attempts in each operation.

Grade	Fundamentals by Examples						Reasoning by Points							
	Attempts			Rights			Attempts				Rights			
	A	M	D	A	M	D	A	S	M	D	A	S	M	D
3	44	4	0	6	0	0	60	52	77	81	43	37	43	62
4	50	35	12	34	22	5	99	90	105	128	97	77	87	108
5	52	46	43	30	36	23	213	209	172	234	164	157	117	181
6	64	48	40	40	34	31	228	221	220	250	159	120	141	156
7	62	55	50	44	42	40	259	209	201	242	175	167	161	206
8	70	71	67	48	54	50	234	248	225	252	196	210	192	234
9	64	60	58	53	44	47	238	251	236	264	205	232	180	238
10	74	69	70	54	58	46	240	253	239	267	213	217	202	250
11	66	63	56	50	54	46	256	273	263	274	232	251	240	257
12	68	64	60	49	53	47	242	240	239	260	215	220	224	238
13	74	74	74	58	61	64	273	273	273	273	250	237	231	256

[1]For the first part of this paper see the *Elementary School Teacher* for October.

The curves show plainly the relative amount of development in each operation and the defects of the various grades. Thus, in Plot 6, fundamentals, in the fifth-grade drill has been

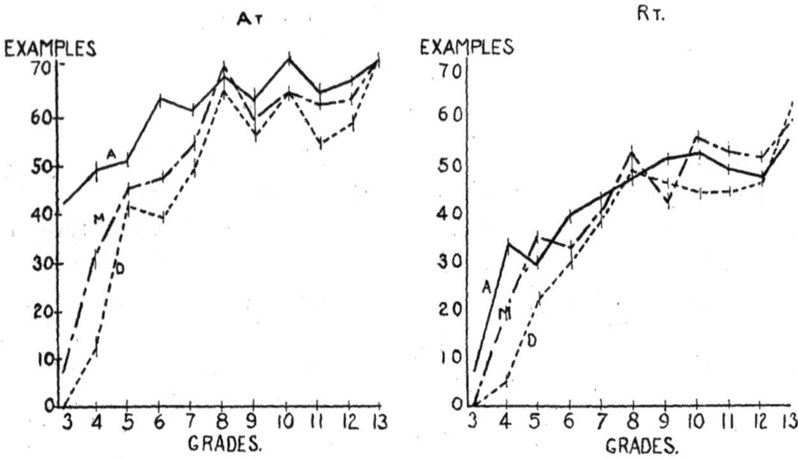

PLOT 6.—Comparative scores in fundamentals by examples. Addition, multiplication, and division as shown in Table III.

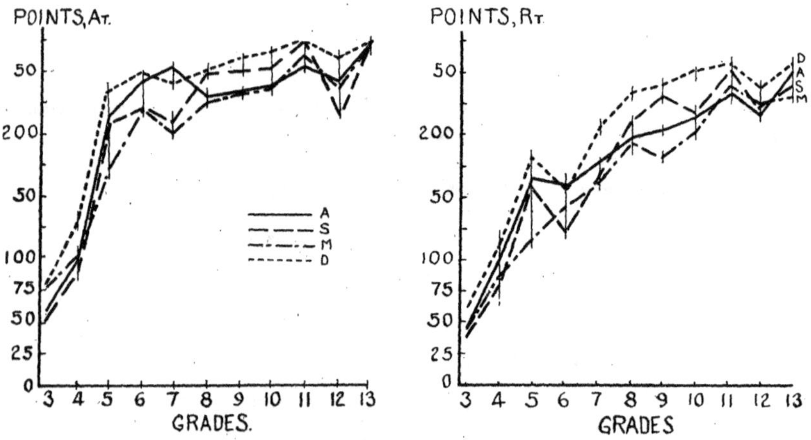

PLOT 7.—Comparative scores in reasoning by points. Four operations as shown in Table III.

given on the multiplication tables and long division, both learned in the grade before but mastered here, to the detriment of addition. Grade 9, on the other hand, is strong on addition and weak on multiplication and division. The form of the curve for any one operation would be very interesting if these were the results of one class for 13 years. Note the form of the curves in the high-school years. Algebra seems to help addition and multiplication which do not begin to decline before eleventh grade geometry, but does not aid division which declines from the eighth grade. However, the variation from grade to grade, which was partially eliminated in the combined results, is very evident here and prevents any such conclusions. For instance, the failure of the tenth grade in division was probably due to a grade defect and not to the lack of practice in algebra, for the thirteenth grade did better in division than anything else. The curves for reasoning permit similar diagnoses of defects and the remedy in each case is evident. Whether such analysis is of value can be told only after a year's remedial work and another test. The most evident fact to be inferred from these curves is that of grade variation and peculiarity. Because a class does well in addition it will not necessarily do well in any other operation, not even subtraction. The cause of such variation and peculiarities must be a subject for psychological investigation before much scientific teaching can be done. The curves obtained seem to the writer further evidence of the rudimentary and chaotic state of our present knowledge.

These results also have some bearing on the much-discussed question of the transfer of mental training from one subject to another. If skill in addition does not influence skill in subtraction, it would seem that there could be little hope of transfer of skill to any other subject. That something is transferred, however, we all know: what it is, is another story. These results seem to uphold the contention of certain psychologists against the value of special training in the development of general ability.

The results have, also, a bearing on the question of the relative degree of difficulty in the four operations. If the examples right are expressed as percentages of those attempted, we have the data presented in Table IV. These same facts are summarized in Table V.

These results make it probable that accuracy of work is a function of the development of the child, and in a way independent of his arithmetical training. Each grade seems to have a

TABLE IV

EFFICIENCIES IN FOUR OPERATIONS IN FUNDAMENTALS AND REASONING

Examples right expressed as percentages of examples attempted

GRADE	FUNDAMENTALS			REASONING			
	A	M	D	A	S	M	D
	per cent.	per cent.	per cent.	per cent.	per cent.	per cent.	per cent.
3	14	0	0	72	71	57	77
4	68	63	42	98	86	82	85
5	60	78	54	77	75	68	77
6	63	71	78	70	55	64	62
7	71	76	80	68	79	80	85
8	69	76	75	83	85	85	93
9	83	73	81	86	93	76	90
10	73	84	66	89	86	87	94
11	76	86	82	91	92	91	93
12	72	83	73	89	92	75	92
13	78	83	87	93	87	85	93

TABLE V

RELATIVE DIFFICULTY OF FOUR OPERATIONS

Derived from Table IV

GRADE	FUNDAMENTALS											TOTALS			CONCLUSION
	3	4	5	6	7	8	9	10	11	12	13	A	M	D	
Easiest	A	A	M	D	D	M	A	M	M	M	D	3	5	3	M
Next		M	A	M	M	D	D	A	D	D	M	2	4	4	D, M
Hardest		D	D	A	A	A	M	D	A	A	A	6	1	3	A

GRADE	REASONING											TOTALS				CONCLUSION
	3	4	5	6	7	8	9	10	11	12	13	A	S	M	D	
Easiest	D	A	DA	A	D	D	S	D	D	DS	DA	4	2	0	8	D
Next	A	S	DA	M	M	MS	D	A	S	DS	DA	4	4	3	4	ASD
Next	S	D	S	D	S	MS	A	M	MA	A	S	3	5	3	2	S
Hardest	M	M	M	S	A	A	M	S	MA	M	M	2	2	7	0	M

certain general degree of accuracy, which after the early years of learning does not seem to increase as one would expect. Within the limits of the accuracy of a class, all combinations of accuracies in the different operations are found, but the extremes for each grade differ by about the same amount. So far as there is any indication of difference in difficulty between the different operations, the results agree with the conclusions of Dr. Stone: For fundamentals, addition being hardest, multiplication or division least difficult; for reasoning, multiplication hardest and division least difficult. In fundamentals, the reason is not hard to find. Much more has been made of the multiplication tables than of the addition tables. Multiplication and division are more complicated processes than addition and harder to teach. It often happens that addition is much neglected after the class is once fairly at work on long division. It seems practically certain that in the present state of our arithmetic teaching each operation and each part or division of a topic is learned by the child as a separate unrelated activity. There is no co-ordination, no welding of separate parts into one science of number, no appreciation of the meaning and purpose of arithmetic as a whole. Accordingly the incidental emphasis of the teacher on one topic or another, due to the varying mentalities of the different classes of the same grade leaves a lasting bias toward skill in one operation or another. It only remains to point out how, in later grade, a high-school class in algebra say, a weakness in one operation masked by a fair general ability, operates to make the best efforts of the teacher of no avail. What is apparently merely a lack of attention or care to detail of the algebra, is really due to a deep-rooted defect of previous training in some important particular skill. Both class and teacher attack the problem of correction blindly and at a place that may need no correction at all. The real benefit comes incidentally and all psychological experiments prove that the overcoming of unconscious habits through incidental unconscious training is very difficult and tedious. The value of complete, all-around training in the early grades in determining general ability in the later grades is very great. And whether or not development is complete and many sided can be told only by such tests and analyses as these.

Leaving now the question of ability, the analysis of the mistakes made will be taken up. The reason why a given ability was not obtained is a question of even greater pedagogical importance than that of what ability was attained. It is this question that the analysis should help answer.

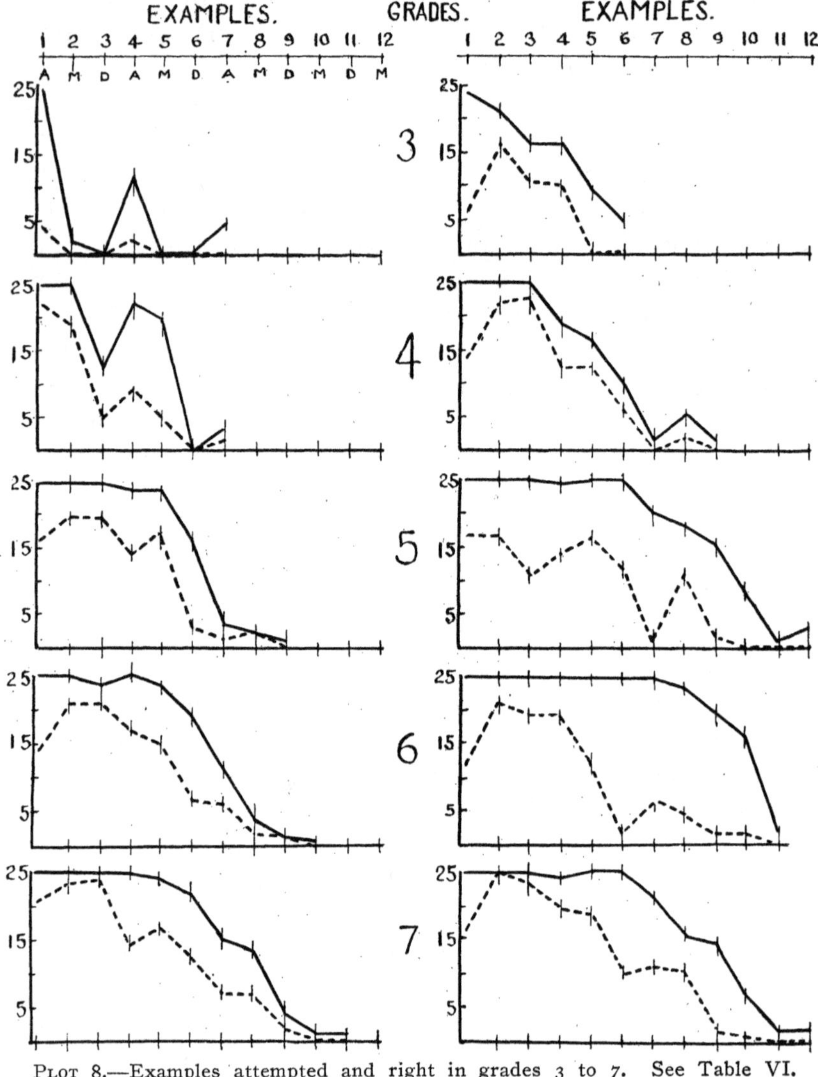

PLOT 8.—Examples attempted and right in grades 3 to 7. See Table VI.

The first step is to gain a comprehensive view of the work actually done by each grade, and this is given in Table VI, plots 8 and 9, which show the examples attempted and right for each grade in both tests. The results have been corrected to a uniform grade membership of 25.

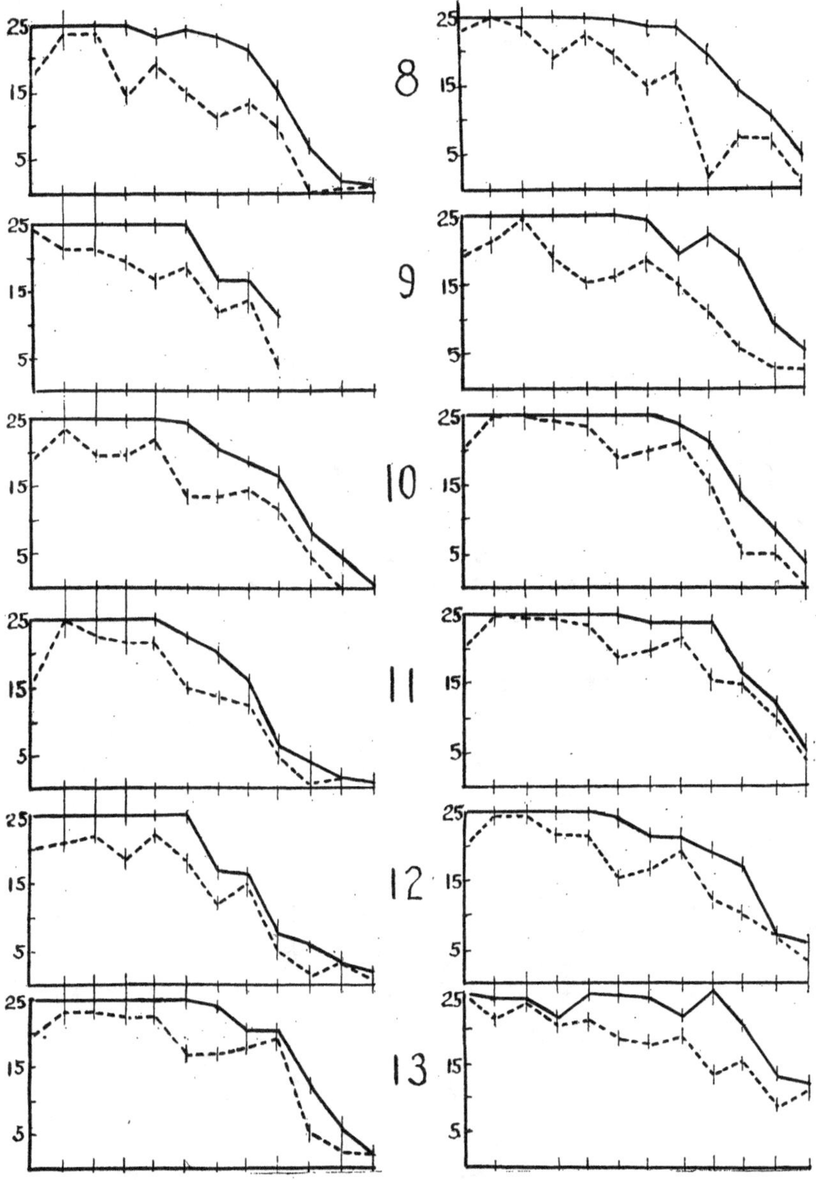

PLOT 9.—Examples attempted and right in grades 8 to 13. See Table VI.

TABLE VI

Grade Records, Attempts and Rights, for Each Example in Both Tests

Results adjusted to uniform grade membership of 25

Part 1. Fundamentals

Examples

Grade	1		2		3		4		5		6		7		8		9		10		11		12	
	At.	Rt.	At.	Rt.	At.	Rt.	At.	Rt.	At.	Rt.	At.	Rt.	At.	Rt.	At.	Rt.	At.	Rt.	At.	Rt.	At.	Rt.	At.	Rt.
3....	25	4	2	0	0	0	12	2	0	0	0	0	4	0	0	0	0	0	0	0	0	0	0	0
4....	25	22	25	19	12	5	22	9	20	5	0	0	3	2										
5....	25	16	25	19	25	19	24	13	24	13	16	3	3	1	2	2	1	0						
6....	25	14	25	21	23	21	25	17	23	14	19	7	12	6	4	2	2	2	2	0				
7....	25	21	25	23	25	24	25	14	24	17	22	12	15	7	13	7	4	2	1	0	1	0		
8....	25	18	25	24	25	24	25	14	23	19	24	14	23	11	21	13	15	10	7	0	2	1	1	1
9....	25	24	25	22	25	22	25	19	25	17	24	18	17	11	17	13	10	4						
10....	25	19	25	23	25	19	25	19	25	22	24	13	20	13	18	14	16	12	8	5	4	0	1	0
11....	25	17	25	25	25	23	25	22	25	22	22	15	19	13	15	12	7	5	4	1	2	2	1	1
12....	25	20	25	21	25	22	25	18	25	22	25	18	17	11	16	14	8	5	6	2	3	3	2	1
13....	25	20	25	23	25	23	25	22	25	22	25	16	23	16	20	17	20	19	11	5	6	3	2	2

Part 2. Reasoning

Examples

Grade	1		2		3		4		5		6		7		8		9		10		11		12	
	At.	Rt.	At.	Rt.	At.	Rt.	At.	Rt.	At.	Rt.	At.	Rt.	At.	Rt.	At.	Rt.	At.	Rt.	At.	Rt.	At.	Rt.	At.	Rt.
3....	23	6	21	17	17	10	17	8	8	0	4	0												
4....	25	14	25	22	25	23	18	12	16	12	8	5	2	0	5	2	2	0						
5....	25	17	25	17	25	22	24	13	25	15	25	11	19	1	17	10	15	2	8	0	1	0	3	0
6....	25	12	25	21	25	19	25	19	25	12	25	2	25	6	23	4	19	2	15	2	2	0		
7....	25	17	25	25	25	23	24	19	25	18	25	10	21	11	15	10	14	2	8	1	2	0	2	0
8....	25	23	25	25	25	23	25	18	25	22	24	18	23	14	23	17	19	2	14	7	11	7	5	1
9....	25	19	25	22	25	25	25	18	25	15	25	16	24	18	19	15	22	11	18	6	8	3	6	3
10....	25	17	25	25	25	25	25	24	25	24	25	16	25	19	23	17	21	14	16	5	8	5	5	0
11....	25	21	25	25	25	24	25	24	25	23	25	18	23	19	23	21	23	15	17	14	13	10	6	4
12....	25	21	25	25	25	24	25	22	25	22	24	15	22	17	22	19	19	12	17	10	6	3	5	3
13....	25	24	24	22	24	24	22	20	25	21	25	18	24	17	22	18	25	13	20	15	13	8	12	11

The most striking fact shown by these results is again grade variation. The different forms of the fronts of the curves, from the convex forms of grades 6 and 7 to the concave variety shown in grade 12, fundamentals, signify different distributions of ability in the grades as will be shown later. Another striking fact is that for so few examples is the efficiency 100 per cent. Except where the example has been tried by but one or two, there is but one place in fundamentals (11th grade, 2d example) where all who tried a problem succeeded in getting it right. In reasoning the results are a little better, there being four cases of perfect scores for example 2 and two cases for example 3. These and the general forms of the curves make it apparent at once that the different examples varied greatly in their difficulty. For instance, in fundamentals, the curves for rights show a marked depression in many grades for examples 1, 4, and 7. But these are the addition examples and this fact but emphasizes the conclusion, reached before from a consideration of the scores for the various operations, that addition is the hardest operation. The excellence of grade 9 in addition could have been inferred from the fact that its curve shows no such depressions. So for other examples and grades.

The total mistakes made are given in Table VII. For comparison these are reduced to mistakes per thousand points. The results, however, give but another view of the growth in accuracy, previously shown in Plot 5; accordingly they are not plotted. Table VII also gives the analysis of mistakes. In fundamentals, addition and subtraction are grouped together (A and S), multiplication and division (M and D), and mistakes in copying or in carrying whether they occurred in one operation or another. These are called mistakes in attention (A). The purpose of this separation was to determine whether failure was due to a lack of knowledge of the addition and multiplication tables, or to a lack of ability to handle such knowledge in an example. The results have been reduced to those for uniform grade membership, and expressed as mistakes per thousand points for purposes of comparison. (Mistakes per two hundred points in reasoning.) It seemed better, also, to use individuals making mistakes rather than mistakes themselves, as a single individual, weak in her knowledge of the multiplication tables, was found to contribute many mistakes in multiplication in a single example. The scores have been called "mistakes" to save time and space, and have been much more accurately determined for fundamentals than for reasoning. In reasoning, as previously explained, mistakes were analyzed into mistakes of understanding (T), mistakes of fundamentals (F), and mistakes of attention (A).

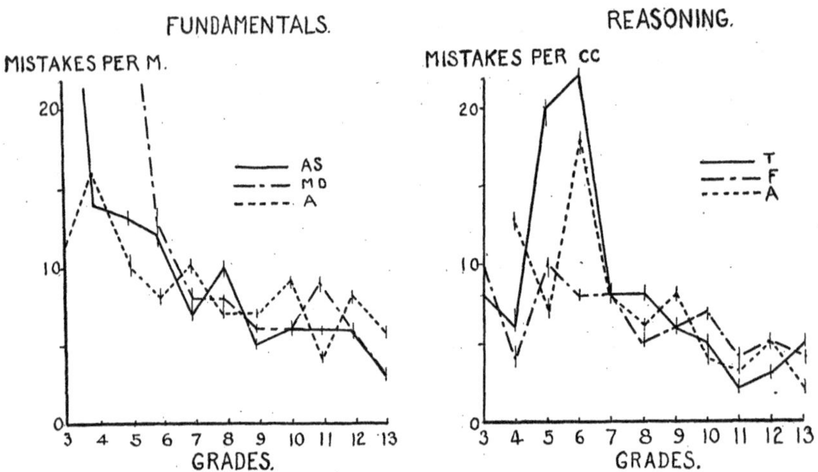

PLOT 10.—Shows mistakes in each grade. For explanation of letters see foregoing text.

In both tests the total score in points is made the basis of the computations of mistakes per thousand in attention. While this is fair from one point of view, it masks the relative size of the different groups. Accordingly, the results have also been expressed in percentage of the total mistakes made for each grade. Plot 11 shows the same results graphically.

The most evident fact to be inferred from Plot 10 is the one noted previously, that after grade 7 the range of variation is fairly constant, and that within this range, the particular type of mistake made is a matter of grade peculiarity. The high values in the early grades are due, of course, to the fact that the learning process for the four operations has not been completed,

TABLE VII

Fundamentals

Grade							Per M			Percentage of TM		
	TM	MM	IM	AS	MD	A	AS	MD	A	AS	MD	A
3	81	89	43	33	0	10	36	0	11	78	0	21
4	76	48	58	16	17	25	14	50	16	28	39	43
5	97	36	73	22	26	25	13	34	10	30	36	34
6	98	32	61	25	12	24	12	13	8	41	20	39
7	69	21	55	15	8	32	7	8	10	27	15	58
8	85	20	70	28	11	31	10	8	7	40	16	44
9	53	15	43	10	7	26	4	6	7	23	16	61
10	68	15	65	17	8	40	6	6	9	26	12	62
11	49	14	42	15	10	17	6	9	4	36	24	40
12	66	17	53	15	7	31	6	6	8	28	13	59
13	57	12	45	12	4	31	3	3	6	27	5	69

Reasoning

Grade						Per CC			Percentage of TM		
	TM	MM	MT	MF	MA	T	F	A	T	F	A
3	51	255	8	10	33	8	10	33	15	20	65
4	37	118	9	6	22	6	4	13	24	16	60
5	109	177	59	29	21	20	10	7	54	27	19
6	160	201	73	25	62	22	8	18	45	16	39
7	75	118	24	26	25	8	8	8	32	35	33
8	69	100	29	18	22	8	5	6	42	26	32
9	72	100	24	21	27	6	6	8	33	29	38
10	57	80	18	24	15	5	7	4	32	42	26
11	38	49	9	16	13	2	4	3	24	42	34
12	48	67	12	18	18	3	5	5	24	38	38
13	50	64	20	17	13	5	4	3	40	34	26

KEY

TM=Total Mistakes. MM=Mistakes per 1000. IM=Individuals making mistakes. AS=Individuals making mistakes in addition and subtraction. MD=Same, multiplication and division. A=Same, Attention. MT=Mistakes in understanding. MF=Mistakes in fundamentals.

SUPPLEMENT DATA

Grade	Total Points		Points A and S	Points M and D
	F	R		
3	917	202	906	0
4	1567	317	1327	340
5	2583	613	1773	809
6	3059	672	2136	923
7	3338	633	2317	1018
8	4324	690	2949	1376
9	3566	720	2455	1112
10	4426	720	3009	1416
11	3602	768	2510	1093
12	3903	712	2703	1200
13	4820	791	3263	1556

and the curves show plainly just where the learning of the different tables is done. In fundamentals, there is again not the evidence of growth that might be expected.

Plot 11 is more significant, as it indicates at once just where remedial work is to be done. In reading this plot however, care must be taken to consult the table, or Plot 10, to determine the

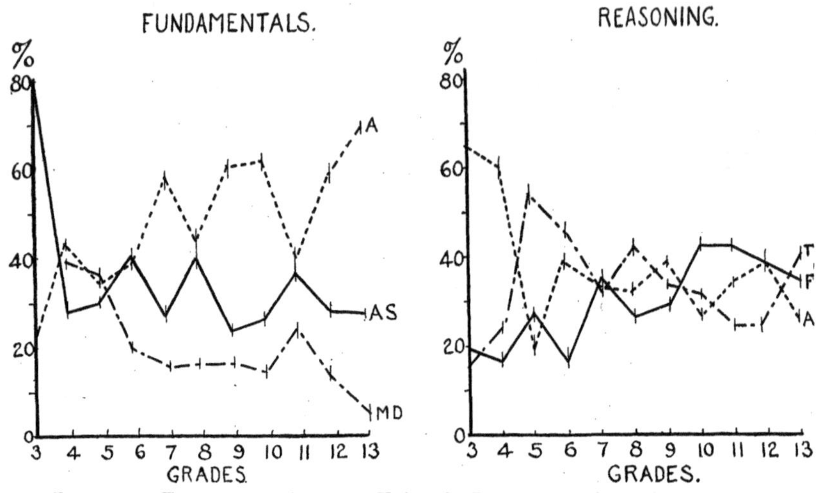

PLOT 11.—For explanation see Table VII and key following table.

actual amount of the mistakes in each group, in order not to be misled by the changes in the relative size of each group. Plot 11 shows that in fundamentals at grade 5 the size of the three groups is the same. That is, the child can direct her attention to her work just about as successfully as she can call upon a knowledge of the various tables needed in this test. Absolutely, the knowledge lags behind the attention as shown in Plot 10; for the test does not make equal demands upon all the operations. From grade 5 on, multiplication receives its proper training, so the curve declines until the mistakes in multiplication become a very small part of the whole. Addition improves so slowly that the percentage the addition mistakes are of the whole remains fairly constant. The child, however, receives, it would seem, no training in the use of her knowledge, and knows how to direct her attention no better at the higher grades than at grade 5. Consequently the relative percentage of the mistakes rises higher and higher. Even absolutely, in mistakes per thousand, the mistakes in attention outnumber the rest in five of the grades from the 7th to the 13th.

In reasoning the subject-matter is different and no direct comparison of the results can be made. It is interesting to note, however, that both in mistakes per cc and in percentages, in five of the grades mistakes in attention or mistakes in fundamentals which is due to the same cause are greater than mistakes in understanding.

This point, it seems to the writer, is an important one. Whatever the explanation, there can be no question of the fact that of all the individuals making mistakes at any given time in a class, at least one-third, and usually two-thirds, will be making mistakes in carrying or copying. The writer well knows that in discovering these mistakes there was much room for error. Yet it is to be remembered that the fact itself was made so evident in the general scoring that a second examination was made for the special purpose of separating these mistakes from the others. Also, the same method was used throughout, and should operate no more unjustly in one grade than in another. It is possible, and may be worth while, to carry the analysis farther.

The last subject to be considered in connection with the test, and to the writer the most important subject, is that of the distribution of ability in the grades. The total scores cover up many important facts and it is important, if any use is to be made of the results in determining future growth, that the present condition of each grade be exactly known.

The twelfth and largest grade has been selected for a detailed study. In Table VIII and Graph 12 are given the individual scores of the 33 members of this grade grouped in various ways. At the top of Plot 12, the individual scores are represented by straight lines drawn to scale. It is evident at once that the extreme variation found in the different grades is also found in the individuals composing the grades. Some degree of variation was to be expected; the question is, how much is normal. The lowest score given is 71; the highest 274: yet both were "passed" through eight years of arithmetic training, to say nothing of the training of the high-school years in mathematics and science. Now a "pass" is supposed to stand for an efficiency of 70 per

TABLE VIII

INDIVIDUAL SCORES AND GROUPINGS, GRADE 12. POINTS ATTEMPTED

Individual Scores	By 10's		By 20's		By 30's		By 40's		By 50's	
	Score	Frequency	Score	Frequency	Score	Frequency	Score	Frequency	Score	Frequency
71.....	71– 80	1	61– 80	1	61– 90	2	61–100	3	50–100	3
88.....	81– 90	0	100	2	120	6	140	12	150	15
96.....	91–100	1	120	5	150	10	180	9	200	8
103.....	101–110	4	140	7	180	6	220	3	250	6
103.....	111–120	1	160	6	200	3	260	5	300	1
103.....	121–130	1	180	3	240	3	300	1		
103.....	131–140	6	200	2	270	2				
118.....	141–150	3	220	1	300	1				
122.....	151–160	3	240	3						
131.....	161–170	1	260	2						
131.....	171–180	2	280	1						
131.....	181–190	0								
135.....	191–200	2								
136.....	201–210	1								
139.....	211–220	0								
145.....	221–230	2								
145.....	231–240	1								
145.....	241–250	2								
151.....	251–260	0								
153.....	261–270	0								
158.....	271–280	1								
161.....										
171.....										
180.....										
194.....										
199.....										
204.....										
221.....										
223.....										
234.....										
241.....										
250.....										
274.....										

cent. at the very lowest, and the mark aimed at is 85–90 per cent. Either the system of marking and examining is very defective or there has been marked deterioration during high-school years in a large part of the class. Perhaps this variation can be made most plain by computing from the normal curve in Plot 4 the average value of the individual score in each grade and expressing the composition of grade 12 in terms of members of the other grades. If this is done it will be found that the

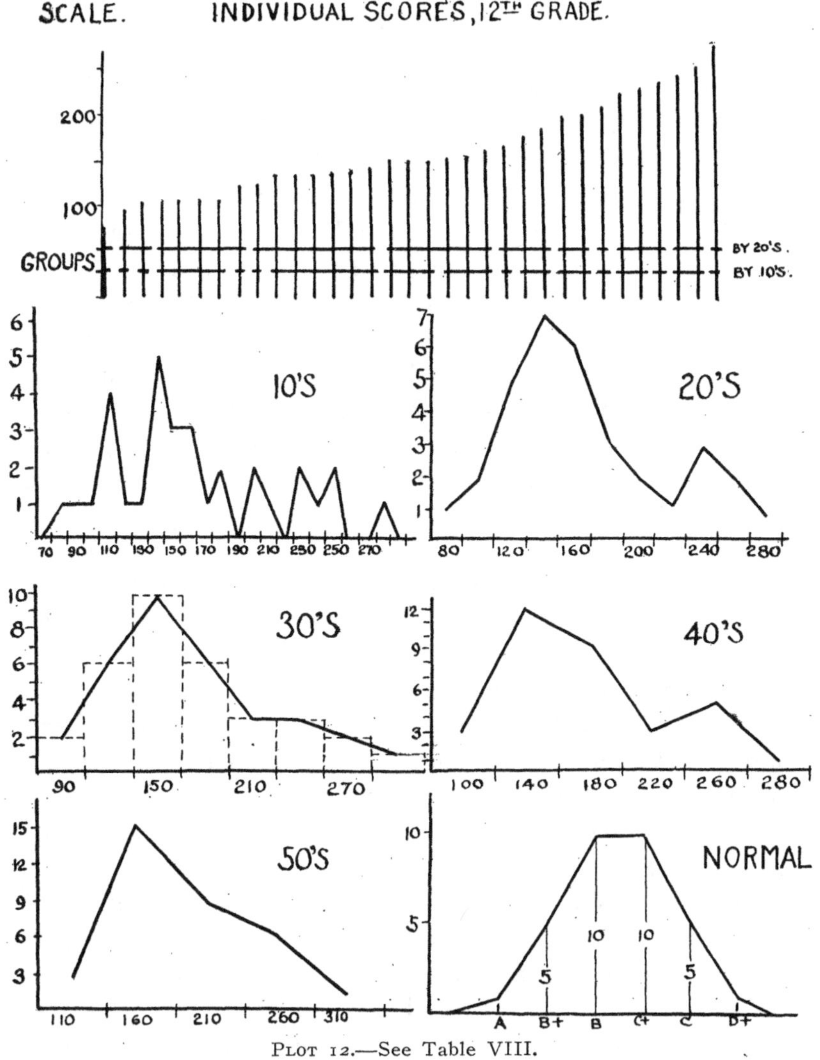

PLOT 12.—See Table VIII.

scores show grade 12 to be composed of 1 member of third-grade ability, 7 members of fourth-grade ability, 12 members of fifth-grade ability, 3 of sixth, 1 each of seventh-, twelfth-, and thirteenth grade abilities, and 7 members whose individual scores are above the average of the thirteenth grade. Over half the class is thus seen to be of less ability than the average ability of the sixth-grade class. This is evidently a subject that needs to be followed through with every grade. The method of doing this is that usually followed in discussions of distribution. The different individual scores are grouped together and the frequency with which any one score occurs can then be expressed by a single number. It is evident that if single scores are used the frequencies will be small, and the number of groups large. By dividing the whole score into equal parts, the number of groups can be decreased and the frequencies increased. The size of the measure to be used in any discussion depends upon the number of individual scores to be studied as well as upon the range of the variation. The highest score made by any individual in fundamentals was 278 points, the lowest 0. There are 11 grades. To allow for some overlapping, it seemed advisable to have more divisions of the score than there were grades, and yet a coarse measure was needed on account of the great variation. On the representation of the individual scores on Plot 12, the heavy black cross lines show the grouping when the total score is divided into periods of 10 points each, and into 20's. These groupings furnish the data for the distribution curves by 10's and 20's given immediately underneath. The divisions of the score are shown along the base line. One hundred and ten in the first graph meaning a group of all the scores from 101–110 inclusive. An inspection of the cross lines or of the table, will show four scores that fall within these limits. Accordingly the curve at this point rises to 4 above the base line. The size of the measure is thus shown along the base line and the frequency of any particular measure by heights above it.

An inspection of the distribution curve by 10's shows a succession of peaks, partially or wholly disconnected, while the same curve by 20's is a continuous curve. The normal distribution curve for any quality or ability in a large number of individuals has been determined, and for a group of 32 normal individuals would take the form shown at the bottom of Plot 12, marked normal. This means that in a class of 32 normal individuals, properly graded, there would be two groups of 10 each, to which the marks B and C+ could be given. On each side of these would be a smaller group of 5 each; one better, B+; one worse, C. Beyond these are two still smaller groups of one each, one of exceptional ability, A, the other very poor, D+. The real ability of the group ought to be taken as that of its central tendency, the central scores about which all the rest cluster, in this case the average of B and C+. In the

TABLE IX

DISTRIBUTION OF ABILITY

Based on individual scores in points. Each grade raised to fifty members

PART I. FUNDAMENTALS

Grade	Scores and Frequencies													
	0–20	21–40	60	80	100	120	140	160	180	200	220	240	260	280
3 At.	13	29	8											
Rt.	36	20												
4 At.		3	16	25	0	3	0	0	3					
Rt.		9	25	12	3									
5 At.			2	5	28	7	2	5	0	2				
Rt.			2	11	25	5	5	2	2					
6 At.				12	3	11	12	7	0	0	0	3		
Rt.			7	8	0	16	8	7	0	0	3			
7 At.				5	2	14	5	16	7	0	0	2		
Rt.				7	5	11	9	16	0	0	0	2		
8 At.						5	7	5	19	2	7	2	2	
Rt.					2	5	7	7	14	1	7	2	2	
9 At.					3	14	3	14	8	3	6			
Rt.					3	17	3	14	6	6	3			
10 At.					2	4	10	4	8	2	4	12	3	
Rt.					4	4	10	8	2	2	8	10	0	
11 At.				6	0	11	2	17	4	0	4	0	4	
Rt.				6	6	8	6	11	2	0	4	0	4	
12 At.				1	3	7	11	9	4	3	1	4	3	1
Rt.				3	6	6	9	12	3	4	4	0	0	1
13 At.						3	3	0	16	9	6	6	3	3
Rt.						3	3	6	13	6	6	3	3	

PART 2. REASONING

Grade	Scores and Frequencies											
	0–3	3–6	9	12	15	18	21	24	27	30	33	36
3 At.	4	4	21	21								
Rt.	12	13	17	8								
4 At.			19	9	6	16	3					
Rt.		6	19	9	6	9						
5 At.						7	11	9	9	7	2	5
Rt.				5	7	21	16	2				
6 At.						4	8	0	9	25	4	
Rt.		4	0	8	9	9	8	4				
7 At.						9	9	0	14	11	0	7
Rt.				2	5	12	14	7	5	5	0	2
8 At.					2	5	7	2	5	7	12	10
Rt.				2	2	5	10	7	10	2	7	5
9 At.							3	5	13	5	19	3
Rt.						5	13	5	8	16	3	
10 At.							11	0	9	14	9	7
Rt.							13	5	13	16	0	2
11 At.							2	2	10	10	14	12
Rt.							4	8	12	6	12	8
12 At.				2	0	2	5	3	2	18	2	12
Rt.			2	2	0	2	10	2	14	10	3	3
13 At.								7	3	13	8	18
Rt.						5	5	10	3	8	8	13

case of grade 12 above, it can be seen at once from the curve by 20's that the central tendency is from 120 to 140. Other curves are given to show the effect of coarser measures. In the case of the curve by 30's, representation by rectangles is also given as this method of drawing the distribution curve is sometimes used to indicate also the size of the measure. In all these curves, however, it will be noted that the individual abilities of grade 12 are in the main grouped about a low score but that there is in addition a smaller group of much greater ability.

For the general study of the distribution of ability in the grades, the measure is taken as 20 points for fundamentals and 3 points for reasoning. This gives 16 groups for fundamentals and 12 for reasoning. Each grade is raised to 50 members for convenience in plotting and all are plotted on the same scale.

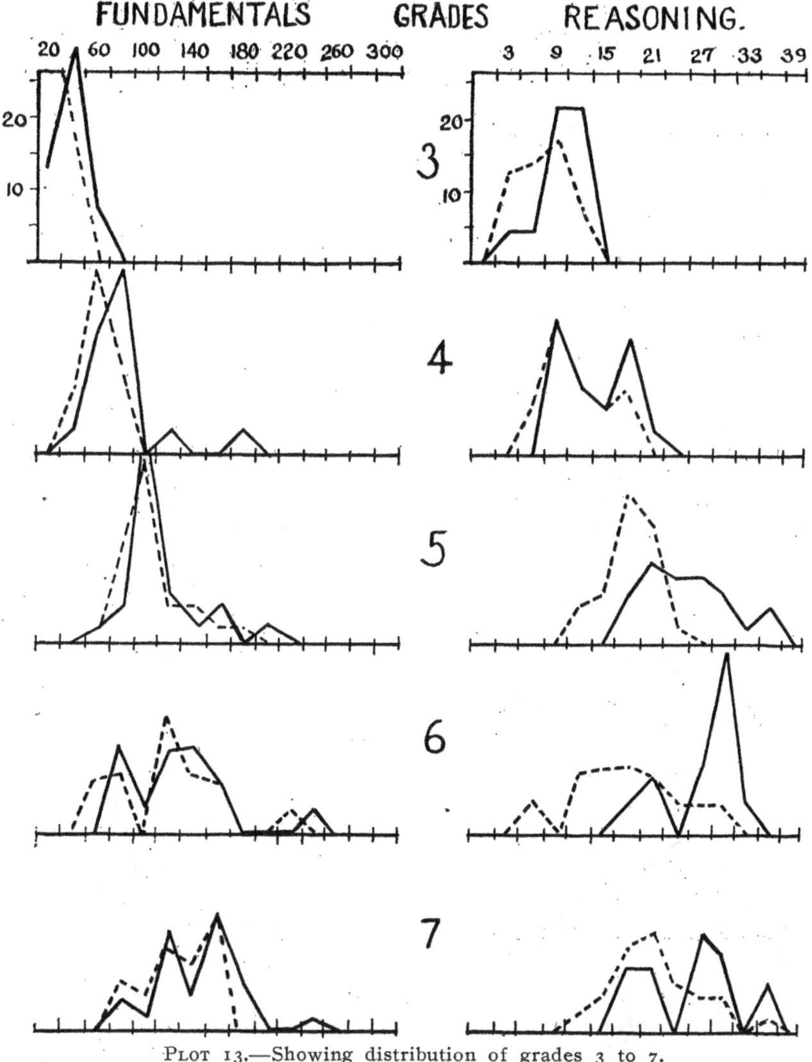

PLOT 13.—Showing distribution of grades 3 to 7.

The full line represents attempts and the dotted line rights in every case. The curves for fundamentals and reasoning are given side by side in order that the distribution of the same grade in the two tests may be compared. The graphs will be known as Plots 13 and 14 and the data for it is given in Table IX.

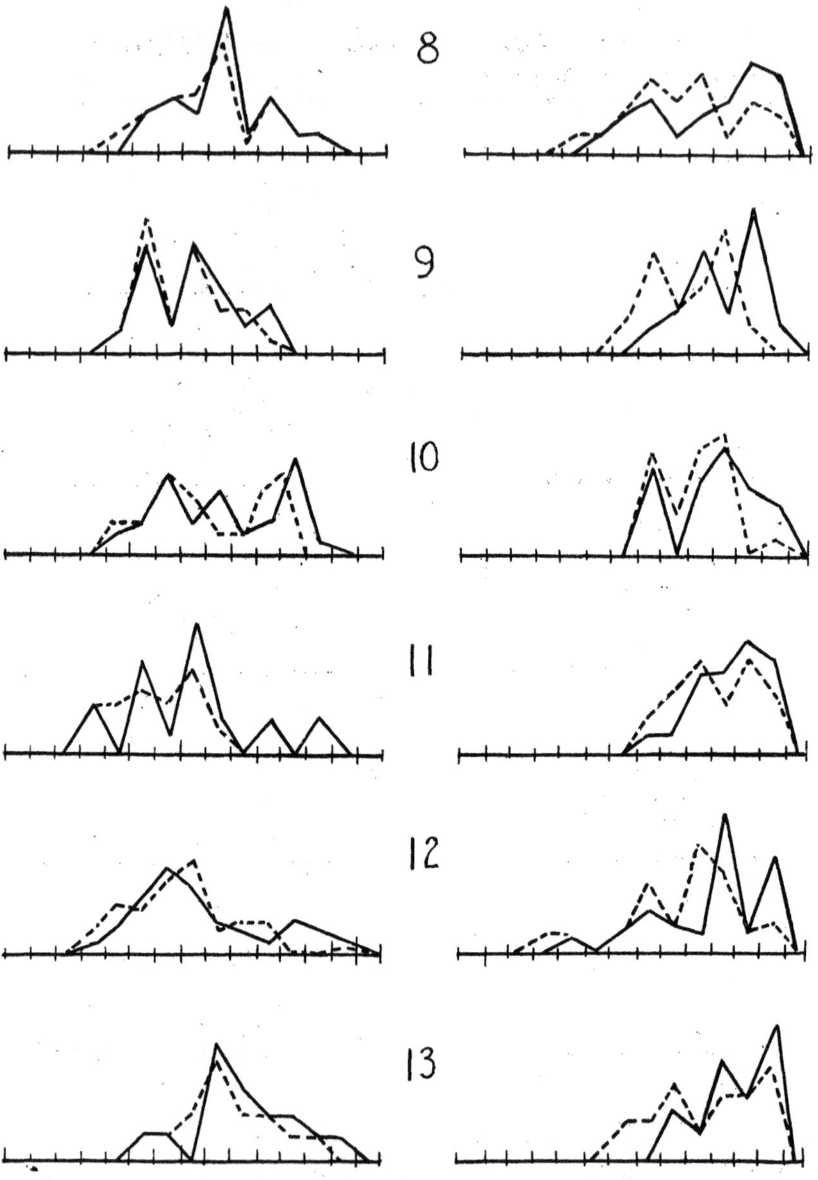

PLOT 14.—Showing distribution of grades 8 to 13.

A very hasty glance at Plot 14 reveals a very irregular distribution of ability in all grades after the fifth, and it seems more than likely that the extent of the variation is much greater than would be normal under any kind of scientific study of individual abilities and needs. It seems to the writer that the determination of the causes of the wide variation in individuals, and the marking out of certain broad classification of individuals according to their peculiar abilities together with the determination of special training adapted for each class is the immediate problem of psychology upon whose solution any beginning of a scientific pedagogy must depend. For it is evident from the Plot that in the early grades the classes are units, but that as the pupils pass from grade to grade, individuals react to the training in different ways, so that the unity of the grade is broken up. It has long been evident that individuals in a class learn enough to pass examinations in very different ways. Some learn understandingly; some mechanically; that is, so that they can do the work set by a particular teacher in a certain way or place, but not so they can use the knowledge gained in any other place or for any other teacher. Whatever the explanation, a poor class, as grade 6, is here found to have a distribution showing several groups of very different abilities, while a good class, as grade 11, reasoning, is here shown to approach the normal distribution. This corresponds with teaching experience. Any teacher working with a small enough class to know the individuals, is conscious of the spur of a compact group of evenly graded children and the drag of the struggle with groups of individuals requiring special handling.

A careful study of the curves for fundamentals will show that the central tendency of the eighth grade is equaled by a large group in no grade except the thirteenth. A small group in the tenth grade is the only exception of any size. This seems to mean that the whole eighth grade has reached as high a degree of ability at the eighth grade as that attained by the high-school grades. The extent of the distribution in this class is greater than would seem right but otherwise it will make a good grade from which to determine what happens to ability in arithmetic during the high-school years.

The curves of Plot 15 permit a score being selected as the typical individual score for a grade; also, another score as the probable individual score that might be reached by the average

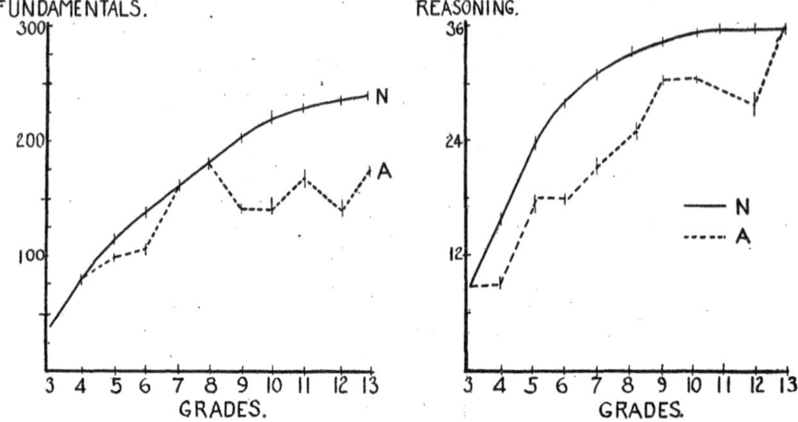

PLOT 15.—Showing normal and actual for each grade. See Table X.

of the class if all received the same benefit from their training as the best group. These values are given in Table X and their graph, 15, gives another possible normal and the departure of

TABLE X

NORMAL AND ACTUAL INDIVIDUAL SCORES DERIVED FROM PLOT 15

	Grades										
	3	4	5	6	7	8	9	10	11	12	13
Attempts—											
Fundamentals, normal	40	80	...	...	160	180	...	220	...	...	240
Fundamentals, central tendency	40	80	100	110	160	180	140	140	160	140	180
Rights—											
Reasoning, normal	9	15	24	...	...	33	...	...	...	...	36
Reasoning, central tendency	9	9	18	18	21	24	30	30	30	27	36

the present state of the school from it. It will be noted that the values in these curves are higher than those in the normals previously established and in most cases, the actual condition somewhat lower. These normals, the one of grade ability and the other of individual ability, furnish standards that make it worth while to attempt special remedial work with both individuals and grades. Their actual value can only be told by use.

From the foregoing tables and plots, it will be seen that this test, while originally purely accidental and experimental in character, and not designed for the close analysis to which it has been subjected, has, nevertheless, yielded many results of value to the writer in his work of supervision. It has shown the need for greater knowledge of what is actually taking place in the child's mind as he passes through grade after grade. It has made plain the uncertainty of the product of the present educational system as well as the value of complete and many-sided training in the early grades if there is to be great ability in the later grades. More than all else it has proved, conclusively to the writer at least, that it is practicable to measure, not only the general condition of arithmetic teaching throughout a school, the growth in ability and efficiency from grade to grade, the defects and needs of any one grade or individual, but the *effects of changes in method or procedure* as well. By a series of tests, through a number of years, it ought to be possible to build up a real science of teaching and to determine by strict experimental methods the truth or falsity of any educational hypothesis. Nor is the method applicable to mathematics alone. In any subject taught in many successive grades, similar comparative testing will not only tend to produce increased efficiency but it will, judging by the results of the present test, furnish a connective thread of growth in the fundamentals of the subject that will produce a unity that is sadly lacking in all present pedagogical effort.

EDITORIAL NOTES

General Reasons for the Decline of Drill

There are many reasons why mere repetition of lessons is no longer practiced in schools. In the first place, there is so much good material to be presented that the teacher feels that the child will not come into contact with the world which science and industry have opened up unless new facts are crowded into every lesson. In the second place it is very difficult to whip up attention and keep alive interest when the subject-matter is familiar and partially mastered. In the third place, it is easy to devise tests which shall show the breadth of a pupil's knowledge and it is difficult to measure the depth and permanency of an impression on the mind. The school which gives the least breadth of training is consequently at a seeming disadvantage even if the depth of its training is greater.

Modern Pedagogical Justifications for Omission of Drill

There are other reasons of the same general type which have contributed to the result that drill has come to be almost a lost art in the modern school. One hears various devices described by which children are to be drilled without being allowed to become aware of what is going on. The same material, we are told, can be presented in various forms; the same principle can be exhibited in various settings; and the ends thus attained which were sought in the old-fashioned drill. Again we find some writers explicitly saying that the mind does not get general training except by sweeping over the whole world. The improvement of experience comes therefore through manifold activities of diverse types, there is no such thing as drilling a few fundamental faculties. The drill of the old school was aiming at a false goal.

School Work in Need of Sifting

It would be futile to criticize this tendency to omit or evade drill if one were armed only with prejudices in favor of the old-fashioned school. Modern reasons must be matched to modern reasons. Let us see if some reasons cannot be briefly presented in favor of drill. First, children in our present-day schools are confused by the mass of material presented to them. They are rushed recklessly from fact to fact and left with fagged minds to wallow in the unorganized mass of new impressions. Many teachers could not organize the material which they give the children so that it would form a coherent, presentable paper for rehearsal before other teachers. How can children organize this material? We shall settle down some day to a few well-selected, well-arranged materials of instruction. We are suffering today from pedagogical surfeit and the absence of drill in our schools is one of the symptoms of this condition.

Repetition Essential to Mental Development

If our studies of brain physiology and functional psychology show one result more clearly than another it is that repetition is absolutely essential to mental development. Mutual development depends upon the organization of the nervous functions in such a way that impulses shall follow fixed paths of discharge. New impulses call for new organizations. One cannot reorganize at ever step, one must establish and fix before he can advance to higher organizations. The question of how education is to organize the individual—whether in higher or lower types of thought and behavior—depends for its answer very largely upon the time given to permanent organization as distinguished from mere temporary organization. The results which have been offered by scientific students in opposition to the doctrine of general mental discipline are often more valuable as criticisms of our present-day methods than as criticisms of the doctrine of discipline. There is many a course in geography which gives no general mental discipline. That does not prove that geography might not give mental discipline of a general type. The question which we ought to be discussing is not whether there is such a training as will discipline the general faculties, but rather how the most permanent effects may be produced through the training which we give.

"Drill" should be reintroduced into our pedagogical vocabularies. It represents a phase of method which is indispensable and clearly justifiable.

NOTES AND NEWS

NEED OF DIFFERENT ELEMENTARY SCHOOL COURSES

That the elementary school may in reality afford equality of educational opportunity, that it may take into account the differences in the social body and the differences in children, it is necessary that a distinction be made between the work of giving children the rudiments of an education and preparing them for a higher academic institution, and the work of giving children the fundamentals of an education and fitting them for early entrance upon life-pursuit, and there is need that separate courses of instruction be provided for the accomplishment of these different purposes.

There are at least three ways of doing this dual work of the elementary school. First an option may be offered in all grades between two courses, one designed for children who purpose to continue their schooling, the other adapted to the interests and needs of children who from choice or necessity expect to complete their education with the grades. A second means is to provide one course of study in the first four grades for all children, and to offer an option in the four grammar grades between two courses, the one designed for those going on, and the other for those expecting to attend no other school. A third means, supplementary to the second, is to organize elementary industrial schools as separate centers of instruction and provide a course of study half of which is devoted to the more practical portions of the fundamental academic branches and the other half to industrial studies and activities.

The second of these suggestions is to be tried in Cleveland this year. Two courses are to be prepared for the four grammar grades—the one adapted to the needs of children of literary taste and going on to the high school, the other to the needs of children looking to early entrance upon life-pursuit. This second course is to be rendered flexible so as to meet the needs of different districts and groups of children through permitting of a maximum and minimum of time that may be given to the several studies, and may be installed at the option of the principal with the consent of the superintendent, but the selection of this course to be optional with the parent.

The third suggestion is to be embodied in an elementary industrial school for boys and girls who are more than thirteen years of age and not below the sixth grade. The course will be two years in length, consisting of two types of work, academic and industrial, and the time of the school will be equally divided between the two. This school will interest boys and girls to whom the regular course is unduly literary and who are not interested in bookish things, and it will also interest those whose economic condition requires them to leave school early to become wage-earners.

The academic studies comprise: English, arithmetic, and geography-history. The English will consist of spelling, writing, reading, literature, and composition. The arithmetic will include accounts and shop problems. The geography-history will deal with the industrial, commercial, and political phases of our national development as well as municipal studies.

On the industrial side the course will include, for boys, benchwork in wood and sheet metal, freehand drawing and design, and mechanical drawing; for girls, sewing and garment-making, cooking and household arts, freehand drawing, design, and construction. Throughout the work will be made intensely practical and be given a direct industrial and commercial turn.

These optional courses designed to meet the needs of children who will probably attend no other schools should, however, by no means lead educationally into a blind alley. They should give such place to the essentials of the three R's and so emphasize neatness, thoroughness, and accuracy in industrial and commercial work, that the child completing such a course would be admitted to manual training or technical high schools and be able, by doing a certain amount of literary work in addition, to gain entrance to an academic high school.

William H. Elson
Superintendent of Cleveland Schools
Frank P. Bachman
Assistant Superintendent

School Gardening and Nature Study in English Rural Schools and in London is the title of Bulletin No. 204 of the Office of Experiment Stations, of the U. S. Department of Agriculture. The Bulletin is written by Miss Susan B. Sipe who has previously rendered similar valuable assistance in the publication of other articles upon school gardening. This bulletin deals with nature-study in the schools of Whitechapel, London, at the Kentish Town Road School, London, with rural school gardens, and with teacher's courses and examinations.

This entire description of what is being done in English schools in natural-history work is filled with the idea of dynamic as compared with what may be called static natural history. Live plants and animals, outdoor studies in great number, the growth of plants in school gardens, the growth of animals in the school garden and about the home are matters of constant mention. The fact that growing plants and animals have large educative results with children seems to be a central factor in the work in English schools, if Miss Sipe's description is representative of conditions in general. The bulletin will be found valuable for all who are interested in supervising or teaching the different aspects of natural history.

O. W. Caldwell

BOOK REVIEWS

Moral Principles in Education. By JOHN DEWEY. "Riverside Educational Monographs." Houghton, Mifflin & Co., 1909. Pp. 61. Price 35 cents, net, postpaid.

This book gives us a new edition of the most important work we have upon the subject of moral education. It is the address given before the National Herbart Society (now the National Society for the Scientific Study of Education) at the Milwaukee meeting in 1897. It is easily the most significant contribution that society has made. There has not been much change in the thought, but considerable improvement in form. The editor's introduction deals with education as a public business and as expert service, and the relations of expert opinion and public opinion, stating clearly a range of problems upon which our administrators may well spend more thought.

The tendency toward extensive analysis of the text, seen in all the numbers of this series (perhaps overdone in some cases) here gives the material in better form for use. The old first section is broken up into (i) The Moral Purpose of the School; (ii) The Moral Training Given by the School Community; (iii) The Moral Training from Methods of Instruction; (iv) The Social Nature of the Course of Study. The original second section becomes (v) The Psychological Aspect of Moral Education. This last section seems to be the least changed in statement. The most striking change is the systematic use of the word "moral" rather than "ethical." The title is now "Moral Principles" rather than "Ethical Principles" and this is followed up throughout the text by a general substitution of the former term for the latter.

It is to be hoped that we shall soon have Dr. Dewey's address at the St. Augustine meeting, 1896, on "Interest as Related to Will" in equally good form. Dr. De Garmo's popularization of it in *Interest in Education* is helpful but does not do away with the need of the original text. FRANK A. MANNY

KALAMAZOO, MICH.

Teaching Children to Study. By LIDA B. EARHART, PH.D. "Riverside Educational Monographs." Houghton, Mifflin Co. Pp. 182. Price 35 cents.

This is a subject we need help upon and every contribution will be of service. Dr. Earhart's thesis, *Systematic Study in the Elementary Schools,* which appeared last year has been rewritten and the tables and other more formal elements have been omitted. The material here consists of a general statement of logical study followed by its application to the work of pupils in the intermediate and grammar grades. The theoretical statement is given first, probably with the intention of formulating the problem, but the result is not altogether fortunate for the exposition afforded is somewhat formal for the students who have not some considerable acquaintance with genetic logic and is scarcely adequate for those who have. Mrs. Young's chapter on this material in *Isolation in the School,* presents the problem rather more effectively and economically. The later sections on "Do Children Possess the Ability to Study Logically?" etc., are more suggestive but not convincing with reference to the aid that here will be gained.

The method used in securing the data is not given concretely. As the author says, "It is difficult to write suggestions, because as soon as written they appear very rigid and lacking in adaptability." The general summary gives ten statements which illustrate this difficulty and also confirm the suspicion one has in reading the preface that recent workers on this topic have overrated, by no means our need, but at least the recentness of the discovery and the value of the development. The "entirely new light" (p. viii) which the editor of the series values for its "newness" (p. xi) and its contribution which is "more than any other document now in print" (p. xii), does not seem to be as novel or as luminous as we had hoped. We are grateful to the author for co-ordinating material on the subject and look forward to Dr. Frank McMurry's *How to Study and Teaching How to Study* for additional material.

One serious defect in the present book arises from the incidental method in which the thinking of children of primary grades is referred to. It may be too strong to say that it seems as if, according to the author, the earlier years could be left to the older more formal ways, but there certainly is not much reference to the basal work done in the recognition of the type of logical thinking appropriate to this stage as illustrated in the reports of Dr. Dewey's work at Chicago.

To many of us the present movement would be made more serviceable if it were less segregated. For some time we have recognized two planes of evolution—one that of brute experience, growth, and development by hard knocks through which one learned at great risk and expense, and a second in which consciousness is able to project a problem and then to try this out by means of the expenditure of a much more limited amount of energy and material. This latter is seen in the best laboratory work. This new light on study seems to have an important connection with this larger movement and would gain, I believe, by relation to it rather than by separation. FRANK A. MANNY

KALAMAZOO, MICH.

Ethical and Moral Instruction in Schools. By GEORGE HERBERT PALMER; *Self-Cultivation in English.* By GEORGE HERBERT PALMER. "Riverside Educational Monographs." Houghton, Mifflin & Co. Each 35 cents, net, postpaid.

These three essays have been of great service to many parents and teachers. The second volume *Self-Cultivation in English* has been more accessible than the others and from the nature of its subject has had more direct influence in schools. The mature thought of a man of knowledge and power in the two great fields of philosophy and literature cannot but be of value when formulated about these practical subjects. Professor Palmer lays great stress upon habit-formation and his discussion is a needed corrective of the tendency to over-stress direct and formal ethical instruction. He does not, however, seem to make clear that just as in every act of perception there is involved a judgment; so the life of the child before adolescence, while clearly having its major activity on the plane of memory and habit, requires very careful and adequate attention to its real needs in higher psychical functions as judgment and reasoning. One can account a function as minor for a time without agreeing to its neglect. The idealistic dualism that brings judgment in as practically a new element at adolescence is too easy a way out. FRANK A. MANNY

KALAMAZOO, MICH.

CURRENT EDUCATIONAL LITERATURE IN THE PERIODICALS[1]

IRENE WARREN
Librarian, School of Education, The University of Chicago

Ashmun, Margaret. Library reading in the high school. School R. 17:618–22. (N. '09.)

Bancroft, Nellie E. The Latin play recently given in the Western high school, Detroit. School R. 17:631–33. (N. '09.)

Benton, Guy Potter. The college fraternity as an ally in maintaining institutional standards. Relig. Educa. 4:334–41. (O. '09.)

Blanchard, Alice A. Story telling as a library tool. Pedagog. Sem. 16:351–56. (S. '09.)

Bobbitt, John Franklin. Practical eugenics. Pedagog. Sem. 16:385–94. (S. '09.)

Boyer, Jaques. A simplified method of teaching experimental physics. Sci. Amer. 101:293, 304, 305. (O. '09.)

Burnham, William H. The hygiene of physical training. Amer. Phys. Educa. R. 14:468–78. (O. '09.)

Burns, Allen T. Educating the church for her social duty. Relig. Educa. 4:358–64. (O. '09.)

Chandler, Edward H. How much children attend the theatre, the quality of the entertainment they choose and its effect upon them. Pedagog. Sem. 16:367–71. (S. '09.)

Chase, H. W. Some aspects of the attention problem. Pedagog. Sem. 16:281–300. (S. '09.)

Clark, Thomas A. The fraternity in the state university. Relig. Educa. 4:327–34. (O. '09.)

Colvin, S. S. The ideational types of school children. Pedagog. Sem. 16:314–24. (S. '09.)

Comstock, Anthony. The work of the New York society for the prevention of vice, and its bearings on the morals of the young. Pedagog. Sem. 16:403–20. (S. '09.)

Courtis, S. A. Measurement of growth and efficiency in arithmetic. El. School T. 10:58–74. (O. '09.)

[1] Abbreviations—Amer. Journ. of Psy., American Journal of Psychology; Amer. Phys. Educa. R., American Physical Education Review; Atlan., Atlantic Monthly; Dial, The Dial; Educa., Education; El. School T., Elementary School Teacher; Good Housekeep., Good Housekeeping; Journ. of Educa. (Bost.), Journal of Education (New England); Out., Outlook; Pedagog. Sem., Pedagogical Seminary; Pop. Educa., Popular Educator; Psycholog. Clinic, Psychological Clinic; Relig. Educa., Religious Education; School R., School Review; School Sci. and Math., School Science and Mathematics; Sci. Amer., Scientific American; Scrib. M., Scribner's Magazine.

CROMIE, WILLIAM J. Youth and the Marathon. Pedagog. Sem. 16:331–36. (S. '09.)

CURTIS, HENRY S. The growth, present extent and prospects of the playground movement in America. Pedagog. Sem. 16:344–50. (S. '09.)

DUBOIS, PATTERSON. The functioning of the Sunday school. Pedagog. Sem. 16:357–60. (S. '09.)

FISHER, IRVING. Public responsibility for the health of infants and children. Pedagog. Sem. 16:395–402. (S. '09.)

FORBUSH, WILLIAM BYRON. Boys' clubs. Pedagog. Sem. 16:337–43. (S. '09.)

FREEMAN, FRANK N. Manual training in the service of physics. School R. 17:609–17. (N. '09.)

GARDINER, J. H. Training in illiteracy. School R. 17:623–30. (N. '09.)

GIBBS, LOUISE R. Making a high school a center of social life. School R. 17:634–37. (N. '09.)

GRADENWITZ, DR. ALFRED. The Brussels popular electrical laboratory. Sci. Amer. 101:312. (30 O. '09.)

GREENE, MARY BELLE. A class of backward and defective children. Psycholog. Clinic. 3:125–32. (O. '09.)

GULICK, LUTHER HALSEY. The opportunity of the physical director. Amer. Phys. Educa. R. 14:461–67. (O. '09.)

HARRIS, M. O'BRIEN. The rank and file in our public schools. Pedagog. Sem. 16:305–13. (S. '09.)

HARRISON, PROVOST, AND SMITH, E. F. The fraternities in the University of Pennsylvania. Relig. Educa. 4:342. (O. '09.)

HEERMANS, JOSEPHINE W. History in the elementary school. Educa. 30: 98–111. (O. '09.)

HEETER, S. L. Conservation of health in the schoolroom. Psycholog. Clinic. 3:121–24. (O. '09.)

HEWINS, C. M. Reading clubs for older boys and girls. Pedagog. Sem. 16: 325–30. (S. '09.)

High School of aerial navigation in France. Sci. Amer. 101:276. (16 O. '09.)

HODDER, MRS. JESSIE D. What is being done for girls who go wrong. Pedagog. Sem. 16:361–66. (S. '09.)

HUEY, EDMUND B. The international congress of psychology. Amer. Journ. of Psy. 20:571–75. (O. '09.)

——(The) inauguration of President Lowell. Out. 93:334–37. (16 O. '09.)

JOHNSON, G. E. Why teach a child to play? Amer. Phys. Educa. R. 14: 500–7. (O. '09.)

JUDD, CHARLES HUBBARD. The department of education in American Universities. School R. 17:593–608. (N. '09.)

KING, HENRY CHURCHILL. The future of moral and religious education. Relig. Educa. 4:293–304. (O. '09.)

LaRue, Daniel Walford. The philosophy of the elementary language course. Educa. 30:74–83. (O. '09.)

Miller, Charles A. A. J. Progress and retardation of a Baltimore class. Psycholog. Clinic. 3:136–40. (O. '09.)

Miller, William T. Vocation-teaching. Atlan. 104:644–46. (N. '09.)

Mitchell, Samuel C. Religious education and racial adjustment. Relig. Educa. 4:316–23. (O. '09.)

Moore, Edward C. Religious education in the Orient. Relig. Educa. 4: 304–16. (O. '09.)

Mussey, Ellen Spencer. The legal relations of parent and child. Good Housekeep. 49:504–7. (N. '09.)

McKenny, Charles. The elementary school and education for social duty. Relig. Educa. 4:353–57. (O. '09.)

Newcomer, Alphonso G. On teaching literature. Dial. 47:276–78. (16 O. '09.)

O'Shea, M. V. Everyday problems in teaching: a disorderly school. Pop. Educa. 27:113, 114. (N. '09.)

Parker, Chester S. Our inherited practice in elementary schools. El. School T. 10:75–85. (O. '09.)

Peters, Fredus N. Scientific and mathematical teaching in the future. School Sci. and Math. 9:751–58. (N. '09.)

Rogers, James Frederick. Physical and moral training. Pedagog. Sem. 16:301–4. (S. '09.)

Sargent, Walter. The fine and industrial arts in elementary schools. El. School T. 10:49–57. (O. '09.)

Scott, Colin A. Social education. Educa. 30:67–73. (O. '09.)

Scott, William A. The college fraternity as a factor in the religious and moral life of students. Relig. Educa. 4:323–27. (O. '09.)

Showerman, Grant. The making of a professor. Atlan. 104:611–19. (N. '09.)

Smith, Mrs. K. W. School-home visiting. Journ. of Educa. (Bost.) 70: 423–26. (28 O. '09.)

Swain, Joseph. Religious education and the public schools. Relig. Educa. 423–26. (28 O. '09.)

Tufts, James H. The school and modern life. Relig. Educa. 4:343–48. (O. '09.)

Wachenheim, F. L. Notes on tuberculosis in school children. Pedagog. Sem. 16:378–84. (S. '09.)

Walker, Charles T. The work of the juvenile protective association. Pedagog. Sem. 16:372–77. (S. '09.)

Walter, Herbert E. An ideal course in biology for the high school. School Sci. and Math. 9:717–24. (N. '09.)

Wilson, Woodrow. What is a college for? Scrib. M. 46:570–77. (N. '09.)

Winship, A. E. The Los Angeles situation. Journ. of Educa. (Bost.) 70: 397–99. (21 O. '09.)

VOLUME X NUMBER 5

THE ELEMENTARY SCHOOL TEACHER

JANUARY, 1910

TRADE SCHOOLS IN LONDON

DR. C. W. KIMMINS
Head Inspector of Schools of the London County Council
London, England

Before entering on the question of trade schools I should point out that in London under the London County Council there is a very elaborate scholarship scheme consisting of Junior, Intermediate, and Senior scholarships which makes ample provision for all the children of exceptional ability in the elementary schools. The normal age of competition for the Junior scholarships is between eleven and twelve years of age, but arrangements are now being made for a further contingent at the age of thirteen for children who develop later than the normal child.

When a Junior scholarship is won the child is transferred from the elementary to a secondary school in which he or she receives free education with a small maintenance allowance at first, which increases considerably at the age of fourteen when, under ordinary conditions, the child might leave the elementary school. If the scholar does well in the secondary school the Intermediate scholarships which are of higher value are open for competition, and the child who is successful may remain at the same secondary school or be transferred to one of higher grade and receive, in addition to free education, a higher maintenance allowance than he received as a Junior scholar. Further, if successful in obtaining a Senior scholarship the boy or girl may go on to Oxford or Cambridge, or technical institutions of university rank in England or abroad for a period of three years with a very substantial maintenance allowance. Thus a pupil may be on the scholarship ladder for over ten years and pass from the elementary school to the secondary school and afterward graduate at one of the ancient universities with practically no cost to his parents since he left the elementary school.

The number of scholarships awarded in each stage is large and will probably be increased still further by the Council should the necessity arise. It may, therefore, be taken for granted that ample provision is made for the specially gifted child, however poor its parents may be. The examinations on which these scholarships are won are based on the ordinary subjects of instruction. In addition to the general scholarship scheme special provisions are made to encourage and endow artistic ability. Scholarships of increasing value are given to students of special promise, and in a scheme now under consideration provision is made for the award of art scholarships to the value of £50 a year tenable for three years.

The brilliant child is therefore well provided for and may eventually become fully equipped for one of the learned professions or one of the higher walks of industrial life.

Other children, though not sufficiently brilliant to gain scholarships for secondary schools at the age of eleven, may be sufficiently clever to be transferred to a higher school of elementary type at the age of twelve and there obtain, though not a trade education, education of a more or less specialized type, and with a higher leaving age than is the case at the ordinary elementary school.

After thus making provision for the abnormal child the problem of problems becomes, How can we prevent the boy or girl of normal intelligence from drifting into the ranks of unskilled labor at the age of fourteen? The difficulty here is seriously increased by the fact that there is not the slightest difficulty in a healthy, moderately well-educated, well-conducted child finding employment at a rate of remuneration which for a child of this age appears very liberal indeed. The point is, however, that in the vast majority of cases such employment does not lead to advancement financially or otherwise, and in a few years' time, after the child has deteriorated intellectually and is less well educated than at the time of leaving school, the employment for which young children are better suited comes to an end and the boy or girl sinks into the ranks of the unemployed or into the lower departments of unskilled labor. It has been found that for the poor type of child it is, under present conditions, quite impossible to insure two or three years' continuous instruction after the age of fourteen unless some grant for maintenance is made which will recoup the parents for the loss they sustain by not letting their children enter unskilled employment.

In order to bridge over the serious gap between the ages of fourteen and seventeen a new type of school, the trade school, has come into existence which is destined in the future to play a very important part in London education.

The origin of this type of school is due to the changed conditions of modern industry and the total disappearance in some, and the gradual disappearance in others, of the apprenticeship system in many of the London industries. The trade school movement has been much influenced more recently by the desire expressed by both employers and employees of the bookbinding and printing trades and the goldsmiths', silversmiths', jewelers', and allied trades for better preparation in technical and artistic preliminary training of boys before entering the workshop and while serving apprenticeship, with a view eventually to raise the standard of work in their particular crafts. This interest has been shown by employers by their keen desire as members of consultative committees to assist the Council with advice in various ways. In the past there was no connection between day schools and the trades and industries of London. These trade schools are now supplying this link. The pupils attending are classed as (1) fee paying, (2) those that have been awarded free places, and (3) scholarship holders with maintenance allowance. It is interesting to note with reference to the latter the great increase in the number of scholarships granted by the London County Council for these schools. In 1905 there were 32, in 1906 there were 310, including 80 for girls to enter the girls' trade schools, while in 1909, 610 have been authorized, of which over 300 are for girls. The competition for these scholarships is very keen indeed. Thus at the last competition for 90 of these scholarships which carry maintenance allowances of £6 per year for the first year, £6 or £10 for the second, and £15 for the third, there were 534 candidates.

The course in the trade schools for boys lasts three years and the general principle that underlies the instruction given is that the pupils' general education is continued and closely coordinated with the particular craft work taught. The amount of time devoted to craft work is about half the total, from about one-third in the first year to two-thirds in the last, and this is taught in a way which is genuinely educational as well as preparatory to the future occupation of the boy.

The staff consists of a headmaster, a chief technical instructor, and assistants who are specially selected and are experts in the particular art or craft they teach and who have also had a workshop training. The staff also includes a science, an art, and an English master.

The following schools work with the definite object of preparing boys for entering specific industries. In the Shoreditch Technical Institute, which has a great reputation as a technical school for the furniture trades and is one of the oldest established of the London trade schools, the maintenance grant is £6 for the first year, £10 for the second, and £15 for the third year, the increase in value from year to year being for the purpose of meeting the increased temptation on the part of the parents to make the boy a wage-earner. The course for furniture and cabinet making at this school consists of English subjects, arithmetic and mensuration, geometry and geometrical drawing, freehand and model drawing, design work associated with wood and metal, modeling in clay, elementary experimental science, workshops and technical drawing, technology of woods and metals, and a large amount of bench work for the use of woodwork and metal working tools. The time allotted to the theoretical and practical workshop lessons is roughly equal to that allotted to the English, mathematical, and science subjects. This school prepares boys to enter the furniture and woodwork trades as cabinet makers, carpenters, joiners, shop fitters, pattern makers, turners, wood carvers, or trade draughtsmen.

In the Central School of Arts and Crafts, which is far and away the finest school of this type in England, there is a special day department to prepare boys to enter some branch of the silversmithing trade or kindred crafts in silversmiths', goldsmiths', or jewelers' work as tracers, engravers, mounters, draughtsmen, etc. Next session there will also be a book-production school in this building, which will give suitable training for boys entering the printing and bookbinding trades. In this school it has been arranged that at the end of the first year the boy shall be apprenticed to firms of good standing, and the time spent in the school after the boy is fourteen years of age will count as part of the period of apprenticeship. The course of instruction will extend over three years, from thirteen to sixteen.

Another interesting school also under the control of the Council is the Brixton School of Building which prepares boys for the building trades and allied professions. In this school boys may qualify as bricklayers, masons, plumbers, painters, architects, builders, and surveyors.

Another trade school which is doing excellent pioneer work is housed in the Borough Polytechnic. In this school the boys have the advantage of working in well-equipped laboratories and workshops used by adult students in the evening classes. This school, while not preparing for any specific trade, gives a general training extending over three years for boys entering the various branches of the engineering trade or any kind of metal work. It is probable that schools of a similar kind will be established in other polytechnics in which there is sufficient accommodation for a school of this type during the day time.

At present most of the trade scholarships for boys are awarded in engineering, silversmithing, bookbinding, furniture and cabinet making, carriage building, wood carving, and for the building trades.

The scholarships awarded to girls are for trade dressmaking, laundry work, upholstery, ladies' tailoring, waistcoat making, corset making, millinery, designing and making of ready-made clothing, and photography. As a rule, trade scholarships for girls are for a period of two years with a maintenance grant of £8 for the first year and £12 for the second year, in addition to free education.

The most important day trade school for girls is the London County Council's school at Bloomsbury. Here there are about one hundred and fifty girls in the first or second year of the course of training. The subjects taken at this school are corset making, dressmaking, ladies' tailoring, millinery, and photography. In all departments there are trade teachers. A very special feature is the art instruction at this school, which has for its object not only the acquiring of technical skill in the drawing required in various departments, but the general cultivation of a refined artistic sense, which is of much importance in all grades of trade work. Two-thirds of the time of this school is devoted to trade instruction and the remainder to the general education of the pupil, with special reference to the requirements of each trade. The subjects of instruction in general education include English, arithmetic, drawing, hygiene, and physical exercises. The school is open five days a week from 9 A. M. to 12:45 P. M. and from 1:45 to 5 P. M.

It is not necessary to enter into any further description of the trade schools for girls as they are based in almost every particular very largely upon the model of the Ecole Professionnelle of Paris, with the exception that in Paris maintenance grants are very rarely given and in London a very large proportion of the girls in each school are scholarship holders.

The fees for the trade schools are very low so that candidates who are unable to obtain scholarships may attend at very small cost, and in many cases where candidates have acquitted themselves creditably at the examination they are allowed free places at the schools though they may have failed to obtain scholarships which carry with them maintenance grants.

In order to insure that trade scholarships are given only to children of parents who are unable to maintain their children at school without assistance, no candidate is eligible whose parents or guardians are in receipt of an income which exceeds £160 a year from all sources. In order to prevent scholarship funds being wasted, the awards are conditional on the candidates passing a satisfactory probationary period of three months at the trade school with no payment for maintenance but simply free tuition, and if at the end of the period of probation an unsatisfactory report on the scholar is received, the scholarship is withdrawn. The parents or guardians of scholars are, moreover, required to sign a declaration that they intend the scholars to enter the trade in which they have received training during the tenure of their scholarships. These safeguards work very satisfactorily and the result is that a very large percentage of scholarship winners find permanent employment in the trades for which they have been prepared.

It will be interesting to hear in the discussion on this paper why it is that in Canada, the United States, Germany, and to a lesser extent France, it is possible to secure good attendance at trade schools without the assistance of maintenance scholarships.

As stated above, the decay of the apprenticeship system has been an important factor in necessitating the establishment of trade schools in which boys or girls may become sufficiently skilful to enable them to enter with intelligence into any department of the workshop in which they may be placed. The trade school, moreover, has a distinct advantage over the old system of apprenticeship for the following reasons:

1. The supervision in a well-equipped trade school is generally of a much more efficient order than even that of a well-ordered workshop.

2. Culture subjects are not neglected, and consequently the general education of the boys or girls is continued in a manner suitable to the trade for which they are preparing.

3. In the apprenticeship system there is a natural tendency for the apprentice to become attached to some special department of the work to the serious neglect of others.

4. In following out a definite curriculum under a well-arranged time-table there is very little waste of time, and the balance of theoretical and practical work is properly maintained.

5. The work of a trade school is generally governed by a consultative committee of experts who are to a large extent responsible for the education of the students being carried on under the best trade conditions.

6. The presence of trade experts with experience of teaching, who are always at hand in the workshop and able to solve any difficulties which may arise, means an enormous saving of time as compared with the case of the apprentice who has to wait the convenience of the foreman for the solution of difficulties.

It thus happens that the boy who has had a continuous course of instruction in a good trade school for a couple of years may have acquired as much skill and knowledge as one who has worked for four years under the conditions attached to an apprenticeship.

Of recent years there has been an enormous advance in London in the establishment of trade schools and in the facilities offered to students of all grades who are anxious to enter the various trades.

The movement with regard to trade schools would have been doomed to failure if employers had not realized the great value of the course of instruction received. The result is that there is no difficulty in finding employment for those who have satisfactorily passed through a full course of training, and it is generally found that in periods of depression the more skilled students from the trade schools retain their employment when others are dismissed.

A very important development in connection with trade schools is the establishment of "Voluntary After Care Committees," the members of which interest themselves in the scholars at the trade schools and take an interest in them after they have been successfully placed in workshops. A committee of this kind is of extreme value, as it can obtain information as to the conditions of work in the various shops and can give valuable assistance to those who are seeking employment, and, moreover, where short periods of apprenticeship are arranged it can see that under the conditions of the indentures the interests of the boys and girls are safeguarded.

A most important element in the success of the trade schools is the alliance of the school with the trade by means of the expert consultative committee. The arrangements which have been found to work very smoothly in London are based on the following regulations:

1. A consultative committee of trade experts shall consist of an equal number of:

a) Representatives of the Council to be selected as far as possible from well-known experts in the subject concerned, or persons of experience in the administration of technical education.

b) Representatives of the trade, one-half of whom shall be representatives of the employers and one-half of the employees.

2. The representatives of the employers and employees shall be appointed on the respective recommendations of the leading associations of employers and trade-unions of the industry concerned.

3. The chairman of the consultative committee shall be nominated by the Council from among the Council's representatives.

4. The consultative committee shall act solely in an advisory capacity.

It will be seen by the above regulations that the functions of the consultative committee are nominally advisory only, but, as a matter of fact, committees in dealing with the proposals of the consultative committees give great weight to their well-considered decisions, and unless this were done it is highly probable that the business men holding important positions, who now serve on the consultative committees, would cease to act.

An important point arises in regard to the trade school, and that is as to the ultimate effect that a general intimate connection with trades may have upon the artistic side of the trade-school work, the standard of taste which prevails in many trades being very far from ideal and the general conditions not being altogether conducive to the development of the artistic faculty;

of the craftsman. It is a matter of extreme importance that this danger should be carefully watched and provision be made to provide facilities and opportunities for the free artistic development of the persons engaged in the various crafts. The great safeguard against such a downward tendency is in the work of the fine arts, and arts and crafts schools where the attendance at classes is not in any way restricted to people engaged only in a trade or industry. These schools, however, give an artistic training, and in the case of arts and crafts schools also provide practical teaching of some of the crafts in properly fitted workshops. The majority of the classes in these schools, however, are untrammeled by commercial or trade considerations and are, therefore, enabled to work out high ideals and to serve a most useful purpose in assisting to lead and cultivate the public taste and to give a knowledge of and create the desire for beautiful things. In fact they may largely be regarded, to some extent at any rate, as culture classes. It is useless making beautiful things unless there is an appreciative public.

In connection with these schools there is an excellent scholarship scheme by which promising artistic material may be given every facility for development under favorable conditions without financial embarrassment. Some of the scholarships thus open for competition are tenable at the most renowned art schools in London.

In addition to the full-time trade schools there are many polytechnics and technical schools in London working in conjunction with employers of labor in connection with the part-time education of certain grades of their employees. Thus boys at the Royal Arsenal at Woolwich, for example, attend for instruction at given times at the Woolwich Polytechnic, all expenses being borne by the War Office. Similarly the apprentices in the engineering workshops of the South Western Railway Company attend day classes at the Battersea Polytechnic.

In connection with the silversmithing trades, in addition to free education for selected apprentices, bursaries are granted by the London County Council at the rate of 8 *d.* an hour for time spent in technical instruction at special day classes in connection with the silversmiths' craft. These bursaries cover traveling expenses and the apprentices' loss of time from their work. Arrangements of this kind are capable of unlimited extension.

In conclusion another point should be made in connection with this subject, and that is the admirable provision made in all parts of London for evening classes in polytechnics and similar institutions in connection with the various trades. These classes are strictly limited to students who are already engaged in the trade, and are taught by teachers who hold important positions in their craft. The enthusiasm with which thousands of young artisans after a long day's work will attend for theoretical and practical instruction in the scientific principles of their trades under skilled craftsmen is one of the most pleasing features in London education.

THE FINE AND INDUSTRIAL ARTS IN ELEMENTARY SCHOOLS, GRADES II AND III

WALTER SARGENT
The University of Chicago

Children who attend schools where instructors encourage drawing and constructive work as an everyday means of expression usually gain remarkable facility during the first year in setting forth their ideas by these means. Through their own invention and the suggestions of the teacher and of their fellow-pupils, they gain command of a wide variety of graphic symbols and simple constructive processes. Expression by means of illustration and construction becomes a matter of course and is carried on with comparative ease.

A change in attitude toward the results is apparent, however, as the children grow older. They soon cease to be wholly satisfied with manual expression as a mere activity without regard to the quality of the product. When during the first year in school the child's impulse to produce something had found an outlet in lines or shapes, the crudity of the result seldom interfered with his exultation as he displayed his production, or caused him to pause before he proceeded to his next attempt. In Grades II and III the product as a product seems to make an impression on the children and gain importance in their estimation. They show indications of caring for the truth of the representation and the quality of the construction, and wish greater knowledge and more adequate means for carrying out their ideas. This newly awakened desire is illustrated by such instances as the announcement of a child who was attempting to represent a ship at sea, that he was going to find some pictures of ships in order that he might know more definitely how the prow of a ship was shaped so he could draw his as it should be. Children who were making nature drawings inquired how to make the bulbs look "round," how to make some leaves look as if they were behind others, how to paint a white narcissus on white paper.

This realization of the need of data in order to represent adequately, and of knowledge of how to put material together if the product is to be satisfactory, offers opportunity to give instruction which the children desire for immediate use and which at the same time enriches their ideas and extends their knowledge of shapes, materials, and processes, and is the guiding suggestion for methods of teaching during these two years.

Based largely on this suggestion, work of the following general character along the lines of representation, construction, and design is recommended as appropriate for children during the second and third years in school.

Representation.—The freedom and facility already gained in drawing make possible a more adequate graphic expression, and the interest of the children in the quality of the results makes worth while a more careful study of objects than was valuable during the first year. A somewhat intensive study of a few typical things conducted by devoting a series of lessons to each, for the purpose of enabling the children to draw these particular things well, is especially adapted to these grades. Such study frees the drawing from some of its crudity and begins the kind of observation which should result later in correct impressions and the ability to record them with some degree of accuracy. Children at this age progress rapidly when they work for several consecutive lessons upon the same topic, expressing it each time in a different way.

For example, if the subject under consideration is a house, after the children have done their best in representing it, attention may be called to particular and significant points: for instance, the desirability that the sides of a house stand vertically. They should examine the houses they are drawing to see if any of them lean. They readily become interested in this geometric relation and will work earnestly over houses on paper and blackboard, in the endeavor to make the sides of the house and its doors, windows, and chimneys exactly vertical. They are then eager to draw villages in which every house stands upright and where fences, poles, etc., are in proper position.

Later they may study houses and pictures of houses to see how gables are shaped, how doors and windows are placed, how chimneys join roofs, etc. They may cut pictures of houses from paper or trace them, and by actual muscular movements over the shapes, gain a clearer perception of them. They may cut patterns for the construction of houses in paper or cardboard and may build houses in the sandbox, which shall embody the ideas thus far gained.

If the material out of which the house is constructed is of particular interest, as in the case of a log house, the problem of learning how to represent this becomes a topic for study.

Again, if the subject for illustration is a bird, the first drawing may be followed by a study of the shape of the bird's head, the way his feet are placed upon the ground, the angle at which he stands. The bird may be drawn on paper, modeled in clay, cut from paper, painted or drawn in color. Pictures may be collected illustrating the bird in various positions and activities, and some of these may be traced and cut out. After a child has gained what he can from observation and his progress in representing a given object seems to have reached its limit for the time, the tracing of good pictures of the object often gives a fresh impulse to his expression. The tendency of tracing when not used with discrimination to become a hindrance to original observation has often prevented teachers from availing themselves of its great value as an occasional stimulation.

After a few lessons the children master the general shape and characteristics of the bird so they can illustrate any story which admits of interpretation in terms of that bird and its activities, and the drawings are informed with all the details and data gained in the several steps.

The interest of the children increases with successive lessons if each presents some new phase. There is a familiar background to which to refer new elements. At first the children are likely to make their drawings much alike. After absorbing items of detail from pictures and objects their productions show great variety and a marked advance in definiteness of shape, correctness of general proportions, and expressiveness of character.

The important advantage of the cumulative effect of a number of consecutive lessons on the same topic is often overlooked, and as a result drawing frequently fails to show definite progress and either ceases to interest or becomes so much a matter of superficial facility that children miss the stimulation that comes with a measurably thorough mastery of a subject. Advancement in ability to draw seems to become evident, not at first in gradual increase of power to draw anything that may be presented, but in learning how to draw one thing after another and thus accumulating a graphic vocabulary.

The interest that is evident when a group of children work together on a single topic, developing the description as they proceed, is a factor that should be utilized. For example, when an illustration of some topic in which the children are interested is started on the board, all are generally enthusiastic in contributing a share to the result. Such topics as are suggested by the school work or outside interests, such as a farm, a city street, a wharf, a market, a harvest field, etc., are excellent. The children show great resourcefulness in composing the scene and offering additional material, and after the first rapid sketching is done they are ready to collect data for correction and improvement of the results.

Constructive work.—Part of the constructive work may with advantage parallel the work in drawing, so that the same things which are being represented in two dimensions may also be constructed in three. That such a relation enriches the value of both means of expression is shown by the increased understanding of form reflected by the drawings, when the same objects are being constructed, and by the amount of data and suggestion which is secured by drawing and embodied in the construction. Such problems as houses, furniture, and the various articles related to studies, games, and occupations, are continually presenting themselves and offer an abundant list of topics.

In most manual problems drawing and construction are both involved in the final result.

In addition to free, illustrative construction, these grades should also present the first steps in well-planned work which requires careful measurements and exact delineation of patterns. This means the beginning of working drawings. During the first year most of the paper cutting that demanded an approach to exact following of a predetermined shape was based upon outlines furnished to the children, such as pictures and patterns. Now the children should begin to make their own patterns and should come to appreciate the value of the rule as an instrument for determining measurements and straight lines with precision. It is not difficult to awaken and maintain interest in the accurate use of the rule if the problems presented involve at first only a few lines and measurements of even inches and later half and quarter inches. The rule used by the children during these years should not contain smaller divisions than quarter inches and the children should be shown how to manipulate it and should be interested in maintaining a relatively high standard of accuracy whenever the work departs from freehand expression and requires an instrument of accuracy.

Bookmarks, tags, weather signals, flags, pin wheels, covers, envelopes and folders for school work, illustrative diagrams such as plans for school gardens, and other projects of this sort give opportunity for planning objects by simple patterns in the flat.

It is important that during these two years a few fundamental geometric relations should be thoroughly apprehended by repeated use. The relations of vertical, horizontal, and parallel are involved in such drawing and construction as the house already suggested. The right angle should also be mastered, so it can be drawn freehand in any position.

In addition to the subjects involving these relations some drill work repeated at frequent intervals is necessary to insure the complete mastery of these relations and ease and confidence in using them. In the third grade such drill may be undertaken with good results. For example, when lines are drawn on the board at various angles, children are interested in trying to draw other lines forming right angles with these, and in testing the results with a cardboard square, or in drawing lines parallel to the given lines and testing their equidistance. They also like to accompany their freehand drawing and construction with occasional drawings of vertical lines on the board, holding the chalk at arm's length and producing the line slowly and steadily to a length of two or three feet and then testing the direction with a plumb line. Horizontal lines and lines to represent given slants should also receive attention. It is of great importance that these geometric relations should be thoroughly mastered so that they may be used with facility. The mind has then an established sense of fundamental relations and a standard for estimating and comparing variations from these.

Design.—The general lines of work suggested for Grade I continue through Grades II and III with higher standards of accomplishment. The problems involve planning simple forms to be constructed and decorating them with suitable ornamentation: such objects as holiday greetings and souvenirs, book marks, valentines, covers for school papers, etc. The decorations may consist of units and borders which the children readily invent by placing pegs and lentils, afterward selecting and drawing the best of these arrangements. The invention of the children at this age can easily be directed along the lines of good types of design by the example of the teacher. Leadership which, by example, directs inventive activities along right lines at first, obviates the necessity of much of that correction and verbal instruction which sometimes seems necessary later if poor arrangements have become fixed in the mind.

The children should continue the rhythmic drawing of borders by repeating units to a time count corresponding somewhat to that of music. After the experience of the first year they are usually able to use more difficult units, to draw them with excellent spacing, and to use them in making decorative borders and simple surface patterns upon the forms they have constructed, employing no other measurements than those rapidly estimated by the eye as the drawing proceeds.

During the second year the children should learn to discriminate hues of color more exactly than in the first year, and should be able to pick out objects the colors of which are more nearly like the samples shown by the teacher. In the third year they may with advantage learn to distinguish color values. The word value is used here to denote the relation of a color to light and dark. In this significance of the term the value of a color changes as the color grows lighter or darker. For example, if white is mixed with green the resulting lighter green is higher in value. If black instead of white is mixed with it the resulting darker color is lower in value than the original green. Children may collect or be furnished with an abundance of color samples and, after selecting those of one color hue, e. g., blue, arrange these so as to form a series of different values, ranging from light blues which are almost white to those which approach black. In a similar manner they may arrange value scales of other colors. Any great degree of accuracy in these arrangements should not be demanded, nor should the number of steps between the lightest and darkest be so many that the children cannot readily perceive the change from one step to another. Five steps between lightest and darkest are sufficient to illustrate fairly well the effects of various values, while seven are as many as can be appreciated by most children in these grades.

Many of the designs made by the children call for color combinations and give opportunity to use the effects of different steps of value in pleasing combinations.

Young children can use water colors to excellent advantage, but during the first three years about all the color expression that is valuable can be secured by collections of samples and by the use of colored crayons. The disadvantages of postponing the use of water colors till the fourth year are probably more than compensated for by the fresh stimulation from the introduction of a new medium at that time, and by the fact that the results obtained by primary children in water colors, which are admired by adults, are almost always chance effects caused by the fluid character of the medium and were unforeseen by

Missing Page

Missing Page

Missing Page

Missing
Page

Missing Page

Missing Page

Missing Page

Missing Page

Missing Page

Missing Page

Missing Page

Missing Page

Missing Page

Missing Page

of what the child thinks about and does, and also be something which he takes pleasure in doing. The moment the joy of work ceases, that moment the artistic element ceases also. "Art is the joy of the workman in his work." Ruskin states that he who works with his hands only is a mechanic; he who works with hands and head is an artisan; and he who works with head, hands, and heart is an artist. Therefore the art work of the child must be, like the dance or the song or the story, a joyful output, stimulated by the more practical work of the day. The whole being is then concentrated—feeling, mind, and body.

As has been said, the child's drawings are akin to his speech,[3] and so the forms he makes are akin to the words of his speech; fragmentary and detached in their relation to each other, but very vitally united to the child's life. It would be as easy and practical to teach him the letters *c a t* before allowing him to say "cat," as it would be to teach him type-forms before allowing him to make a life-form. He talks spontaneously of the things which interest him, and he draws or models just as spontaneously those things he cares about. He draws these, just as he speaks of them, hoping his ideas may be understood; and he should be encouraged to draw or model, just as he is encouraged to talk—for the sake of expressing an idea clearly, never to show off his skill.[4] *All* criticism here should tend to lead him to discover wherein his expression is not clear or complete; it should help him

[3] "In fact, drawing for a very young child is so thoroughly a language that we may be wrong in considering it in any degree an art expression. One is startled to see how easily a child of this age (under six) declares a mass of meaningless lines to be a man, a horse or an engine."—Barnes, *Child-Study and Art Education.*

Messonier thought drawing the basis of primary education. He said: "It is the only language which can express all things. An outline, even if ill-shaped, conveys a more exact idea of a thing than the most harmonious sentences in the world. Drawing is absolute truth, and the language of truth should be taught everywhere."

[4] "Art is interpretation—there must always be an idea to express."

"Wherever art is practiced for its own sake and the delight of the workman is in what he does and produces, instead of what he interprets or exhibits, then art has an influence of the most fatal kind on brain and heart, and if long so pursued issues in destruction both of intellectual power and moral principle; whereas art devoted humbly and self-forgetfully to the clear state-to find out about things and get a better image. For instance, if he draws a man without arms, ask him how the man can put on his hat, etc.; or if he has reached the landscape stage and has placed a horse in the sky, ask him on what the horse stands.

Instead of type-forms preceding the expression of feeling or ideas, it is out of the expression of ideas that type-forms and technique may easily be developed. A child will draw straight lines by the hour to represent a mouse running to its hole, a train moving on the track; or he will draw a square (accurately, too) to represent a policeman going around the block; or a circle round which the children march. Other type-forms, oblongs, triangles, diamonds, etc., are easily produced, if only they are related to an idea which interests the child; in other words, related to those things of which he has experience—father, mother, animals, toys, family occupations, or home utensils. He will draw a line to represent a walk he has taken, placing on either side houses, trees, playmates, or any objects of interest he has passed; and usually both his line of direction and its relation to the objects are true.

Thus form, like words, becomes necessary to the child as a means of expression, not as an abstract, mechanical thing; and skill in modeling or drawing the things he wishes is acquired easily and quickly. Knowledge of size and number also becomes a matter of necessity in the same way. Even an adult will verify his instinctive conception of the number of a chicken's toes, the shape of its body, and the size of its head, if he attempts to draw it, especially from memory. The boy in kindergarten does better as a rule than the adult; for he can draw an engine with a knowledge of the form, size, number, and relation of its parts which sends his cadet-teacher on a tour of inspection.

In the beginning, nothing is more important than the necessity of making the various senses alert and bright by constant and systematic use. The

ment and record of the facts of the universe is always helpful and beneficent to mankind, full of comfort, strength, and salvation."—Ruskin.

"The reason we give instruction in art is that we may familiarize men and women with divine ideas, first as they appear in the representations of those clear-sighted men who have seen them first, and then as they appear in nature itself. In this way we convince them that nature is but the visible, audible, and tangible expression of divine ideas."—Thomas Davidson.

perceptive faculties should be made accurate, the memory correct, the thinking and willing powers strong and true by direct use on things. These capacities and faculties diminish very rapidly for lack of use, and at certain stages the organism refuses to work, and the best impressions possible are dull and fleeting. Mental structure must be made by children coming into contact first hand with things, receiving and assimilating all possible sense impressions, and making all possible movements and reactions.

Therefore when the child is interested in trying to make these objects, it is the time to encourage him in every possible way, or later he will have lost his keen interest.

The derivation of one form from another scarcely seems to have a more conscious place here than would the grammatical construction of his sentences before he had learned words. He tries to seize upon forms as he seizes upon words, because he needs them for a purpose; later he both puts them together and pulls them apart.

The question naturally arises as to the place of decorative art in the kindergarten. If by decorative art is meant the making of borders and patterns, it occupies a very small place.[5] The child loves repetition and rhythm, but if he must labor long and painfully making and placing each unit of his design or border, the object of the work is defeated; he will become bored and tired and hate the work.[6] He certainly should never be set to making "abstract design," for there is no such thing in kindergarten or out. Decorative design means the making of a harmonious pattern in a given space for a given purpose. There are few opportunities for the kindergarten child to practice this, because,

[5] "All of a child's spontaneous drawings before he is six years old are pictorial. Mrs. Maitland found only 5 per cent. of the children at this age drawing geometrical designs and only 3 per cent. using ornaments. In illustrating stories, Barnes found less than 1 per cent. using ornamental forms; Lukens found 2 per cent. using geometrical designs and decoration combined. As we have repeatedly said, drawing is for these young children a language akin to speech."—Barnes, *Child-Study and Art Education.*

[6] "To subordinate a child to type-forms, to things, to the Parthenon, to the practice of decorative design, or even to manual training is *materialism.*

"These things, like the Sabbath, are made for man, for the child, not the child for them. They must be simply his to help him to the best utterances of himself, to sincerity, genuineness, unconsciousness, and power. Imagination is expression; technique is that phase of expression which helps realize more perfectly the vision, the inner image."—John Dewey, *Psychology of Drawing.*

as a rule, the objects he has to decorate demand patterns too small for him to make without physical injury. Even when he does make designs, he is rarely, if ever, prompted by a conscious aesthetic motive, but rather by the same laws of repetition and rhythm which prompt him to dance, skip, or sing. It is obvious in the light of the above, however, that he should choose and arrange his own units to suit his own taste. Moreover, the medium must be such as will give quick results, so that he may be conscious of the product as a whole. "Product and climax" should be near enough together for him to realize the reward of his labors. One form of this kind of decorative design is excellent, however, and that is stringing beads. If the beads are carefully selected as to color and form, the child is particularly happy in making combinations out of them. But even in this simple form of design, when uninteresting units and vulgar colors are given him to combine, it is as harmful as would be the hearing or singing of discordant and vulgar music, particularly because first impressions are so lasting.

A vessel deep man's virgin spirit is:
When the first water poured therein is foul,
The sea might pass and not wash out the stain.

—De Musset.

There is a phase of decorative art which helps arouse aesthetic feeling in the child. This is the putting of things in right places. Setting any object in the room in a suitable and harmonious place; hanging a picture; putting a flower into a vase; arranging a shelf; choosing a cupboard-curtain—all these are matters of decorative art. Little children are striving for balance constantly, and they like regular, symmetrical arrangements. Setting a table furnishes a practical piece of work, out of which may be developed knowledge of form, size and number, as well as some feeling for space-relations and color. Laying out a garden plot leads to absorbingly interesting and widely varied ideas as to form, size, number, and space-relations.

The aim of the art work of the kindergarten seems to be largely confined to the following points: (1) cultivation of imagination and expression; (2) increased power of observation;

(3) some manual training; (4) a slight degree of aesthetic feeling.

As to the four media commonly used for accomplishing the above results, clay, paints, paper, and crayons, clay is perhaps the best for the youngest children; for, in it, solids can be represented as solids, without the confusion which results from having to represent an object of three dimensions on a flat surface. Clay develops the larger muscles, not the finer ones, *if properly handled;* mistakes can quickly be rectified without spoiling the whole; and clay furnishes a natural and easy transition from work in solids to work in the mass on a flat surface; that is, work in high relief, to be followed by work in low relief. This makes an easy step to painting in flat washes, and then the representation of solids on a flat surface. Clay can be utilized in the making of borders (if children are interested in decorating a room). It gives opportunity for quick repetition of any interesting unit, which in turn gives rise to invention and logical thinking on the part of the child. Nothing is better than clay for pictorial or representative work for children of kindergarten age and even younger.

While clay deals particularly with form, painting gives the child a chance to revel in color; and paper-cutting combines both color and form. The latter has its dangers, but may be successfully used in the hands of a skilful teacher.

The use of crayons (large ones) should be encouraged constantly,[7] and it is the chief business of the teacher to watch each individual child and develop his power to see more accurately. This will not be done by placing objects before him for him to copy,[8] but by having him work from memory after he has become

[7] "During the cataloguing stage from two to six a child should do a great deal of drawing. He should draw figures on large surfaces, which should be so placed as to encourage activity of the central muscle masses. The subjects should be men, women, babies, animals, toys, and the like. Expression being the important thing at this period, all criticism should be made subordinate and incidental enough, so as not to discourage effort or weaken zest.

"All art development at this period is a by-product of general doing and thinking, as it must largely always be."—Barnes, *Child-Study and Art Education.*

[8] "But the child is interested in objects only from the standpoint they play

familiar with the object, has felt of it, talked about it, knows its uses, its life, its resemblance to other objects in color, form, size, etc. Then after he has made his drawing, the teacher can stimulate his curiosity by skilful questioning to go back to the object for a more correct impression.

It is impossible to separate art work from the other activities of the kindergarten. Everything which aids the child's vision, or which increases his artistic ability; everything which calls forth his choice and use of color, form and arrangement, or stimulates into action his power of expression, belongs to the child's realm of art. The art work of the kindergarten is by no means confined to the use of clay, paint, paper, crayon, or beads. Like the warp of the weaver, it is intimately connected with the whole pattern.

So much for the aims of the kindergarten art work. Now, as to method, there is but one thing to be said, and that must needs be said with emphasis: All depends upon the teacher. If there is one thing more than another which Froebel insists upon, it is that the teacher shall be what she expects the child to be.

in his life, their use, their function, their purpose or service. Hence there is crudity, lack of proportion, lack of qualities of structure and form, hence symbolism serves as a sign, not as a conveyance. It serves to stimulate, to vivify; its main value is reactive, freeing the child and giving him hold upon his own imagery. It must first be judged from this standpoint, its liberating power.

"But the reaction ought to go to the point of forming a new mode of vision on the part of the child, and allowing this new mode of experience to control his motor expression; otherwise, after a certain point is passed, slovenly habits both of seeing and moving are acquired.

"The first consideration is the doing, the use; after use comes method, the how of doing. Now method must exist not for its own sake, but for better self-expression, fuller and more interested doing.

"Hence these two points; technique must grow out of free imaginative expression; it must grow up within and come out of such expression; it must always and at once be turned back into such imaginative expression.

"The object is meant to fulfil a function, to stimulate to look again; an image is formed, then the movement is controlled by that new vision. Thus technique arises normally. When the technique is mechanical, there is no meaning, no idea to it, and there results this psychological evil that the imagery is as uncontrolled as before; no new mode of seeing is acquired. It is so completely an abstract that it ceases to be an element of the original object and not a universal one at that."—John Dewey, *Psychology of Drawing.*

In this case, it means to be alive to the world of beauty in which she lives, and be able in a fair degree to represent it. In every other mode of expression, such as walking, talking, singing, or dancing, the child has ample opportunity for imitation. The same thing is true in the industrial activities; but almost never does he see anyone modeling, painting, or drawing. When the teacher herself has had her own aesthetic sense awakened and her power of expression trained, she will then, and then only, be able to direct the child's first efforts.

EDITORIAL NOTES

Dr. Harris

The death of Dr. W. T. Harris, former commissioner of education of the United States, gives us all reason to pause in the business of life and pay respect to one who exerted a large influence in American education. Dr. Harris first came into general notice as the central figure of a group of devoted students of Hegelian philosophy in St. Louis. At the same time that he and his associates were studying philosophy he was attracting the attention of school men by his aggressive organization of the public schools of that city. He wrote and edited many books; some of them were books for children, some were treatises on philosophy. Among the largest of the publication enterprises which he undertook was the editing of *Webster's Dictionary*. He was a pioneer in his support of the kindergarten, and of manual training. He was always open to all that was strong in the newer education.

In the office of commissioner he brought together the elaborate reports which have made him known wherever educational interests are regarded.

In the latter years of his life he laid aside the active duties of public office and retired to his literary work. Friends have sought his council and public gatherings of school men have extended to him no uncertain welcome. He has left a great name behind, and more than that, he has left behind many large contributions to American intellectual life.

The Contents of the Book

The appearance of a book entitled *Psychology and the Teacher* from the pen of a writer so well known as Professor Münsterberg is sure to attract the attention of teachers in all parts of the country. The book is made up of three sections. The first deals with the ethical aim of education and discusses in a broad way some of the general questions of values in human life. The conclusion of this part of the book is that education should improve the individual, physically, socially, and mentally. The second part of the book takes up certain general psychological problems, such as the relation between mind and brain, the nature of attention, association, habit, imitation, and other mental processes and capacities. This is the psychological part of the volume. The third part discusses courses of instruction and certain general matters of organization. In this part many conclusions of the author with regard to how schools should be organized are set forth in definite and emphatic terms. One final descriptive statement may be added: all this discussion is completed within the compass of 325 pages. The special topics must accordingly be treated in the most summary fashion and many of the conclusions must be stated without elaborate justification.

The book is interesting as an indication of Professor Münsterberg's attitude. Some years ago he was looked upon as the arch-skeptic, opposed to educational psychology and all mixing of science with the work of instruction. He tells us now that all he asked for at that time was caution. He wished to stimulate investigation by his skepticism. He now rejoices that the serious workers saw his subtle motive and went actively about the development of educational psychology. The toilers have been successful in searching out many truths, and now the skeptic has turned reviewer and epitomizer and has summarized all this and mixed it with a little ethics and a little advice as to how schools should be conducted; and thus has given to the world a book on psychology and the teacher.

The Author's Attitude

Some years ago Professor Münsterberg criticized the then current discussions of brain physiology and education on the ground that the educational applications had no roots in the physiological theories. We turn therefore with greatest interest to his chapter on "Mind and Brain." It discusses such questions as the causal or parallelistic relation between mind and body. These are problems in metaphysics; they are not very actively discussed, even by technical psychologists. What teachers need and what they want today is some concrete description of nervous organization.

Metaphysics as a Substitute for Psychology

Assume, however, that we have read up to the section of the book which deals with applications. Here one feels at every step that the conclusions run far beyond the data presented anywhere in the book. Thus, turning at random, one reads such pronouncements as these: "It is a psychological mistake to begin too early with physics. The mental equipment for botany and zoölogy and physical geography is much earlier at the disposal of the child" (p. 288). Or again on the next page, "The overestimation of the perception as against the conception, is one of those superficialities of pedagogy which are in harmony with many features of our time, but which cannot be excused and certainly should not be supported by true psychology." Perhaps these statements are true, possibly not—at all events they are not proven. Where is the evidence that the child should study erosion before he studies the mechanics of weight and motion? Where is the evidence that our education is "short" on *the* conception?

Dogma as a Substitute for Experiment

During the period of Professor Münsterberg's observation of the development of educational psychology two changes have taken place which are not recorded in this book. Teachers do not rely as much as they used to on dicta about physics and other like matters. Teachers are today trying out these questions and they are more interested in experiments in education than in anyone's opinion. Secondly, the science of educational psychology has passed into the stage of concrete analyses of

Experimental Education

the mental processes of school children. We are not talking now about association and attention in general terms. We have a body of very definite material on writing and reading and modern languages. The school problem is not one that any writer can deal with in a few casual observations.

The Book as an Example to Avoid

The book will be a disappointment to some, a stumbling-block to others. It is not a summary of the empirical work which has been done in our field. It is not a body of new results. It is the kind of a book which used to be written when Professor Münsterberg first began to break away from his skeptical forebodings. It will be read half through by many who know Professor Münsterberg's name and then will go on the shelf with the other psychologies which have not affected educational practice. The progress of the movement toward a science of education is impeded by such books. Let those of us who are at work in the field speak clearly in this matter. We desire an end of advice from those who write in large, vague terms. We know what science is: it is the direct experimental attack upon our school problems. The author who addresses us should show his qualification by making it clear that he knows that we know that education will not change its course one jot, whether he believes in parallelism or causal relation, whether he thinks that physics should follow physical geography or turn up somewhere in its elementary forms in the fifth grade. Educational psychology of the vague general type has been superseded by experimental education, and opinion by carefully analyzed results.

Charles H. Judd

NOTES AND NEWS

The first volume of the *Report of the Commissioner of Education* for the current year was published early in December. This is the earliest date at which the report ever appeared. The directories of superintendents, college officers, and normal-school officers will be of value not merely as historical references, but as practical means of reaching the educational public. The volume also contains a statement of educational progress which is unusually full, especially with reference to movements in the various states of the United States. The reports of a number of commissions in various states are reported in full, and exhibit not merely the legislation actually consummated, but also the grounds on which this legislation was based. The reviews of foreign education are significant in the light which they throw on the problems which are under most vigorous discussion in this country, such, for example, as trade schools, moral training, and broadening of the scope of school activity.

During the Christmas week many educational meetings were in session. One of the very significant meetings which may have escaped the notice of many teachers was the meeting of Section L of the American Association for the Advancement of Science. Section L was organized four years ago for the purpose of taking up in a serious scientific way the study of educational problems. Its presidents have been Commissioner Brown, Professor Dewey, and Dean Russell. Its earlier meetings were devoted to general problems, especially those related to science teaching and to college organization. The meeting which was held in December was somewhat broader in its scope than the earlier meetings. Especial attention was given to the formulation of programmes for scientific investigations. Problems in statistical and experimental treatment of education were outlined very fully, and committees to take up some of these problems were organized.

A new journal bearing the title *The Journal of Educational Psychology* is announced under the editorial management of Messrs. Bell, Seashore, Bagley, and Whipple. The journal is to be published by Williams & Wilkins Co., of Baltimore, and is to contain material on all phases of mental development and experimental education. Journals of this type have been published in Germany for some time. The American journal which is to publish its first number in January certainly should attract the attention of teachers as a very definite contribution to the educational problem from the point of view of psychologists.

BOOK REVIEWS

Practical Nature-Study. By JOHN M. COULTER, JOHN G. COULTER, AND ALICE JEAN PATTERSON. New York: D. Appleton & Co., 1909.

It seems to the reviewer that there are few problems in education today which are more pressing than that of nature-study in the elementary school. Scientific knowledge and the scientific method of thought are playing a very large part in modern life, and they deserve to play a much larger part than they do. At the same time with the growth of cities, a larger and larger proportion of the people are being removed from daily contact with wild nature as it existed in the past—a contact that doubtless meant more educationally than many realize. These conditions make it imperative that the nature-study problem be given serious attention by all who are concerned in general education, for as long as nature-study remains in its present chaotic condition, everyone who thinks seriously about it must admit that the schools are failing to answer a very evident and a very important demand.

This little book written jointly by Dr. John M. Coulter, Dr. John G. Coulter, and Miss Alice Jean Patterson is, to my mind, the most sensible and helpful publication along this line that has yet appeared. It does not claim to be a final solution of the problem, but merely an aid in that direction. It deserves to be widely read and studied and used by teachers and superintendents, and if this is done, a long step will be taken toward giving this important subject the kind of place that it ought to have in the schools.

The book consists of four parts. Part I deals in a general way with different phases of the subject under the following headings: "Nature-Study and Agriculture," "The Training of the Working Teacher," "The Mission of Nature-Study," "The Dangers of Nature-Study," "The Principles of Nature-Study," "The Spirit of Nature-Study," and "The Child and Nature-Study."

The first chapter deals with a subject concerning which many people appear at the present time to be misinformed. We hear much talk about nature-study having proved a failure, and elementary agriculture being a subject worthy to take its place because it is nearer to life. On this point, the authors say: "Elementary agriculture can get no nearer to life than nature-study should, and nature-study aims to get near to a broader if not higher aspect of life than pertains to agriculture alone." In the chapter entitled, "The Mission of Nature-Study" the educative results of nature-study are summed up as follows: "A sustained interest in natural objects and the phenomena of nature; independence in observation and inference; some conception of what an exact statement is; some conception of what constitutes proof." Under the last statement, the authors make the following remarks: "This is the crying need of the men and women of today who make and hold the most impossible connection between cause and effect. It is in this very broad field that charlatanism of every sort flourishes like a noxious weed, and unless this situation is changed through the schools, the dupes will continue to multiply. . . . . Nature-study presents unrivaled opportunity for training in proof, for it is found that a single observation is rarely trustworthy and that additional facts are apt to modify conclusions."

The first chapter in Part II consists of a "Topical Outline by Grades and Seasons," and is the course used at present in the Training School of the Illinois State Normal University. The course is the result of a gradual evolution from a beginning made in 1892 by Dr. Charles A. and Mrs. Lida B. McMurry. Since that time, Professor B. P. Colton, C. W. Whitten, J. P. Stewart, and Miss Alice Jean Patterson have each had a hand in bringing it to its present form. The course has thus been worked out in a practical way under the most favorable circumstances and is one of the most efficient courses in the subject that has yet been arranged. It should be an exceedingly helpful guide to any teacher endeavoring to handle the subject. The second chapter of Part II consists of a series of typical lesson plans which should be very helpful in giving inexperienced teachers the method of procedure.

Part III contains an "Outline in Nature-Study and Elementary Agriculture for Rural Schools" and twenty-six other short chapters on various topics mostly designed to give the teacher of nature-study a necessary fund of information and further to illustrate the method of attack. It is in some of these chapters that certain material is introduced which is, to my mind, of questionable value. An illustration of this is the chapter entitled, "Selecting, Judging, and Storing of Seed Corn." Selecting seed corn is neither science nor nature-study, but rather an art which rests on science. The crucial question in this whole matter is: "Shall we teach the arts in the schools, or shall we teach the science which underlies the arts?" If the chapter had been headed "Heredity," much of the same material could have been used and the same practical benefit derived, but the goal would have been a principle, a general notion with many applications, instead of a particular notion of how to do one particular thing for which many of the children will have no use in actual life.

Part IV of the book is not essentially different in its nature from Part III except that the material suggested is adapted to the upper grades.

I predict for the book on the whole a very wide influence, and believe that it will lead to a careful observation of the work that is now being done in the Training School of the Illinois State Normal University, which, I judge, largely inspired the writing of the book.

J. L. Pricer

Urbana, Ill.

Changing Conceptions of Education. By Ellwood P. Cubberley. "Riverside Educational Monographs." New York: Houghton Mifflin Co., 1909. Pp. 70. Price 35 cents.

In the introduction to this work it is stated: "In these days when some of our educational workers are doubting the power of educational history to give practical guidance to the teacher, it is a particular pleasure to offer this illuminating historical treatment of the problem of educational reconstruction." The material is presented in three sections: I, "Changes in the Nature of Our Life;" II, "Changes in the Conception of the School;" III, "New Conceptions and Present Tendencies."

The first part restates the topics relating to the transition from predominantly rural to predominantly urban conditions, and leads up to the "problem of providing a proper environment and of utilizing this excess leisure time in profitable training—one of the most serious as well as one of the most difficult problems now before us." Next are shown the various periods in the development of the American school, and an excellent summary is given of the important new factors in the function of the school. The third section shows some of the probable steps about to be taken. "To convey to the next generation the knowledge and the accumulated experience of the past is not its only function. It must equally prepare the future citizen for the tomorrow of our complex life."

FRANK A. MANNY

KALAMAZOO, MICH.

Education for Efficiency. By CHARLES W. ELIOT. "Riverside Educational Monographs." New York: Houghton Mifflin Co., 1909. Pp. 58. Price 35 cents.

The editor of this series states in the introduction that "the measures for the hourly judgment of teaching" "are to be found in those qualities of the human personality which have an abiding worth under the tests of our civilization. They are the measures of personal culture and social efficiency. The teaching that fosters these ends succeeds; the teaching which neglects them fails." The social factor, according to the author, appears in "effective power for work and service during a healthy and active life" and in the fact that "training for power of work and service should be the prime object of education throughout life, no matter in what line the trained powers of the individual may be applied."

These ends toward efficiency are considered under "The Training of the Senses and the Care of the Body;" "The Imparting of the Habit of Quick and Concentrated Attention;" "The Cultivation of the Critical Discernment of Beauty and Excellence in Things and in Words and Thoughts, in Nature and in Human Nature;" "The Judicial Faculty for the Wise Employment of Liberty;" "The Passion for Truth or the Fact as Distinguished from the Guess or Imagination;" "The Native Power of Some Enthusiasm or Devotion."

The second section is entitled "The New Definition of the Cultivated Man." Arnold's and Emerson's modifications of earlier ideas of cultivation, the inclusion by one of science and by the other of manual labor are accepted, although President Eliot finds it necessary to include athletic sports in the term manual labor. Further qualifications which have received increased emphasis during the last hundred years are "character," a combination of "the knowledge of literature with knowledge of the 'stream of the world,'" acquaintance with those parts of "the infinite human store" which enable a man "with his individual personal qualities to deal best and sympathize most with other human beings," "new varieties of constructive imagination." These elements give us the "man of quick perception, broad sympathies, and wide affinities; responsive, but independent; self-reliant, but deferential; loving truth and candor, but also moderation and proportion; courageous, but gentle; not finished, but perfecting."

FRANK A. MANNY

KALAMAZOO, MICH.

BOOKS RECEIVED

AMERICAN BOOK COMPANY, NEW YORK

Practical Agriculture. By JOHN W. WILKINSON. Illustrated. Cloth. Pp. 383. $1.00.

Physical Laboratory Manual for Secondary Schools. Revised Edition. By CHARLES F. ADAMS. Cloth. Illustrated. Pp. 192. $0.60.

T. Y. CROWELL & CO., NEW YORK

Crowell's Shorter French Texts. With Introduction, Notes, and Exercises. General Editor, J. E. MANSION. Cloth. Pp. 55 to 88. $0.25 each. 13 vols.

GINN & CO., BOSTON

Primer. "The Language Readers." By JOHN H. WADE AND EMMA SYLVESTER. Illustrated. Cloth. Pp. 112. $0.20.

First Reader. "The Language Readers." By JOHN H. WADE AND EMMA SYLVESTER. Illustrated. Cloth. Pp. 136. $0.35.

HARPER & BROTHERS, NEW YORK

Decisive Battles of America. Edited by RIPLEY HITCHCOCK. Illustrated. Cloth. Pp. 396. $1.50.

HOUGHTON MIFFLIN CO., BOSTON

Ethical and Moral Instruction in Schools. By GEORGE HERBERT PALMER. Cloth. Pp. 55. $0.35.

JOHN LANE CO., NEW YORK

Mental Discipline and Educational Values. By W. H. HECK. Cloth. Pp. 147.

LAIRD & LEE, CHICAGO

The Standard Guide for Locomotive Engineers and Firemen. By ED. TURNER. Leather. Illustrated. Pp. 198. $0.75.

THE MACMILLAN CO., NEW YORK

The Life and Adventures of Robinson Crusoe. Part I. By DANIEL DEFOE. Edited with Introduction and Notes by CHARLES ROBERT GASTON. Cloth. Pp. 349. $0.25.

The Pupils' Arithmetic Primary Book. Part I. By JAMES C. BYRNES, JULIA RICHMAN, AND JOHN S. ROBERTS. Cloth. Pp. 216. $0.26.

Outlines of General History. By V. A. Renouf. Edited by WILLIAM STARR MYERS. With Maps and Illustrations. Cloth. Pp. 499. $1.30.

The Nature-Study Idea. By L. H. BAILEY. Cloth. Pp. 246. $1.25.

The Pupils' Arithmetic Primary Book. Part II. By JAMES C. BYRNES, JULIA RICHMAN, AND JOHN S. ROBERTS. Cloth. Pp. 218. $0.30.

Selections from the Addresses, Inaugurals, and Letters of Abraham Lincoln. Edited with Introduction and Notes, by PERCIVAL CHUBB. Cloth. Pp. 208. $0.25.

RAND, McNALLY & CO., CHICAGO

The Century Spelling Book: A Book on the Study and Use of Words. By J. B. ASWELL, JOE COOK, AND S. G. GILBREATH. Cloth. Pp. 182. $0.26.

SWAN, SONNENSCHEIN & CO., LTD., LONDON

Hegel's Educational Theory and Practice. By MILLICENT MACKENZIE. With an Introductory Note by J. S. Mackenzie. Cloth. Pp. 192.

TEACHERS COLLEGE, COLUMBIA UNIVERSITY, NEW YORK CITY

The Teaching of Arithmetic. By DAVID EUGENE SMITH. Cloth. Pp. 120.

THE UNIVERSITY OF CHICAGO PRESS, CHICAGO

Child Religion in Song and Story: Walks with Jesus in His Home Country. By GEORGIA LOUISE CHAMBERLIN AND MARY ROOT KERN. Edited by ERNEST D. BURTON. With Songs. Cloth. Pp. 251. $1.38.

The Child and His Religion. By GEORGE E. DAWSON. Cloth. Pp. 124. $0.82.

WORLD BOOK COMPANY, YONKERS-ON-HUDSON, N. Y.

Primer of Sanitation. By JOHN W. RITCHIE. Illustrated by Karl Hassmann. Cloth. Pp. 200. $0.50.

CURRENT EDUCATIONAL LITERATURE IN THE PERIODICALS[1]

IRENE WARREN
Librarian, School of Education, The University of Chicago

ABBOTT, ALDEN H. Non-urban high school in Massachusetts and New York. II. Educa. R. 38:444–58. (N. '09.)

ASHMUN, MARGARET. Library reading in the high school. School R. 17: 701–4. (D. '09.)

BARNES, CLIFFORD W. Moral training through the agency of the public school. Jour. of Educa. (Bost.). 70:533–36. (25 N. '09.)

BENNETT, CHARLES A. Which of the manual arts shall be taught in the schools? Educa. 30:151–57. (N. '09.)

BLACKWOOD, ALEXANDER L. The relation of science to the student and his needs. Educa. Bi-mo. 4:81–87. (D. '09.)

BROWN, J. STANLEY. The moral atmosphere in secondary schools. Relig. Educa. 4:457–61. (D. '09.)

BROWNE, EDITH A. The school lecture. School W. 11:407–9 (N. '09.)

BUCKLEY, SARA CRAIG. Some of the problems that confront us as educators. Educa. Bi-mo. 4:111–16. (D. '09.)

BUTLER, NICHOLAS MURRAY. The Carnegie Foundation as an educational factor. Educa. R. 38:399–405. (N. '09.)

CALDWELL, OTIS W. Natural history in the grades. El. School T. 10: 131–38. (N. '09.)

CARLTON, FRANK T. Educational ideals and values. Relig. Educa. 4: 445–51. (D. '09.)

———. Continuation schools. School W. 11:415–16. (N. '09.)

COPE, HENRY F. Character development through social living. Relig. Educa. 4:401–9. (D. '09.)

[1] *Abbreviations.*—Atlan. Educa. Journ., Atlantic Educational Journal; Educa., Education; Educa. Bi-mo., Educational Bi-monthly; Educa. R., Educational Review; El. School T., Elementary School Teacher; Harp. W., Harper's Weekly; Journ. of Educa. (Bost.), Journal of Education, (Boston); Journ. of Educa. (Lond.), Journal of Education, (London); Psycholog. Clinic, Psychological Clinic; Pub. Lib., Public Libraries; Relig. Educa., Religious Education; R. of R's, The American Review of Reviews; School R., School Review; School W., School World; Sci. Amer. Sup., Scientific American Supplement; Teach. Coll. Rec., Teachers' College Record.

CORNELL, WALTER S. The need of improved records of the physical condition of school children. Psycholog. Clinic. 3:161–63. (N. '09.)

DAVIS, BENJAMIN MARSHALL. Agricultural education: the United States Department of Agriculture. El. School T. 10:101–9. (N. '09.)

DREVER JAMES. The essential elements of a complete school system. Journ. of Educa. (Lond.). 41:748–50. (N. '09.)

———. Education by experience: the physiological basis of success. Sci. Amer. Sup. 68:362–63. (4 D. '09.)

———. Effects of football reform at Columbia. R. of R.'s. 60:730. (D. '08.)

EVANS, HENRY RIDGELY. A survey of educational literature, 1908, 1909. Atlan. Educa. Journ. 5:5, 6, 38. (D. '09.)

EVANS, W. A. The hygiene of schools and school children. Educa. Bi-mo. 4:88–92. (D. '09.)

FISHER, GEORGE J. Character development, social and personal hygiene. Relig. Educa. 4:392–401. (D. '09.)

GREENWOOD, JAMES H. Formal systematic instruction in moral training. Relig. Educa. 4:465–67. (D. '09.)

HANNA, JOHN CALVIN. The moral atmosphere in secondary schools. Relig. Educa. 4:461–65. (D. '09.)

HOBART, FRANCES. Reaching the rural population. Pub. Lib. 14:373–77. (D. '09.)

HOBSON, SARAH M. Diet of school children. Educa. Bi-mo. 4:93–98. (D. '09.)

HODGE, RICHARD MORSE. The content of a Sunday school curriculum. Relig. Educa. 4:430–33. (D. '09.)

JOHNSON, FRANKLIN WINSLOW. The social organization of the high school. School R. 17:655–80. (D. '09.)

KELLY, BEATRICE M. The selection of juvenile books for a small library. Pub. Lib. 14:367–72. (D. '09.)

KILPATRICK, W. H. Date of the first school in New Netherland. Educa. R. 38:380–92. (N. '09.)

KOHN, ALFRED D. Social hygiene in the schools. Educa. Bi-mo. 4:117–21. (D. '09.)

LEE, JOSEPH. The boy who goes to work. Educa. R. 38:325–43. (N. '09.)

MAIN, JOSIAH. The correlation of high school science and agriculture. Educa. 30:135–45. (N. '09.)

MEADER, CLARENCE L. The present educational situation in Russia. School R. 17:681–93. (D. '09.)

MIERS, H. A. The true object of higher education. School W. 11:401–4. (N. '09.)

MITCHELL, G. R. The most popular English works studied in schools. School W. 11:410–12. (N. '09.)

Paddock, Miner H. Holopaideutical teaching. Journ. of Educa. (Bost.). 70:536, 537. (25 N. '09.)

[illegible] S. Chester. Our inherited practice in elementary schools. El. School T. [illegible]48. ([illegible] '[illegible])

———. Professor Sadler on schools in 1929. Jour. of Educa. (Lond.). 41: 747, 748. (N. '09.)

Sabin, Frances E. An experiment in high school publication. School R. 17:713–16. (D. '09.)

St. John, Edward P. Method of school and church in moral and religious education. Relig. Educa. 4:418–23. (D. '09.)

Sandiford, Peter. Report of the English consultative committee on education. Educa. R. 38:393–98. (N. '09.)

Sargent, Walter. Fine and industrial art in elementary schools. Grade I. El. School T. 10:110–20. (N. '09.)

Scott, Colin A. Social education. Educa. 30:163–72. (N. '09.)

Shaw, Albert. College reform and football. R. of R's. 60:724–29. (D. '09.)

Shelly, C. E. The factors of risk and of safety in school athletics. School W. 11:404–7. (N. '09.)

Shepherd, John W. The nature study problem in large cities. Educa. Bi-mo. 4:99–104. (D. '09.)

Siebert, Albert. The development in physical education in Germany. Mind and Body. 16:249–53. (N. '09.)

Skinner, Ernest B. Some hints on the uses of limits in geometry. School R. 17:694–700. (D. '09.)

Smith, Frank Webster. The normal school ideal. III. Educa. 30: 158–62. (N. '09.)

Soares, Theodore G. Religious training for the high-school age. Relig. Educa. 4:451–57. (D. '09.)

Spindler, Frank Nicholas. Psychology of motor development. Educa. 30:146–50. (N. '09.)

Starbuck, Edwin D. Should the impartation of knowledge be a function of the Sunday school? Relig. Educa. 4:424–29. (D. '09.)

Storr, Francis. The art of translation. Educa. R. 38:359–79. (N. '09.)

Struthers, John. The reading of public school children. Relig. Educa. 4: 468–78. (D. '09.)

Taussig, Albert E. The prevalence of visual and aural defects among the public school children of St. Louis County, Mo. Psycholog. Clinic. 3: 149–60. (N. '09.)

Terman, Lewis M. Education against nature: the confessions of a pedagogue. Harp. W. 103:17, 31. (20 N. '09.)

Thomas, Isaac. The Bible as a textbook in the public high school. School R. 17:705–12. (D. '09.)

VAILE, HARRY S. The public library as a factor in public education. Educa. Bi-mo. 4:149–53. (D. '09.)

VANDEWALKER, NINA C. Froebelian literature in kindergarten training. El. School T. 10:121–30. (N. '09.)

VOTAW, CLYDE W. Method of school and church in moral and religious education. Relig. Educa. 4:410–17. (D. '09.)

WAGNER, ALVIN E. Retardation and elimination in the schools of Mauch Chunk Township. Psycholog. Clinic. 3:164–73. (N. '09.)

WHITEHEAD, T. The true function of a pupil-teacher center. School W. 11:413–15. (N. '09.)

WINSHIP, A. E. Are our schools behind the needs of the times? Journ. of Educa. (Bost.). 70:479–81. (11 N. '09.)

WITTICH, GEO. Elements of strength and weakness in physical education as taught in public schools. Mind and Body. 16:254–56. (N. '09.)

WOOLMAN, MARY SCHENCK. The making of a girls' trade school. Teach. Coll. Rec. 10:1–67. (S. '09.)

VOLUME X NUMBER 6

THE ELEMENTARY SCHOOL TEACHER

FEBRUARY, 1910

IS THERE A RELATION BETWEEN THE AMOUNT OF SCHOOLING AND FINANCIAL SUCCESS IN LATER LIFE?

OTHA BOWMAN STAPLES

1. *The problem.*—While unanimity is lacking among the statisticians who have made a study of elimination, or the number of children who drop out of school at various stages, they are all practically agreed that not more than 50 per cent. of all the children enrolled in the schools complete even the eight grades of the elementary school, while only one in ten goes through the high school.

This investigation was undertaken with a view to ascertaining what the actual effect of elimination has been upon a representative group of adults, taking their later financial success as the criterion by which to measure the effect.

2. *The method of investigation.*—Five hundred adults now engaged in productive activity, and representing practically all the activities of a typical community, were asked regarding the date of leaving school and their present income. The data were secured at Lake Geneva, Wis., a town of some 3,800 inhabitants, and situated in an agricultural and dairying region. The five hundred respondents constitute about 75 per cent. of the voting citizens. With few exceptions all the professional and business men of the town were canvassed. The 25 per cent. not canvassed were chiefly common laborers and artisans, which classes are nevertheless the most largely represented in the investigation. As to numbers in various grades of occupation the order would

be: carpenters, day laborers, teamsters, painters, merchants and shop-keepers, stonemasons, plumbers, butchers, clerks, barbers, etc., concluding with six to ten each of physicians, lawyers, and ministers. And in addition to those immediately in the town forty-four farmers living in the adjacent vicinity were canvassed as to the same facts.

With a view to securing as correct data as possible the object of the investigation was explained to each respondent and an

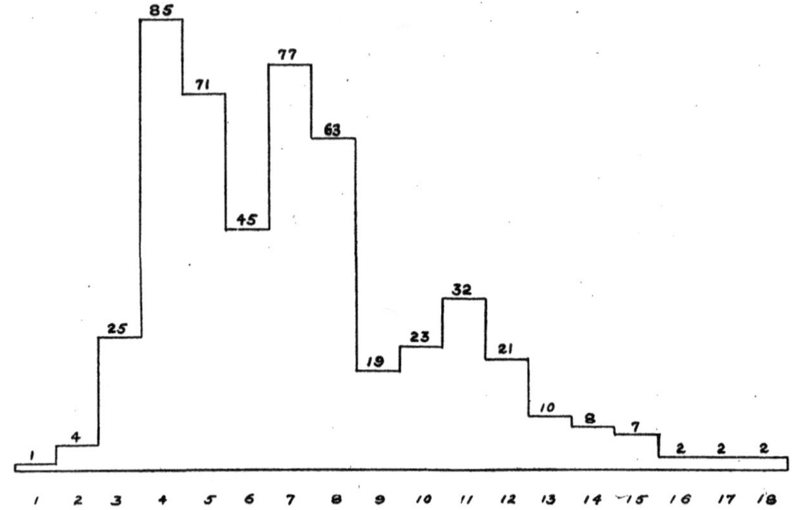

CHART I.—Distribution according to years of school attendance.

effort made to lead each one to feel that he had an opportunity of making a definite contribution to a study which might prove of some value to education in general. This seemed to be sufficient inducement to cause practically all of the respondents to make earnest endeavor to give correct data as to how many years each attended school. A check on the data as to compensation, or incomes, was made through the city treasurer, who is also assistant cashier of the principal bank of the town. Being a native of Lake Geneva, and having held both these positions for several years, he was able to render valuable assistance in checking up the data after it had all been secured.

3. *Explanation of charts.*—The next step was to find a

method of comparing these two sets of data, namely, those relating to school attendance and those relating to income, so as to ascertain how much correlation, if any, exists between them. This was done by means of the charts which follow. Arranging each set of data according to the "normal distribution curve" as represented in Charts I and II we are at once struck with a general resemblance between the two distribution curves, although they differ more or less in details. That is to say, taking up

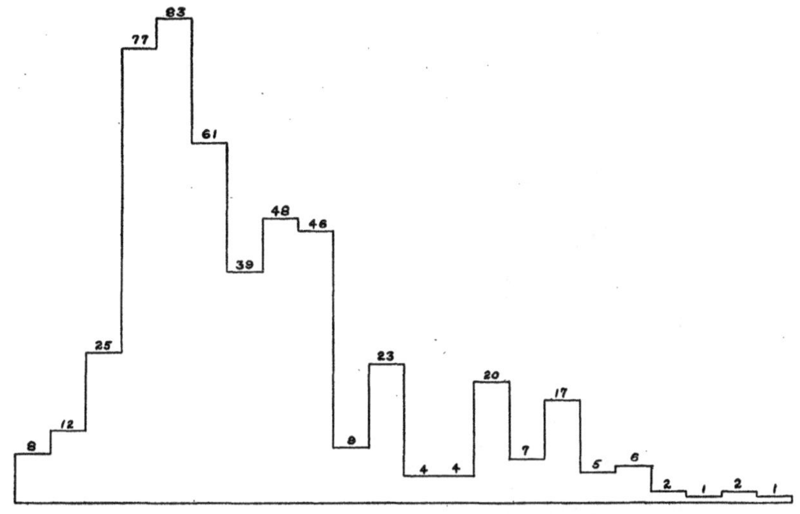

CHART II.—Distribution according to present salaries.

Chart I we observe that the entire range of years in school attendance is from one to eighteen; but 341, or 68 per cent. of the entire number, attended school from four to eight years, with comparatively few attending less than four or more than eight years. Making similar observation of Chart II we find that the salaries or incomes range from $200 to $6,000; but 354, or 71 per cent. of the entire five hundred, receive between $500 and $1,000, only twenty people receiving less than $400, and seventeen more than $2,000.

Passing from this more general comparison of the distributions, in which we see a gross similarity, let us take up Chart III, in which by the use of cross-hatching and a more definite method of comparison we get an exact expression of correlation between the number of years these five hundred individuals attended school and their respective salaries or incomes.

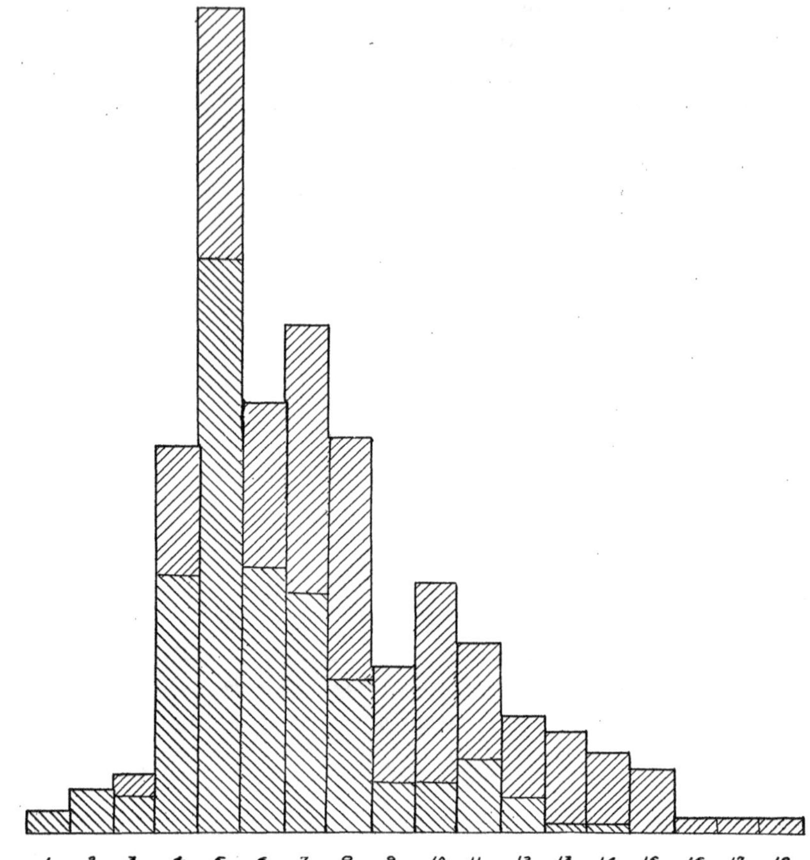

CHART III.—Oblique lines from upper right to lower left indicate those receiving more than $700; obliques from upper left to lower right those receiving $700 or less.

By actual count we find that half the entire number of individuals received over $700 as salaries or incomes; the other half of course receiving $700, or less. Therefore by using oblique lines from upper right to lower left to represent those who receive over $700, and oblique lines from upper left to lower right to represent those receiving $700, or less, and by arranging the entire number of respondents in columns according to the number of years they attended school, it becomes evident at a glance that the majority of those receiving $700 or less, attended school less than eight years, whereas the majority of those receiving over $700 attended school more than six years.

In Chart IV we use a similar method, though here we have the obverse of Chart III. That is, we find by actual count that 243, or practically 50 per cent. of the entire five hundred people,

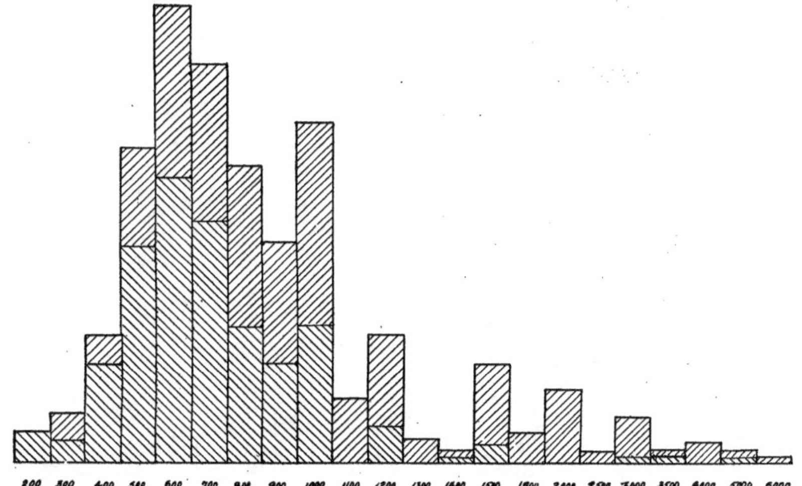

CHART IV.—Oblique lines from upper right to lower left indicate those in school more than six years; obliques from upper left to lower right, those in school six years or less.

attended school six years or less. Therefore in this chart we have arranged the entire number of cases in columns corresponding to their various salaries or incomes, representing those who attended school six years or less by oblique lines from upper left to lower right, and those attending school more than six years by obliques in the opposite direction.

The same general parallelism between the number of years in school and the size of the salaries or incomes appears as in Chart III, namely, the majority of those attending school six years or less receive the smaller salaries, while those attending more than six years receive the larger salaries. For example, we find only thirteen people who attended school six years or less receiving over $1,000, while only twenty-eight people who attended school more than six years are receiving less than $600. Or to state the same thing in still other terms, if we use the result of this study as a criterion, any individual who has attended school more than six years has 68 chances to earn more than

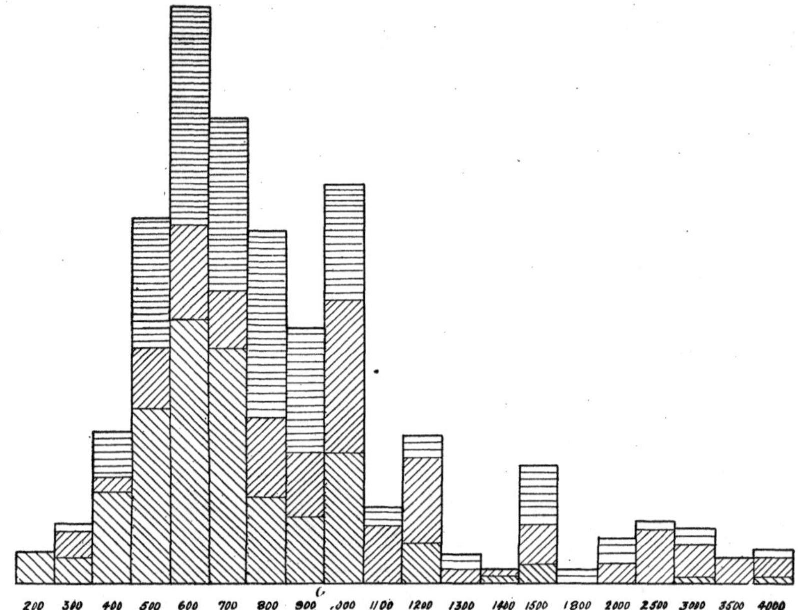

CHART V.—Obliques from upper left to lower right indicate those in school five years or less; obliques from upper right to lower left those in school nine years or more; horizontal lines, those in school from six to eight years.

$700, as against 32 chances that he will earn less than $700. Whereas, if he has attended school less than six years the chances are as 68 to 32 in favor of his earning less than $700 a year.

Chart V is an attempt to make still more apparent the correlation between these two sets of data. The whole number of respondents is divided into three approximately equal groups with reference to the number of years they attended school, although it turns out that there are 172 in each of the extreme groups, or thirds, and only 156 in the middle third. The first third represents those who attended school five years or less, the middle third those who attended school from six to eight years inclusive, and the last third those who attended school nine years or more; and as heretofore they are all arranged in columns corresponding to the various salaries they received. Those who attended school from six to eight years are represented by horizontal lines, those who attended five years or less by obliques from upper left to lower right and those nine years or more by obliques in the opposite direction.

It is readily seen that the large majority of the middle third as to school attendance also constitute the large majority of the people who receive the medium salaries or incomes. By actual count we find the number who attended school from six to eight years and who received less than $500 a year to be only eight, while 27 of this group receive more than $1,000 a year. That is, over 77 per cent. of those in the middle third of school attendance receive from $500 to $1,000 a year. Comparing the other two groups, or thirds, we find that of the 172 in the lowest third of school attendance, 136, or over 78 per cent., receive not over $700 a year as salaries, whereas of the 172 in the highest third as to school attendance 133, or over 77 per cent., receive more than $700.

But it may be asked, "What about the considerable number, approximately one-third of the entire five hundred, between whose school attendance and incomes there is no appreciable positive correlation?" For example, turning to Chart IV, it will be observed that there are five people who attended school over six years receiving only $400, and five others with over six years' school attendance receiving only $300. On the other hand in the same chart will be found six people whose school attendance was less than six years, but whose salaries are $1,200, and four with less than six years' schooling whose salaries are $1,400, $3,000, $3,500, $5,000.

An entirely adequate solution or explanation of all the negative correlation need not be undertaken, but there are some facts which strengthen the general conclusion that the correlation is more intimate than the charts indicate. In the first place, referring to the ten above mentioned in Chart IV whose schooling was more than six years but whose salaries were only three and four hundred dollars it should be said they are women clerks in stores and shops of different kinds. Again in Chart IV, it may be observed that 18 of those receiving only $500 attended school more than six years. Of those eighteen five are women teachers. These fifteen comprise the entire number of women respondents and help to explain part of the negative correlation. That is to say, the data of these somewhat lower the percentage of corrrelation between the amount of schooling and compensation for the reason that women of equal schooling as a rule receive lower wages.

Age is another factor which helps to explain some part of the lack of perfect correlation. By examining the records of the individuals whose school attendance is below six years, but whose salaries are above $1,200 we find that with few exceptions they are men from forty-five to sixty. They appear to be well endowed by nature; they found their life-work early, and have pursued it diligently. The one who receives $5,000 is president of a bank and also a prosperous farmer, age 54. The one receiving $3,500 is postmaster and also president of a large hardware company, age 56. On the other hand the young men who have recently completed high school and college and have gone to productive work are in the main receiving comparatively low salaries because of lack of experience, while their school attendance is of course comparatively high. Then, too, the schooling of the ministers was high as compared to their salaries.

It may justly be argued that the social and financial standing of a child's family will largely influence his income as an adult. That is to say, it is admitted that the child receives much training and assistance in the home, and in his social environment outside the school, which makes for or against his future financial success. But it should be remembered that the social and financial influences which make for the future success of the child likewise contribute to the prolongation of his period of schooling; whereas if the social and financial condition of his family be such as to limit him with reference to his future financial success these same conditions will likewise tend to decrease his period of schooling. In other words, there is a complete parallelism between social condition in the family and period of schooling. If the facts presented in the above tables with regard to period of school are treated merely as symptoms of a more fundamental fact the interpretation of the result may be more complete, but it will be in no wise in conflict with the obvious implication that there is a marked correlation between school attendance and income in later life.

4. *Conclusions.*—1. That in the five hundred individuals canvassed there is a correlation of about 68 per cent. between the length of time they attended school and their salaries.

2. That in the remaining 32 per cent. of negative correlation fifteen of the cases may be explained by the fact that being women they receive relatively low wages.

3. That age and experience also help to explain part of the negative correlation; young men of more education but less experience often receiving lower salaries than older men of less education but more experience.

NATURAL HISTORY IN THE GRADES

OTIS W. CALDWELL
The University of Chicago

III. THIRD GRADE

A general review of the plants and animals used in grades one and two should constitute the first work in the third grade. This review is needed in order first to keep clearly defined the individual characteristics of different things that were studied and second to recall and re-establish the more difficult matters that were encountered in such processes as relate to climatic changes and the life round of the three types of animal life used most extensively in the second grade. It will be well to introduce into the third-grade room in autumn some cocoons, tadpoles or young frogs by means of which to review and extend the work that was done in the preceding spring. Related types as the salamanders and newts are found as a regular part of the lists of materials suggested for the grade, but these are all the more profitably used if preceded by a brief review study of the toad, the cecropia moth and cocoon, the story of how the pigeons built their nests and reared their young, and by the preparation of lists and brief discussion of the different groups of materials as trees, insects, rocks, soils, and weather phenomena, which have already been studied.

The topics included in this grade are:

1. *Animal life.*—Squirrel or some similar animal kept by the grade; further study of the life cycle and feeding habits of the toad, the salamander, showing its external gills, its form and behavior as compared with the toad; the cabbage butterfly grown through its metamorphoses and the parts mounted to illustrate the life cycle; water insects—dragon flies and mosquitoes, the swimming, feeding, and resting habits of adults and particularly of the young that may be kept in the school-

room aquaria; effects of insects upon garden plants as of the caterpillars upon the currant bushes which are under the especial care of this grade and which when caterpillars appear are sprayed or sprinkled by the grades, some of the caterpillars being kept in cages for study; oriole, song-sparrow, night-hawk, humming bird, brown thrush, blackbird, cow-bird, warblers, a few observations upon bird migration, upon the nesting and feeding habits of these birds, especially upon the ways in which warblers feed upon scale insects upon trees; if possible study in some detail the nesting habits of at least one kind of bird comparing it with the pigeon work done in the preceding grade; some discussion of the balance of life between insects and birds, and in aquaria and ponds between insects and fish, toads, frogs, etc.; add any common land animals of the region not already included in preceding grades, and use true stories descriptive of wild and domesticated animals of this and other regions; the possession of pet animals and children's literature dealing with animal life fit well into this grade.

2. *Plant life.*—In addition to the review of the trees studied in the preceding grade, add the mulberry, box-elder, and two or three others of the most available kinds. Study the form of these and in discussion and sketches establish definite ideas of the characteristics of the different trees that are used. If good enlarged photographs of typical trees of the kinds that are included are placed on the walls they will be helpful, and will be sufficiently unlike those of the vicinity which the pupils are studying to allow all the originality that may be wished. Such photographs may be secured from R. B. Hough, Lowville, N. Y., and also from other sources, but local trees that the teacher or others may have taken in the general vicinity of the school are quite as good and have the additional advantage of the local "color" that adds so much both to teacher and pupil. In the next grade more extended work with the lumber industries is suggested, and this individual study of trees in this grade will assist greatly in the following work.

Acquaintance with plants of the vacant lots of the region should be extended, including the rag-weed, cockle-bur, wild parsley, butter-print, and burdock. The names and general characteristics of the plants and animals that are growing in the aquaria in the room should be made the basis of a few lessons. The most extensive work of this grade is done with the bulbs, which will be separately discussed at the close of this article. This work is carried on throughout the latter part of the autumn, winter, and early spring, both in connection with the garden and with the indoor study.

3. *Garden work.*—Instead of having the whole grade have one, or but two or three gardens, as suggested for the lower grades, a better plan for this grade is to have each group of three or four pupils have a garden together, or if abundant space is available, to have each pupil possess one garden entirely alone. Outdoor studies of the soil, planting, germination, watering, weeding, cultivation, characteristics of the plants in different stages of their growth, and the care that they need to keep them in proper condition are the leading topics that relate to the garden work for this grade. The children make their own plans for their gardens, and under the advice of the teacher select the plants that they are to grow. This must be carefully guarded lest they will select things that are not possible for the region or for the area at their disposal. The suggestions of the teacher are usually sufficient to determine proper selection by the pupil. It will be found best usually to have each pupil grow a few kinds both of vegetables and of flowering plants. A good plan is to divide the bed into a vegetable garden and a flower garden so that all may have a chance at all both useful and ornamental plants that are available for general use. In the next year the pupils are asked to plan for their gardens by making drawings to scale showing just the amount of space to be used and the use to be made of each part of it, and a statement of the appearance that is imagined when the plants are grown. In the third grade this planning is carried on under the close supervision of the teacher. In this way the class and teacher work out the plans before the time for the outdoor work. This serves to increase the interest in the garden and to give definiteness and meaning

to it. In connection with the fourth-grade outline, one or more detailed sample plans for gardens will be presented.

It will be of interest and value to grow in the schoolroom during the latter part of the winter or early spring some of the seeds that are to be used later out-of-doors in order that the pupils may get an idea of the characteristics and appearance of the plants that they are to grow, and may learn to distinguish them from the weeds of the garden.

The earth materials and meteorological materials for this grade are not arranged as separate groups but are treated, in so far as they appear at all, in connection with the garden work. Considerable study of the soil and of the conditions that are favorable for the successful growth of the plants of the garden are constantly discussed, the center of the natural-history work of the grade being the garden and bulb work, hence the inclusion of these things here rather than in separate topics.

4. *The indoor work with bulbs.*—General outlines for this work were given in the October, 1909, *Elementary School Teacher,* to which reference is made, and knowledge of which will be assumed in the following discussion. It is the present purpose rather to give an outline of a few of the detailed problems that the pupils can do with profit in the schoolroom. Enough bulbs should be supplied to allow each pupil to have one each of the kind selected for the main work and also to supply several kinds of less common bulbs for general possession and study by the entire grade. The paper white narcissus, Chinese sacred lily, or hyacinth are probably best for the experimental work. But for comparison there should be provided a good supply of several other kinds, as hyacinths, crocuses, tulip, Freesias, Amaryllis, and scilla. This year part of the children of the grade have been given paper white narcissus, part have been given hyacinths, and the rest Chinese sacred lilies, while the grade as a whole has a few each of several other kinds of bulbs. Considerable discussion as to the best way of planting the bulbs in question was had before the work began, and then each child did his planting under the direction of the teacher.

After planting, the bulbs were well watered and placed in a dark and cool room, where they should be kept for weeks, until after the holiday season unless they grow more rapidly than is expected. They need to be watered just enough to keep the soil from drying out, but care must be taken to see that the soil is not wet enough to allow the bulbs to decay. In this way the roots should start in a short time, and should be well under way before there is any appearance of the stem and leaves. The plants may be brought up to the schoolroom at any time after the roots are well started, and forced for winter or early flowering. Some of the potted bulbs may be planted out-of-doors by being buried in the soil or under straw, and may be brought into the schoolroom at any time that is wished. Great care must be taken to see that the earth and plants thaw out very slowly else the plants will be killed. This is best done by putting the pots first into a cool basement room for a few days, then into the schoolroom.

With the planting done, experimental work with the bulbs and a study of their parts is begun. One study as suggested by the following directions, consists of opening tulip bulbs lengthwise to determine what parts are present and how they are arranged with reference to one another. By use of a bulb that has stood in water for a few days determine where the roots arise, where the stem is, how the leaves are arranged and how they inclose the growing point. This study should be carried farther by use of bulbs that have been cut crosswise, and sketches of the bulbs in different views should be made. By use also of one or two bulbs that have been planted for a week or ten days the nature of the different parts will be interestingly shown. From this point of view further study may be made of similar bulbous plants that are growing in the room.

Another experiment that has proven valuable consisted of growing three sets of plants in different places which afforded different lighting and possibly different temperature. The pots were placed in a dark closet at the time when the bulbs were planted and others, planted at the same time, were placed in the windows, and still others in a dark cool basement room as previously described. The closeted plants developed root systems, but produced blanched leaves and no flowers, those placed in the window soon put up their leaves and flower stocks but had developed meager root systems and finally produced small and but few flowers, while the plants that were started in the basement produced abundant roots and when brought up to the schoolroom produced large leaves and large and abundant flowers. Much interest was shown in following the development of these three groups of plants grown under different conditions. A fourth group of potted bulbs has been buried out-of-doors, and when it is brought into the room it doubtless will serve excellently as a comparison with the three groups here described, and should make possible valuable inferences as to the behavior of bulbous plants relative to soil, temperature, and light.

Another valuable series of experiments consists in determining the amount of water used by a plant and the relation of this to the amount of growth of the plant. In a fruit jar a measured amount of water was placed. Suspended to a stopper in the top of the jar a bulb was fastened, so that its lower end touched the top of the water. The cork was sealed with paraffin so that no evaporation of water from the jar could occur. The entire apparatus was weighed carefully and the weight recorded. Sketches were made of the apparatus at intervals to show the changes as they occurred. Gum labels placed on the outside of the jar served to determine whether the water was lowered from day to day. When the water was lowered and the growth such that the weight remained practically constant, interesting questions arose as to whether the growth took place directly from the water removed from the jar. Obviously some simple explanations were necessary, such as the statement that the plant took some of its food from the air about it. A further instructive experiment consisted in comparing the weight of a bulb with the weight of the whole plant that finally grew from it. It may be questioned if in this experiment we are not dealing with factors some of which are too elusive for pupils even much older than these and we must recognize that such is true. But the gross results were determined, and farther than this it would be unwise to attempt to go with children.

In one class the experiment with the bulb grown in a jar led to a study of the amount of water in the soil. The class weighed some soil, then dried it carefully, of course not being able to remove all of the water, but removing all that ordinary drying would remove, and then by weighing the dry soil determined the loss by weight, which, as they could readily understand, was a water loss. It is not intended that any extended study of the soil should be taken up until in the fifth grade. Many interesting experiments offer themselves in connection with this study; the reaching for light by plants, as shown in the window or by plants inclosed in a box so as to be lighted from but one side, budding, flowering, and seed-making, depth of planting that gives best results, differences between growth from large and small bulbs, and from those that were used by the class last year and new bulbs.

Two somewhat special features of the bulb work are being tried in this grade this year. One is to have the children grow a dozen or so pots of especially fine varieties as the newer hyacinths, crocuses, and Freesias, which, if successful, the children will present to other grades or to outside interests to which the grade may wish to contribute. Secondly, a fine Amaryllis has been secured for this grade which the grade is expected to care for and pass on at the opening of the next school year to the next third-grade class. It is hoped that another Amaryllis may be cared for by this grade and carried through all of their grade experience, and disposed of as they see fit when they finish the eighth grade.

AGRICULTURAL EDUCATION

AGRICULTURAL COLLEGES, INCLUDING EXTENSION WORK, DEPARTMENTS OF AGRICULTURAL EDUCATION, AND SUMMER SCHOOLS FOR TEACHERS

BENJAMIN MARSHALL DAVIS
Miami University

Of the many agencies now promoting agricultural education in elementary and secondary schools the most important are the state agricultural colleges, for they are the "only teaching institutions that are in possession, at first hand, of the essential facts of rational agriculture." Until recently they have been too busy perfecting their own organization, and too greatly occupied in developing and promoting the scientific aspects of agriculture to give much attention to outside educational matters. It is difficult to determine just when the agricultural colleges began to take an active interest in the public schools. Dean L. H. Bailey says:

> More than any other institutions they stand for democracy and nativeness of education, for their purpose is nothing less than to reach the last man on the last farm by means of the very things by which that man lives (28, p. 40).[1]

This idea of bringing the college to the people found its first expression in various sorts of extension work dealing with the farmers directly. Now this work is well organized and is doing great service. Through farmers' institutes, farmers' conventions, farmers' excursions to the college, instruction trains, demonstration farms, and other means, the man on the farm is having the college brought to him. These efforts of the colleges are now appreciated; so much in fact, that it is often difficult for a college to meet the demands for this kind of outside instruction. But the farmer has not always had this friendly attitude. He was slow to recognize the value of what he called "book farming." Perhaps it was in these early days of agricultural extension that

[1] The references are to the bibliography at the end of this article.

some of those in charge thought it worth while to give some attention to the coming generation of farmers, to the children in the public schools.

Doubtless many individuals connected with agricultural colleges had put this idea into practice and had helped to introduce agricultural subjects in some of the public schools long before any college took official notice of this means of extension. The first college to take this matter up was the Agricultural College of Cornell University. Reference has already been made to this work under the Nixon law of 1897.[2] It assumed considerable importance at once. The report of 1898 concerning this work says:

> Thirty thousand teachers are enrolled on our lists and have received leaflets, and many have attended lectures explaining the methods of presenting nature-study work in the schools. Sixteen thousand children have received those leaflets which are especially adapted to their needs (20, p. 1611).

This work is administered by a department of the college known as the Nature-Study Bureau and consists of publications, correspondence, organization of boys' and girls' clubs, and lectures and demonstrations for teachers. Other agricultural colleges soon took up similar work in their respective states until now nearly all are doing more or less extension work among the public schools. At present agricultural colleges are assisting agricultural education in the elementary and secondary schools (*a*) by various extension methods, (*b*) by organizing departments of agricultural education and (*c*) by conducting summer schools for teachers.

Extension methods vary somewhat in different states. This is probably due to differences in local conditions, state support, and policies of the colleges themselves. Usually each college develops one particular method of reaching the schools although it may use several. Several colleges follow the Cornell plan (29, 30) of regular publications for teachers and pupils, for example, the agricultural colleges of Kansas (31), Ohio (32), New Hampshire (33), and Rhode Island (34). Purdue Uni-

[2] This *Journal,* Vol. X, No. 4, p. 169.

versity, Indiana University, and Pennsylvania State College published regularly for a while leaflets on nature-study. Others publish occasional bulletins on various phases of public-school agriculture, for example the agricultural colleges of Massachusetts (35, 36), Illinois (37), Minnesota (39), Tennessee (38), and California (40). Material designed to aid teachers is sometimes prepared by faculty members of an agricultural college to be published by the state department of education or by some school magazine, for example from the agriculaural colleges of Illinois (42) and Michigan (41).

These extension publications are distributed free of charge and often large editions have to be reprinted to meet the demand. The extension bulletin of Ohio State Agricultural College (32), for example, is printed in editions of from 10,000 to 20,000. The mailing-list is made up anew each year from responses to notices that names will be dropped from the mailing-list unless requests are renewed. Pupils of the public schools are expected to carry on some work suggested by the college and report upon this work in order to receive the bulletin regularly. In this way the extension department is kept in close touch with the teachers and pupils of the state. The bulletin serves several purposes: it is a means of communication between the college and the schools; it presents various phases of agriculture of interest to the pupils; it assists in organizing agricultural clubs among the public-school children; it is the organ for promoting interest in rural-school improvement, such as consolidation of rural schools and beautifying school grounds.

Each agricultural college has more or less correspondence among teachers and pupils but some colleges have encouraged it and made it a feature of their extension work. This method has the advantage that comes from establishing a sort of personal relation between the college and the individual. But the work involved in a correspondence dealing with several thousand individuals is enormous and almost impossible for an agricultural college, were personal answers given to each letter. A regular publication is necessary to outline and suggest work to be reported upon. The correspondence is really one-sided, for answers to individual letters may be given in the next publication or in circular letters. Only a small percentage requires personal answers. The office work is thus reduced to filing and checking reports and preparing mailing-lists. The most extensive work of this kind has been carried on by Cornell University. "Uncle John," who is supposed to read the letters, is more widely known and is more popular among the young people of New York rural communities than any other member of the university. This method is also used by the agricultural colleges of Ohio and Rhode Island. The Agricultural College of Florida conducts a correspondence course in agriculture for teachers, enrolling in 1908–9, 438 teachers.

The most successful form of agricultural extension among public-school children has been agricultural clubs (43, 44). They are now organized in nearly every state and are not only a means of imparting a knowledge of agriculture to their members, but they have a wholesome reaction on the communities in which they are organized. The following is a statement of the work of boys' clubs of Louisiana:

> This year, 1909, we have about 2,000 boys in our agricultural clubs. Next year we expect to have 10,000. I shall devote all of December, January, and February to the organization of these clubs in every parish in Louisiana. The corn crop in Louisiana this year exceeds in yield by 50 per cent. the crop of 1908, and it is generally admitted that a large part of the increase is due to the interest created in corn during the last two years by the boys that are in the boys' clubs. The best corn show ever held in Louisiana was that of the boys' clubs at the State Fair at Shreveport the first days of this month.[8]

The most complete state organization of boys' and girls' clubs is in Nebraska (43). Here the State Agricultural College and the State Department of Education work together. The organization consists of a state association, and county and local or district associations. The central or state association meets once a year and is composed of delegates from county associations.

> A special course in agriculture and domestic science for boys and girls will be given at the State University Farm, beginning Monday, January 17,

[8] From a letter of Professor V. L. Roy, Department of Agricultural Education, State Agricultural College of Louisiana.

and ending Friday, January 21, 1900. This course is planned for the delegates from each county of boys' and girls' agricultural and domestic science associations. Special arrangements have been made with the professors at the University College of Agriculture to give a course of instruction lasting five days. . . . . The laboratories at the Agricultural College will be at the disposal of the delegates from the different counties during this week and professors from the college will give the instruction. The course is filled with interesting and instructive lectures and demonstrations (43, p. 11).

The agricultural colleges reach the public schools in various other ways. The extension department of Ohio State Agricultural College gives its attention almost wholly to rural schools. The superintendent of agricultural extension in this institution believes that the most important work of his department lies in improving the rural schools, not only by helping to introduce agriculture, but by interesting the patrons in consolidating small district schools, in making other improvements, and by encouraging the teachers to adjust their school work to fit the needs of the communities in which they live. The Mississippi State Agricultural College gives a short course of one week each winter in the county agricultural high school. Many colleges send representatives to address teachers' institutes and other teachers' meetings. They also furnish judges for boys' corn shows, and corn and stock-judging contests.

The early extension work of agricultural colleges among the public schools was intended to awaken an interest in agricultural affairs. It was mainly propaganda for arousing a favorable sentiment toward the subject. The more recent work has had for its aim the actual introduction of certain phases of agriculture into the schools, and to render assistance to teachers who wish to teach the subject. The demand on many colleges for this kind of work has become too great to be properly met by the regular extension departments. To meet this situation special departments are being organized. These are usually known as departments of agricultural education. In the Agricultural College of Minnesota the department is called agricultural pedagogics, and in the Agricultural College of Missouri it is called the department of rural school education. The following tabulation shows the organization of these departments up to date:

State	Year	Head of Department
Alabama	1909	L. W. Duncan
California	1909	Ernest B. Babcock
Illinois	1905	D. O. Barto (secondary agr. ed.)
	1909	Fred L. Charles (elementary agr. ed.)
Indiana	1908	George L. Roberts
Idaho	1909	Edwin E. Elliot (O. M. Osborne, asst.)
Louisiana	1909	V. L. Roy
Michigan	1908	Walter H. French
Massachusetts	1907	W. R. Hart
Minnesota	?	D. D. Mayne
Missouri	1909	R. H. Emberson
Nebraska	1909	J. L. McBrien (University extension)
North Carolina	1909	I. O. Schaub
Oklahoma	1909	E. E. Balcomb
Pennsylvania	1909	Thos. I. Mairs
Wisconsin	1909	K. L. Hatch

The agricultural colleges of Arkansas, Delaware, Maine, North Dakota, South Dakota, Vermont, and Washington give courses in education to their students who expect to become teachers. The Agricultural College of Tennessee added a department of agricultural education temporarily in 1908 for one year and expects to re-establish it. A number of other colleges have signified their intention to establish departments of agricultural education as soon as practicable.

It will be seen from the above summary that most of these new departments began their work in 1908 and 1909. This is probably due, at least in part, to a provision of the Nelson amendment of 1908 (22, 28, p. 5) whereby "said colleges may use a portion of this money (referring to additional appropriation) for providing courses for special preparation of instructors for teaching the elements of agriculture and mechanic arts."

Massachusetts in 1907 made a special appropriation of $5,000 for this work (28, p. 41). In addition to the regular instruction given during the school year and summer school for teachers, the department conducted, in 1908 and 1909, conferences on agricultural education (36). At the conference of 1909, a committee appointed in 1908 made a report outlining a series of exercises "of experimental character that should serve as material for the teaching of agriculture in the common schools" (35).

The departments of agricultural education in other colleges are just getting under way, and it is therefore not possible at this time to give any report of their work beyond a few brief statements. Boys' clubs and teachers' institutes are receiving special attention in several states. In Missouri the schools of the county in which the University of Missouri is located are taking up the study of agriculture under the direction of the professor of agricultural education who visits the schools with the county superintendent, gives instruction in the seventh and eighth grades and makes suggestions to the teachers for carrying on the work. The University of Illinois is pursuing a similar plan. In Indiana the department was established especially to enable the students of Purdue University to comply with the state law requiring teachers in the public schools to have some professional training. In general, these new departments seem to regard the development of agriculture in high schools as an important part of their work. Mention should be made in this connection of the co-operation of the College of Agriculture of Cornell University and Teachers College of Columbia University for the training of students for special work as teachers of agriculture in high schools and normal schools. "Appropriate courses in agriculture are taken at Cornell University and the study of educational problems at Teachers College" (28 p. 36–37).

The number of agricultural colleges giving summer courses for the benefit of teachers is increasing rapidly. During the present year courses were given in the agricultural colleges of the following states: Connecticut, California, Georgia, Illinois, Massachusetts, Michigan, Minnesota, Mississippi, North Carolina, North Dakota, Ohio, Oklahoma, Oregon, Tennessee, and perhaps others. These courses last from three to eight weeks and are well attended. The indications are that the attendance and interest will increase and that summer schools of agricultural colleges will become a considerable factor in elementary and secondary agricultural education.

BIBLIOGRAPHY

Only publications referred to by number in the text are given. In this list will be found representative publications of agricultural colleges concerning various phases of agricultural education. No attempt has been made to make it complete. Many of the facts of the text have been obtained from personal letters.

28. *On the Training of Persons to Teach Agriculture in the Public Schools.* LIBERTY HYDE BAILEY, Washington, D. C.: U. S. Bureau of Education, Bulletin No. 3 (1908), pp. 53.

The subject is discussed in three parts: I. The nature of the problem in (*a*) elementary schools, (*b*) high schools, (*c*) special schools; II, The means of training the teachers (*a*) those already in service, (*b*) new teachers; III, The general outlook; the significance of normal work in the colleges of agriculture.

29. *Cornell Nature-Study Leaflets.* New York State College of Agriculture of Cornell University, Albany, New York: State Department of Agriculture, Nature-Study Bulletin No. 1 (1904), pp. 607.

This volume is made up of selections, with revisions, from the Teachers' Leaflets, Home Nature-study Lessons, Junior Naturalist Monthly, and other publications from the College of Agriculture of Cornell University.

30. *Rural School Leaflet.* New York State College of Agriculture of Cornell University, Ithaca, N. Y.

Vol. I of this publication began in September, 1907. It is published monthly in the interest of the rural schools. It takes the place of the various other nature-study publications sent out by this institution: *Teachers' Nature-study Leaflets,* beginning in 1897; the *Junior Naturalist,* from 1901 to 1904; *Nature-Study Quarterly,* beginning in 1899; *Home Nature-Study Lessons,* beginning in 1900, new series in 1904.

31. *Agricultural Education.* J. H. MILLER, editor. Manhattan, Kansas: Kansas State Agricultural College. Vol. I began November, 1908.

No regular dates of publication are announced, but it is intended that at least four numbers will be issued each year. Each number takes up somewhat in detail some one subject; Vol. I, No. 1, *A Corn Primer,* pp. 46; No. 2, *Plant Breeding,* pp. 92; No. 3, *A Study of Insects,* pp. 52; No. 4, *Insects Injurious to Farm Crops,* pp. 91; No. 5, *Boys' and Girls' Contest Number,* pp. 22.

An educational series of four numbers appeared in 1907, being special editions of *The Industrialist,* a weekly publication of the College. Previous to 1907 occasional numbers devoted to agricultural education appeared from time to time.

32. *The Agricultural College Extension Bulletin.* A. B. GRAHAM, editor. Columbus, Ohio: Ohio State Agricultural College. Vol. I began October, 1905.

Each volume consists of nine numbers published monthly. Each number treats some subject of interest to teachers and pupils of rural schools. Each year one number is devoted to the centralized schools in Ohio.

33. *New Hampshire College School Bulletin.* E. DWIGHT SANDERSON, editor. Durham, N. H.: New Hampshire State College of Agriculture. Vol. I began May, 1908.

This is a quarterly publication in the interest of New Hampshire schools. Contents of Vol. I, No. 1, *Agriculture through the Rural Schools;* No. 2, *Soil Studies;* No. 3, *Seeds and Seedlings;* No. 4, *Seed Testing.*

34. *The Nature Guard.* A. E. STONE, editor. Kingston, R. I.: Rhode Island State College of Agriculture. Vol. I began October, 1899.

This leaflet is issued monthly from October to May. It is the official organ of the Nature Guard and Junior League of Improvement Societies of Rhode Island. Each number has from four to eight pages and is usually devoted to one subject; for example, the title of No. 63 is *Experiments with Soils.*

35. *Public School Agriculture.* W. R. HART. Amherst, Mass.: Massachusetts State College of Agriculture. Special Bulletin (1909), pp. 32.

This is the Report of the Committee Appointed at the Conference on Agricultural Science at Amherst, Mass., 1908. Fifty-four exercises in elementary agriculture are outlined.

36. *Proceedings of the Conference on Agricultural Science. Ibid.* (1908), pp. 43.

Four papers are published as follows: "The Place of the School Garden in the Development of Science Teaching," W. A. Baldwin; "Administrative Phases of Agricultural Instruction," C. H. Robison; "Physics and Agriculture," R. W. Guss; "Chemisry and Agriculture," Charles Wellington.

37. *Extension Bulletins Relating to Agricultural Education.* Illinois State Agricultural College, Urbana, Ill.

Consolidation of Country Schools, E. Davenport (1903, 2d ed., 1904), pp. 56. *Developing the Farm Boy,* Fred H. Rankin (1905), pp. 26. *The Grout Farm Encampment,* Arthur J. Bill (1906), pp. 42; *Second Encampment, ibid.* (1907), pp. 40. *Dairy Lessons,* Wilbur J. Fraser (1907) four parts, one lesson in each. *The Next Step in Agricultural Education,* E. Davenport (1908), pp. 22. *Sugar Beets and How to Grow Them,* Fred H. Rankin (1908), pp. 7. *How to Run Farm Machinery,* Fred R. Crane (1908), pp. 39.

38. *A Manual for High Schools.* JOSIAH MAIN.. Knoxville, Tenn.: Tennessee State College of Agriculture. Special Bulletin (1909), pp. 32.

A scheme for correlating agriculture with other high school sciences is worked in with considerable detail.

39. *Rural School Agriculture.* W. M. HAYES *et al.* St. Anthony Park, Minn.: University of Minnesota, Bulletin No. 1 (1903), pp. 200..

"Exercises in this bulletin . . . . have been prepared for use of teachers in the rural schools of Minnesota." This publication is of especial interest because it represents one of the first efforts of agricultural colleges to assist teachers by preparing concrete lessons in an agricultural subject. A revised edition of this bulletin appeared as Bulletin No. 2 in 1907. A comparison of the two bulletins shows an interesting shifting of point of view as to matter presented and method of presentation.

40. *Suggestions for Garden Work in California Schools.* E. B. BABCOCK.

Berkeley, Cal.: California State Agricultural College, Circular 46 (1909), pp. 48.

This contains a history of the movement, what teachers have done, what teachers can do, instructions for teachers beginning garden work, how to secure special preparation for teaching nature-study within California and list of publications.

41. *An Elementary Laboratory Study of Crops.* Jos. A. Jeffery. Lansing, Mich.: State Department of Education, Bulletin No. 26 (1907), pp. 28.

An Elementary Laboratory Study in Soils. Jos. A. Jeffery. *Ibid.* Bulletin No. 27 (1908), pp. 36.

An Elementary Course in Horticulture. S. W. Fletcher. *Ibid.* Bulletin No. 28 (1908), pp. 31.

42. *The Study of Farm Crops, Farm Animals, Horticulture and Agriculture.* A. D. Shamel, E. Davenport, and J. S. Blair. Taylorville, Ill.: C. M. Parker, *The School News* (1900–4).

About fifty short articles on the above subjects were published in the *School News* and afterwards reprinted by the publisher in form of leaflets, and sold at one cent each in quantities of ten or more. They had a wide sale and no doubt contributed much toward arousing an interest in agriculture in the public schools of Illinois.

43. *Nebraska Boys' and Girls' Association State Contest and Convention.* Val. Keyser and E. C. Bishop. Lincoln, Neb.: University of Nebraska, Bulletin series XIV, No. 12 (1909), pp. 20.

This bulletin contains announcement of the State Convention of 1910 of the Boys' and Girls' Association of Nebraska. Other bulletins concerning this Association have appeared from time to time, e. g., *Selecting Corn for the Contest,* Ser. 12, No. 25; *Planting Corn for the Contest,* Ser. 12, No. 12 (1907); *Selecting Potatoes for the Contest,* Ser. 13, No. 11 (1908); *Cooking and Sewing,* Ser. 13, No. 14 (1908).

44. *Boys' Agricultural Clubs.* D. J. Crosby. Washington, D. C.: U. S. Department of Agriculture, Yearbook for 1904, pp. 489–96.

This article gives a description of "the boys' exhibit of corn at the Louisiana Purchase Exposition, the development of boys' clubs in Illinois and other states, and school fairs; and discusses the educational value of the work done by such organizations."

THE FINE AND INDUSTRIAL ARTS IN ELEMENTARY SCHOOLS, GRADES IV AND V

WALTER SARGENT
The University of Chicago

The previous article in this series stated that one distinguishing characteristic of the beginnings of manual expression is satisfaction in occupation, almost regardless of the product. Later appears an interest in the quality of the product and a desire that it be a somewhat adequate expression of an idea. This interest gives value to the sort of intensive work suggested for Grades II and III, where in addition to the free drawing and constructive work used as a means of describing ideas of current interest, a few things were to be selected and studied somewhat thoroughly in a series of lessons, each one of which presented or emphasized some particular aspect or detail of the object or process of construction. In these careful records of observations drawing ceases to be merely the making of symbols that can be recognized when used as illustrations of a story, and becomes a sincere effort to interpret truly a particular object. For example, if the drawing is of a Norse boat, the children forget for a time the historical associations in the attempt to represent that special form of boat correctly. A new interest enters in: that of trying to make the particular thing in view exist again on paper. The drawing has a content of its own. When after such drawing the children turn again to illustration of history requiring the Norse boat, they do so with increased power of expression. The results of intensive study of this sort should be a relatively thorough knowledge of a few objects, geometric relations, and processes, with a corresponding confidence in the use of them, and the satisfaction that arises from having mastered certain definite things, and from a realization that well-directed, persistent effort is likely to bring desired results.

In constructive work the teacher of manual expression has early to decide between a policy that leans toward giving children the freedom of all tools and materials at as early an age as these can be handled with safety—for example, bench tools for wood-working in primary grades—or toward utilizing somewhat completely the possibilities of simpler materials and implements, regarding these as adequate to that stage of expression and a fitting introduction to more difficult undertakings. Where the second policy is adopted and interpreted freely, the pleasure of thorough accomplishment usually makes the need of stimulation by novelty less urgent. The incitement of new tools and materials can be reserved till appropriate times. Thus may be avoided the necessity for continually checking the development of the ability to enjoy exploring the possibilities of a few things, and for interfering with the habit of undertaking whatever task is at hand with courage and good will.

The mastery of one implement and process after another may be so guided as to aid rather than hinder originality, and is ultimately necessary to freedom of expression. Such mastery develops those worthy accompaniments of free expression, namely appreciation of technical skill and constructive honesty, ability to think constructively, to plan processes intelligently, and to experience the satisfaction of contributing a piece of work that is well done.

In the desire to develop originating power and not simply technical excellence, we should not lose sight of the importance of developing also the inclination and skill to carry projects to completion and not simply to originate them.

Manual expression should awaken pleasure in the sort of work which requires sustained effort. This should not be confused with the pleasure in spontaneous play. Every man should find pleasure in his work and in his play, but no sane man continues play after it has become irksome, and no man of character drops his work whenever it is irksome. The interest arising from the projection or presentation of new things is easily awakened. The interest which is developed by carrying a project through to completion after the first burst of enthusiasm has passed is of a much slower growth but is more trustworthy, and if systematically strengthened, becomes a motive which can be relied upon.

We turn with aversion from the sight of a school where children are trained simply in mechanical processes. They are making with their hands things which their desires had no part in suggesting nor their heads in planning. But the other extreme, that of a group of earnest, highly trained teachers compelled to spend their best strength trying to make any serious work seem worth while to classes of blasé upper-grade or high-school children who have "had it all before," and who regard these efforts with mild contempt, is a phenomenon that occurs with sufficient frequency to merit consideration.

Such children have been deprived of the sort of work-interest which is necessary to save work from becoming commonplace. A man is unfortunate who has never been trained to suggest and direct his own work, but on the other hand, a large part of one's work will inevitably consist in dealing with matters one never suggested nor desired. One is also unfortunate who has never developed a habit of dealing with such matters cheerfully and effectively simply because they are there and must be done.

The following suggestions for work in representation, construction, and design emphasize the points in technical development which the abilities of the children seem to indicate as particularly appropriate to these grades, and which are factors necessary to freedom of expression.

Representation.—Grades IV and V present an important problem to the instructor in drawing. In many exhibitions of drawing one is impressed by the spontaneity and vigor of graphic expression during the first three grades, and by the failure in the upper grades of any adequate fulfilment of the promise given in the lower. If, seeking a reason for this, we visit schools and watch children at work, we usually find, as was suggested in the last article, that during the second year in school, and more especially during the third, there is added to interest in the mere activity of drawing an interest also in the quality of the product and a desire that it represent the object more adequately. This suggests that failure to make reasonable progress after the third or fourth year is due either to continuation of general drawing without emphasis of particular phases appropriate to the needs of these grades, or to a too abrupt change into adult methods. The intensive study of a few objects, to each of which a succession of lessons is devoted, was suggested for Grades II and III, to meet this changed attitude of the children toward their work and to make certain that ability to draw should keep pace with appreciation of representation.

At some time near the fourth year in school most children appear to lose interest in making crude sketches. They become conscious of and are in danger of being discouraged by their lack of skill. The sort of direction given to their observation and expression determines largely the development of ability during the remainder of the school course.

The method most commonly followed at this time is to introduce the study of the principles of perspective, especially those relating to foreshortened circles and to rectangles at different levels above and below the eye. While the knowledge of these principles is necessary to correct delineation, the application of them to actual objects is a complicated process, and anything more than an incidental reference to them requires greater expenditure of time and effort than is justified in these grades. The children are so fully occupied with direct comparison of object with drawing in the attempt to make the representation "look right" to the eye that they can seldom be led to refer for intellectual confirmation, to a principle which defines how the thing should appear under the given conditions. The immediate impression resulting from comparing the visual image of the object with that of the drawing to see if they fit is the important factor. The questions, "Does it look like that object?" and "How can you make it look like that?" are usually more effective at this age than explanations of the technical grammar of graphic expression. If the child's own observation will not carry him far enough, sketches made for him, which satisfy his eye, will usually interpret the facts of appearance sufficiently to enable him to express the problem in hand.

It seems wiser, therefore, during the fourth and fifth years in school to treat perspective effects incidentally, and postpone, if possible, problems involving definite study of them. This gives time for necessary practice with things easily understood, instead of requiring children to learn advanced principles without experience sufficient to make them practical working schemes.

The latter method often results in an accumulation of formulae for representing perspective appearances, rather than a trustworthy working knowledge. It is a difficult task to induce a child in these grades to draw a book correctly in perspective. When it is successfully done it is usually an indication that he has followed his instructions, rather than that he has seen the thing as he has represented it.

An important matter, and one which appeals strongly to children at this age, is that of correct proportions as a necessary element in truthful and satisfying representation. They readily discern whether a drawing is "too tall" or "too short" as compared with the object, and they develop ability to estimate relative lengths of parts with some degree of precision.

For example, in such a drawing of a toy boat as Fig. 1, a child will take great interest in representing the hull of the boat in its proper proportions, and in adding the keel so that its size bears the right relation to the hull. He can easily be led to proceed with much care, showing just where the mast should be placed and how tall it should be to be like the model. In a similar way he may be led to find much satisfaction in estimating the slant and length of each line with considerable accuracy. Constructed objects such as toys offer excellent opportunity for drill in the matter of correct proportions. Some such drill in correct drawing is necessary to mastery of this means of expression. Without it drawing may easily become a promoter of careless habits, and the interest in doing a thing well may remain unawakened.

A common method of obtaining correct proportions is to

hold the pencil at arm's length and use it as a measure. Aside from the fact that it is practically impossible to teach young children to use this method with any trustworthy results, the assistance obtained by such measurements, even when they are skilfully taken, is of extremely doubtful value for children. Progress in ability to draw correctly depends largely upon the power to compare visual images and discern their likenesses and

FIG. 1

differences. Pencil measurements substitute a mathematical computation for a visual perception.

For example, in Fig. 2 the pupil can measure and ascertain that the width of the tumbler at the top is two-thirds of the height of the image, and with this information can plan his drawing correctly. On the other hand, if he will indicate the top and bottom of his tumbler by lines of indeterminate length and place two splints to represent the sides, moving them till the included shape satisfies his eye, he will discover that he can thus determine the proportions with great accuracy. If one looks at *a*, which is the shape to be represented, and then at *b*, he sees immediately that *b* is too narrow, while the image of *a* fits that of *c*, and the similarity of proportions satisfies the eye. The source of this satisfaction is not due to any confirmation from a mathematical estimation of width and height but to an immediate sense of correspondence of images. This sense develops rapidly with exercise. In Grades IV and V much should be done toward training the eye to swift and unerring discrimination. Unless this is done drawing will be as halting and uncertain as are mathematical processes when the worker is not sure of the multiplication table.

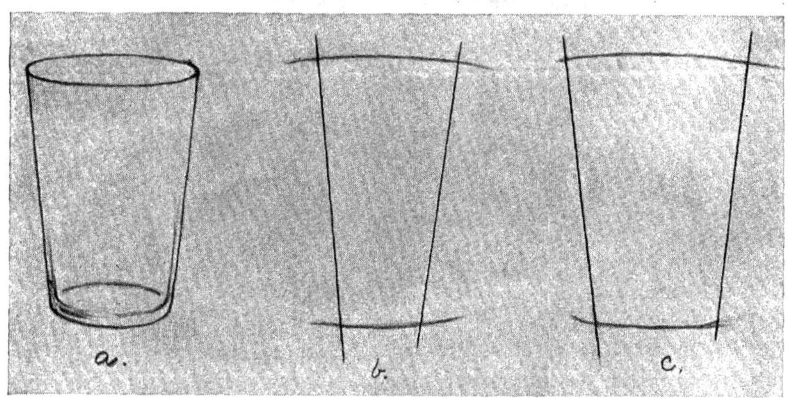

FIG. 2

Pencil measurements might be recommended as a final verification, except for the fact that they are seldom so trustworthy, even when carefully taken, as the visual perception which has received an amount of training equal to that required for the mere process of learning to take pencil measurements.

The representation of objects by splints gives excellent practice in judging proportions. There are no lines to be erased. Such representation is a helpful introduction to drawing the object with pencil.

The sort of observation which leads to most perceptible progress often may be stimulated by having pupils exchange seats and talk over the drawings made by other children, indicating by sketches or otherwise how they think improvements may be made.

To avoid mechanical slowness there should be alternation of lessons in making rapid sketches which express as much as

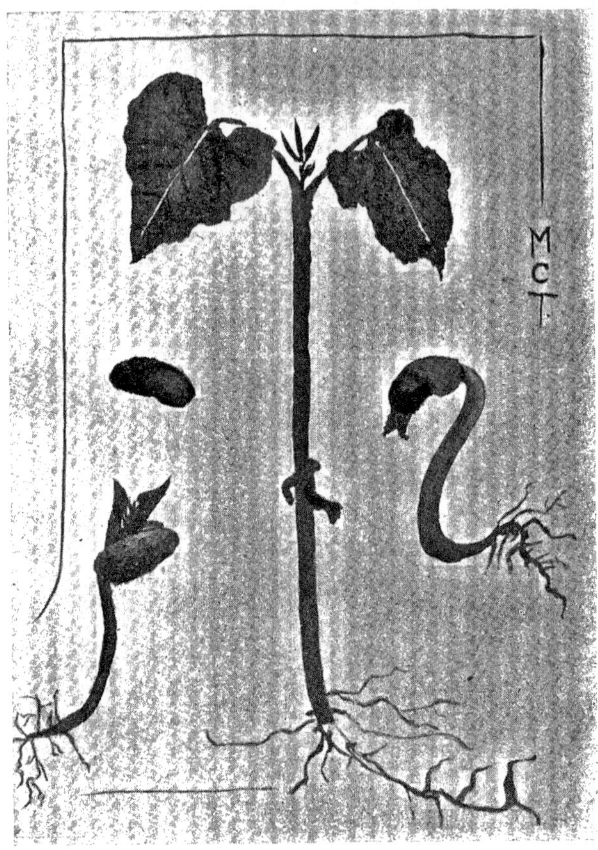

FIG. 3

possible by a few lines or brush strokes, with other lessons where a single drawing is carried to completion by being worked over and made as correct as possible.

Nature drawings in water color or brush and ink call for careful representation of proportions and shapes as well as beauty of form and character of growth (Fig. 3). As an accompaniment of drawing, modeling is an exceedingly valuable means of leading children to appreciate characteristics of objects and to think of them as occupying three dimensions.

Construction.—Skill to handle new implements and more refractory materials, a greater satisfaction in good workmanship, and ability and willingness to undertake more careful preparation in the way of plans and patterns before cutting into the material for final construction, are noticeable in children in these grades as compared with those in Grades II and III. Problems will vary with the conditions of different localities. Some instructors prefer to use constructive work as a center for other subjects. Others plan a course to develop appreciation of industries and occupations, and still others choose as a basis for problems, the immediate needs and interests of school and home. Whichever line is emphasized, much of what is valuable in the rest may be included, and in any case opportunity will be offered for experimentation with plans and designs and for increased mastery of tools and materials.

The following recommendations are based on the line of work which finds its suggestions chiefly in the needs and interests of the particular school and home environment. Children are usually ready to propose an abundance of practical projects.

Many objects useful and interesting to the children may be made from tough paper and later from cardboard. This material can be shaped by folding, cutting, and pasting so easily that it stimulates invention and is especially adapted for objects which are to be planned by means of patterns. Continued use of the rule with the addition of compasses and 45°-triangles and more complete control of scissors give children the mechanical means for planning and completing objects.

Envelopes for street-car tickets, Christmas cards, invitations, clippings, etc., call for careful patterns and measurements so that the envelope may be of the required size. Picture mounts, portfolios, sketchbook and lesson covers, and boxes of various kinds are among the suitable objects.

The sort of working-drawing required in making patterns for these, acquaints children early with this means of predetermining the shape material shall take, and is the best sort of preparation for later making drawings which represent three dimensions. Some of the patterns involve drawing to scale and translating two dimensions into three.

With vellum, lining papers, tape, paste, sewing-linen, and a punch, the cardboard work may be extended to include interesting and simple forms of book-binding, for example, notebooks, pocket

FIG. 4

memorandum pads, needle cases, book covers, portfolios, clipping files, etc. (Fig. 4).

Weaving is an occupation of universal interest. It develops some acquaintance with textiles and processes and calls for knowledge of design and color. The looms for small articles may be of the simplest construction, such as can be made by the pupils themselves. Clay work in tiles and simple pottery shapes is another valuable medium of expression of form in definite terms, and together with weaving furnishes a means of developing concrete interest in some industries of the present and past. Some of the domestic activities of sewing and cooking should form an important part of the work of these grades, especially of Grade V.

Simple forms of woodwork which can be done mostly with the knife are well adapted to these grades and give some familiarity with the material which is useful as an introduction to bench work in upper grades. For most of this work, thin wood which can easily be prepared in the rough and does not require bench tools, is sufficient.

Among the projects most frequently suggested by the children are pencil sharpeners, pen and pencil boxes, paper cutters, brush and water-cup holders, string and fishing-line winders, windmills, weather vanes, waterwheels, games, models for bridges, derricks, etc., toy carts, sleds, boats of various kinds, kites, flying machines, tops, pin-hole cameras, toy houses and furnishings, bird houses, etc.

Design.—The two places of design before described, that of practice in repeating units at consistently related intervals, and that of planning and decorating objects, should continue.

In addition to borders previously suggested, pupils should repeat units over surfaces, spacing the distribution by the eye unaided by mechanical measurements (Fig. 5).

The spacing of printing on covers for school work, the planning of margins, titles, etc., on school papers, so that language, spelling, and arithmetic papers may present a good appearance, and the simple decoration of constructed forms, furnish appropriate problems. When an object is to be decorated it is usually best at this age to limit and define the problem. For example, if a folder or box cover is to be ornamented the element of decoration may be limited to a plain band border. The pupils then experiment with different widths of margins and of border lines, to determine the spacing which produces the most pleasing effect. Another example may be the careful spacing of one element on a given surface, such as a title to be printed upon a cover.

In all these problems the results depend for their effect upon well-related spaces. The cover titles are printed in plain letters carefully planned so that the letters will appear neither crowded nor scattered, and so that the completed title shall exactly fill the area previously determined for it on the page. By thus limiting the elements which children are allowed to use attention is concentrated upon an attempt to make the best possible

FIG. 5

arrangement of what is given. This tends to develop appreciation of consistently related spaces which is a fundamental element in good design. It is necessary for children to learn that the most important question in design is not how much can be included in the space, but what is the best disposition of appropriate material. This can be emphasized at first by furnishing the elements and leaving to the children only the problem of their disposition, which at this age is fully sufficient.

When the given elements are simple, children in the fifth grade usually choose the best spacing, if they experiment with, and discuss, different possible arrangements. For example, when the problem is to design the spacing for two stripes across a rug which is to be woven, if the children cut patterns of the rug and place two splints or pencils across to represent the stripes and

FIG. 6

move these back and forth to see the effect of different spacings, they will generally select as the final choice an arrangement similar to Fig. 6, which is pleasing.

The ability, which is apparent at about this age, to appreciate good spacing, should be developed from year to year till it becomes unerring in its judgment. Thoughtful experimentation is the most effective method of developing this ability.

In the fourth year and during each succeeding year children should have general practice in the use of water color in connection with nature and object drawing. Special emphasis may be placed upon the study of color hues or the steps by which one color merges into another. If samples of two colors adjacent in the spectrum, for example, green and yellow, are placed at a little distance apart the children can collect and arrange samples so as to form well-graded steps from green to yellow. Later they may represent these steps with water color. The children should also learn to make even, flat washes of color over given areas.

A reasonable standard of accomplishment has been reached at the end of the fifth year in school if to the increased facility in graphic expression which comes from continued general practice has been added definite training in quick perception of relative proportions of shapes and slants of lines, so that the mind is able to retain and compare the image of the object with that of the representation and discern their correspondences and differences. This is likewise true if children can bring to their constructive expression such acquaintance with new tools as gives them new mastery of material, and such knowledge of patterns as enables them to think out processes and forecast results more intelligently, and such constructive interests as lead them to find satisfaction in originating projects and carrying them to a worthy completion. And it is true, too, if they find increased pleasure in well-related spaces, in the best solution of simple problems in design, and in the greater familiarity with color that comes from continued study aided by the addition of a new medium of expression in the form of water colors.

EDITORIAL NOTES

The modern school programme is very much overcrowded. Some of the causes for this condition have been pointed out so often that they are fully recognized. We live in an age which can boast of more forms of knowledge than could any other age. Each new form of knowledge asks for admission to the course of study. In the second place, there is an increasing demand for activity outside of the school. Social life, the demands for training in music or art, or some other refinement are much more exacting than they were a generation ago. In the larger communities vacations tend to grow longer, the school day is condensed into a half-day session, and the hours of study are thus steadily contracted. In the third place, it is being urged on every hand in explicit terms and in a thousand silent acts that children qualify earlier for the productive occupations of life. Boys leave school to go to work. Parents are impatient of the slow progress of their children toward the goal of independence. For these and many other reasons our school programmes are crowded.

The Demand for Economy

There is one type of recommendation which is coming to be heard more and more in these latter days. It is recommended that we return to the good old course of study. That was simple and economical and should be restored. Anyone who will examine that older course of study in detail will be convinced that it was not economical. It contained a great deal which was very trivial. There was much needless repetition and much padding in order to fill out the year. Thus the reading books were full of the most impossible stories, unjustified either by their appeal to children's interests or by their value for the training of the mind. The examples in arithmetic were piled mountain high in order to give enough work to fill out the long courses in

We Cannot Return to the Older Condition

arithmetic. The advanced geographies were made larger chiefly by increasing the size of the maps and adding more names of localities. To return to these meager courses in the world of today would be like turning back from our trolleys and steam engines to horse cars and canal boats. The course of study must be enriched in order to comport with modern life.

If the new subjects have a right to recognition, the older subjects certainly have an equal right. To drop out or evade arithmetic for nature-study is just as irrational as to hold that there is no room for nature-study. The experiment of getting on without arithmetic and spelling and writing has been faithfully tried in many schools and it can safely be said that no school can dispense with these subjects. They are essential. The method of economizing by omitting them may have seemed simple and direct but it was not a true solution of the problem.

Nor Can the Older Forms of Knowledge Be Omitted

What we need is a reworking of each part of the course with reference to the whole, a series of detailed economies rather than some general adoption of either the new or the old. One of the greatest obstacles in the way of this reworking of the course is the fact that very few of our educators can take a broad view of the whole field. Our tendency is toward specialization, toward departmental teaching. The only expedient known to the specialist is to put out that which does not belong within his own subject. His own subject, on the other hand, he enthusiastically expands.

Difficulty Growing Out of Departmental Teaching

There is hope, however, in the fact that in all departments compound courses are being worked out. Thus the students of science are beginning to plan combination courses containing much that is essential and little that is trivial. The students of geography and industry are unifying their interests. The work of history and English is being combined. Thus through combination is economy being effected.

Combination Courses

These combination courses realize in a new and most productive form what Herbart advocated in his doctrine of correlation. Many early interpreters of the doctrine looked for external connections whereby one subject might be attached to another. This external linking did not work out the internal economy which was needed in order to renovate each subject. When, however, there is organized into a single compact course all the various materials which can be unified into a single type of study, then all of the contributing sciences and subjects are genuinely worked over and true economy is attained. Our elementary school needs more combination courses. Combination of arithmetic, geometry, and algebra should be worked out; combinations of physics, geography, and anthropology; combinations of all with English in its broadest sense. These combinations must be worked out in detail, not omitting the essential of any of the subjects nor destroying the opportunities for drill in each. Thus shall we bring about at once condensation and expansion, economy and enlargement of the school programme.

Revive the Principle of Correlation

There will be a tendency on the part of all who are primarily interested in single subjects to object to this fusing of lines of thought which have been laboriously differentiated through the growth of science and modern scholarship. There is, however, full justification for this course in history, for in its early history the race learned to know the world in large, undifferentiated terms. So must the child. The specialist has undoubtedly mastered the world in greater detail than did his ancestors, but the breadth of his view is less.

For economy and breadth, for large preparation for future specialization, combination courses are the hope of our common schools.

BOOK REVIEWS

How to Study and Teaching How to Study. By F. M. McMurray. New York: Houghton Mifflin Co., 1909. Pp. 324. $1.25.

Dr. McMurray might well claim to be the chief exponent of the movement which has become prominent in the last five years toward more general attention to the problems involved in training children to study. Books on methods of teaching have emphasized the selection and arrangement of subject-matter, the conduct of the recitation and classroom management, but little attention has been devoted to the technique of directing children how to study. Dr. McMurray has been gradually developing his subject for several years in his classes at Teachers College.

The principal topics considered are eight "factors in study" to each of which a chapter is devoted. The first factor in effective study is stated as "the provision for specific purposes." The treatment is a combination of the Herbartian requirement of definitely formulated aims and the Dewey emphasis on the pupils' conscious needs.

"The supplementing of thought" is the second factor treated. The technique of a "discussion recitation" is described. The third factor, the "organization of ideas," involves training children to group the material studied under main points, and sub-points, to make briefs, to neglect non-essentials, to cultivate thoroughness in study. The other factors in study which are treated are: (4) judging of the soundness and worth of statements; (5) memorizing (by association, reflection, and organization); (6) the using of ideas; (7) provision for a tentative rather than a fixed attitude toward knowledge; and (8) provision for individuality (cultivation of initiative). Each chapter has three divisions: (*a*) the necessity and nature of the process; (*b*) the ability of children to carry on the process; and (*c*) practical suggestions for training children.

The style is non-technical, at times rather "gossipy," but always comprehensible, and adapted to the ordinary teacher. This is worth noting as so many recent books for teachers are so technical as to be incomprehensible. There is a wealth of concrete illustrations.

The rather strict Herbartian organization which prevailed in the earlier McMurray method books, and to which exception is often taken, is not so much in evidence. It is evident, however, that factors 1, 2, 3, and 6 are statements of the formal steps.

The following criticisms are suggested: (1) The book is more a discussion of "general method" and less a specific treatment of "how to study" than is desirable. (2) Some parts seem labored and comparatively pointless, e.g., the first part of chap. viii. (3) Apart from the use of the results of the investigations of Earhart, Stone, and Corman, the book does not give evidence of much acquaintance with the results of recent "experimental education."

Thus the chapter on memorizing is largely a summary of the chapter in James's *Principles of Psychology,* and there is no mention of the work of Ebbinghaus and Meumann.

S. C. PARKER

Habit-Formation and the Science of Teaching. By STUART H. ROWE. New York: Longmans, Green & Co. Pp. xvii+308.

This book was written for the purpose of calling attention to the fact that education has to do with many forms of development which cannot be defined in terms of ideas or knowledge. Ideas, the author holds, represent the relatively temporary and unassimilated phases of experience, while habit, which is the term set over against the term idea, refers to the organized, automatized aspects of experience. It has been one of the cardinal mistakes of educational practice to emphasize information and general ideas and other forms of explicit cognition. What is needed in the science of education is a study of those forms of development which do not come to clear explicit cognition but depend upon organizatons which are not recognized.

There is much emphasis in the book on a certain type of drill, not the drill which merely reiterates information until it is learned, but the type of drill which gives the child enough contact with his environment to master it and organize his reactions into settled attitudes. This special form of drill requires methods which the teacher should master. How to initiate a reaction and direct it, how to guide the child from his native instincts as the starting-points to better adjustment to the environment as the end, these are the problems of method. Method is not merely the arrangement of information, not primarily the presentation of ideas.

The reader of this book is impressed with the difficulty of defining habit. Habits of thought are referred to frequently, and habits of interpretation are also noted as desirable. Habits are now like reflexes, now like fixed modes of thought. Habit is in all these uses too inclusive a term. It covers all of the fixed modes of mental organization and certainly ought not to be contrasted with the term idea.

In the second place, one wonders whether there has been such an unqualified mistake made in the assumption of the school that its business is the development of ideas. Our author like many recent writers has found in instincts a model for school work. But human culture is what it is because we have developed out of the instinct stage of evolution into the idea stage. That there is something more significent than idea is a thesis which calls for long defense.

This book will serve to call attention to the current emphasis on habit-psychology and will, at least by its criticisms, call out the defenders of the doctrine that mental life is enriched chiefly by new ideas.

CHARLES H. JUDD

CURRENT EDUCATIONAL LITERATURE IN THE PERIODICALS[1]

IRENE WARREN
Librarian, School of Education, The University of Chicago

ADAMSON, J. W. The history of education as a professional study. Educa. T. 62:489–92. (D. '09.)

(An) ancient Quaker school. Journ. of Educa. (Lond.). 41:850–56. (D. '09.)

ANGIER, ETHEL M. A new plan of teachers' annuities. Educa. 30:229–33. (D. '09.)

BALDWIN, W. A. The high school, its weaknesses and suggested modifications. Journ. of Educa. (Bost.) 70:505–7. (2 D. '09.)

BENNETT, CHARLES A. Visiting manual training schools in Europe—II. Man. Train. Mag. 11:109–34. (D. '09.)

BOWEN, CLARENCE WINTHROP. Congress of American scholars. Harp. W. 101:24, 25. (25 D. '09.)

BOYER, JACQUES. Ninth annual Lepine exhibition of toys in Paris. Sci. Amer. 101:468. (18 D. '09.)

BRANNON, MELVIN A. Higher education and the farm. Educa. R. 38: 451–60. (D. '09.)

BUTLER, NICHOLAS MURRAY. The American college under fire. Educa. R. 38:515–21. (D. '09.)

CALDWELL, OTIS W. Natural history in the grades. El. School T. 10: 157–62. (D. '09.)

CAMP, WALTER. Personality in football. Cent. 79:442–57. (Ja. '10.)

COCKERELL, T. D. A. The Darwin celebration at Cambridge. Pop. Sci. Mo. 76:23–31. (Ja. '10.)

COURTIS, S. A. Measurement of growth and efficiency in arithmetic. El. School T. 10:177–99. (D. '09.)

[1] Abbreviations.—Cent., Century Magazine; Educa., Education; Educa. R., Educational Review; Educa. T., Educational Times; El. School T., Elementary School Teacher; Good Housekeep., Good Housekeeping; Harp. W., Harper's Weekly; Ind. Educa., Indian Education; Journ. of Educa. (Bost.), Journal of Education (New England); Journ. of Educa. (Lond.), Journal of Education (London); Journ. of Geog., Journal of Geography; Lit. D., Literary Digest; Liv. Age, Living Age; Man. Train. Mag., Manual Training Magazine; New Eng. Mag., New England Magazine; Out., Outlook; Pop. Sci. Mo., Popular Science Monthly; School R., School Review; School W., School World; Sci. Amer., Scientific American; Scot. Geog. Mag., Scottish Geographical Magazine; Tech. World Mag., Technical World Magazine.

CRAMPTON, C. WARD. Education by play. Educa. R. 38:488–92. (D. '09.)

CRAWLEY, A. E. Physical education. School W. 11:446–48. (D. '09.)

Culture and training. Liv. Age. 46:52–54. (Ja. '10.)

DAVENPORT, EUGENE. Industrial education a phase of the problem of universal education. Man. Train. Mag. 11:135–48. (D. '09.)

DAVIS, BENJAMIN MARSHALL. Agricultural education: United States Bureau of Education. State Department of Education. State legislation. El. School T. 10:163–76. (D. '09.)

DODD, ALVIN E. Better grammar grade provision for the vocational needs of those likely to enter industrial pursuits. Man. Train. Mag. 11: 97–107. (D. '09.)

DOGHERTY, CHARLOTTE E. School management. Educa. 30:207–9. (D. '09.)

DUNN, S. O. A school for railroad managers. Tech. World. Mag. 12: 502–8. (Ja. '10.)

EARHART, LIDA B. Department of elementary school problems: an experiment in teaching children to study. Educa. 30:234–44. (D. '09.)

(The) enlargement of Harvard. Harp. W. 103:17. (18 D. '09.)

FITZPATRICK, FRANK A. William Torrey Harris: an appreciation. Educa. R. 39:1, 2. (Ja. '10.)

GILBEY, WALTER. The educative value of the modern museum. Liv. Age. 46:18–26. (Ja. '10.)

GORDON, MALCOLM KENNETH. The reform of school athletics. Cent. 79: 469–71. (Ja. '10.)

GOVE, AARON. Contributions to the history of American teaching (II). Educa. R. 38:493–506. (D. '09.)

GOW, JAMES. Teachers' registration council. School W. 11:441, 442. (D. '09.)

Harvard's eleven-year-old freshman. Lit. D. 39:1033–37. (4 D. '09.)

HINSDALE, ELLEN C. Coeducation again. School R. 18:36–39. (Ja. '10.)

KELSEY, FRANCIS W. The fifteenth Michigan classical conference. School R. 18:40–42. (Ja. '10.)

LEWIS, W. D. College domination of high schools. Out. 93:820–25. (11 D. '09.)

LYONS, H. G. The scope of modern geography. Scot. Geog. Mag. 25: 617–35. (D. '09.)

MAIN, JOSIAH. Some factors in the making of a high-school course in agriculture. Educa. 30:220–25. (D. '09.)

——. University extension in Tennessee high schools. School R. 18: 29–35. (Ja. '10.)

MANNY, FRANK A. The background of the certificate system. Educa. 30: 199–206. (D. '09.)

MANNY, FRANK A. Dividing line between secondary and elementary schools. Educa. R. 38:461–68. (D. '09.)

ORMSBEE, MARY R. Household science in New York. Good Housekeep. 50:3–11. (Ja. '10.)

RUSSELL, JAMES E. The school and industrial life. Educa. R. 38:433–50. (D. '09.)

SADLER, M. E. Education in England. Ind. Educa. 8:147–52. (N. '09.)

———. Education in India. School W. 11:457–59. (D. '09.)

———. Teachers and the religious lesson. Educa. R. 39:32–52. (Ja. '10.)

SALISBURY, ROLLIN D. The teaching of geography—a criticism and a suggestion. Journ. of Geog. 8:49–55. (N. '09.)

SCOTT, COLIN A. Social education. Educa. 30:210–15. (D. '09.)

SISSON, EDWARD O. Genius of the American high school (II). Educa. R. 38:469–84. (D. '09.)

SMITH, DAVID EUGENE. The International Commission on the teaching of mathematics. Educa. R. 38:507–14. (D. '09.)

SNEDDEN, DAVID. Educational tendencies in America. Educa. R. 39:13–31. (Ja. '10.)

STEVENSON, JOHN J. College diversions. Pop. Sci. Mo. 76:71–75. (Ja. 10.)

STRUNSKY, SIMEON. College contests of the future. Cent. 79:458, 459. (Ja. '10.)

SUPER, CHARLES. Contributions to the history of American teaching (III). Educa. R. 39:53–60. (Ja. '10.)

TERMAN, LEWIS M. The pathology of school discipline: being a chapter out of the annals of flagellation. New Eng. Mag. 41:479–84. (D. '09.)

THOMPSON, F. V. The commercial high school and the business community. School R. 18:1–11. (Ja. '10.)

WEEKS, IDA AHLBORN. Notes on sectarianism in higher education. Educa. R. 39:82–93. (Ja. '10.)

WELSH, CHARLES. Can we teach literature? Educa. 30:226–28. (D. '09.)

WILLARD, EUGENE BERTRAM. The study of the child. Educa. 30:216–19. (D. '09.)

VOLUME X NUMBER 7

THE ELEMENTARY SCHOOL TEACHER

MARCH, 1910

STUDIES AND STUDY-VALUES IN ELEMENTARY SCHOOLS OF LARGE CITIES

SUPERINTENDENT WILLIAM H. ELSON
AND
ASSISTANT SUPERINTENDENT FRANK P. BACHMAN
Public Schools of Cleveland, Ohio

In a social order like our own, where there is no central authority directing educational movements, developments in education are modified more or less by local conditions. What these developments are, to what degree they are alike, and in what ways they differ can only be determined by summarizing and comparing the educational activities of different localities.

The influences determining the development of rural and village schools are different from those acting upon the schools of small cities, while the forces acting upon education in small cities are again different from those modifying the school work of large cities. A comparison of any aspect of the school activities of these units, or of phases of work in a single unit, whether it be rural communities or small or large cities is both interesting and instructive.

STUDIES COMPRISING THE ELEMENTARY CURRICULUM

No educational theme is at present claiming more attention, at least in large cities, than the question of the course of study. A country-wide demand has arisen that the elementary-school curriculum be simplified, that the component studies be revalued, and that the three R's be again given their rightful place in the schools. Local authorities are asking what branches make up the elementary curriculum in other cities of like size, in what grades are the different subjects taught, what time values are given to the several studies, what place is assigned the three R's?

Table I shows the several studies taught in the elementary schools of fifty of our largest cities and the number of this fifty teaching each branch:

TABLE I

Studies	Reading	Spelling	Grammar	Lang. and Comp.	Writing	Arithmetic	Algebra	Geometry	Geography	History	Civics	Music	Drawing	Manual Training	Cooking	Sewing	Physical Training	Physiology	Hygiene	Elementary Science	Bookkeeping	Typewriting
Number of the fifty cities teaching each branch	50	50	38	50	50	50	19	3	50	50	18	50	50	41	32	41	46	46	44	30	5	1

In the first fifty cities of the country, twenty-two different subjects find place in the curriculum of the elementary school. Reading, spelling, language and composition, writing, arithmetic, geography, history, music, and drawing are taught in all. Of the remaining number, grammar, manual training, sewing, physical training, physiology, and hygiene are taught in thirty-eight or more, while cooking is given place in thirty-two, elementary-school science in thirty, algebra and civics in eighteen and more, bookkeeping in five, geometry in three, and typewriting in one.

Reading, spelling, language and composition, writing, arithmetic, geography, history, music, and drawing, it may therefore be said, constitute the core of the elementary course of study in American cities of size; in addition 80 per cent. give instruction in grammar, manual training, sewing, physical training, physiology, and hygiene; 60 per cent. make place also for cooking and elementary school science, but it is only here and there that other subjects are taught.

GRADES IN WHICH STUDIES ARE TAUGHT

Table II shows the branches included in the elementary courses of study of fifty of our largest cities, the number teaching each branch, also the grades in which each is taught and the number teaching the given subject in the respective grade:

TABLE II

	No. of Fifty Cities Teaching	Grade in Which Each Is Taught and Number of the Fifty Cities Teaching in Respective Grade							
		I	II	III	IV	V	VI	VII	VIII
1 Reading....	50	50	50	50	50	50	50	50	50
2 Spelling.....	50	40	47	50	50	50	50	50	50
3 Grammar ..	38	..	1	3	5	14	25	34	35
4 Language and Composition ..	50	46	46	47	50	50	50	48	48
5 Writing.....	50	48	50	50	50	50	50	46	43
6 Arithmetic	50	35	46	50	50	50	50	50	50
7 Algebra.....	19	..	..	..	..	..	..	2	19
8 Geometry...	3	..	..	..	..	..	..	1	3
9 Geography..	50	4	9	32	50	50	50	46	32
10 History.....	50	8	9	11	17	31	39	48	50
11 Civics.......	18	..	..	..	..	..	..	6	18
12 Music	50	50	50	50	50	50	50	50	50
13 Drawing....	50	50	50	50	50	50	50	50	50
14 Manual Training..	41	21	21	21	20	22	28	35	35
15 Cooking	32	..	..	..	..	1	2	28	28
16 Sewing	41	..	..	5	13	29	37	27	13
17 Physical Training..	46	46	46	46	46	46	46	43	43
18 Physiology	46	21	22	23	30	36	35	38	40
19 Hygiene	44	35	36	38	38	43	41	40	38
20 Elementary Science ..	30	24	24	24	24	25	25	25	26
21 Bookkeeping	5	..	..	..	..	..	..	..	5
22 Typewriting	1	..	..	..	..	..	..	1	1

Reading, spelling, language and composition, writing, music and drawing are the only studies, it will be observed, that are actually or practically taught in all the grades of the schools of the fifty cities under consideration. Though grammar finds place in other grades, it is confined in the main to the last three. With regard to arithmetic, there is a growing movement to either omit altogether or to make the work in it during the first two years incidental, regular and systematic instruction beginning only with the third. In cities, where algebra or geometry are taught, one would expect these studies to supplant arithmetic, but this is not the case; they seem to be taught not as supplementary to arithmetic, but as separate and additional branches. Few cities give place to geography before the third grade, and this instruction is confined largely to the fifth, sixth, and seventh years, and though it is taught in the eighth grade, there is a tendency to complete the work in this branch in the seventh. Despite the attractiveness and educative value of historical materials, only here and there is history taught before the fifth grade, and it is taught by all the cities

TABLE III

	Grade							
	I	II	III	IV	V	VI	VII	VIII
Reading	+	+	+	+	+	+	+	+
Spelling	+	+	+	+	+	+	+	+
Grammar	..	..	..	..	..	+	+	+
Language and Composition	+	+	+	+	+	+	+	+
Writing	+	+	+	+	+	+	+	+
Arithmetic	..	+	+	+	+	+	+	+
Algebra	..	..	..	..	..	..	..	+
Geography	..	..	+	+	+	+	+	+
History	..	..	..	..	+	+	+	+
Civics	..	..	..	..	..	..	..	+
Music	+	+	+	+	+	+	+	+
Drawing	+	+	+	+	+	+	+	+
Manual Training	..	..	..	..	+	+	+	+
Cooking	..	..	..	..	..	..	+	+
Sewing	..	..	..	..	+	+	+	..
Physical Training	+	+	+	+	+	+	+	+
Physiology	..	..	..	+	+	+	+	+
Hygiene	+	+	+	+	+	+	+	+
Elementary Science	+	+	+	+	+	+	+	+

in question in but one, the eighth. As a rule manual training is combined during the first four years with drawing, and notwithstanding it is given separate place in some cities in the fifth and sixth, the real work in this branch is confined largely to the seventh and eighth years, so also with cooking for girls which takes the place in these grades of the manual training for boys; sewing on the other hand seemingly finds its proper place in the fifth, sixth, and seventh, yet where sewing is taught in the seventh, cooking is as a rule confined solely to the eighth. Though physical training and hygiene are practically taught in all the grades in all the cities where they have been introduced, physiology is taken into account more generally in the fourth and thereafter. Likewise, with elementary science, where it is given place, it is taught on the whole in all grades.

The grades in which the studies, comprising the elementary curriculum in cities of size, are taught, notwithstanding variations, are indicated on the preceding page.

Table III shows the principal studies comprising the elementary course of study in large cities and the grades in which each is generally taught.

STUDY-VALUES

Though a seemingly large number of studies find place in the curriculum of the elementary schools of large cities, these are by no means regarded of equal importance. The significance attributed to a study is indicated by the time devoted to it.

Table IV shows the percentage of the total time of the elementary school given in 1907–8 to each study in eleven typical large cities, it also shows the average percentage of the total time assigned each branch:

TABLE IV

	Boston	New York	Chicago	Rochester	Cincinnati	Indianapolis	St. Louis	Milwaukee	Kansas City	San Francisco	Cleveland	Average Per Cent.
Reading	26.25	32.50	40.26	17.77	14.13	17.80	17.90	22.79	14.50	30.93	26.31	23.74
Spelling	*a*	*b*	*b*	5.28	9.57	5.33	6.39	8.07	10.70	5.23	5.94	7.06
Grammar	*a*	*b*	*b*	2.39	3.25	2.16	*a*	*a*	*a*	*a*	3.63	2.85
Language, Composition and Supplementary Reading	20.14	*b*	*b*	7.98	11.37	18.03	10.05	13.27	11.20	10.56	12.18	12.75
Writing	*a*	5.81	4.88	5.08	5.41	7.86	11.05	6.86	9.66	3.77	5.73	5.71
Arithmetic	16.41	13.40	11.02	18.60	18.78	11.97	14.98	14.71	15.10	16.59	16.40	15.26
Geography—History	10.06	10.77	9.65	16.95	13.28	9.66	11.50	9.55	14.10	12.82	9.36	11.60
Music	4.47	4.85	6.37	4.79	4.87	6.85	8.18	6.92	6.60	5.38	5.46	5.88
Drawing	6.85	8.90	6.95	4.78	6.05	9.45	9.98	6.92	11.50	4.52	4.91	7.34
Manual Training	6.15	4.65	9.85	7.83	2.16	2.16	2.38	6.23	*c*	1.80	4.73	4.79
Physical Training—Physiology and Hygiene	7.09	13.05	5.17	6.57	7.40	8.65	5.32	4.61	4.00	5.23	5.31	6.58
Elementary School Science	2.51	6.01	5.80	1.99	3.79	.....	2.92	.....	3.11	3.11	....	3.65

a. Included in language; *b.* Included in reading; *c.* Included in drawing.

There is considerable variation, it will be observed, in the value accredited the same subject in different cities and in that ascribed different studies in the same city. This, however, is true for the eleven in review, and doubtless for all large cities, namely, that reading is taken to be of first importance; to it is ascribed on the average 8.48 per cent. more of the total time of the elementary school than to arithmetic, almost twice as much as to geography and history combined; while practically as much time is accredited to it on the average as is devoted to music, drawing, manual training, physical training, physiology, hygiene, and elementary-school science taken together. In a word, almost one-fourth of the total time of the elementary school of these eleven typical large cities is given to the teaching of reading.

Of second importance is arithmetic, to which is credited practically every sixth day the school is in session. The third in order is language and composition, followed closely by geography and history.

Of fourth importance are spelling, writing, music, drawing, manual training, and physical training, physiology and hygiene, while grammar and elementary-school science are being ranked as fifth in significance.

GROUP-VALUES

Further light is thrown upon the value ascribed the different studies in the elementary schools of large cities, if these studies are grouped and the values assigned the different groups compared. The studies of the elementary school may be classified as the three R's, the fundamentals, and special subjects.

Table V shows the per cent. of the total time, of the elementary schools of eleven typical large cities, given in 1907–8 to the three R's, to the fundamentals, and to the special subjects, also the average per cent. of the total time devoted to each group.

From Table V and taking the average there given as the basis of judgment, the three R's, it would seem, are regarded in large cities as the subjects of first rank, to them is assigned six-tenths of the total time of the elementary school or in other words, upon the teaching of children to read, write, and cipher is expended six-tenths of the energies of the teacher and six dollars out of every ten levied for elementary education.

If to reading—employed to comprise spelling, language,

and grammar—to writing and to arithmetic there are added geography and history, and these branches taken together are characterized as fundamentals, to them is accredited, in cities of first size, almost three-fourths of the time of the elementary

TABLE V

	Boston	New York	Chicago	Rochester	Cincinnati	Indianapolis	St. Louis	Milwaukee	Kansas City	San Francisco	Cleveland	Average Per Cent.
The Three R's: Reading—Reading, Spelling, Grammar and Language; Writing; Arithmetic ..	62.80	51.71	56.16	57.10	62.51	63.15	60.87	63.70	61.16	67.08	70.19	61.49
The Fundamentals: Reading; Writing; Arithmetic; Geography; History	72.86	62.48	65.81	74.05	75.79	72.81	71.87	73.25	75.26	79.90	79.55	73.05
The Special Subjects: Music; Drawing; Manual Training; Physical Training—Physiology and Hygiene; Elementary School Science ...	27.06	37.46	34.14	25.96	24.27	27.11	28.78	24.68	25.21	20.04	20.41	26.82

school, while but one-fourth is credited to the special subjects or to the so-called "fads and frills." With such a conception of the values of studies prevailing, there seems little immediate danger of the "fads and frills" or of the special subjects, notwithstanding their increasing worth, taking possession of our city schools and of the fundamentals being given a subordinate place in the education of the rising generation.

NATURAL HISTORY IN THE GRADES

OTIS W. CALDWELL
The University of Chicago

IV. FOURTH GRADE

The nature materials recommended for this grade are:

1. *Animal life*.—Further study of two or three kinds of common fish, their structure, uses of the parts of the body; nesting habits of one or two kinds if the nests can be found reasonably near the school building; where the eggs are placed and how they are cared for, the behavior of the young; optional individual and group field-study of fish in neighboring pools and streams; recognition acquaintance with the cat-bird, red-wing, blackbird, red-start, nut-hatch, kinglet, and the quail if it is available; the bird calendar and further study of bird migration should be continued; feeding and nesting habits of birds should be continued by study of some particular bird's nest if a convenient one may be had; economic value of birds as shown in the feeding habits in the particular nest referred to above, and also as shown in the habits of the birds in the garden throughout the season's garden work (see garden work below); the common snakes should be noted and should be thought of as valuable factors in the life of the region, not considered harmful as they are usually supposed to be; a further acquaintance-forming study of such insects as the coddling moth, plant lice, ant lion, and others that are common to the garden and field; spiders; the hibernation of animals in the winter season as shown by a study of their condition in the late autumn and again in the early spring. Spiders will be taken as the topic for fuller illustration of the method of treatment at the close of this list of the materials that are used.

2. *Plant life*.—Arrange a list of the trees that furnish food for the birds of the region and consider their importance with reference to the economic value of birds, the desirability of

having birds in the locality for other than economic reasons; collect fruits of trees which are edible for birds and for man or other animals, and discuss the relation of trees to the whole animal life of the region; the general uses of timber by men, elementary lumbering processes studied mainly by means of good stories about logging and lumbering; visit a good lumber yard if possible and ascertain the regions from which the timber used in the local region comes (see geography); the natural history

FIG. 1.—Individual plots of the fourth grade. The first cultivaton, weeding, hoeing, caring for the walks.

of the trees is to be emphasized but needs to be related to the use of their products; acquaintance with the local wild flowering plants in the autumn and spring, including a half-dozen of each; the care and growth of common edible and decorative plants in the garden during which there is secured some knowledge of the nature of a plant and its relation to the earth.

3. *Garden.*—The garden work of this grade should be done with each pupil having an individual plot in which he may grow plants of his own choice in so far as that choice is possible and harmonizes with the general plan of the garden (Fig. 1);

each pupil should be made responsible for the care of his garden and should own the results therefrom; each will need careful direction as to planting and cultivation, watering, removing the products at the right time and in the proper way, but with all there should be maintained the feeling of responsibility and ownership from which the best results come; plans and drawings to scale should be made before the time for the outdoor work to begin; also attention should be given to starting from slips and cuttings some of the things that are to be needed in the garden; in the autumn seeds for the next year's use should be collected, labeled and put away where they may be safely kept; during the progress of the garden work, constant attention should be directed to watering, drainage, condition of the soil, weeds, and their effects upon other plants, insect enemies of garden plants; a few of the methods to be used as protection against these insects should be discussed; the effects of the birds and other animals of the garden as the toad upon the well-being of the garden; a garden record should be kept and will serve well as the basis of language work, and for the art work.

In making the detail plans for the individual gardens, care must be taken to see that pupils do not include too much material, and that it is so arranged that when grown some things will not shade the others (Fig. 2), or that in case of flower gardens some plants will not hide others. In one garden which I visited last year there was a row of castor beans around the outside of the bed inside of which was a row of petunias, which in turn inclosed a small bed of sweet alyssum. Had all of the castor beans grown they would have had much less space than they needed even with several times the space allotted to this whole plot, and those that were able to grow so completely shaded the things within the garden that the latter received no light and could not have been easily seen had they grown. Within this group of gardens several illustrations were seen of this lack of proper planning. While the pupil should make his plan and decide in the main what he will grow, this plan and the things selected should be so carefully supervised that failure will not result. It is sometimes argued that pupils should be allowed to have these failures in order that the results of their work may be shown to them. There still remain after the plans are well made plenty of chances for demonstrating the results of improper work. There are here presented figures showing the preliminary plans made by fourth-grade pupils (Fig. 3), also the garden of another pupil after it is far enough along to show whether the plan was successful (Fig. 2).

FIG. 2.—A fourth-grade boy's combination vegetable and flower garden. Parsley, lettuce, and onions in the first and sweet alyssum and balsam, or touch-me-not, in the second. Some of the plants have been removed for use.

4. *Earth materials.*—In connection with the third grade, study was made of evaporation from the soil and the relation of soil to growth of the bulbous plants that were the center for much of the nature-work of that grade; further study should be made of the formation of soil through erosion and decay of rocks; removal, carrying, and deposition of soil as it is shown in streams, along the lake shore, and in laboratory experiment;

relation of plant and animal decay to soil formation; effect of winds upon soils; kinds of soils that are best for agriculture (see geography for location of best agricultural regions).

5. *The work with spiders.*—In taking this topic to illustrate in a more detailed way the kind of lessons that are used in this grade, it is not to be inferred that the topic is emphasized in the grade to the exclusion of other topics. The spider work

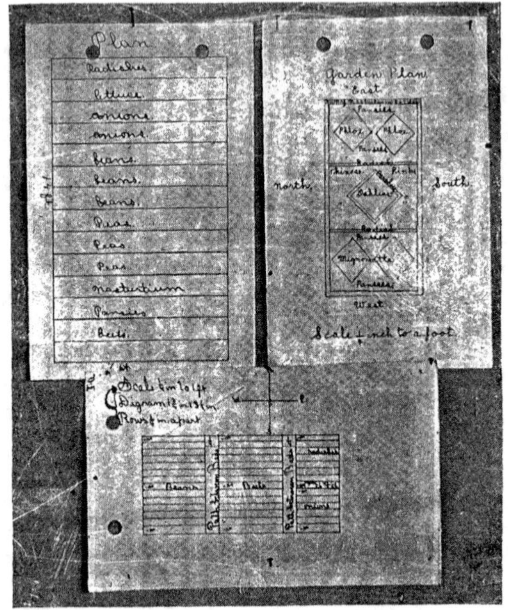

Fig. 3.—Children's garden plans.

consisted of ten lessons together with the voluntary and individual field work that the children did outside of school time. Spiders were brought into the room before the time for the first lesson and at the time that the lesson was to begin one of the spiders had spun a web part of the way down from the ceiling. It was taken as the starting-point in the work. The ten lessons as they were given by Miss Lackner, the teacher of this grade, are as follows:

First lesson: Observed spider spinning web from the ceiling, and tried to determine where the web comes from, and how it is spun. The spider was seen to crawl part of the way back up the web after it was almost to the floor, and the pupils saw that the web was rolled into a small gray ball and carried by the spider. They tried to determine how the web was carried. The web was examined under a hand lens. The question as to the source of the web was not decided, but afforded much interest. It was suggested that all pupils who wished to do so should bring into the schoolroom before the next lesson, two days later, any spiders that they could find. The question as to what are the parts of the spider's body and how they are arranged was taken up but not determined in this lesson.

Second lesson: Many spiders had been brought into the room and kept in a cage which the children called the "spider hotel," and much interest was shown in the different kinds, the differences in behavior of those that were turned out in the room, and the different ways in which they were spinning their webs. "Where are spiders found?" was the question at first taken up and the experiences showed that many sources had been discovered. "Of what use are spiders' webs to them?" "How are they able to move so rapidly?" and "How do they spin the webs?" were constant questions. The children could not agree in their observations concerning the number of legs that the spiders have, nor as to the part of the body on which they are attached, and these points were left for following lessons. The interest was intense and the pupils individually without suggestion sought assistance from various sources. At this point in the work one of the girls found a fine yellow and orange specimen which she wished to keep in a cage by itself, for which arrangements were made. It was placed in a glass fruit jar, and within a day began to lay its eggs and weave the web by means of which the eggs were inclosed (Fig. 4). A better demonstration could scarcely be desired. The eggs were laid upon the leaf with which the spider had been brought into the room, and the building of the web about the eggball proved of interest to adults as well as to the children. While this had been occurring another female spider had been brought into the room within a small pasteboard box. The box containing the spider was placed in a glass dish, the bottom of which was much wider than the pasteboard box. Soon the spider laid her ball of eggs, then she began to anchor the box in the center of the bottom of the glass dish. Web was placed from all sides to the wall of the dish, but with the first handling of the dish the box moved somewhat, when at once additional webs on all sides were placed so that even with the dish turned on edge the box

FIG. 4.—A spider's "egg ball"; eggs laid and the web woven in the schoolroom.

did not slip. This was a response to new conditions that interested and surprised everyone. In inverted flower pots in the garden the children found spiders and their eggs. The children concluded that the spiders had gone into "winter quarters" and examined them diligently for evidence upon this point.

Third lesson: This lesson was used in reading from books upon the spider's web, how it spins, life of the ground and water spiders, how spiders "fly" through the air, the mother and young spiders. The study that the children had made furnished an excellent basis for this reading about things that they had not been able to see in this study.

Fourth lesson: A further study of the structure of the spider's body. Diagram on the board of the spider's body, ending by a diagram made by the teacher in which the pupils assisted by describing the parts, using the following names for them: abdomen, spinneretts, thorax, the eight legs, the seven parts, the eight eyes, and the feelers.

FIG. 5.—A child's board drawing representing his idea of the spider and its web. Not a drawing of any particular web.

Fifth lesson: Form and construction of spider's webs. Drawings of webs in different stages of construction as seen in the schoolroom and as remembered from the individual outdoor studies. The teacher had prepared upon the board a most carefully made and complete drawing of a spider, which was used for final discussion of the structure of the spider's body. A sample of the drawings by the children is shown in the picture (Fig. 5) which represents a pupil's drawing unchanged by the teacher. One child had watched a spider spinning its web and was called upon to describe the process. This child had remained within the schoolroom during the recess period. I was going through the hallway near the room and, chancing to look within, saw the boy lying on his face in the corner of the room beneath a small table. Stepping into the room

FIG. 6.—Photograph of a spider's web. Taken early in the morning with dew upon it. Illustrates structure and form. Photograph by T. L. Hankinson.

to see what he was doing, I was met with the request: "Don't make a noise; there is a spider here and he is spinning his web and I want to see how he does it." I watched in silence for a while, and started to leave the room when the boy said: "I hope recess isn't over; the children will come in and I'm afraid the spider will stop." This child was able to describe the spinning from first-hand observation, and while doubtless some errors were made, his report was given in the real spirit of an investigator.

A photographic illustration of the form and structure of a spider's web is shown in Fig. 6.

Sixth lesson: Written lesson on the spiders, their webs, their uses to the spiders, their structure, the home of spiders, their eggs and young; drawings to illustrate the descriptions.

Seventh lesson: An oral report along the same lines of the written work but given at the elementary school's opening exercises before pupils from the other grades.

Eighth lesson: One child had found in the library a book which contained some interesting descriptions of spiders—a book that was not known to the teacher or the other pupils. The children read from this book and discussed it from the point of view of their previous work.

Ninth lesson: Spiders had been noted with webs floating in the air and some of the reading that had been used had spoken of this phenomenon. An experiment with a spider having this habit was tried in this lesson—an experiment that is suggested in Hodge's *Nature Study and Life.* On the top of a pencil that was supported in the center of a basin of water one of the spiders was placed. After making several attempts to escape, the spider began to spin a web and to let it float out into the air. The children were warned not to jump away in case the web should strike them, and when it did strike one of them the spider immediately crawled along the web and escaped from the water by way of the child's head. This experiment was repeated many times with much interest to all.

Tenth lesson: The use of pictures of spiders, final study of a spider to determine certain controverted points, and a final written paper.

Some of the books that will be found helpful are *The Spinner Family,* by Alice Jean Patterson (A. C. McClurg & Co., Chicago); *Nature-Study and Life,* by C. F. Hodge (Ginn & Co., Chicago); *Stories of Our Shy Neighbors,* by Mrs. M. A. B. Kelly (American Book Co., Chicago); *Nature-Stories for Young Readers* (Animal life), by Florence Bass (D. C. Heath & Co., Chicago); *The Common Spiders of the United States,* by J. H. Emerton (Ginn & Co., Chicago).

ENGLAND AND HER RETARDED CHILDREN

HERBERT LEATHER
Manchester, England

Although the English Education Act of 1870 placed upon the school boards the responsibility of dealing with all children of school age, it was not until thirty years afterward that the claims of retarded children to educational consideration were recognized by the central government. An alarming and steady increase of lunacy, together with an accompanying decline in the physical condition of English people generally, has caused public attention to be focused with increasing concentration upon the problem of the feeble-minded child and the conditions under which he is propagated. Recently several of the larger school boards, notably those of London, Liverpool, Birmingham, Glasgow, Manchester, and Bradford made independent inquiries with a view to ascertaining the number of retarded children of school age under their jurisdiction. Some startling discoveries were made. Large numbers of unfortunate children, who by their defects were able to evade the law of compulsory school attendance, were found to be living under such conditions of pure animalism as constituted a grave menace to the social system.

Miss Dendy, of Manchester, who has devoted her life to the interests of the feeble-minded, conducted an inspection of 40,000 pupils attending the schools of Manchester, and 500 cases of abnormal mental defect were observed and classified. These figures give a percentage for school pupils slightly in excess of 1.2 per cent., but taking into account the cases which are confined to the home, Miss Dendy calculates the proportion for all children of school age at 2 per cent.; and it is interesting to note the opinion of experts in lunacy that such children are usually the offspring of mentally defective parents. The complexity of the general problem is apparent in the fact that of some 250,000 persons in England and Wales who may be accounted as of deficient intellect, only half have been certified for permanent detention in homes. As a result of the inquiries, special schools for retarded children were founded in the large towns. The general intention was that the children should receive simple instruction in small classes under specialist teachers, until such proficiency in studies had been attained as would enable them to be drafted into the common schools. But in practice the theory proved quite unworkable. Often the children were admitted to the special schools without any attempt at classification; pupils who were merely mentally backward were associated with epileptics and idiots. The teachers had to be ceaselessly active, and many bear permanent marks of the violence of their pupils in the early days of the special school system. And as curricula were based upon the requirements of the common schools the work of the pioneer special centers was carried on under almost impossible conditions.

When the pupils left the special schools it was found that they were unable to do work which called for effort of a sustained character. In speaking of the general results of the special school system, Dr. James Kerr, medical officer of the London County Council Schools, reports:

> A considerable proportion of the pupils show little moral restraint, some are almost without speech, some seem incapable of work, others work without progress or intelligence; very frequently too they are addicted to staying out or even wandering at night, and many of this class come into the hands of the police. Some have bad habits, and immoral tendencies are common. Many are capable of control while in the special school, but speedily become irregular and uncontrollable on leaving it. About one-third will be capable of materially contributing to their livelihood after leaving, one-third will partially contribute but require an after-care association of some kind to watch over them, whilst the remainder should not be allowed to mix with the rest of the community, but should receive some kind of custodial treatment.

In the case of Bradford it was found to be characteristic of special school boys that though they could do some kinds of work and generally found situations when they left school, they never kept their places and were always on the streets, being dismissed usually, not for physical inability to do the manual work required of them, but for some eccentricity of conduct.

> Our experience in Manchester [runs the report], is that the boys very often get work when they leave the special school, but they keep it only for a short time. The best of them keep their places only so long as they can be considered to be boys. When it comes to a question of men's wages they are turned adrift. Nobody wants them. Others who are presentable in appearance and of good address get place after place, but are rarely in employment for any length of time. Undoubtedly the newly introduced Employers' Liability act will further militate against the chances of work for the mentally backward.

Of the cases which passed through the special schools of London during a fixed period, only 12 per cent. were eventually reported as being in receipt of good wages and only 34 per cent. were classified as satisfactory with regard to their moral condition.

Perhaps the most practical work of the early special school experiments was the classification of cases according to their distinctive defects. It was at first a most difficult matter to distinguish between the backward type of pupil and the defective; but generally speaking it is now recognized that the first class comprises those children who have a definite sense of responsibility in what they undertake; and their innate slowness of conception is not so fatal as, in later life, to prevent them from earning a living. In a physiological sense such cases would be normal. Within the second class may be grouped such cases as are marked by a notable degree of irresponsibility, which may or may not be accompanied by slowness of perception; but there is nearly always present some physiological defect—faulty formation of the palate, of the organs of sight and hearing, of the spine, or of the skull, which causes the pupil to be insensible to the usual methods of the school tutor. "No school training can cure the feeble-minded child" has been the experience of the pioneer English experiments in this field.

It was not until 1899 that the government, roused by the spade-work of the large towns, passed the Defective and Epileptic Children Act which empowered, but did not compel, the authorities to provide for such children in every locality. This act recognizes defective children as a class as distinguishable from the sane and the insane, and provides legislation for them up to the age of sixteen. Being permissive, this act has not been generally adopted. Apart from the towns, only three counties have set it in force—Cheshire, Shropshire, and Surrey. In all there are now 179 special schools accommodating 11,000 children.

While it is not compulsory upon education committees to provide schools for weak-minded children, it is compulsory upon parents to avail themselves of such schools when these are provided, and when they are directed to do so by the responsible education authority. This arrangement leads to many difficulties; for parents desiring to have their children specially instructed will move into districts where such instruction is provided; while parents wishing to avoid attendance at special schools for their children evade the law by moving out of the area provided for. At the present time children can be admitted into special schools at the age of five and can be legally detained until the age of sixteen years; so that in the eye of the law mental defect ceases automatically at the latter age.

The absurdity of this legislative action has been repeatedly proved by the results of after-care committees in nearly every town. Recent returns from Liverpool show that only 18 per cent. of ex-special-school pupils provide satisfactory reports, while the Birmingham committee supplies satisfactory records for 16 per cent. of the cases under observation. It is evident therefore that the work of the special schools is at present nullified for want of legal provision for the permanent detention of the worst cases in custodian homes.

If a child in the primary school is thought to be of defective mentality, he is sent by the teacher to the local special school for examination by the medical officer, after which he is retained in the school on probation and ultimately is (1) returned to the ordinary school as not being defective; (2) dismissed as being too defective; (3) retained in the special school until the age of fourteen or sixteen. For imbeciles (class 2) there is no provision whatever, save that provided by the poor-law authorities.

In order to carry on the work of the special schools, the Lancashire and Cheshire Society for the Permanent Care of the Feeble-Minded was formed several years ago mainly through the initiative of Miss Dendy. An estate of 500 acres had been purchased by the trustees of David Lewis—a millionaire merchant prince—for the purpose of establishing a colony for epileptics, and as the whole of the land was not needed for this object, a freehold-site of 20 acres was given by the trustees to the new society. Upon this land three houses and a day school were erected; and at a later period the same trustees provided a convalescent home and country schools for the purposes of the society's work. According to the report of the Royal Commission recently issued, this experiment is the most complete yet made for permanently providing for the feeble-minded. At first a small school for little boys was opened, followed by a similar school for girls. Next a schoolhouse was added; and as, with the growth of members, there was not sufficient accommodation, an adjoining farm was rented. In the farmhouse the older boys sleep, these being drafted thither as soon as they are too old to sleep with the little boys. From the first the principle has been adopted that no children older than thirteen years shall be admitted, many are received at a much younger age; hence there is little difficulty in maintaining harmonious discipline. By means of co-operation with the Cheshire County Council and the education authorities of Manchester, Salford, Bolton, and Blackburn a regular yearly income is guaranteed on behalf of the children sent from these districts and as there is a substantial grant from the Board of Education on behalf of the younger inmates under school instruction in the home, its committee is able to meet other financial calls from private sources.

The cost of the children at Sandlebridge is $100 per head per annum; the cost of keeping an ordinary law-breaker is $120 per annum, while that of a convict amounts to $200 per annum. So great has been the success of the experiment that three years ago an adjacent estate was purchased. It had on it a very good farm house, a large mansion—Warford Hall—with a lodge and cottage. It has also splendid gardens and greenhouses and seventy-four acres of good land. The hall has been adapted to the needs of the older girls and at the present time the equipment is perfect. There are now close on two hundred boys and girls on the estate, of ages ranging from ten to twenty.

There are about one hundred acres of land under cultivation. Eight of the boys work on the farm and twelve in the gardens, and as they are encouraged to believe that the whole place with the animals, etc., belongs to them they take great pride in their work and its results. The boys who sleep at the farm rise in summer at 5:45 A.M., work with the men until breakfast, and after prayers go out again to work until dinner time. They work again on the farm until tea, the monotony being pleasantly relieved by an occasional journey to town with produce, helping with the threshing-machine, hay-making, etc. After tea, unless there is pressure of work, their time is their own save that they must wash themselves thoroughly and clean their boots. Two or three of the boys have small plots of land upon which they devote much energy. They are allowed to sell what they produce. When the evenings are spent indoors the form of recreation is decided by each in turn; one night it will be singing, another night games, another reading aloud. The hour for retiring is 8 P.M. There are six practical men on the farm who do not leave the boys at work under them until they see them under the care of the matron or one of the teachers. On Sunday, which is always kept as a day of reading, singing, and walking, simple services are held in the schoolhouse, the big boys and girls having separate rooms for this purpose. When the festivals of the year occur—Shrove Tuesday, Easter, May Day, Christmas—little treats are given which are greatly appreciated by the young people.

It has been found that the girls are less easy to manage in some respects than the boys, as they are more quarrelsome, more restless, and more delicate. Under the supervision of two laundry instructors the girls do all the washing for the colony, which includes a resident staff of twenty-six, in addition to the children. The girls also do a great deal of knitting and sewing and go through an extensive course of physical exercises. They are dressed as prettily as possible, and the home feeling is fostered by considering their tastes as to work whenever possible. It is curious to note that many of them prefer laundry work to any other, though many of them are fond of light tasks in the garden, such as weeding, cutting lavender, etc. Such work, however, is given rather as a privilege than as regular employment.

A great point is made of good manners; it is found quite possible to make all the pupils behave so well that there is no objection to better-class children associating with them. The toilet, meals, play, and school are all made means of conveying lessons in good manners. It has been found that cold has a marked effect upon retarded children and great care is taken in the Sandlebridge colony to secure cosy conditions at all hours and seasons. Throughout the experiment the fact has been emphasized that it is easy to control feeble-minded children if they are never allowed to indulge animal passions. It has been found that a mature weak-minded girl who has once gone wrong can only be reclaimed under forcible detention; hence the emphasis laid by the Sandlebridge authorities upon the importance of early admission to the colony.

In addition to the usual subjects taken by special-school pupils —including simple games and songs, nature-study, manual work. as joinery, etc., basket-making, chair-caning, cookery and needlework for girls, drawing and brushwork, with modeling—both boys and girls at Sandlebridge learn to knit, darn, and sew, and do rug-work. They knit all their own vests, and many, their own stockings. The health of the children, which is supervised by a special medical officer, is excellent, as is shown by the fact that there have only been three deaths since the school was opened five years ago. During the same period three pupils have been discharged, and seven removed by parents. The farming operations are eminently satisfactory. The milk supply alone last year reached $2,000 in value. Stock is raised without the necessity of purchasing fodder during the winter months, sufficient hay being produced on the farm for the purpose. Potatoes, wheat, oats, mangels, and cabbages are the most successful crops raised. The glass and kitchen gardens form another profitable department. The balances of profit on the working of the farm and gardens for the last two years are $2,250 and $1.600 respectively.

The report of Dr. Eichholz, the eminent specialist in mental disease, who visited the school last year, runs:

The children now in residence have been selected for training after very careful scrutiny as to which children are fit for a colony school of this type, a distinction having to be made so as to exclude imbeciles on the one hand and those who are educable in day schools on the other. On the educational side of the institution every effort is made to develop such slender powers as the children possess by means of the usual schoolroom subjects, manual work, physical exercises, and music, this department being very ably conducted.

On the domestic side the children show great improvement in physical appearance and in vigor of movement. Good manners, a proper attitude to work, fair play, and the cultivation of a neighborly feeling are matters upon which stress is laid both in school and home. The opening of Warford Hall for older girls, the separation of the younger boys' home from the rest of the colony, are new features which go to make organization and classification less difficult than before. With the industrial provision for adolescents and adults added to their school, the committee are able to regard their institution as a model scheme of administration for handling the whole problem of the feeble-minded at every stage.

It is worthy of note that Manchester, the center of English industry, is fully alive to its educational responsibilities for those whose misfortunes are indirectly due to the exacting demands of modern industrialism upon the mental and physical constitution of the workers. For the mentally retarded there are the special schools and the Sandlebridge Colony; for the crippled, the lovely home and school at Swinton; for the children in the poorer districts, the country school at Mobberley, where batches of pupils are taught throughout the milder months; for the epileptic, the David Lewis Colony. Birmingham has already opened an institution modeled on the lines of that at Sandlebridge and important developments on behalf of retarded children are now being carefully planned in many English educational centers.

THE FINE AND INDUSTRIAL ARTS IN ELEMENTARY SCHOOLS, GRADE VI

WALTER SARGENT
The University of Chicago

Children in Grade VI have generally reached a stage of maturity where they are able to enjoy working with sustained purpose for a result that requires a considerable length of time for its realization and that demands thoughtful and somewhat complicated planning. They take pride in a high quality of workmanship in their production and find satisfaction in its usefulness, even though that usefulness is for the benefit of society at large and not directly for themselves. An appreciation of the beauty of well-related proportions and fine outlines is increasingly apparent. Children at this age will occupy themselves with problems of design that demand, as a book cover does, the experimental arranging of title, ornament, and other elements until the space relations are most pleasing.

In representation the children desire a knowledge of how to picture objects so they will appear to be solid and in various positions and at different angles. All these attitudes toward the manual arts are often evident earlier than the sixth year in school, but at this time they furnish sufficiently strong motives to lead the children to sustained effort for the sake of solving a problem in representation or of mastering tools and processes that these may be a means of freedom and sureness in execution, or of planning and arranging forms and colors so that the result may be pleasing to the eye.

Perhaps the most significant attitude of mind characteristic of children in Grade VI is the awakening of the desire to be connected with the activities of the outside world, and to do something worth while. Life in the country offers abundant opportunity for such occupation. Each child as he comes to suitable age can assume some responsibility, the meeting of which contributes directly to the welfare of the family. The garden, the wood pile, the poultry yard, the kitchen, give concrete opportunities in which the relations to family welfare are immediate and evident.

In large towns and cities outlets for activities which make the boy or girl a responsible contributing factor in the social system are not so obvious. Products are bought ready made. Children become accustomed to regard things as the equivalent of money, rather than of labor. Moreover, the providing of all school supplies by the town or city often presents with its evident advantages the disadvantage of leading children to feel that the municipality is an impersonal, inexhaustible source of supply. In cities also appear in Grade VI symptoms of that deflection of children from schools into industries which reaches its height at the end of Grade VIII. The fact confronts us, that about four-fifths of all children leave school by the end of the eighth grade and go to work. The seriousness of this situation is found in the fact that these children are too young to enter vocations which call for skill or offer opportunity for development. Such occupations as those of errand boys and cash girls are typical of what is open to children in the cities. The majority appear to drift about with no industrial interests or vocational outlook and take whatever pays best. They spend important formative years in employment which offers slight prospects of advancement. This experience tends to produce an unfortunate attitude toward work as something which contains within itself no interest nor scope for realizing ambitions.

A small proportion of the children will rise through these circumstances, but not the majority, unless vocational interests and right attitudes toward work are awakened before they leave school.

The educational system with its high schools and its growing number of technical schools offers increasingly excellent industrial opportunities for those who will remain. The somewhat appallingly large proportion who do not remain makes pertinent the question as to whether schools completely fulfil their function by providing advanced opportunity for those who will take it, or whether in addition elementary schools ought not to give a training planned definitely to awaken industrial interests and to promote industrial efficiency and satisfy the desire to do something worth while and to have a part in the world's activities. The final form which this training will take must be determined by wide experimentation, but the evident need that children should have a part in some work which develops a realization of the interdependence of individuals in modern civilization and of the responsibility of each, of the fact that what the municipality furnishes is produced or supplied by its individual inhabitants, and of the meaning of industrial life, gives some hints of the lines along which experiments should be tried.

The most promising answer yet made to this problem is that the time devoted to handwork in Grade VI, VII, and VIII should be increased to at least five hours a week, the extra time being taken from drawing, arithmetic, and physical exercise, as these activities are involved in constructive work, and that this time be devoted to making material which the city or town uses in its supply department. In this way a commercial standard would be furnished and at the same time financial complications would be avoided, and since the city can buy these materials at any time, the projects may be changed frequently enough to escape a too mechanical routine. Such work would frankly undertake the production of articles in quantity and by such industrial methods as division of labor and organization of a system by which poor work might be traced to its producer.

While such work may not supersede what is now known as manual training it may share the time with it, and it possesses certain important educational advantages. For example, supposing the project to be a portfolio, if each boy in the class makes one complete, and then the class is divided into groups and each performs a single operation, the great economy in time and material and the consequent increase in producing power is at once evident. Moreover, the repetition of a process, if not too long continued, instead of dulling the mind, awakens it to invent devices for performing these processes more rapidly and accurately. All danger of automatic routine may be avoided by the use of good judgment as to when the project shall be changed.

The interest shown by such a class when the school supply team calls to take the product is sufficient proof that the motive of personal ownership is not necessary as an inducement to do good work.[1] These contributions to the system readily awaken a new appreciation of school material in general and of all public property and its relation to individuals. Work such as this gives to the boy who goes into industrial employment a realization that any process to which he is assigned is part of a whole, and it is likely to awaken a demand on his part to know and master the whole. It is not unreasonable to hope that such "work teaching" which awakens interest in effective ways of doing things may bring discontent with unskilled occupations and a desire for more thorough industrial and technical training.

Certain dangers attending the introduction of industrial education into elementary schools readily suggest themselves, but they can scarcely exceed the dangers arising from the present lack of any suitable provision for properly satisfying the desire to come into touch with the activities of the world and the readiness to join with others in making a contribution to the general welfare.

In connection with the regular school programme the following suggestions for work in representation, construction, and design emphasize the phases which the abilities of the children seem to indicate as particularly appropriate to Grade VI.

Representation.—The use of drawing as a means of plain description should continue in connection with other school subjects. The work of Grades IV and V should have developed a habit of keen observation and correct representation of relative proportions and slants of lines in the objects drawn. That of Grade VI should develop still more power and freedom in representing the facts of form and structure. Definite progress toward this end is made when pupils develop a habit of thinking out the directions and limits of lines before these are drawn, by carrying the brush or pencil over the paper experimentally in the path the line is to take.

[1] These considerations are based largely on the results of an experiment tried in Boston by Frank M. Leavitt and described in detail by him in the *Manual Training Magazine* for June, 1908.

If the subject to be represented is a plant form the direction of the stem is thus thought out, and the location, direction, and size of the leaves are calculated stroke by stroke. This pause for a correct estimation of each movement makes certain that the child thinks about the line before instead of after he draws it. This order of procedure makes progress certain, but demands painstaking care. A great amount of earnest mental effort as well as manual practice is necessary if one learns to draw with any degree of correctness. Careless drawing is easy, but serves no valuable utilitarian or aesthetic end. Correct drawing is difficult

FIG. 1

to attain and the effort is not always pleasurable, but if it is undertaken in earnest the eye becomes sure in its judgment and truthful delineation grows to be a habit. This habit should be established at this time, and a proper presentation of each subject will furnish an incentive for correctness to which children readily respond. For example, maps and routes call for plain explanatory drawing in which correct proportions are a necessary framework with which no freedom can be taken. Children readily appreciate this fact and are interested to draw such routes as a stranger might depend upon in finding his way about town (Fig. 1).

Plant forms, on the other hand, involve proportions and shapes which constitute elements of beauty. Exquisite representations of plant shapes appear when the plant is held in the sunlight so as to throw its shadow on a sheet of paper, and the child stands where he can see only the shadow. He finds the structure of stems, the shapes of large masses, the foreshortening of leaves

FIG. 2

and flowers, and the delicacy of grasses and thistledown perfectly translated into terms of black and white. This interpretation is a greater incentive than the best verbal instruction. His brush and ink give results that look like shadows and he is stimulated to try to equal the perfection of the actual shadow thrown by the plant he is trying to represent (Fig. 2). The child who learns to

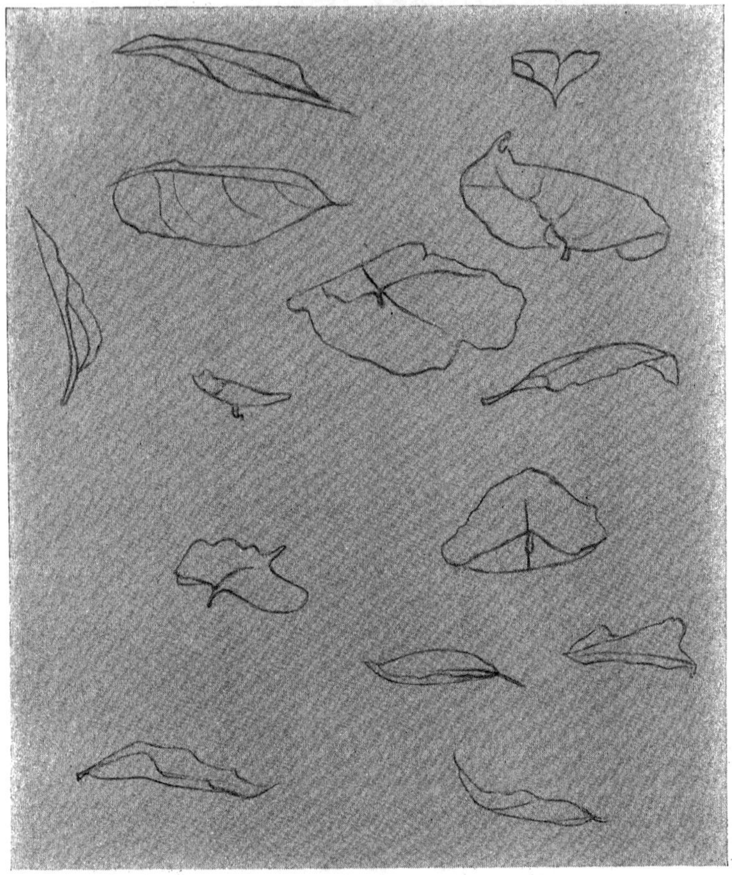

FIG. 3

represent things *as they are* gains a knowledge of form which will enable him to justify his courage when later, with increased aesthetic judgment, he ventures to alter the actual to conform to his ideal, and thus produces designs and compositions embodying natural forms.

Another subject appropriate to Grade VI is the representation of a few simple objects to show how each appears in several different positions: for example, a leaf held at various angles (Fig. 3) or a half apple turned successively in a number of directions. A topic such as this becomes a problem the solution of which the children are to work out. They are also interested in representing the solidity of objects such as boxes. One favorite juvenile method is to draw two squares and connect the corners

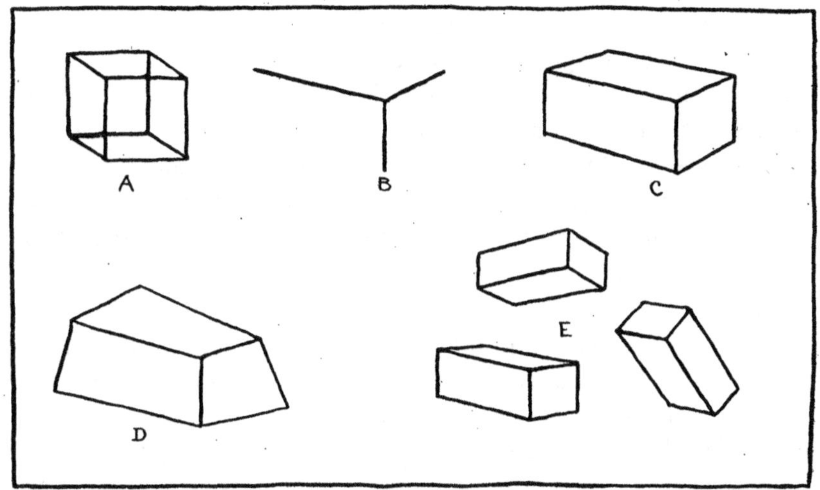

FIG. 4

(Fig. 4, *a, b*). They readily learn that three lines give the key to the structure and position of the box and that the other lines follow respectively the general directions of these (Fig. 4, *c*). Their first attempts at completing the box are frequently like Fig. 4, *d,* but practice in treating this figure as a problem in construction by trimming down the top and sides till these are satisfactory representations of rectangular faces soon results in a convincing picture of a rectangular solid. The children are then ready to experiment with different slants of the first three key lines to see the effect in changing the apparent position of the solid (Fig. 4, *e*). Nothing seems so readily to develop ability to represent rectangular solidity and later to draw from actual objects as this constructive drawing from imagination. Mention of the principles of formal perspective, such as convergence of lines or the relation of the object to the level of the eye, does not seem to be necessary or helpful at this time.

Construction.—A desire to produce things which have a definite use, and a willingness to spend time mastering tools so that they may be utilized as an added means of dealing with material are characteristic of this grade. The making of simple mechanical apparatus, such as is involved in toys that work, and the production of things that are of evident use in the school and home are especially appropriate to this grade.

In planning courses in woodworking, Grade VI seems in most localities to be the most suitable place for introducing the children to bench work. This involves the use of tools which demand strength and skill. If bench work is postponed until this grade it comes at a time when the stimulus of new material and means of handling it are especially effective.

Two ways of organizing woodwork have been evident during the history of manual training. One prescribes a series of forms involving constructive elements and processes so graded that there is logical progression in difficulty and complexity. In some cases the problems are isolated parts of construction given for the purpose of developing technique without regard to any use to which the result shall be put, as in the Russian system. In other cases, as in sloyd, the results are objects which will be of use when completed, but so chosen as to insure a logical progress in the order of tools and processes involved.

The other method of organizing woodwork is based on the argument that a constructive problem in its entirety involves three steps: First, the idea of an object suggested by a need for it, so definite in character that the conditions shall furnish the worker with a means of reasoning out just what the size, form, and construction of the object should be to best fulfil the needs. For example, if the object is a bird house, its shape, the size of the door, and other details will be determined definitely by knowing the habits and size of the bird for which it is to be built and the locality in which it is to be placed. Secondly, after ideas of the object in its completed form are clearly defined the most fitting method of construction should be reasoned out and patterns or working drawings made which show the number of parts needed and their exact shape and size. In this way the greater part of the constructive thinking may be done beforehand in terms of drawings and patterns, so that work in material may be predetermined and not experimental. In actual experience elementary school pupils can seldom plan perfectly beforehand and need some experimentation with material which often modifies the first plans. Thirdly, the tools needed and the knowledge of how to use them should be provided as necessity arises.

Woodwork with bench tools is in itself so interesting and at this age so suggestive of world activities that, however it may be presented, there is seldom any lack of enthusiasm on the part of the children. In fact, every system of woodwork cites as testimony to its suitability the great interest it arouses in the children.

Children trained by the first method are likely to develop a fine consciousness of ability to deal with material and a pride in excellent construction, but to be somewhat lacking in power to plan and to design. Generally the majority of a given class produces good work. Those trained by the second method have excellent opportunity to develop judgment and ability to plan how conditions may be met, but often the majority of a given class fails in the technical skill required to put their ideas into creditable material form. A few usually produce excellent results.

In actual practice, a combination of the two methods is generally followed. The children begin with given models by means of which the class can be taught as a whole and attain a certain degree of mastery of tools. After a year or two, those who show sufficient skill to justify undertaking individual projects are allowed to do so. By this means a standard of workmanship is maintained and the desire to produce an independent piece of work acts as a strong stimulus. A class model, while requiring the same processes of all pupils, need not result in mechanical uniformity. Fig. 5 shows the variety of design available in so common a stock model as the pen tray.

The constructive work for boys and girls of Grade VI should

bring them into contact with outside industries in the home and neighborhood, for example, sewing, cooking, constructive work, agriculture, etc. Experiments along the line of industrial work which produces by industrial methods material for use in the school system promise exceedingly valuable results.

Design.—The two phases of design before described, that of practice in repeating units at consistently related intervals, and

FIG. 5

that of planning and decorating objects should continue. The pupils should have practice in distributing more carefully worked-out units over surfaces. The frequent free-hand repetition of a single well-chosen unit trains judgment as to what constitutes tasteful distribution of pattern on a surface, and develops an individuality of style such as comes only when the hand repeats a well-mastered form, as in penmanship.

The projects in sewing and constructive work are among the best opportunities for design, and give scope for choice as to the finest shapes, proportions, and decorations. For example, in the pen trays (Fig. 5) the comparison and discussion of outlines and relative proportions involve excellent problems in design. At this age appeal may be made directly to a response in terms of

Fig. 6

aesthetic pleasure. The question, "Which looks best" generally calls forth thoughtful replies.

As in Grade V, the best results in decoration are usually obtained by limiting a problem to a few elements, as a border where the only choice is in margins and modification of corners, or a lesson cover with its printing and perhaps a monogram or other suitable ornament. Special occasions which call for invitations, menus, announcements, and souvenirs, such as valentines (Fig. 6), offer opportunities for good arrangements of spaces.

Continued use of water colors develops ability to discriminate colors more accurately. The children should learn to mix paints so as to match any given sample or produce any desired color. Special emphasis may be placed upon color values or the changes in effect when a color passes into light or into dark. The children should make charts showing five values of the same color in carefully graded steps between black and white.

A reasonable standard of accomplishment has been reached at the end of the sixth year if drawing grows more free and correct, because each line is carefully calculated, and if representations of objects show their solidity and position, if more difficult tools are mastered and the children are enabled to make things which appeal to them as worth while as a contribution to general or individual needs. All such things involve intelligent planning. And the desired object is achieved if the children are able to design simple constructive problems so that the results will be not only adequate to their purpose but tasteful in form and ornament and if ability to match colors and to discriminate between different tones is increased.

EDITORIAL NOTES

Libraries not Fully Utilized by Teachers

The possibilities of the library in connection with school work have never been fully realized by teachers. The teacher, like the average citizen, draws books from the library and reads them and hands them in again without having done anything to make the material in the books readily accessible in the future. How often one remembers vaguely that he read a month ago just the facts which he now needs for immediate use, but the source of the needed information has been forgotten and the facts themselves have grown very hazy in memory. If one had only made a note! Such a note properly recorded would be useful not only for one's own private use but also for the use of others. When a teacher refers a class to the library in a general way there is very little chance that the reference will be productive. If, on the other hand, a teacher will give children a few precise references, the use of the library will be encouraged and made productive. What is needed in our schools is more systematic, intelligent use of libraries.

Supplementary Reading

We are all convinced that supplementary reading has come to stay in our schools. The best kind of supplementary reading is that which the children get by going to books in the library. Such supplementary reading not only yields information but it gives training in the methods of research which will be of lasting benefit throughout life. A body of facts which the pupil has "run down" in the library is very much more significant for his training than a body of facts set forth in some short book which requires nothing of the pupil but the effort of reading. The difficulty which the child encounters when he tries to "run down" the facts for himself are the familiar difficulties of finding readily what is in a large collection of books. The searching of books is an art in itself. Someone must go over the books and make the matter in them accessible. Someone must help the child at first to approach books intelligently. Thus we come again to the conclusion that teachers should learn to use books and to guide children in the use of books.

Training of the kind which has been advocated in the foregoing paragraphs can be very advantageously gained in the school library. Let a grade with the help of the teacher begin to make a card catalogue of a few subjects. Here are perhaps ten books on American history, and each one contains some material on Washington. Where is this material? Let a card or series of cards be made referring to all of the significant passages on Washington. Again, the grade is studying Asia. Where can anyone find information about Asia? Let all the references be compiled by the grade. Once the child has contributed to the preparation of a card catalogue he will see the value of the big catalogue in the public library. He will realize the value of an index. He will open with some interest Poole's *Index* and like aids to the library user. The teacher will find that the work of next year will be made lighter and that there will be a genuine stimulus to research in the achievements of the grade of the year before.

What to Do in the School Library

Even if the teacher were not interested in developing this kind of ability in the pupils there would still be ample reason for urging on members of our profession the importance of becoming acquainted with library methods. No one who teaches can afford to fall behind in his acquisition of new facts, and the only way to keep up with new facts is to collect them systematically. The librarians of this country have carried the methods of systematic classification of library material farther than it has been carried anywhere else in the world. In the last two decades this country has taken the unquestioned lead in all matters of library technique. Teachers cannot afford to be ignorant of this technique. The librarians have perfected the art of using books; we who depend on books must learn their art.

Teachers May Learn Much from Librarians

School Librarians

There are promising signs that the future will realize very fully this transfer of the librarian's art to the school. Here and there libraries are found in close co-operation with the schools through the enterprise of librarian and interested teachers. Public libraries are establishing branches in schools. These can be made more than mere distributing centers; they can be made and are being made centers for wholesome training in methods of using books. Finally, there is a very great demand for librarians especially trained in the handling of children's books. The Pittsburg library has a school for the training of children's librarians, and the demands for the products of this school far outrun the available supply. All these signs are encouraging. They indicate what can be done now that attention is turned in this direction. They also serve to call the attention of each individual teacher to his and her opportunity of taking advantage at the earliest possible moment of all that is to be derived from systematic methods of using books.

BOOK REVIEWS

Questions in School Hygiene. By GUY MONTROSE WHIPPLE, edited by CHARLES DEGARMO. Cornell Study Bulletins for Teachers, No. 4. Syracuse: C. W. Bardeen, 1909. Pp. 88.

This book, which is the fourth of a Series of Bulletins edited by Professor Charles DeGarmo and the third of the series written by Professor Whipple, contains about one thousand questions, systematically grouped and classified under the headings of the hygiene of education. The general topics treated are: the schoolhouse and its site, grounds, construction, form, size of rooms, illumination, desks, heating and ventilating, sanitation, vision, the hygiene of reading and writing, hearing, the hygiene of the mouth, throat, nose, school diseases and accidents, medical inspection and growth, with special reference to sex hygiene, fatigue, overpressure, rest, pauses, and programme arrangement. Under each of those topics there are from eight to fifty well-selected page and chapter references to standard authorities. Attention is also called to four American journals which contain articles on school hygiene, a few of the best German works, and five German periodicals.

The Bulletin is designed for use in college, normal or training-school classes, teachers' associations, parents' clubs and similar organizations. When viewed from the standpoint of its purpose and method it "is devised to stimulate the interest of students and teachers, to afford a guide for reading and discussion, and a means for promoting and testing the intelligent assimilation of the subject-matter it represents."

Aside from the interrogatory form of soliciting reports and discussions, the author skilfully intersperses the questions with brief statements which call for analysis, enumeration, classification, description, or explanation; a definition, comparison, outline, or sketch is sometimes required.

The comprehensive scope of the questions may be inferred from the subjects indicated. The form of the questions, which are, as a rule, "single" and unambiguous, varies considerably. A few may be answered with "yes" or "no"; some are direct, others indirect; many are based on references, a few on direct observation; some imply answers, others offer varying degrees of suggestion.

The reviewer's experience leads him to believe several of the questions would have more significance to the average reader if they gave one or two direct suggestions as to what to look for. The following question, which is one of six in the Bulletin of the particular type in mind, will serve as an illustration. (44) "For what games or sports ought provision to be made on the playground, e. g., baseball, basket-ball, handball, horizontal bar, swings, etc.?" This question definitely directs the reader and at the same time stimulates further thought and investigation. Two or three examples in place of five would have been sufficient.

The question just quoted will also serve to illustrate the limits of the field outlined in this connection, since this is the author's nearest approach, aside from a question on the playground movement, to the needs and difficulties of *directed* play from the standpoint of hygiene and development. There are no questions bearing directly on the meaning of play and its educatonal value to those who take part.

There are some questions of a type illustrated by the following: (386) "Define the terms 'heterophoria' and 'heterotropia.'" (393) "What is 'exanopsic amblyopia'?" The lay reader will no doubt infer the answers to these must be contained in some one, or perhaps more, of the references listed under the twenty authors named under "Vision." This is somewhat typical. The references are not closely classified or evaluated and many of the questions turn the attention to books rather than school conditions.

That this book is, however, full of valuable and interesting questions could be shown by calling attention to the subject-matter of any one of its pages. Under the heading of "School Desks," for instance, we find, aside from the references, questions whch call attention to periods of growth, sex differences, evil effects of bad posture, relative values of desks and tables, habits of posture, necessity of exercise, and so on.

Some questions taken at random are:

(435) "How many books are read by the average child during his second school year?"

(550) "Are adenoids more common among the poorer classes? Why?"

(558) "What is the difference between stuttering and stammering?"

(708) "Unless in most vigorous health the school teacher should not teach in the Sunday school. Why not?"

The method used in this book, which brings the reader face to face with practical educational problems and schoolroom situations by means of well-selected and pointed questions, is rapidly growing in value and influence. It is from this kind of concrete material and searching criticism that education will gain much toward securing a body of rational and systematized knowledge.

BIRD T. BALDWIN

THE UNIVERSITY OF CHICAGO

Music in the Public Schools. A Manual of Suggestions for Teachers.

This recent publication may well be considered a good sign of the times. For the past few years teachers of music have been gradually awakening to the seriousness of the study of music in the child's life, and to the necessity of having such study in definitely graded form.

The writer of this manual, with a keen appreciation of the needs of the child, has prepared a course of study for eight years' work with a definite outline for each week of each year, for the guidance of the teacher. This outline will prove especially helpful to teachers who find themselves confronted with the necessity of teaching music, having little preparatory training, while to teachers of experience many of the suggestions may increase the value of their own courses of study.

Nearly all of the essentials of music-study, namely song interpretation, perception of good music, voice training, and the reading of music notation, are given due attention—the first three showing a mark of great progress in the treatment of school music; we say "nearly" all, for there is yet to be desired a place for original or conceptive work, which is the basis of all song-study.

It is a welcome day when the poetic content of song is considered. In this book the material has been wisely chosen in reference to the poetic as well as melodic content; most of it is simple in the ideas involved, therefore within the child's interest and comprehension.

If the definite technical work which the author has outlined for the first three years could be left until a later period, and more time put upon song singing (the necessary technicalities being taught so simply that they are learned almost unconsciously by the children), together with original work, the course would be broader, and a more certain musical basis would be laid for the work of the succeeding years.

ELIZABETH HOAR

ETHICAL CULTURE SCHOOL
NEW YORK CITY

CURRENT EDUCATIONAL LITERATURE IN THE PERIODICALS[1]

IRENE WARREN
Librarian, School of Education, The University of Chicago

ACHER, E. A. Spontaneous constructions and primitive activities of children analogous to those of primitive man. Amer. Journ. of Psy. 21: 114–50. (Ja. '10.)

ADAMS, MELVIN O. AND ATWOOD, WILLIAM T. The new Dartmouth. New Eng. Mag. 41:521–30. (Ja. '10.)

BACHMAN, FRANK P. The school superintendent and his training. Educa. 30:368–73. (Fe. '10.)

BALLIET, THOMAS M. Undergraduate instruction in pedagogy. Educa. 30: 335–43. (Fe. '10.)

BATT, DR. MAX. Library work in Great Britain and Germany. Pub. Lib. 15:51–53. (Fe. '10.)

BENNETT, CHARLES A. Visiting manual training schools in Europe–III. Man. Train. Mag. 11:214–36. (Fe. '10.)

BOUGHTON, ALICE C. Penny luncheons. Psycholog. Clinic. 3:228–31. (Ja. '10.)

BRICKER, G. A. Shall secondary agriculture be taught as a separate science? Educa. 30:352–56. (Fe. '10.)

BRUERE, ROBERT W. The work of the New York association for improving the condition of the poor in saving child life. Pedagog. Sem. 16: 450–56. (D. '09.)

[1] Abbreviations.—Amer. Educa., American Education; Amer. Journ. of Psy., American Journal of Psychology; Cent., Century; Child L., Child Life; Educa., Education; Educa. Bi-mo., Educational Bi-monthly; Educa. R., Educational Review; El. School T., Elementary School Teacher; Good Housekeep., Good Housekeeping; Harp. W., Harper's Weekly; Journ. of Educa. (Bost.), Journal of Education, New England and National; Journ. of Educa. Psychol., Journal of Educational Psychology; Journ. of Geog., Journal of Geography; Liv. Age, Living Age; Lib. Journ., Library Journal; Man. Train. Mag., Manual Training Magazine; New Eng. Mag., New England Magazine; Pedagog. Sem., Pedagogical Seminary; Pop. Educa., Popular Educator; Psycholog. Clinic, Psychological Clinic; Pub. Lib., Public Libraries; School B., School Bulletin; School and Home Educa., School and Home Education; School R., School Review; Sci. Amer. Sup., Scientific American Supplement; Teach. Coll. Rec., Teachers' College Records.

Burnham, William H. The scientific study of hygiene. Pedagog. Sem. 16:437–41. (D. '09.)

Caldwell, Otis W. Natural history in the grades. El. School T. 10: 270–76. (Fe. '10.)

Carmen, George N. Co-operation of school and shop in promoting industrial efficiency. School R. 18:108–14. (Fe. '10.)

Cooper, Edward H. Children's books. Liv. Age. 46:316–18. (29 Ja. '10.)

Crawford, Caroline. The function and development of the arts of movement. Educa. Bi-mo. 4:156–64. (Fe. '10.)

Cronise, Caroline C. The art work of the kindergarten. El. School T. 10:240–47. (Ja. '10.)

Daniels, Joseph M. College athletics and physical education. Educa. R. 39:144–55. (Fe. '10.)

Davis, Benjamin Marshall. Agricultural colleges. El. School T. 10: 277–86. (Fe. '10.)

Dawson, George E. A characterization of the prevailing defects in backward children and a method of studying and helping them. Pedagog. Sem. 16:429–36. (D. '09.)

Findlay, Maria E. Froebel's principles and current idealism in England. Child L. 11:231–35. (D. '09.)

Fleischman, Frank. A boy prodigy and the fourth dimension. Harp. W. 104:9. (15 Ja. '10.)

Flint, Lillian C. Pensions for women teachers. Cent. 79:618–20. (Fe. '10.)

Geissler, L. R. The measurability of attention by Professor Wirth's method. Amer. Journ. of Psy. 21:151–56. (Ja. '10.)

Goldthwait, Joel E. The importance of training the growing child in correct postural habits. Pedagog. Sem. 16:455–46. (D. '09.)

Greenwood, James M. William Torrey Harris: educator, philosopher, and scholar. Educa. R. 39:121–43. (Fe. '10.)

Gregory, W. M. Secondary school geography in the middle West. Journ. of Geog. 8:110–16. (Ja. '10.)

Gwinn, Joseph M. Tendencies in the content of the courses of study in state normal schools. Educa. R. 39:156–64. (Fe. '10.)

Harger, Charles Moreau. Industrial fellowship in university work. Sci. Amer. Sup. 69:79. (29 Ja. '10.)

Hart, Hastings H. The care of the dependent child in the family. Pedagog. Sem. 16:464–72. (D. '09.)

Hill, Patty Smith. The future of the kindergarten. Teach. Coll. Rec. 10:29–56. (N. '09.)

Hopkins, Ernest Martin. The critical period for the American college. Educa. R. 39:165–75. (Fe. '10.)

JOHNSTON, W. DAWSON. The library as a reinforcement of the school. Amer. Educa. 13:208–11. (Ja. '10.)

JOHNSTONE, E. R. The welfare of feeble-minded children. Pedagog. Sem. 16:447–49. (D. '09.)

JUDD, CHARLES H. On scientific study of high-school problems. School R. 18:84–98. (Fe. '10.)

KILPATRICK, VAN EVRIE. Department of elementary school problems: emancipating the individual pupil. Educa. 30:375–85. (Fe. '10.)

KIMMINS, C. W. Trade Schools in London. El. School T. 10:209–19. (Ja. '10.)

KIRK, EDWARD C. The dental disabilities of school children. Psycholog. Clinic. 3:217–23. (Ja. '10.)

KNOWLES, A. C. The army signal school. Sci. Amer. Sup. 68:407. (25 D. '09.)

LADD, A. J. The function of the teachers college: II. Educa. 30:344–51. (Fe. '10.)

LINDSAY, SAMUEL MCCUNE. Exploring the new world for children. Pedagog. Sem. 16:459–63. (D. '09.)

MCANDREW. The college influence on public high schools. School B. 36: 89–93. (Ja. '10.)

MACVANNEL, JOHN ANGUS. The materials of the kindergarten. Teach. Coll. Rec. 10:1–28. (N. '09.)

MANNY, FRANK A. Some programmes in the school arts. Educa. Bi-mo. 4:165–69. (Fe. '10.)

NISHIYAMA, SEKIJI. Japanese elementary schools. Educa. 30:364–67. (Fe. '10.)

NOYES, WILLIAM. The ethical values of the manual and domestic arts. Man. Train. Mag. 11:201–13. (Fe. '10.)

NORTHRUP, WILLIAM PERRY. Good and bad air and its effect upon children. Pedagog. Sem. 16:442–44. (D. '09.)

O'SHEA, M. V. On making commands to children effective. Pop. Educa. 27:225–26. (Ja. '10.)

PARKER, S. CHESTER. Our inherited practice in elementary schools. El. School T. 10:228–39. (Ja. '10.)

PYLE, WILLIAM H. The psychological basis of moral training. School and Home Educa. 29:179–87. (Fe. '10.)

REESE, CARA. Chicago's school buildings. Good Housekeep. 50:208–15. (Fe. '10.)

SARGENT, WALTER. The fine and industrial arts in elementary schools, grades II and III. El. School T. 10:220–27. (Ja. '10.)

SARGENT, WALTER. The fine and industrial arts in elementary schools, grades IV and V. El. School T. 10:287–300. (Fe. '10.)

SARGENT, WALTER. The place of manual arts in the secondary schools. School R. 18:99–107. (Fe. '10.)

SEASHORE, CARL E. The class experiment. Journ. of Educa. Psychol. 1:25–30. (Ja. '10.)

STAPLES, OTHA BOWMAN. Is there a relation between the amount of schooling and financial success in later life? El. School T. 10:261–69. (Fe. '10.)

THORNDIKE, EDWARD L. The contribution of psychology to education. Journ. of Educa. Psychol. 1:5–12. (Ja. '10.)

THORNDIKE, EDWARD L. Promotion, retardation, and elimination. Psycholog. Clinic. 3:232–40. (Ja. '10.)

TRACY, S. E. The occupation treatment for sick children. Pedagog. Sem. 16:457–58. (D. '09.)

TUPPER, FREDERIC ALLISON. Moral training in the public school: a symposium. Journ. of Educa. (Bost.). 71:117–23. (3 Fe. '10.)

WHIPPLE, GUY MONTROSE. The spelling of university students. Journ. of Educa. Psychol. 1:31–33. (Ja. '10.)

WHITE, FRANK MARSHALL. The babies who work. Harp. W. 54:12–13. (8 Ja. '10.)

WILLIAMS, S. HORACE. The educative value of manual training–III. Man. Train. Mag. 11:252–60. (Fe. '10.)

WILSON, LOUIS ROUND. The public library as an educator. Lib. Journ. 35:6–10. (Ja. '10.)

WINCH, W. H. Some measurements of mental fatigue in adolescent pupils in evening schools. Journ. of Educa. Psychol. 1:13–23. (Ja. '10.)

YOUNG, ELLA FLAGG. The public high school. School R. 18:73–83. (Fe. '10.)

VOLUME X NUMBER 8

THE ELEMENTARY SCHOOL TEACHER

APRIL, 1910

PROVISION FOR GIFTED CHILDREN IN PUBLIC SCHOOLS[1]

J. H. VAN SICKLE
Superintendent of Schools, Baltimore, Maryland

During the past decade much attention has been given in public-school systems to the problem of the backward, delinquent, and defective children who clog the lower grades of our schools and retard the progress of the children of normal mentality. Their presence in ordinary classes imposes upon the teacher the necessity of devoting an undue portion of time and attention to the few from whose education society will benefit least, to the disadvantage of the many who can better profit by the instruction given; and hence it has come about that in many city-school systems special classes are provided for children of subnormal intellect in which they may receive an education suited to their peculiar needs. This is good policy for two reasons: every such child has a right to enough education to make him as useful as the limitation of his natural endowment will permit; and economy in administration is observed by so much segregation of the backward as will permit the teaching of normally constituted children in reasonably large classes. This cannot be done in a manner fair to the children in our schools when 50 per cent. of the teacher's time and energy must be given to 5 per cent. of the children in the class. So the movement for special classes for the few—possibly 2 per cent. of the whole number—who cannot

[1] Paper read before the Department of Superintendence of the National Education Association, March, 1910.

profit by instruction as given under ordinary school conditions is undoubtedly in the right direction. I would go farther and say that another group of children, numbering possibly 8 or 10 per cent. of the whole school enrollment, intermediate in mental grasp between the extreme cases and the great body of average children, should receive such individual attention as cannot be given in large classes. It does not fall to my lot today to discuss the proper handling of these two groups of children, but I desire to leave no doubt in your minds as to the very great importance which I attach to the proper instruction of the slower children. Most of them will later develop marked strength, and it is by no means safe to conclude that the slow child of today will be the slow child two years hence.

The topic assigned to me assumes that there are children at the other extreme of ability for whom also special provision should be made. These are the pupils of more than ordinary power who should not be restricted to exactly the same curriculum nor held to the moderate pace which is necessarily set by the ability to progress shown by the great body of children. President Eliot has often called attention to the importance of discovering these capable individuals and giving them opportunities commensurate with their abilities, so that society may use them "to lift the whole population to a higher plane of intelligence, conduct, and happiness." Theoretically, most people are willing to admit that the general tendency in a democracy is to bring all men to a common level; that the level toward which we tend is the level of the average intelligence rather than that exemplified in the genius; and that the only way to lift the whole population is to develop capable individuals to take the lead in the lifting. It cannot be denied that the graded school system, by its tendency toward uniformity, has operated toward making us satisfied with a medium level of attainment. Undoubtedly, one of its effects has been to raise many individuals to a higher level than they might otherwise have attained, and this is good; but, on the other hand, it has made many other individuals satisfied with lower attainments than those of which they were capable, and this is not good. It is not easy to break the "cake of custom" that fifty years of uniformity have created; but now that such signal process has been made in the proper education of children at the lower levels of ability, we may hope for at least equally valuable results from special attention to children of exceptionally strong mental endowment. For the purpose of this discussion these children are spoken of as "gifted." By the gifted child we do not mean the genius in the sense of which Mr. Galton uses the term. We refer to a more numerous class of children endowed with somewhat more of intellectual power and energy than the great mass of children in our schools. Of course there is no clear-cut line of division anywhere between the various groups. They shade into each other, and we shall often be in doubt as to the group in which a child belongs; but even under such circumstances there is a gain for education, because we shall sooner solve a problem by recognizing it as a problem than by ignoring it altogether. Statistics are available showing about how many subnormal children there are among every one thousand, but we do not know how many gifted children there are among every one thousand children born into the world. We do not know because we have not been looking for them. Under the operation of school attendance laws, instead of easily getting rid of the dullards and laggards, as we too often formerly did, we are undertaking not to crowd them out but to hold them and teach them, and it is an easy problem to discover who they are. They force themselves upon our attention. We cannot be ignorant of their presence. Too often, on the other hand, we fail to notice that some children in our classes might do much more work than we are requiring of them. From time to time a few, by reason of their special aptness, have commanded our notice, but we have not considered that they needed any special opportunities. We have, as a rule, held that these bright children would in some way take very good care of themselves, and that if a child had any special ability he would make his way in spite of all obstacles. This may be true of the extremely limited number of individuals included in Mr. Galton's definition of genius; for he holds that the actual genius is the only genius; or, in other words, that the only individuals of superior native ability are the ones who have demonstrated that superior ability by actual accomplishment; and conversely, that those who have not actually demonstrated the possession of superior native powers do not possess them. He rules out the extremely important factor "opportunity." According to Lester F. Ward,

> The only true test of genius (ability) is trial. But unless the conditions for trial are present there can be no trial, and without trial under favorable conditions there is no basis for judging whether there be genius or no.

Ward's position in this matter, though somewhat over-sanguine, is to my mind more reasonable than Galton's.

> Great men [he says] have been produced by the co-operation of two causes, genius and opportunity; neither alone can accomplish it. But genius is a constant factor, very abundant in every rank of life, while opportunity is a variable factor and chiefly artificial. As such it is something that can be supplied practically at will. The actual manufacture, therefore, of great men, of the agents of civilization, of the instruments of achievement, is not a utopian conception but a practical undertaking . . . . it consists in the extension to all the members of society of an equal opportunity for the exercise of whatever powers each may possess.

How slight an opportunity to develop whatever powers they may possess have children who drop out of school and enter the ranks of unskilled labor as soon as the law permits! Often a parent is unaware that his gifted child is the possessor of any special talent unless so informed by the teacher. When so informed, not infrequently a parent will keep his child in school even at the sacrifice of the small but important pecuniary aid which the child's labor would afford. By dealing thus with parents whose only capital is their labor, teachers are able to aid very materially in bringing genius and opportunity together. But keeping children in school is not enough. Adherence to fixed and unchangeable courses of study and to inflexible schemes of classification fall far short of furnishing equal opportunity to all in our schools. Total lack of systematic procedure would equally fail to secure the desired equality of opportunity, for stimulation and guidance must be well organized and constant. We hear of isolated instances of such stimulation and guidance, but not often of well-organized schemes which may be applied on a large scale, as in a city system of schools.

There is a considerable body of literature on the subject of backward children, the lower 10 per cent. of our enrollment, but very little on the upper 10 per cent., the gifted. Mr. Kendall's presentation of the case of the ablest pupils, two years ago, is the only one giving definite plans of prodecure that I can find in the *Proceedings of the National Education Association.* The Mannheim scheme of classification (briefly described on pp. 43–47 and 121–23 of *Bulletin No. 376, Bureau of Education,* entitled "The Auxiliary Schools of Germany") makes special provision for the abler pupils by grouping them in separate divisions. The "Report of the Committee on Provision for Exceptional Children in the Public Schools," presented at the Cleveland meeting of the N. E. A., devotes the greater part of its space to abnormal and subnormal children. Only one page is devoted to provision for exceptionally capable children, and the attitude taken by the committee is that the problem, while immensely important, remains unsolved. Their position will be made clear by the following quotation (*Proc. N. E. A.,* pp. 350, 351):

> In our conception of what the gifted child should do, we are inclined to look too exclusively upon the shorter time in which he can accomplish the tasks of the conventional course of study. Until we comprehend that for the gifted child a somewhat different atmosphere should be provided, that, too, a different curriculum should be developed, we shall accomplish little.
>
> While the saving of time is not unimportant, the really important consideration is the ideal of effort and accomplishment which the child is forming. It is essential, therefore, that these gifted children have the stimuli that will react upon them in such a way as to cause them to become as vigorous in will as they are acute in intellect; for there is reason to believe that great achievements in leadership are due more to strength of will than to mere intelligence.

In the same volume Dr. Charles A. A. J. Miller, of Baltimore, devotes a half-page to this topic (p. 959). The "Report of the Committee on Six-Year Course of Study" is suggestive, especially in recommendation 4 (*Proc. N. E. A.*, 1908, p. 627). A year later the same committee made a report (*Proc. N. E. A.*, 1909, 498–503) in which there appear twelve brief statements of plans designed to meet the needs of pupils of varying ability. In the same volume (pp. 175–82), Mr. Walter Siders presents an excellent discussion of certain phases of the subject.

The value of any plan must be measured by its results. We cannot expect complete and convincing reports of results in the early stages in the operation of any plan; but where, as in Indianapolis, Worcester, Baltimore, and elsewhere, special provision made for the abler pupils has been in operation for several years, a tentative statement might at this time be possible. For instance, where high-school credits have been earned by elementary school pupils, it would be possible to make a numerical statement of that particular kind of result and to say something specific as to the class rank of such pupils upon graduation from the high school. Such a statement would be of more value for comparison than an indefinite remark to the effect that by means of a given plan "many pupils save considerable time" or "some pupils are able to complete the high-school course in three years." Instead, therefore, of indulging in indefinite statements, I shall attempt to give a brief statistical report of measurable results accomplished by means of a plan, common to several cities, which, beginning in a small way in the fall of 1902, we have been using in Baltimore. The plan, in brief, is to allow pupils who have done strong work in the sixth grade, with the approval of their parents, to take up extra studies of high-school grade while doing the regular work of the seventh and eighth grades of the elementary school. These studies are Latin, German, advanced English, and, in exceptional cases, some of the mathematics of the first high-school year. Pupils who take this work are transferred to a convenient center in which enough pupils may be gathered together to allow the instruction to be organized on the departmental plan. We started in 1902 with one center, enrolling 173 pupils, and that year we admitted pupils of the eighth grade as well as the seventh. In 1903 and later, admission was limited to pupils just entering the seventh grade. We now have four centers with an enrollment at present of 571 pupils in these preparatory seventh and eighth grades. For three years one of these centers has been allowed, by way of experiment, to keep selected pupils for an extra year. Such pupils spend but two years in the high school. Other preparatory pupils ordinarily spend three years in the high school; but in either case, for preparatory pupils the time required for high-school graduation after the sixth elementary grade has ordinarily been five years, whereas six years would have been required had it not been for the high-school credits earned in the elementary school.

The preparatory arrangement was in only a formative and transitory stage during 1902–3, 1903–4, 1904–5. High-school adjustments also were quite difficult at first. Hence, of pupils promoted to high school in 1903, 1904, and 1905, a majority were unable to graduate in three high-school years. With the preparatory class promoted in June, 1905, the tide turns.

Promotion from Preparatory	Total Graduations from High School	Graduations in Three Years	Graduations in Four Years
1903	27	4	23
1904	42	8	34
1905	39	27	12
1906	48	42	6
1907	(Not yet available)	39	(Not yet available)

In other words—

At High-School Graduation of	Preparatory in Two Years	Preparatory in Three Years	Preparatory in Four Years
1906	..	4	(Could not be)
1907	..	8	23
1908	..	27	34
1909	16	42	12
1910	25	39	6
	41	120	75

The first preparatory-school pupils were graduated from the high school in 1906. By June, 1910, 236 in all will have graduated. Of these, 41 were in the high school proper but two years; 120 were in high school three years, and 75 four years. Among the latter were 57 who spent but one year—the eighth—in a preparatory center, the one which was opened in 1902. While these 75 pupils who, in the early days of the plan, spent four years in the high school did not save any time, they enjoyed marked advantages. They earned 13,050 credits, or an average of 174 each; whereas the number required for graduation was on'y 150. It is quite evident that the high-school course pursued by these pupils, though not shortened, was made much fuller and richer than it would have been had they entered from the ordinary eighth grade.

To make clearer this general statement about the 75 preparatory pupils who spent the usual four years in the high school, a few particular instances are selected. Fourteen girls, graduating in 1907, gained an average scholarship rank of 46 in a class of 147, or 27 places above the middle of the class. Two of these girls stood, respectively, first and seventh in the class, and four others were among the first twenty in scholarship rank. The average number of credits earned by members of this company was 162. Twenty-two girls graduating from the high school in 1908 secured average scholarship rank of 48 in a class of 160, or 32 places above the middle of the class; and three of them stood, respectively, first, second, and third in the class, while four others ranked among the first twenty. The average number of credits earned by those in this group was 166. Nine preparatory boys, graduating from the high school in 1907, won an average scholarship rank of 34 in a class of 103, or eighteen places above the middle of the class; and four of them ranked among the first ten in their class. The average number of credits earned by members of this company was 192—very greatly in excess over the required 150. Thirteen preparatory boys graduating from the high school in 1908 won an average scholarship rank of 49 in a class of 120, or eleven places above the middle of the class. The average number of credits earned by members of this group was 189, an excess of 39 over requirements.

A study of individual records of high-school graduates who came from the preparatory classes shows in general that a notable gain was experienced in one of two ways: either the student gained a year or more in time, securing the high-school diploma in three years or less instead of taking the customary four years; or the student, though spending four years in the high school, was able to rank among the honor graduates of his class and to secure a much broader and richer training than the regular four-year student secured. In a relatively larger number of cases where the student took a third preparatory year in the single center offering this extra preparatory year, distinct gain was experienced in both these directions at the same time, because the high-school diploma was secured after only two years in the high school proper, and the student also stood among the honor graduates.

Six preparatory-class boys who spent three years in preparatory class and only two in high school, and who graduated in June, 1909, won a rank of 34 in a class of 133, or 32 places above the middle of the class, and two were among the first twenty in the class. Eight girls from the same preparatory class, graduating from the high school at the same time, made an average rank of 21 in a class of 161, or 59 places above the middle of the class (in Baltimore boys and girls go to different high schools). One of these girls stood second in her class and three others were among the first twenty. The average number of credits earned by this company of boys and girls was 165, or 15 in excess of requirements. Two hundred and thirty-six preparatory pupils will have been graduated from the high schools in the four years ending in June, 1910. This is not a large showing when we consider that in these four years the same high schools (three out of the five in our city) have graduated 1,342 pupils; but the plan is very new compared with the usual one, and a number of obstacles must yet be overcome. Some parents do not fully understand the plan. Not all teachers can be quite impartial in their attitude toward a scheme of work which takes away from the regular classes some of the more desirable pupils. Furthermore, many pupils entering the seventh grade are timid about going to a strange school located at a point somewhat distant from their homes; and so it happens that only about one-third of those recommended as capable of taking up the extra preparatory work avail themselves of the opportunity offered. If the work were carried on in every large school so that pupils could enter upon it without being transferred away from the home school, doubtless more would attend; but unless there are enough enrolled at one point to form at least three classes, the teaching cannot be economically provided for. For this reason we are using for the preparatory classes only selected centers, and for the further reason that our plan enables us to utilize schoolrooms in portions of the city where the population is decreasing and where consequently some schoolrooms have become vacant.

There are now enrolled in our preparatory classes in the elementary schools 571 pupils, and in the high schools, exclusive of students to graduate in June, there are now 223 students who were promoted from preparatory classes. Mr. Ward's statement that genius is not restricted to any rank of life is borne out, in the case of our preparatory pupils, by the interesting fact that in these classes are to be found boys and girls representing every rank of the social order and wide variety of home conditions. To take this material and, following Ward, make "leaders and builders of civilization" out of it is an ambitious undertaking—so ambitious that we do not aim so high; but, judging by the energy and enthusiasm that these se'ected pupils put into their work, and the marked success which they have so far attained as measured by school standards, we are quite certain that they will display somewhat more of energy and efficiency in whatever field of life-effort they enter than if, during their school days, they had become contented with a lower level of effort and attainment.

DEFINITION IN THE SPELLING RECITATION[1]

J. W. SEWELL
Supervisor of Grammar Grades, Nashville, Tennessee, Public Schools

I. THREE WAYS OF DEFINING

Logical definition requires so full a knowledge that it can state (1) the proximate genus to which the notion signified by the word belongs, and (2) the distinguishing property, or quality, which will set it distinctly aside from all other members of that genus. Some illustrations will help to make the matter clear. For example, the notion *brittleness* is to be defined. The ending *-ness* indicates quality; the notion belongs to the genus quality. But that would, so far, mean the same as *hardness, lightness, happiness, paleness,* etc. So we must find the particular quality which sets aside *brittleness* from others of that genus; and putting the distinguishing quality after the proximate genus, we derive the definition, "Brittleness is the quality of being easily broken."

To define accurately, then, requires exact classification, which means broad information. It also requires a critical faculty, a nicety of discrimination, to include just the essential quality and to exclude all qualities that are not essential.

Obviously, you will say, it is an impossibility to get real definitions from school children; pupils in the lower grades, even those in the upper grades, have neither the wide information which gives them the ability to classify notions nor the critical discrimination which would enable them to know essential from non-essential qualities.

Yet this is not altogether true. Not all definition is scientific, nor is it always built after the logical pattern already examined. To begin with, children are not so poor, after all, in their ability to define, provided the notion to be defined is not foreign to their

[1] This article leads the editor to suggest the desirability of a similar test in some school which does not emphasize the progressive use of logical definition.

experience or by its very nature difficult for anybody to define. Ask a child what *mansion* means, and he will probably say, "A big, fine house." Not so bad. But ask him if he means the city hall; he will say, "No, I mean a big, fine house to live in—a big, fine home." Such a definition should satisfy any sensible teacher.

Try the word *caravan*. One will say, "A lot of camels." "Is it a drove out loose in the desert?" "No; a line of camels loaded with goods." That is a pretty good definition too. Many examp'es like these will be quoted from actual exercises later in this paper.

Definitions of this kind, if they contain just the right thought, are the best of all. If a child repeats the words of the dictionary, it is possible he has the idea in mind; but when he gives an accurate definition in his own colloquial diction, the teacher knows that the actual picture has passed through the child's mind and that the definition is backed up by actual understanding. The native colloquial diction of the child is a thing that deserves encouragement, whereas it is often treated with contempt or at least indifference; and more often still the over-careful teacher takes pains to "correct" every phrase that the child naturally uses for the expression of an idea. By colloquial diction I do not mean the loose combination of vulgarism, slang, and idiom ordinarily thrown together into a sort of linguistic junk-heap by the dictionary-maker and called "colloquial." What is slangy, I should ca'l slang; what is provincialism or solecism I should call by the respective term. The term colloquialism should be the name for the strong native English of conversation, of the familiar letter, and of the playground. It is the lusty idiom, the long-lived vernacular. It dates back beyond Chaucer, much of it; and it will flourish—not only among the children and the unlearned, but among those who talk with vigor, with native freedom and unstudied directness—long after the sturdy old rhetorics are moth-eaten, long after some prim, lexiconed preceptors have closed their serious and musty labors.

The teacher's duty, therefore, is not to reprove the child's colloquial language as s'ovenly or ignorant, but to accept it as correct and honest, a foundation for a broader and more e'egant and sonorous vocabulary. Not only would such an attitude cause the English language of the schoolroom to be less foreign and repugnant, but a most useful avenue would therein be found for the reception of new ideas in all studies of the school course.

There is yet another means of definition with which the young student is almost equally ready; also it is a favorite and doubtless an indispensable method that the dictionary writer has of making clear the meaning of the word he is defining. This is by the use of synonyms. One of the commonest devices for presenting a thought that is new to the mind is by comparison. The whole content may be so unfamilar that to attempt the standard method of classification and limitation by means of the logical definition may be quite useless. Of what use would it be to an Eskimo to tell him the class to which an orange belongs, and the difference between an apple and an orange? But if a snowball be used to illustrate the size of the fruit and the taste of some confection brought by the visitor be cited to convey an idea of the flavor, a conception will dawn in the mind which may be enlightened later into sufficient understanding.

Just so with words. Turn at random in the dictionary and see to what extent synonyms are used in defining: for example, *gratify,* "to please, to indulge, to humor, to requite, to recompense"; *recess,* "a withdrawing, retirement, intermission, an alcove, a niche." Hence, if a word that is new to a child be identified with a familiar one by means of a synonym, he at once appropriates the new word.

Identification by means of synomyms is obviously not the same process as logical definition. It is not a mental process of so high an order as that. Whereas logical definition places a notion in its proximate genus and selects from its qualities that which differentiates it from other members of that genus, the use of a synonym indicates that the general implication of the word is comprehended sufficiently well to recognize that two or more notions roughly or accurately cover the same ground. Thus they are taken as wholes and compared as wholes.

Consequently we may expect children in the lower grades to use synonyms freely in their definitions. The logical definition is beyond the powers of most of them; the colloquial definition may not be attainable on account of inability to trim between even familiar notions; but the vaguest hold that one has on a word will make it possible for him to offer a word that he regards as of similar meaning and therefore identical—a synonym of it.

In these two methods, colloquial definition and use of synonyms, the teacher has the most direct approach to the minds of pupils. A new word, *purloin,* occurs in the lesson. It is utterly unfamiliar. The teacher says, "It means to take what doesn't belong to you; to steal"; and no dictionary will ever make the idea plainer than that.

By these two methods, young children who have not yet learned to draw fine distinctions may express their understanding of words. At the beginning of practice in definition, say in the 4-B grade, the attempts are of course awkward; but they are in the right direction, since they are endeavors to give expression to a shadowy idea.

To illustrate these attempts, and to show the processes of mind natural to a child at this age when he is attempting to appropriate and reproduce a dictionary definition, we select the words *station, caution, patience, familiar,* and *terror* from a lesson. After taking the suggestions of his teacher, the child goes to his dictionary and stores away (he thinks he does) the definitions. In recitation they appear about thus:

1. "A *station* is where people get on the train."
2. "*Caution* means to look out, to take care."
3. "*Patience* is being quiet, not fussing."
4. "*Familiar* means what you know right well."
5. "*Terror* is when you are scared a whole lot."

In 1, there is no genus, only partial description; in 2, a noun is defined as a verb; in 3, clear knowledge is indicated, even if only partly expressed; in 4, an adjective is defined as a noun; in 5, an abstract noun lacks the genus, and the specific difference is quaintly worded. Yet I do not hesitate to say that, as 4-B definitions, these are good enough, every one; the essentials of each idea are evidently grasped. A pupil of this grade is not expected to know the parts of speech. The means by which he got the substance of these five words into his mind was the vehicle of colloquial, free definition or fairly good synonyms.

Of course, these two methods must give way gradually to more mature and accurate methods. How this is to be done, how in some general way and at indefinite periods some progress is to be made, will appear from the tests detailed below. But a necessary caution to teachers just here is that perfect definitions must not be expected of children until they are far along in the course of study.

II. A TEST AND ITS RESULTS

From the regular textbook, one hundred words were selected out of the assignment for the respective school year, and these were handed to the teachers of fourth-year, fifth-year, and sixth-year pupils. The words had been studied in the dictionary some weeks before, and had been used in sentences in class. Given as a test thus, without warning, the words were defined naturally, with no possibility of an artificial recitation from memory in terms that might not be understood. Given to one large school only, it was assured that children of much the same environments should define all the words. In all, about six thousand definitions were tabulated so as to assign each to one of the three methods discussed in the preceding pages.

Grade	Colloquial Definition	Synonyms	Logical Definition
	Per cent.	Per cent.	Per cent.
4-B	89.5	1.5	9
4-B	82.2	3.5	14.3
4-A	73.7	15.3	11
4-A	51	43	6
5-B	71	24	5
5-B	42	43	15
5-A	80	15	5
5-A	39	16	45
6-B	35	35	30
6-B	17	21	62
6-A	21	5.5	73.5
6-A	16	14	70

Allowing for difference in quality among the teachers, the table shows a striking progression, almost regular, in working away from the less scholarly up toward the more scholarly methods of defining words.

Interesting examples of colloquial definition will be quoted to show how satisfactory these may be:

Fourth Grade

Iceberg: "a big piece of ice in the cold ocean"; "frozen water floating down a stream."

Sausage: "ground meat that comes from a pig."

Machinery: "lots of work"; "steel stuff to thrash corn and wheat."

Strait: "a small body of water that goes like a gate."

Pineapple: "a plant that grows in the ground with its head out."

Caravan: "a drove of men on camels on the desert."

Mechanic: "a man that fixes things."

Patient: "a doctor's sick person"; "one you wait on"; "to wait long and be still"; "to be quiet and take things as they come."

Patience: "to wait and not to grumble"; "what it takes to train fleas."

Bashful: "ashamed to talk"; "scared to come out"; "if some one would ask you to say a piece and you would not and you would cry and be so fretful."

Speechless: "a person who has been told something dreadful and hardly can stand it."

Dumb: "is when you can't talk; speechless is when you are too frightened to speak."

Fifth Grade

Wisdom: "You know a lot."

Vision: "something that you see at night"; "something seen in a dream."

Mosquito: "a long slender fly that has a long bill"; "an insect that flies around at night and bites."

Butterfly: "a fly that has slick dust on its wing."

Perseverance: "sticking to a thing"; "not to stop till you win."

Examples of synonyms and logical definitions are not quoted, for the reason that these are in dictionary language and would not be in any way unusual.

III. SUMMARIES AND CONCLUSIONS

1. Definition does not consist in memorizing and reciting ponderous phrases from the dictionary. These may be utterly foreign to the child's mind. He may deceive himself by learning mere forms; he may deceive his teacher thereby; but certain it is that mere memorizing is not definition.

If what he gets is a definition, it must be so expressed as to tie the new word to something in the child's conscious experience. If it happen to be a synonym, it must identify the new term with some well-known term which is part of his ready language and his actual knowledge. That which he takes in as a definition, if really a definition, must be current coin receivable by him at full face value.

2. In the tabulation by grades above, observe—

a) That the colloquial definitions decrease in almost a regular way from about nine-tenths of the whole in the 4-B Grade to about one-sixth of the whole in the 6-A Grade.

b) That the logical definitions increase almost as rapidly as colloquial definitions decrease, from about one-tenth of the whole in 4-B to nearly three-fourths in the 6-A.

c) That the number of synonyms varies according to the nature of the words to be defined, but that more of them are used about the middle of the course. Probably this is because few synonyms are attainable in the Fourth Grade, and they are not greatly needed in the Sixth, since by that time pupils are able to use logical definitions freely.

3. Do not refuse to recognize the value of colloquial English in definition. At some stages in the child's education, the colloquial idiom is particularly useful as a vehicle for taking in as well as giving out ideas. As shown in the examples quoted, these definitions are frequently accurate, sometimes remarkably incisive, remarkably direct and complete. In other cases they are very loose: they define a noun as a verb, an adjective as an adverb; they place the notion in almost any large group not proximate; they may present on'y a familiar phase or example instead of a definition. In the lower grades colloquial definitions are not only unavoidable but acceptable. In the Fifth Grade they should be taken sparingly; and above that grade they should be set aside as rapidly as possible in favor of logical definitions, since herein is a more extensive, more elegant, and more accurate vocabulary.

4. When synonyms are allowed as definitions, the teacher should be certain that the synonym offered is better understood than the word to be defined. For example, for the word *curiosity,* the pupil should not give the synonym "inquisitiveness"; for *revive,* "reanimate"; for *fascinate,* "captivate"; for *caution,*

"wariness" or "admonition." In none of these instances is there evidence that the child has gained a new thought.

5. As to the progress of definition from grade to grade, only general suggestions may be given, for much depends upon the nature of the words in each lesson.

In the Third and Fourth Grades, few exact definitions should be expected. Not only does the pupil lack ability to classify and discriminate so as to form logical definitions, except perhaps those of terms in arithmetic, geography, etc. which he has fully learned; he lacks also the *vocabulary* for expressing nice shades of thought, and his stock of useful synonyms is limited. Hence most children have to fall back upon colloquial, loose definition.

In the Fifth Grade, much the same condition prevails. The pupils have perhaps improved in their ability to handle the dictionary, so that one-third or more of the words should be accurately defined. A'so more synonyms have been gathered, and a large percentage of these will be used.

In the Sixth and Seventh Grades, attention should be paid to correct parts of speech in the definitions chosen. For example, pupils in these grades should not be allowed to say, "*Jocose* means to be jolly," or "*Census* means to count all the people."

In these grades should be emphasized another matter which is too commonly neglected. Children usually suppose that the purpose of the dictionary is to give the pronunciation of a word, its derivation, then its various meanings—that is all. This idea accounts for a large number of errors to be found in the written work of pupils in high schools as well as in grammar schools—such sentences as, "The girl will *unfurl* the package of candy"; or, "The man fell down and hurt his canopy" ("covering over the head"); or, "The apple was *precocious*" ("maturing early"). Actual school sentences these are. The *application* of words, as well as their meanings, must be learned, and in the Sixth and Seventh Grades much of this work may be done. In assigning the lesson, the teacher may point out beforehand some words that will be troublesome, and warn the pupils to find in the "big dictionary" illustrative sentences that will show the one or more applications.

Furthermore, when synonyms are chosen for definition, they should now fit closely the word to be defined. For example, "robber" would not do as a synonym of *pirate;* nor should "controversy" be accepted as an exact equivalent of *wrangle.*

The Eighth Grade should give more attention to etymology and word analysis. Students in this grade should learn that the derivation of the word and the present meaning are not necessarily the same: *circumscribe* must not be defined as "to draw around," nor *philology* as "love of words."

Pupils in this grade ought to be able to define and use in their current sense certain less common newspaper terms, such as *ultimatum, cuisine, expansion, reciprocity, optimist,* etc. Merely to give a general idea of their sense is no test of skill in definition.

In all this work, the necessity for free oral discussion in the class cannot be over-emphasized. In no other way can teachers expect their classes to conquer the many linguistic problems.

6. One who has had much experience with the struggles of children with definition cannot forbear a word of regret that a simple dictionary for children does not appear to exist. The smaller the volume, the more condensed and consequently more general and colorless, are the definitions. Great progress has been made in almost all other lines in elementary school work, but the pupil in the lower grades confronts all the difficult puzzles that his grandfather did—he is dazed by the ponderous roll of words if he finds a definition in full, or he is cheerfully bethumped with synonyms most foreign and incomprehensible.

It may be replied that only fairly mature minds are able to grasp definitions, which must of necessity be abstract and fully expressed—therefore they cannot well be simple. But children from Fourth Grade up must search for the meaning of words, and it does seem that a consistent attempt to use simple language in the smaller dictionaries might be successful. If perhaps five thousand to eight thousand words of the ordinary grammar school vocabulary were made into a volume, the more usual meanings of these given in simple language, and brief illustrative sentences added to help the child, the whole matter of definition might be removed from danger of the slough of despond.

AGRICULTURAL EDUCATION
STATE NORMAL SCHOOLS

BENJAMIN MARSHALL DAVIS
Miami University

It is the business of state normal schools not only to train teachers but also, as far as conditions permit, to find out by experiment in practice schools, what to teach and how to teach it. When both aspects of the work of these schools are considered, the important relation which they bear to agricultural education, particularly in elementary schools, becomes apparent. The problem of the normal school in this matter is twofold: (*a*) to meet the rapidly growing demand for teachers who are able to give satisfactory instruction in elementary agriculture, and (*b*) to reduce the subject to a proper pedagogical basis, in other words to determine what phases of this great subject may be undertaken in the elementary schools under average school conditions both from the standpoint of the child and of the teacher.

The following is a brief summary of the efforts of the state normal schools to find a solution of this twofold problem. The data have been gathered from one hundred and thirty-seven of the one hundred and forty-five schools now actively engaged in training teachers.[1]

When the diverse social, educational, and industrial interests of the country as a whole are considered it is to be expected that these differences will be reflected in the types of instruction given in the various normal schools. To these differences brought about by conditions more or less local are to be added those due to tradition. The older schools are usually less elastic and adaptable than the newer ones. Bailey regards the latter fact as a very serious obstacle in the way of a general introduction of agriculture into these schools. He says, "One cannot look to all the existing normal schools in the older states, or even to any

[1] Just now the nine state normal schools of Oregon are closed, owing to lack of financial support from the state.

considerable part of them, for the training of teachers for this kind of work" (28).[2] This statement must be qualified for there are many exceptions. For example, the Johnson State Normal School of Vermont has been offering courses in agriculture for over eight years, while the one at Laramie, Wyoming, recently established, does not give courses in agriculture but prepares its graduates to teach in cities.

The number of graduates of state normal schools that teach in agricultural communities varies exceedingly not only in different states but among the schools of a single state. Reports from seventy-six show that twenty-eight have from 60 to 100 per cent. of their graduates going into schools of rural communities; twenty-seven have from 20 to 50 per cent.; and twenty-one have from 1 to 10 per cent. Of the twenty-eight having from 60 to 100 per cent. of their graduates teaching in rural communities, twenty are offering instruction in agriculture and fifteen require it; of those having from 20 to 50 per cent., twenty offer instruction in agriculture and nine require it; of those having from 1 to 10 per cent., eleven offer agriculture and three require it. If this proportion should apply to all the schools it would seem to indicate that the number of graduates of normal schools going into agricultural communities is quite large, perhaps larger than generally supposed. It indicates also a tendency of the schools to adapt their work, at least to the extent of introducing agriculture, to the needs of the communities where their graduates teach. This estimate is only approximate and only inferences may be drawn from it. It does not take into consideration the large number of students who take a portion of the course and who for the most part go into the country to teach. One normal-school president says: "There are very few of our graduates who teach in rural schools, but there are multitudes of our undergraduates who do so." This statement suggests another phase of the problem of normal-school instruction which has received little or no attention, viz., what recognition in the course of study or character of instruction should be given to the

[2] The references are to bibliographies of previous articles of this series and to bibliography at end of this article.

fact that so many who attend the normal school for part of the course drop out and become teachers in rural schools? For example, in the school just referred to, the instruction is evidently adjusted to meet the needs of students who expect to teach in city schools. No agriculture is taught although "multitudes of the undergraduates" become teachers in rural schools, and in the state itself agriculture is the chief industry.

The development of agricultural instruction in state normal schools has on the whole kept pace with the growth of the general interest in the subject. It is hard to say just when this subject was first taken up. Probably the first institution to begin this work under the name of agriculture was the Rock Hill State Normal School of South Carolina, which offered courses in agriculture as early as 1895. The Johnson State Normal School of Vermont offered its first course in agriculture in 1901, and about this time the subject was introduced in some of the state normal schools of the Middle West (45).

In 1906 a report on "Preparation of Teachers to Give Instruction in Elementary Agriculture" was prepared for the Joint Board of the California State Normal Schools trustees (46). This report showed that the normal schools of Minnesota, North Dakota, Nebraska, Missouri, and South Carolina were attempting to prepare teachers to give instruction in elementary agriculture; that some attention was being given to the subject in the normal schools of Illinois, Utah, and Oklahoma; that nothing was being done to furnish such training in the schools of Iowa, Kansas, Michigan, Ohio, Pennsylvania, Alabama, North Carolina, or New York, but that several of these schools were, however, getting ready to undertake the work as soon as possible.

In a study of ninety-one state normal schools reported to the National Education Association in 1907, it was shown that seventy-five believed in an instruction in agriculture, and were either giving it in some form or desired to do so. Sixty-one of this number were either offering courses or had made plans for such courses for the following year. Seven of these were giving only a little agriculture in connection with other science courses. Eight were doing still more in connection with school gardens and were planning to extend the work. The remaining forty-six were giving definite courses in agriculture (47).

During the present school year, of one hundred and thirty-seven state normal schools, eighty-seven are now giving some instruction in agriculture. In fifty-two of those offering courses, twenty-two are elective and thirty required. Of those not giving instruction in agriculture, thirty-seven give it incidentally in connection with botany, nature-study, or some other course in science, and nearly all those giving courses in agriculture also give some attention to the subject in other science work, particularly in botany and nature-study.

It will be seen from the above that normal schools are rapidly introducing agriculture. The number of schools offering such courses has increased from about 20 per cent. in 1906 to more than 50 per cent. in 1909. Indeed, the demand for well-qualified instructors in agriculture for normal schools exceeds the supply. One normal-school president says that he tried for over one year to secure a competent instructor. Davenport says: "The call is sharp from the normal schools of the Middle West which have this year (1909) taken some of the best trained and most promising teachers of this class" (48, p. 144). The call is not alone from the Middle West but the East as well. During the present school year one of the normal schools of the New England states secured a teacher who, at the time of his appointment, was professor of agricultural education in an agricultural college of the Middle West.

Letters from presidents and others connected with normal schools not now offering agricultural instruction indicate that in many of these schools plans are under way to introduce the subject as soon as possible. Included in this number are the normal schools of New York and Pennsylvania, none of which now offers such instruction except incidentally with nature-study and other subjects.

The character of the work in agriculture varies much in different schools. But there is one feature of the instruction that is common to all, viz., as evidence of the newness of the subject and of the fact that it is in an experimental stage. In some schools the work in agriculture is only in name, much better instruction being given in other schools in courses in nature-study.

The time given in the course of study varies from ten weeks to two full years, the average being less than one year. One interesting reaction following the demands for agricultural instruction is to be found in the readjustment in science courses, especially in the biological sciences. The title agricultural botany and agricultural zoölogy frequently occurs in courses of study. One fails to find in some of these, however, justification for the new titles, for the instruction remains much the same, with emphasis on morphology. The attitude of certain teachers of biology toward their subject is well illustrated by the following extract of a letter received from a member of the faculty of a large state normal school. "I obtained over one dozen kinds of water animals one day from a pool when the science (biology) teacher said he saw none in it. He was sending to New York City for crayfish when a brook near the building was full of them. The boys (in training school) had made nets and would have been glad to have caught the animals for him." Perhaps the influence of such a teacher was partly responsible for the ignorance of a practice teacher (a senior) who stood in a bed of marigolds and asked if there were any marigolds in the garden. The introduction of agriculture will no doubt have much to do in changing this attitude.

> It will in the end exert a profound influence upon the teaching of general science. There is no manner of doubt that the masses of people are best benefited by the teaching of science in its applied form. . . . . Agriculture is evidently to be the pioneer in this business of the adaptation of science to the common affairs of life in the schools that are attended by the masses, and if this is true its incidental service may be even greater than its direct. In the meantime it is vastly significant that the schools where teachers are made have at last commenced to study real life in one of its most concrete forms (48, pp. 45–46).

Normal schools have so far been too much occupied in providing for instruction in agriculture to give much attention to the pedagogical problems of the subject. These problems concern (*a*) the organization of courses in the normal school itself, and (*b*) methods of teaching the subject in the public schools. Naturally, the former has been the first to receive attention. The organization of work in agriculture has been in two directions, one in the science work already referred to, and the other in the purely agricultural courses recently introduced.

Special efforts of adjustment have affected nature-study more than other science studies. Many believe that as far as the elementary schools are concerned agriculture should have the nature-study aspect, or as some prefer to say, nature-study should have an agricultural trend; that since nature-study has to do with material drawn from the child's immediate environment, and since a large part of this environment is more or less agricultural (consisting of animals and plants under control of man) a good course in nature-study forms an adequate preparation for a teacher to give such agricultural instruction as will meet the needs of rural schools, and at the same time enables a teacher to make use of school gardening and other practical or economic phases of the subject in city schools (49).

The particular direction in which nature-study has been most modified in its readjustment has been in the school garden (50). It has been found that the school garden may serve as a very effectual means of unifying most all nature-study work. Children are not only able to "grow things" in gardens, but in doing this work successfully have had to solve many of the problems that are fundamental to agriculture. The character of the soil, the conservation of water by cultivation, the protection of plants from insect and other enemies, and many other factors of successful plant growing are encountered. Many normal schools have regarded this readjustment of nature-study and other science work as sufficient to meet the demands for agricultural instruction in the training of elementary teachers, and are working with this end in view. Some of the normal schools of California, Illinois, Massachusetts, New Jersey, and other states, and many of those schools now offering courses in agriculture, have made substantial progress in the readjustment of science work.

Instruction in agriculture as a separate subject in normal schools is now in an experimental stage. Yet certain work and methods seem to have proved successful. The first publication of work adapted to normal schools was in the form of a textbook based on teaching experience in the Kirksville, Mo., State Normal School (51). Recently a very concrete treatment of the problem has appeared as a government publication. It is an account of what is actually being done and how it is done in a typical normal school. The writer says in his introduction,

> The aim of the normal school is to prepare young men and women to teach in the elementary schools of the state. The young people who attend come from farms or smaller towns, and when they go out to teach they are called upon to give instruction in what is known as elementary agriculture. To meet this demand, a department of agriculture was established four years ago. The course at first extended through one term's work but has been lengthened until practically two full years are now devoted to agricultural instruction. The work has attracted many young people, and the success with which they have subsequently instructed others along these lines indicate that the instruction has been effective. Not all the problems in teaching agriculture have been solved but it may justly be claimed that a few of the more difficult of them have been solved (52).

Other similar publications of successful practice which has been tested by the work of students when they become teachers will contribute much toward the pedagogical efficiency of the subject.

From the standpoint of methods of teaching the subject in the public school, little has been done. A very promising beginning of the study of this question was made at the Peru Nebraska State Normal School in February, 1909, when the Normal Agricultural Society was organized. The purpose of this society is to aid teachers in "handling the new subject of agriculture in public schools of the state." Those interested in its organization have expressed the hope that "it will become a pedagogical laboratory for testing and discovering methods to improve and extend the teaching of agriculture throughout the schools of Nebraska." The director is the head of the department of agriculture in the Peru Normal School and conducts for the society a column in the *Nebraska Farmer* which is to be the official publication of the society (53).

An interesting experiment limited to one phase of agriculture is now being conducted at the Western Illinois State Normal

School at Macomb in co-operation with the Illinois State Agricultural Experiment Station. A soil experiment field of two and one-half acres has been provided by the normal school. The school

as its share of the responsibility, takes full charge of the field operations implied in the plans. Such co-operation provides for both scientific and educative values in the work and it is proposed to make the results as far reaching as possible. Not alone to teachers and prospective teachers will it be valuable but as well to persons now engaged in agricultural practice (54).

A few helps to teachers have been worked out in normal schools and published, for example, from Cape Girardeau, Mo. (55), and Chico, Cal. (56). They consist of discussion of agricultural subjects suitable for public schools, and methods of instruction.

There is one large class of normal-school students already mentioned that is not adequately provided for. This class is made up of students who wish to teach in rural schools and who can spend only a year or part of a year in preparation, and is the largest in states where emphasis is placed on examination for certification. These students attend primarily to prepare for examinations.

It has been the custom in most schools to provide for these students by offering short review courses. Often instruction in elementary agriculture and sometimes in manual training forms a part of this work, and is really the only part that takes into consideration the life of the community in which these students are to teach. These short courses are generally regarded by normal-school teachers as unsatisfactory, both on account of the shortness of the time given and the irregular preparation of the students themselves. Although the situation is recognized as a difficult one very little has been done to improve it. There are several schools, however, that have undertaken to give their students of this class some real preparation for this work as teachers. Some have arranged with local public-school authorities for a one-room rural school to be used as an observation or practice school. Others have built or have control of a one-room schoolhouse and have endeavored to make it a model of its kind so as to show concretely the possibilities of a rural school. For example, the Kirksville (Mo.) State Normal School has a well-appointed single-room schoolhouse. It has been

designed and constructed to show that a rural school anywhere can have all the conveniences and comforts offered in any city building. The children are transported in covered vehicles to and from school. It is a model school so far at it can possibly be made such. It is to exemplify the best things which a school board and a good teacher with up-to-date facilities can do in and for a rural school.

Special provision is made for instruction in manual training, elementary agriculture, and home economics.[3]

Two somewhat similar plans for rural education should be mentioned in this connection. Both of these have the larger possibilities of teaching in rural communities in view. One is a course of two years called "rural arts" given by the Harrisburg (Va.) Normal and Industrial School for Women. The course requires high-school graduation for admission. The object is to

give its students a training of mind, heart, and hand which will fit them for efficient service in rural schools, and for intelligent and appreciative participation in the life of rural communities. It will not attempt to train farmers; it cannot be expected to turn out agricultural experts. Its work will be limited to those phases of farm life in which women usually, or frequently, or may properly participate, and to that portion of agricultural instruction which may properly be given by female teachers in elementary and high schools.

The course includes besides some of the regular normal courses, horticulture, elementary agriculture, rural sociology, poultry raising and bee culture, dairying, forestry and floriculture, and theory and practice in rural arts.[4] The other is a course of two years known as "rural industrial education" given by the Ohio State Normal College of Miami University. Its requirements for admission are the same as for other college courses. This

[3] *Bulletin First District Normal School, Kirksville, Mo.*, IX, No. 1 (1909), 9–16.

[4] *Bulletin State Normal and Industrial School, Harrisburg, Va.*, I, No. 1 (1909), 88–92.

course is expected to meet the needs of township superintendents, principals and science teachers of high schools in rural communities, and to enable these teachers to adapt the work of their high schools more nearly to the life of the school communities. The course includes education, school administration, rural sociology, agriculture (two years), forestry, botany, manual training, rural education, methods of rural school organization, physical geography, trigonometry and surveying, and physics of farm machinery. In planning this course, which is at present a tentative one, the influence of the high school of an agricultural community on the elementary schools was carefully considered. Most of the teachers in the elementary schools of these communities are graduates of these high schools. They seldom receive further training. Therefore, with a high school organized to meet the needs of the community, its influence should thus extend to the elementary schools through its graduates who become teachers.[5]

Any account of the work of the state normal schools in agricultural education would be incomplete without some special reference to the teachers themselves who are engaged in this work. Many are doing their work under considerable disadvantage. This applies not only to the fact that agriculture is a new normal-school subject to be adapted to new conditions but also to the fact that it has been added as an additional subject to a teacher's already overcrowded programme. One teacher writes that he is offering agriculture this year for the first time, but is expected also to teach physics, chemistry, botany, zoölogy, physiology, geology, and physical geography. Several teachers have bought small farms primarily in order that their students might have the advantage of actual field experimentation.

With the earnest body of teachers now beginning to take up the work and with the progress already made it seems likely that the demands for agricultural instruction in the training of teachers in state normal schools will soon be met. The real test of the value of this training is in the work of the teacher who goes out from the schools and it is now too early to pass judgment.

[5] *Bulletin, Miami University,* Series 8 (1910).

BIBLIOGRAPHY

The facts of the text have been obtained chiefly from personal letters, normal-school catalogues, and reports of presidents of normal schools to state officers of education. Only those publications referred to by number in the text are included in the following list:

45. *Outline of the Courses in Science.* Madison, Wis.: Board of Regents of State Normal Schools (1901), pp. 32.

Each of the subjects of instruction in the state normal schools is briefly outlined. About seven pages are devoted to agriculture and include purpose of subject, scope (soil, plant and crops, animals and stock), and plan.

46. "Shall Teachers Be Prepared to Give Instruction in Elementary Agriculture?" B. M. DAVIS. *The Western Journal of Education,* May, 1906, pp. 5–15.

This is a report submitted to the Joint Board of the California State Normal School Trustees at its annual meeting held at Chico, Cal., April 15, 1906. It discusses the organization of agricultural education in the United States, agriculture in the elementary schools, work in Canada, N. E. A. report on industrial education in schools for rural communities, work of the normal schools, the problem as concerns the California normal schools including a tabulation of answers to questionnaire sent to all the county superintendents of the state, and a discussion of the work of the normal school.

47. "What Has Been Done by Normal Schools and Agricultural Colleges for Popular Education in Agriculture." E. E. BALCOMB. *Proceedings of the National Education Association for 1907,* pp. 1069–75.

This report is a summary to answers to letters to the president of each agricultural college, to each state normal school, and to certain other schools of the United States.

48. *Education for Efficiency.* E. DAVENPORT. Boston: D. C. Heath & Co., (1909), pp. 184.

Its subtitle is "A discussion of certain phases of the problem of universal education with special reference to academic ideals and methods." The book is in two parts: the first, a discussion from general educational standpoint including education for efficiency, industrial education with special reference to high school, as a phase of the problem of universal education, educative value of labor, culture aim and unity in education; the second, an illustration of the principles discussed in first part as applied to agriculture—including agriculture in the high school, in the elementary school, in the normal school, and the development of agriculture—what it is and what it means.

49. "The Organic Field of Nature-Study." GEORGE H. HUDSON. *Nature-Study Review,* Vol. III, No. 5 (1907), pp. 129–35.

A scheme is given outlining the subject in considerable detail in two parts: one, the physical or practical, the other, the psychical. Both are amplified by a discussion which follows.

50. "School Gardens for California Schools." B. M. DAVIS. Chico, Cal.: *State Normal School Bulletin No. 1* (1905), pp. 79.

This is a manual for teachers. It discusses the history of school gardens and their educational importance, the plant and its relations, plant propagation, instruction including aim and scope, practical work, correlative subjects, adaptation to school conditions, etc. The annotated bibliography of nearly three hundred titles is a summary of the literature of the subject up to 1905.

51. *Agriculture through the Laboratory and School Garden.* C. R. JACKSON AND L. S. DAUGHERTY. New York: The Orange Judd Co. (1905), pp. 419.

"The preparation of this book was undertaken, primarily, that the classes in agriculture in the State Normal School of Kirksville, Mo., might have in one book the directions for all the laboratory experiments and exercises, and such information as would enable them to understand the results of these experiments."

52. "Normal School Instruction in Agriculture." N. J. ABBEY. *U. S. Department of Agriculture, Office of Experiment Stations, Circular 90* (1909), pp. 31.

This circular "sets forth in a brief way the manner in which agriculture is taught at the Maysville State Normal School, No. Dakota." It contains a discussion of why normal schools should train teachers in agriculture and the place of agriculture in the normal school curriculum. Most of the circular is a detailed account of the work, including textbook instruction, class exercises, laboratory instruction, typical laboratory exercises, apparatus, the school garden, the model school, visiting a rural school, field excursions, methods, correlation, and difficulties.

53. "Normal Agricultural Society." CHARLES R. WEEKS. Peru, Neb.: *State Normal School, Special Circular* (1909), p. 1.

This circular gives history, purposes, and plans of this organization.

54. "Western Illinois State Normal Experiment Field." J. T. JOHNSON. Macomb, Ill.: *State Normal School, Circular No. 1* (1907), pp. 4.

The circular contains statement of purpose, location, and plans of conducting the soil experiment field.

55. "A Correlated Course of Study in Agriculture, Geography, and Physiology for Rural Schools." E. A. COCKEFAIR. Cape Girardeau, Mo.: *State Normal School, Special Bulletin* (1909), pp. 63.

It contains daily programme of recitation; general outline including such subjects as seed, corn judging, corn selection, corn breeding, how corn grows, the soil, crops, foods, live stock judging, markets, dairying, gardening, fruit growing, forestry, cooking, sewing, home decoration; elaboration of outline.

56. "Course in Nature-Study and Elementary Agriculture." RILEY O. JOHNSON. Chico, Cal.: *State Normal School, Special Circular* (1908), pp. 8.

The work outlined in this circular is designed for the ungraded schools of California. There are three parts: (1) an outline of the work, (2) a specimen lessons, and (3) a list of references.

OUR INHERITED PRACTICE IN ELEMENTARY SCHOOLS

S. CHESTER PARKER
The University of Chicago

IV. FREE SCHOOLS AND THE LANCASTERIAN SYSTEM

This is the fourth of a series of papers which aim to illustrate a method of studying the history of education in which the emphasis is placed on educational practice in its relation to social conditions. The Lancasterian monitorial or mutual instruction system, which prevailed in the larger cities of the United States during the first quarter of the nineteenth century serves as an admirable illustration in contrasting this kind of history of education with the history of educational theory.

This system was imported from England in 1806 for use in New York city schools. It derived its name from the use of the more capable children as instructors of the others who were organized in small groups, and from its exploitation by Joseph Lancaster.

Some histories of modern education do not mention the Lancasterian system at all, in others it is given only passing comment as a discredited method, and in general, writers express surprise that the system should ever have been considered or used. These same authors will present at length the theories contained in the *Great Didactic* of Comenius published in 1657, but which was forgotten for two centuries and only re-discovered in 1841. Yet the theories of Comenius for the improvement of the technique of instruction in elementary schools were practically unknown in America, while the Lancasterian methods which aimed at the same result, were being used as the basis of rapid improvement in elementary education.

In some respects Comenius and Lancaster were quite similar. They were both practical teachers who invented many improved devices which were used successfully in practice, and they were both enthusiastic about the possibility of formulating a mechanical method which would, in a way, work itself. The following quotation from Comenius serves to represent the ideas of such a method held by both men.

The art of teaching, therefore, demands nothing more than the skilful arrangement of time, of the subjects taught, and of the method. As soon as we have succeeded in finding the proper method it will be no harder to teach schoolboys, in any number desired, than with the help of the printing-press to cover a thousand sheets daily with the neatest writing, or with Archimedes' machine to move houses, towers, and immense weights, or to cross the ocean in a ship, and journey to the New World. The whole process, too, will be as free from friction as is the movement of a dock whose motive power is supplied by the weights. It will be as pleasant to see education carried out on my plan as to look at an automatic machine of this kind, and the process will be as free from failure as are these mechanical contrivances when skilfully made.

From the standpoint of present day theory in which freedom and individuality is emphasized the mechanics of the Lancasterian system may seem absurd, but if we consider it in the light of the lack of public provision for education in the first quarter of the nineteenth century and in contrast with the unintelligent wasteful methods of instruction then in vogue in elementary schools, we can better appreciate the exaggerated hopes for the system expressed at that time. Such men as Governor De Witt Clinton, of New York, Governor Wolcott of Connecticut, William Russell, editor of the *American Journal of Education,* John Griscom, noted scientist and educator, who through a period of more than twenty years believed in the system, were not visionaries to be led astray by an irrational device. Governor De Witt Clinton's tribute to the system is best known. In 1809, he said:

When I perceive that many boys in our school have been taught to read and write in two months, who did not before know the alphabet, and that even one has accomplished it in three weeks—when I view all the bearings and tendencies of this system—when I contemplate the habits of order which it forms, the spirit of emulation which it excites, the rapid improvement which it produces, the purity of morals which it inculcates—when I behold the extraordinary union of celerity in instruction and economy of expense—and when I perceive one great assembly of a thou-

[1] Comenius, *The Great Didactic* (Keatinge), p. 248.

sand children, under the eye of a single teacher, marching with unexampled rapidity and with perfect discipline to the goal of knowledge, I confess that I recognize in Lancaster the benefactor of the human race. I consider his system as creating a new era in education, as a blessing sent down from heaven to redeem the poor and distressed of this world from the power and dominion of ignorance.[2]

Governor Wolcott of Connecticut in his message to the legislature in 1825 said:

If funds can be obtained to defray the expenses of the necessary preparations, I have no doubt, that schools on the Lancasterian model, ought as soon as possible to be established in several parts of this state. Wherever from two hundred to one thousand children can be convened within a suitable distance, this mode of instruction, in every branch of reading, speaking, penmanship, arithmetic, and bookkeeping, will be found much more efficient, direct and economical, than the practices now generally pursued in our primary schools.[3]

The testimony of a prominent contemporary professional educator is of the same nature as that of the two governors quoted. William Russell was editor of the first successful American educational periodical, the *American Journal of Education,* published from 1826 to 1830. Mr. Russell was one of the most important schoolmen of the period, in touch with educational movements in Europe and America, interested in the training of teachers, in Pestalozzianism, and other methods of improving teaching. In 1826 he edited a *Manual of Mutual Instruction,* containing directions for organizing instruction on the Lancasterian plan and a history and justification of the method. In the preface it is stated that the volume is issued in response to repeated calls which had been made "at the office of the *Journal of Education* for information concerning the system of mutual instruction, and for works calculated to assist teachers in introducing it." This little volume of 121 pages is a most instructive source of information as a contemporary description of the development of the system in New York City, Albany, New Haven, Boston, and elsewhere. Mr. Russell strongly

[2] W. O. Bourne, *History of the Public School Society of City of New York,* p. 19.

[3] Wm. Russell, *Manual of Mutual Instruction* (Boston, 1826), p. 102.

favored the system and even printed an argument of fourteen pages in favor of adopting it in colleges.

The enthusiasm of Dr. John Griscom for the monitorial system lends additional evidence of its significance. Mr. Griscom's travels published as *A Year in Europe* is one of our best sources for information concerning schools of that period. In 1805 he opened the first course of popular lectures on physics and chemistry given in New York City. He was the principal organizer of the Society for the Prevention of Pauperism and of the New York House of Refuge (1824). Mr. Griscom had been impressed with the successful operation of the monitorial system in the New York elementary schools and had visited the High School of Edinburgh where, he said:

> I saw a school, eminent almost to a proverb for the elevated tone of its classical attainments, entirely under the regimen of the monitorial system. Such was the success attending it, that it was universally admitted that the 150 boys under the head master made a more rapid progress, were more thoroughly taught, and pursued their studies with more vigor and alacrity, than in any institution in which the monitorial system was not adopted.[4]

Impressed with the necessity of a similar high school in New York City, Mr. Griscom organized a stock company, erected a three-story building, employed a competent assistant, and in 1825 opened a school which soon contained 650 scholars. It continued in successful operation until 1831 when the building was sold to the Society of Mechanics and Tradesmen who desired it for a school which they maintained.

The previous discussion has shown the enthusiastic belief in the value of the monitorial system which prevailed among political leaders, scientists, and professional educators. Certain factors in the social situation which justified such enthusiasm may now be examined. Two of these are especially important, first, the lack of public support for free schools, especially in the Middle Atlantic states, and second, the growth of cities and the resulting concentration of ignorance, vagrancy, pauperism, vice, and crime.

[4] *Memoir of John Griscom*, LL.D. (New York, 1859), p. 202.

1. The lack of public provision for free schools was almost universal in the Middle Atlantic states, while in New England, where the early Puritan spirit had provided laws which required schools to be maintained, the actual practice in many places at the beginning of the nineteenth century was to have a very inferior school for only a few months out of the year. In Boston only private tuition schools existed to teach children to read. Yet children had to be able to read before they were admitted to the public writing or grammar schools. As a consequence hundreds of children of poor parents grew up in ignorance. Not until 1818 were public primary schools established in Boston.

In New York City up to 1806 there existed only private and parochial tuition schools and a few private charity schools. In 1806 was opened the first school of the Free School Society, a private corporation which soon maintained free charity schools on a large scale. There was no local public Board of Education in New York City until 1842, although moneys for the support of schools were received from the State Common School Fund from 1815, and from local tax beginning 1829. In Pennsylvania there were no public free schools except "pauper schools" until 1834. Similar conditions existed in the other Middle Atlantic states.

As late as 1840 in New York City, even with the facilities provided by the (Free) Public School Society, only 60 per cent. of the children of school age were under instruction; and in Brooklyn only 30 per cent., the commissioners of common schools of that city attributing the inferiority to the district system which prevailed there. In Williamsburg only 14 per cent. were under instruction. The cost of instructing a child in New York about 1840 was $2.70 a year. In Brooklyn the cost was a little over $3.00. During the life of the New York Public School Society (1805–54) the annual cost of instruction per child seldom exceeded $5.00, varying from $1.37 in 1822 to $5.83 in 1852.[5]

If these figures are compared with the amounts spent today for free public instruction we can realize the change that has

[5] Bourne, *op. cit.*, p. 509 (xxxii).

taken place. The median annual cost per child for elementary schooling in 1902–3 in some fifty cities in the North Atlantic states was found by Strayer to be $28.50, one city spending as much as $55.00.[6]

The only kind of instruction that could be hoped for in free schools in the first part of the nineteenth century was *cheap* instruction. The Lancasterian system provided such instruction. This, no doubt, was the chief social reason for its adoption, but it must not be forgotten that contemporary evidence indicated that its *effectiveness* in training the large groups of children which it was desirable to handle in city districts, made it superior to the methods of instruction commonly pursued.

2. The second social factor which bore an important relation to the adoption of the Lancasterian system, was the growth of cities. In 1800 there were in the United States 6 cities having a population of over 8,000; in 1810 there were 11; in 1820, 13; and in 1830, 26. The population of the six largest cities in 1800 is shown below.[7]

Philadelphia	69,403	Boston	24,937
New York	60,489	Charleston	20,473
Baltimore	26,114	Salem	9,457

In these cities existed concentrated ignorance, vagrancy, pauperism, vice, and crime. Public-spirited citizens who were concerned about the degraded social condition of the lower classes in the cities, organized societies to study and improve it. Thus in New York City there was organizd in 1817 the Society for the Prevention of Pauperism. This society undertook the establishment of a savings bank, an apprentices' library, and other enterprises. Defects in the penitentiary system were attacked, especially the confining of vagrant children with hardened criminals. A private subscription of $17,000 was raised for the establishment of a House of Refuge for Juvenile Delinquents, which was opened in 1825.

The same peculiar social problems of city life were uppermost in the minds of the citizens who established free schools on

[6] G. D. Strayer, *City School Expenditures* (Teachers College, 1906).

[7] A. F. Weber, *Growth of Cities in the Nineteenth Century*, p. 21.

the Lancasterian basis. This fact was expressed by De Witt Clinton in the same speech from which was quoted his eulogy of Lancaster.

A number of benevolent citizens had seen, with concern, the increasing vices of the city, arising, in a great degree, from the neglected education of the poor. Great cities are, at all times, the nurseries and hotbeds of crimes. Bad men from all quarters repair to them, in order to obtain the benefit of concealment, and to enjoy in a superior degree the advantages of rapine and fraud. . . . . The mendicant parent bequeaths his squalid poverty to his offspring, and the hardened thief transmits a legacy of infamy to his unfortunate and depraved descendants. . . . . In this state of turpitude and idleness, leading lives of roving mendicancy and petty depredation [these children existed] a burden and disgrace to the community.[8]

A similar situation confronted the leaders of the movement for the establishment of free primary schools in Boston (1818).

These gentlemen had long been united in forwarding various projects for the amelioration and improvement of the condition of the poor. It was mainly through their exertions that the "Provident Institution for Savings" had been put into operation, and its success had encouraged them to further efforts in the same direction.[9]

The several points that have been discussed thus far, namely, the enthusiasm for the Lancasterian system, the lack of provision for free public instruction, and the concentrated ignorance and depravity existing in the growing cities, may be studied to advantage in connection with the development of public schools in Pennsylvania. The state constitution adopted in 1790 contained this provision: "The legislature shall, as soon as conveniently may be, provide by law for the establishment of schools throughout the state, in such manner that the poor may be taught gratis."

For many years the legislature did nothing more than seek to aid churches and private schools to provide free education for the poor. There was no law for this purpose, even, until 1802, and it merely provided that the tuition of poor children attending a school in any neighborhood should be paid by the overseers

[8] Bourne, *op. cit.*, p. 17.

[9] Wightman, *Annals of the Boston Primary School Committee*, p. 18.

of the poor from the public fund. The law compelled parents to declare their poverty, in other words, to pauperize themselves, and in a slightly modified form was the only general provision for free education in Pennsylvania, down to 1834, when the state established a free public school system for all children.

A special law of 1818 established Philadelphia as the "First School District of Pennsylvania," and authorized the district to maintain free public schools for "indigent orphan children or children of indigent parents." These were "pauper schools" but were organized under the control of a public Board of Controllers. The law required these schools to use Lancaster's methods in their most approved state. "Philadelphia had no free schools open to the children of the rich and poor alike, until after the law of 1818 had been amended, in 1836, so as to admit all children without distinction."[10]

Previous to this public provision for educating poor children in Philadelphia, philanthropic individuals and societies had been active in the same cause. Thus in 1799, three young men opened a night school for poor children, and two years later organized "The Philadelphia Society for the Establishment and Support of Charity Schools." In 1807, another similar association was formed which opened schools for boys and girls on the Lancasterian plan.

The law of 1818 which provided for the establishment of free public "pauper schools" in Philadelphia was the result of the activities of a "Society for the Promotion of Public Economy," which was organized to relieve the distress among the poor during the winter of 1816–17. One of the committees of the society was on public schools. It investigated the possibilities of the Lancasterian system and framed the law which the legislature was induced to pass.

The close connection existing between this early movement to establish free schools in Pennsylvania and the use of the Lancasterian system is suggested in this paragraph by Wickersham.

> The special acts relating to education in Philadelphia and in the counties above mentioned, were prompted by a new plan of school man-

[10] Wickersham, *History of Education in Pennsylvania*, p. 287.

agement, called Lancasterian, after its author, Joseph Lancaster, which began to take root in Pennsylvania about 1809. Schools conducted on this plan were established at Philadelphia, Lancaster, Columbia, Harrisburg, Pittsburg, Milton, Erie, New Castle, Greencastle and perhaps at a few other places.[11]

The economy of this system which appealed to legislators who were not willing to appropriate money for the elementary education of any but pauper children may be judged from the ratio of teachers to pupils. In Philadelphia in 1819, there were 10 public Lancasterian schools, with 10 teachers and 2,845 pupils, or one teacher for 284 pupils; in 1834, 20 schools, 31 teachers and 6,767 pupils, or one teacher for 218 pupils.

The important service of the Lancasterian schools in Philadelphia is stated by Wickersham in these words:

> The Lancasterian schools served the good purpose of hastening the adoption of the free school system, by gradually preparing the way for the heavy taxation the support of such a system necessarily incurs. They did more; they awakened thought and provoked discussion on the question of education in all its aspects, the result of which was a more enlightened public sentiment on the subject. In addition, to the Lancasterian system Philadelphia and Pennsylvania are deeply indebted for another thing. It brought with it the idea of the necessity of trained teachers, and this idea outlived the system of which it was a part, and became permanently incorporated into the educational policy of the city and the state. The establishment of a Model School for the preparation of teachers was provided for in the law of 1818, and as a school of this kind it was the first established in the country. In 1821 this school was attended by five hundred and sixty-four pupils, and teachers were prepared therein not only for the schools of the city, but to some extent for those in other parts of the state.

It is evident from the preceding discussion that the social situation in American cities at the beginning of the nineteenth century justifies and explains the enthusiastic belief which prevailed in the usefulness of the Lancasterian system. The two characteristics of the system upon which this belief was based were its cheapness and its effectiveness in handling large groups of children. It was cheap because it employed monitors. It was

[11] Wickersham, *op. cit.*, p. 270.

[12] *Ibid.*, p. 289.

effective because it embodied the results of a careful study of every detail of classroom management and the reduction of these details to an exact system.

Effective "school keeping" involves two types of problems or factors which Bagley has distinguished as the "routine factors" and the "judgment factors." The routine factors are defined as those measures which aim to build up a number of specific habits in the various individuals of the group and to organize a system that will take care of the mechanical details. The judgment factors concern the variables which it is necessary to consider, the constant readjustments which a teacher has to make in the interests of the individuals constituting the group.

The history of education has been written largely from the standpoint of the second type of teaching problems, as if the whole problem of effective teaching consisted in such complete provision for individuality as Rousseau advocated in the Émile. This point of view would seem to imply that the handling of children in a group is simply a concession to financial necessity and that the tutorial education advocated by the educational reformers to whom so much space is usually given, namely Rabelais, Montaigne, Locke and Rousseau, is the best realization of the aim of education. To those who hold this view, any teaching process that includes elements similar to military drill is non-educative.

In opposition to this interpretation, it may be maintained that both types of training are essentially educative, that the routine elements in school work have a positive, permanent value for the individual as well as the "judgment" factors, that each needs to be provided and that it is better to have the first without the second than to have neither, that effective military drill is better than a loose, lazy, idle, passive, inattentive, slipshod existence which encourages the formation of many bad negative habits, and few good positive habits.

The prevailing "school keeping" at the beginning of the nineteenth century was of this latter type. It was not effective either from the standpoint of routine or educative individual attention. It was predominantly country "school keeping," and the methods of the country school had been adopted in the city schools which were usually small and in charge of a single teacher. That is, instead of taking advantage of the possibility of forming a number of large schools with several teachers in different rooms having charge of children of the same age, many small one-room schools were located in different parts of the towns. The "country-school" or district-school methods employed in these schools were described in the first paper. The teaching was such that a child "had the privilege of forty minutes' worth of teaching and three hundred and twenty minutes' worth of sitting still," the master's time being all consumed with hearing individuals recite their lessons, making pens, setting copies, and keeping order. The systematic grading of schools was practically unknown at the beginning of the century.

Even in the well-organized public primary schools of Boston, which merely taught the elements of reading, writing, and spelling, there were in 1820 four classes in each school all under one teacher.[13] In New York City as late as 1829, out of a total of 24,952 children attending school, 15,320 were in 430 private schools which employed 432 principal teachers and 259 assistants. This averaged 1 to 2 teachers and 33 pupils per school.[14] We read of "a handsome two-story brick building erected in 1792" in Boston, in which "in one apartment Writing and Arithmetic is taught; in another, Spelling, Reading, English Grammar and Geography." Other schools described were of either one or two rooms.[15] I have read of a four-room school building erected at this time in which a teacher in each room conducted a school on the district plan having children of all ages and using the method of individual recitation.

Thus we see that the mechanics of school keeping, the routine factors in school management, were given little consideration and as a consequence an enormous amount of waste existed. There was just as little consideration of the judgment factors, that is of provision for educative individual attention. Improve-

[13] Wightman, *op. cit.*, p. 58.

[14] Bourne, *op. cit.*, p. 121.

[15] Wightman, *op. cit.*, p. 8.

ment along this line was not affected until the influence of Pestalozzian methods was felt, to a limited extent in the second quarter of the century, but not to any considerable degree until the Oswego movement in 1860. Improvement in the routine factors of teaching began much earlier and received its chief impulse from the Lancasterian system.

The Lancasterian system marked an advance over contemporary practice in the following respects:

1. In making a careful and complete study of classroom management and of the mechanics of instruction. This has been a prominent element in the work of most successful educational institutions and systems, and the schools of Lancaster would be classed with those of John Sturm, the Jesuits, and the Brethren of the Christian Schools which were acknowledged in their day to be the most effective schools in existence.

2. Just as economy was a fundamental element in the financial organization, so it was in the school routine. While the routine of passing of classes, taking attendance, changing work, etc., was organized so as to consume a minimum of time, the teaching was so organized as to keep all the pupils employed all the time. It is said that Lancaster invented the mottoes, "A place for everything and everything in its place" and "Let every child at every moment have something to do and a motive for doing it."

3. Special attention was devoted in the construction of the schoolroom to lighting, ventilation, slant of floor, seating, elimination of noise, etc. Great ingenuity was shown in devising apparatus that would assist in teaching, such as sand tables for writing, blackboards, reading charts, etc.

4. Children were carefully classified according to attainments into larger or smaller groups, and in some cases a child could recite with one group in arithmetic and another group in reading or spelling.

5. Studying and learning were made active social processes rather than passive individual processes. A child was always studying or working or reciting as a member of a group, producing some objective result to which the monitor or the rest of

the class gave attention. Emulation was the chief social instinct stimulated, as was the case with the Jesuits and parallel results were secured. There was much marching back and forth and alternation of seat work and standing recitations.

6. Teachers were carefully selected and trained, and they undertook teaching as a permanent career. For their guidance manuals of instruction were prepared giving detailed directions for school keeping, another parallel to the efficient schools of the Jesuits and of the Brethren of the Christian Schools.

EDITORIAL NOTES

Private Gifts to Public Schools

The announcement that Mr. Carnegie has decided to give three million dollars for the purpose of improving the schools of ten cities raises the very interesting general question of the advantage and methods of using private benefactions for institutions which have heretofore been regarded as very exclusively public in character. It has been a common experience in American education for private benefaction to establish and maintain higher institutions of learning, but we have regarded the public school as an enterprise to be maintained wholly through public funds. It has frequently been suggested that the endowment of public schools might improve the character of these institutions, but the problem of administering such private endowments has not often arisen in any concrete form.

Experience of the City of Indianapolis

There is one interesting case of such private benefaction left to a city school system in the Gregg Legacy, which places in the hands of the Board of Education of the city of Indianapolis a very considerable sum of money to be used annually in the training of teachers. This fund has been expended in sending teachers of the Indianapolis school system away for purposes of advanced study. In some cases a teacher has been sent to Europe or one of the higher institutions for a whole year. In other cases the period of study provided has been much shorter, covering a summer school or a single term of study in some educational institution. Those who have observed the working of this plan in Indianapolis are very enthusiastic about its effect on the teaching corps. The possibility of further study acts as an incentive to the teachers to maintain a higher grade of regular work. Furthermore, the advantages gained through the period of study are brought back to the school system in the form of reports and classes, which can be led during the winter by those who have had the advantage of study, and in increased efficiency on the part of those who have enjoyed the benefits of the fund.

Administration by Public Officials

The administration of this Indianapolis fund has been relatively simple because the fund has been in the hands of the regular offices of the school system. Whatever the superintendent of schools considered to be advantageous for the system as a whole could be fostered through the use of this fund. It is by no means as easy to see how an outside committee of administrators could improve a school system which was not prepared in its own organization to administer such a fund. The outside board or committee would find it extremely difficult to form an adequate opinion of the efficiency of teachers and to distribute the funds to them in anything like an adequate fashion.

Could Such Funds Be Used for Pupils?

Improvement of the teachers suggests itself as the first avenue for the expenditure of such a private benefaction to the public schools. Other types of activity, however, can be suggested especially with reference to the pupils in the schools. There are many pupils who are said to leave school because of the economic demands made by the family that the younger members of the household contribute to the family support. It would be an extremely interesting task for a committee supplied with private funds to inquire into the cases of such students and, where they were found at all worthy, to pay a part or the whole of the income which they would gain from leaving school and entering the factories. We should then have a definite experiment which would help us to solve the vexed question of whether our public life is losing through these early withdrawals from the school.

Mr. Staples' Conclusion

Mr. Staples was able to show, in an article in the February number of the Elementary School Teacher, a very close relation between income in later life and the period of one's schooling. A small investment from a private fund might raise the efficiency of a great number of children to a point where the community would profit in later generations by this investment in pupils as much as by an investment in the teachers themselves.

Growing Unity of Educational Interests

One of the very impressive features of the recent meeting of the Department of Superintendence of the National Education Association was the variety of interests that were represented at this meeting. We frequently make the remark that our school system is becoming more and more of a unit. Colleges see their relation to the problem of elementary school work. The normal school and the college are approaching each other in the type of work which they undertake, and the high school, standing between the elementary school and the upper schools, constitutes a link of the most intimate sort in the chain of educational succession. Certainly this remark with regard to the unity of our school system was justified in the various lines of activity represented at the recent meeting of the superintendents. College teachers of education were present at this meeting and held important sessions. There were societies for the study of physical education dealing with problems that related to all grades of schools. Papers on the major programmes dealt not only with instruction in the common schools but also with the relation of such instruction to all types of institutions and to all types of specialized work.

This concrete exhibition of the unity of our educational system is a very welcome indication of the advance that has been made in recent years in bringing together all kinds of teachers. The time was when there were no college teachers of education and no organizations that would have brought together those interested in higher education and those interested in the elementary schools. That period of separation is past and whatever can be contributed in the way of scientific studies or by way of efforts toward a unified course of studies throughout the schools, is now recognized as a legitimate part of institutional work of all grades.

BOOK REVIEWS

Genetic Psychology: an Introduction to an Objective and Genetic View of Intelligence. By E. A. KIRKPATRICK. New York: Macmillan, 1909. Pp. xv+373.

The author takes for the subject of his treatment the development of mind in its broadest sense and from the various points of view from which it may be regarded—animal evolution, the racial and the individual development of man. Since our knowledge of the mental life of animals is an inference from their structure and behavior, the first half of the book is taken up with the discussion of these matters. The latter half of the book deals in general with consciousness and its development. The method of treatment then is first to describe the development of physiological and nervous structure, then of behavior, and finally the mental activity corresponding to this development.

After a brief chapter on the development of the sense organs and motor apparatus there follows a detailed description of the behavior of all grades of animals from the single-celled amoeba to the highest vertebrates, as it has been determined by experimental investigation. This discussion is, in the opinion of the reviewer, much too detailed and is not written in such a way as to make prominent the manner in which animal behavior develops. The mind of the general reader will be left with a mass of unrelated details. The developing behavior might also be more closely correlated with the development of the nervous system.

The treatment of behavior concludes with two chapters on the instincts and the development of behavior in the individual—"the acquisition of habits and ideas." In the consideration of ideas the author of course abandons the objective treatment. There is a later chapter on types of learning which treats of essentially the same subject—the development of the individual—and it would seem that these could better be brought into closer relation with each other.

Following a chapter on the criteria and general characteristics of consciousness comes the most convincing and illuminating part of the book, a chapter drawing a comparison between the mental life of man and of animals. The mental life of animals is shown to be comparable in general not to our clearly analyzed ideas or perceptions but to our undifferentiated, purely practical mental reactions to our surroundings. The human endowments of imagery and conceptual thought, together with their vehicle, language, are the means of developing the typically human consciousness out of the infant consciousness which starts on the level of the animal. The lower processes are then transformed by this higher development.

The various grades of conscious process, sensory, perceptual, conceptual, etc., are worked over again in the next chapter from the point of view of their function in adaptation to the environment instead of from the descriptive point of view. There are also added to conscious adaptation the physiological processes as lower forms of "intelligence." This classification together of physiological and conscious processes as "intelligence" seems to the reviewer unnecessarily to neglect the differences between them and to rest in many cases on mere analogy, as when the acquirement of immunity to disease is compared with learning.

The chapter on learning is divided according to a similar classification to those just mentioned into physiological, sensory-motor, representative, conceptional and combination learning. Under the last head is discussed the learning activity in some of the school subjects, as writing and reading.

In general, the reader feels that the book is more satisfactory in its detailed treatment than in its general organization. The same material is treated in different places from slightly different points of view and this is confusing. In many places also the general lines of development might be brought out more clearly instead of treating the facts in isolated groups and allowing the reader to trace the course of development, as in the chapter on "Types of Animal Behavior."

The student of education, however, will find much in the book that is valuable. It enforces the general point of view of mental life as a development and traces the course of the development in detail. The author gives evidence of a wide acquaintance with the facts and gives a comprehensive list of sources at the end of each chapter.

F. N. FREEMAN

THE UNIVERSITY OF CHICAGO

The Ninth Yearbook of the National Society for the Study of Education: Health and Education. By THOMAS DENISON WOOD, A.M., M.D. Chicago: The University of Chicago Press, 1910. Pp. 108. 75 cents net.

This volume gives, in the compass of 108 pages, a comprehensive and systematic statement of the various lines of activity which the school may undertake in order to improve the physiological condition of pupils and to build up, through physical exercise, strong, healthy bodies.

After a brief introduction, the first section of the book gives an account of the health examinations which should be made when children enter school and during the successive years of their study. The material thus collected at several centers in this country is of very great value in determining the norm or standard of physical health which should be maintained in the schools. Elaborate tables are here presented summarizing the results of such investigations, and blanks are described in detail which should be filled out during the physical examinations. Attention is also directed specifically to the chief physiological defects whch will be observed in children.

The second section is a brief one and deals with the problem of ventilation and cleanliness in the school building. This section is not exhaustive, but it suggests a number of problems to which the teacher's attention should be directed. With the aid of the bibliography, which appears at the end of the book, the section can be made very instructive.

Two sections now follow, one dealing with the hygiene of instruction, where the problem of fatigue and eye-strain and sleep are discussed, and a section on health instruction in which a plan is outlined for teaching the children personal hygiene. This part of the book might have been elaborated to very great advantage, as the ordinary teacher undoubtedly finds it very difficult to select the problems which can be taken up appropriately in a course in hygiene.

A final section on physical education gives in detail the various exercises which can properly be used with school children. A number of games are also mentioned and an appropriate sequence of these games is suggested.

Taken as a whole, the volume will be very useful in calling attention to the various aspects of physical health in the school. The whole topic is one which is receiving great attention at the hands of teachers, and anything which opens up the field in such a comprehensive way will be welcome. The book would make a very valuable introduction for teachers' meetings on the subject of physical health.

C. H. J.

CURRENT EDUCATIONAL LITERATURE IN THE PERIODICALS[1]

IRENE WARREN
Librarian, School of Education, The University of Chicago

ALEXANDER, JOHN W. The need of a National Academy and its value to the growth of art in America. Craftsman. 17:607–18. (Mr. '10.)

BARTON, WILLIAM E. The library as a minister in the field of religious art. Relig. Educa. 4:594–603. (Fe. '10.)

BURSTALL, SARA A. Independent study in schools. School W. 12:44–46. (Fe. '10.)

BUTLER, NATHANIEL. The teacher as a constructive force. Relig. Educa. 4:550–60. (Fe. '10.)

(The) confessions of a teacher (I). Journ. of Educa. (Bost.) 71:201–3. (24 Fe. '10.)

COPE, HENRY F. Textbooks on morals and ethics. Relig. Educa. 4:575–81. (Fe. '10.)

DIXSON, ZELLA A. The share of the library in religious education. Relig. Educa. 4:588–93. (Fe. '10.)

(The) educational value of the camera. Craftsman. 17:647–56. (Mr. '10.)

FAUNCE, WILLIAM H. P. Church and religious education. Relig. Educa. 4:527–30. (Fe. '10.)

HEFFRON, JOHN L. The moral value of the teaching of the physiology and hygiene of sex in the public schools. Relig. Educa. 4:543–49. (Fe. '10.)

HODGE, RICHARD M. Time-relations of church and school. Relig. Educa. 4:568–72. (Fe. '10.)

HRBEK, SARKA. The library and the foreign-born citizen. Pub. Lib. 15:98–104. (Mr. '10.)

HUGHES, JAMES L. Definite tests for the moral efficiency of state schools. Relig. Educa. 4:561–68. (Fe. '10.)

KNOX, RAYMOND C. Moral and religious training in college associations. Relig. Educa. 4:582–85. (Fe. '10.)

MACLEISH, MARTHA H. The home in religious education. Relig. Educa. 4:572–75. (Fe. '10.)

[1] Abbreviations.—Amer. Educa., American Education; Craftsman, The Craftsman Magazine; Educa. R., Educational Review; Harp. W., Harper's Weekly; Journ. of Educa. (Bost.), Journal of Education (Boston); Psycholog. Clinic, Psychological Clinic; Pub. Lib., Public Libraries; Relig. Educa., Religious Education; School W., School World; South. Educa. R., Southern Educational Review; Teach. Coll. Rec., Teacher's College Record.

MELL, P. H. The college attitude toward the high school. South. Educa. R. 6:17–20. (Ap., My., Je., and Jl. '09.)

MURRAH, W. B. Right views of education. South. Educa. R. 6:1–9. (Ap., My., Je., and Jl. '09.)

O'GRADY, HARDRESS. The teaching of French in the training colleges. School W. 12:49–50. (Fe. '10.)

PRITCHETT, HENRY S. Advertising the colleges. Harp. W. 104:9, 34. (19 Fe. '10.)

RAYLEIGH, PETER. Education in China. Educa. R. 18:30–39. (Fe. '10.)

ROSE, WICKLIFFE. Education as a public business. South. Educa. R. 6: 10–16. (Ap. '09.)

SADLER, M. E. The relation of elementary schools to technical schools, day and evening. School W. 12:41–44. (Fe. '10.)

SCHLEGEL, GEORGE S. The Reading free dental dispensary. Psycholog. Clinic. 3:249–54. (15 Fe. '10.)

SEIPMANN, OTTO. Education in England and abroad. School W. 12:50–53. (Fe. '10.)

SNEDDEN, DAVID. The movement for vocational education and its probable effects on liberal education (I). Amer. Educa. 13:252–55. (Fe. '10.)

WILSON, LOUIS N. The library and the teaching profession. Pub. Lib. 15:93–98. (Mr. '10.)

WINSHIP, A. E. Vocational training in the public schools; what are the real causes of the present movement? Journ. of Educa. (Bost.) 71: 143. (10 Fe. '10.)

WITMER, LIGHTNER. The restoration of children of the slums. Psycholog. Clinic. 3:266–80. (15 Fe. '10.)

WOODHULL, JOHN F. The teaching of physical science. Teach. Coll. Rec. 11:1–82. (Ja. '10.)

VOLUME X NUMBER 9

THE ELEMENTARY SCHOOL TEACHER

MAY, 1910

REPEATERS IN THE UPPER GRAMMAR GRADES

EDWARD L. THORNDIKE
Teachers College, Columbia University

The question suggested by our title is important for several reasons, which will be made clear after the facts have been presented.

The facts are as follows: A "repeater" is, for our purpose, defined as a pupil who is reported by school officers (1) as doing the work of the grade for the second time, or (2) as having spent more than a year (or half-year in the case of systems with 14, 16, or 18 grades in the elementary school) in the grade. I have data from ten cities chosen at random as to the number of "repeaters" per hundred pupils enrolled in the case of each of the last three grammar grades (grades 6, 7, and 8 in eight cities; 7, 8, and 9 in one city; 5, 6, and 7 in one city). I have similar data in the case of each of the last two grades (6 and 7) in the eleventh city. For the average of the cities the number of repeaters per hundred pupils enrolled is:

In the second from the last grammar grade............14.3
In the next to the last grammar grade................12.6
In the last grammar grade...........................12.4

For the median of the cities the number of repeaters per hundred pupils enrolled is:

In the second from the last grammar grade...........11.4
In the next to the last grammar grade...............11.8
In the last grammar grade.......................... 8.1

In view of the nature of the data I should estimate the central tendencies as 12.5, 11.5, and 9 for the three grades in order. Table I gives the facts in detail.

TABLE I

RATIO OF NUMBER OF "REPEATERS" TO TOTAL NUMBER OF PUPILS, FOR EACH OF THREE GRADES IN ELEVEN CITIES

School	Second from Last Grammar Grade	Next to Last Grammar Grade	Last Grammar Grade
Aurora, Ill.	.071	.065	.055
Chester, Pa.	.188	.179	.141
Decatur, Ill.	....	.118	.081
Galesburg, Ill.	.318	.263	.450
Jamestown, N. Y.	.096	.119	.088
Kansas City, Mo.	.224	.212	.127
New York City (a few schools only)	.148	.157	.073
Quincy, Mass.	.109	.092	.097
Springfield, Ohio	.119	.043	.020
Wheeling, W. Va.	.052	.057	.037
Williamsport, Pa.	.102	.077	.075
Median	.114	.118	.081
Average	.143	.126	.124

The data are for October, 1909, except in the case of five cities. In Jamestown they are for December, 1909; in Galesburg they are for 1898; in Springfield they are for June, 1907 and 1908; in Williamsport they are for June 1907 and 1908; in Kansas City they are for June 1905 and 1907. For the data for 1907 in the last three cities I am indebted to Ayres, *Laggards in American Schools,* p. 74. For the data for Aurora, Chester, Decatur, Jamestown, Quincy, and Wheeling I am indebted to the superintendents of schools in those cities. For the New York data I am indebted to several principals of schools. The Galesburg figures are the proportions *of those promoted* who spent more than a year in the grade.

These facts disprove the opinions expressed or implied by Ayres and others that if a pupil fails of promotion in grades 6, 7, or 8 he is practically sure to be eliminated. On the contrary two-thirds or more of those failing of promotion in grades 6, 7, or 8, seem to continue in the grade. The percentage of pupils failing of promotion is known to be about 15 for grades 6 and 7 and 12½ for grade 8. The percentage of repeaters is, in our eleven cities, about 12.5 for grade 6, 11.5 for grade 7, and 9 for grade 8.

This rough estimate for cities in general can be checked by getting the actual percentage which the proportion remaining over a year is of the proportion failing of promotion in the same grade. I have data permitting the calculation of this percentage, subject to the chance variations of different years, for seven cities. The median results are that seven out of ten students failing of promotion in grade 6 or 7 continue in the grade, and five out of ten in grade 8. On the whole the most likely estimate seems to be that of the non-promoted in grades 6, 7, and 8, respectively, seven-tenths, seven-tenths,and six-tenths became "repeaters." The data are given in Table II. They are

TABLE II

PERCENTAGE WHICH THE PROPORTION REMAINING OVER A YEAR IN THE GRADE IS OF THE PROPORTION FAILING OF PROMOTION IN THE SAME GRADE
DATA FOR LAST THREE GRADES IN SEVEN CITIES

School	Second from Last Grammar Grade	Next to Last Grammar Grade	Last Grammar Grade
Chester, Pa....................	55	66	35
Jamestown, N. Y..............	107	85	29
Kansas City, Mo..............	80	85	75
New York, N. Y.*............	98	98	44
Springfield, Ohio..............	68	39	45
Williamsport, Pa..............	70	77	79
Wheeling, W. Va..............	27	26	46
Median..................	70	77	45

* One school only.

inadequate for any one city, not only because the proportion remaining over a year had to be in some cases from a different year than that from whose record the proportion failing of promotion was found, but also because demotions, trial promotions, and the like greatly complicate the records. For example, the number failing of promotion in the first grade is in one city recorded as 50 per cent., or three times the number repeating that grade (.185). Of course there were not really 31.5 per cent. who fai ed of promotion but did not repeat the grade. This city reports only 27, 26, and 46 per cent., respectively, of the non-promoted in grades 6, 7, and 8 as repeating the grade, but it reports only 35, 60, 55, 51, and 25 as corresponding percentages for grades 1 to 5. So it would be absurd to conclude that in that city the great majority of those failing in grades 6, 7, or 8 leave school before the next November. If one did he would have to conclude also that half of the pupils failing in grades 1, 2, or 3 left school before the next November!

Though thus inadequate for any one city, the data give a result for the median of the seven cities which, though probably too low and very unreliable, is very much more reliable than any person's guess. It is therefore a very valuable check on the more roundabout result for the eleven cities.

So far then as the facts reported by school officers go, *the pupil who fails of promotion in grades 6, 7, 8 is almost as likely to continue in school as the pupil who is promoted.* Roughly he is, by our records, nine-tenths as likely to do so. For, of all the pupils in grade 6 or grade 7, only four-fifths continue to the next grade; while of all the pupils in the last grammar grade the percentage continuing is probably even lower.

As I have elsewhere stated emphatically, the mass statistics of school reports need to be supplemented by individual educational histories. The facts of elimination, retardation, extra promotions, repetitions of grades, and the like can be measured adequately only by such histories of individuals. And I am fully aware of the complexities, inconsistencies, and ambiguities of school records. But the reports concerning the number of children repeating the last three elementary school grades, even after full allowance is made for possible errors, show three facts beyond a doubt:

First of all, retardation is seen to be an important feature of the late as well as the early grades. It has been shown elsewhere that the percentages of failure of promotion are as great for late as for early grades, with the exception of grade 1. The data reported in this article show that these pupils are not saved from retardation by the worse fate of immediate elimination. As a matter of fact the same pupil is *more likely* to be retarded in the late grades than in the early.

Secondly, to estimate the number of pupils who continue to any given late grade it is not correct to divide the enrolment of that grade (say grade 6) by the number of pupils beginning should in one year six or so years before. The dividend should be the number of pupils beginning that grade in one year. This will be, on the average, only seven-eighths of the enrolment for grade 6, eight-ninths for grade 7, and nine-tenths or ten-elevenths for grade 8. The estimates made by Ayres of the number of pupils continuing to grade 6 and beyond are thus much too high. The objections which have been made to the estimates in the United States Bureau of Education Bulletin on *The Elimination of Pupils from School* on the ground that failure of promotion and consequent repetition of a grade are far more frequent in grades 2, 3, and 4 than in grades 6 to 11 are shown to be without foundation in fact.

In the third place, the facts show that in so far as failure of promotion is an adequate measure of intellectual dulness, the retention of pupils in grades 6, 7, or 8 is not at all highly selective for intellect. Failure of promotion is, of course, far from a perfect measure of dulness; and nothing like an exact measure of the extent to which the more gifted pupils in grade 6 continue in school to grade 7, the more gifted in grade 7 to grade 8, and so on can be made from present knowledge. But the rate of progress in school is correlated with intellectual gifts to some degree, and the so frequent continuance in school in the last three grammar grades by pupils who fail of promotion is significant. The facts reported here certainly could not exist if the length of a pupil's continuance in school paralleled at all exactly his intellectual ability.

On this important question of the nature of the selection for continuance in school and college we have far too few facts. They are substantially the following: (1) The relative proportions of children of different ages in the different grades through to college graduation show that the children who reach a given grade (after the first two or three) at a late age are likely to leave school earlier than the others. This can be proved to be the case for age at entrance to grades 3, 4, 5, or 6 and probably holds for grades 7–12, and even for college classes. But in view of the facts reported in this paper slow progress in the last three grades does not seem to have so great an eliminating force as slow progress in earlier grades. (2) Dearborn has found a rather slight relation between continuance to high school and scholarship (as tested by marks) in late grades of the elementary school. (3) Several school officers have reported the opinions of teachers concerning the causes why pupils leave school. By these opinions intellectual inferiority is a real, but by no means an exclusive, cause.

At present we have some rough idea of how many pupils continue to any grade up through high school, how many fail of promotion in that grade, and how many stay in that grade for more than a year. But we know almost nothing about the qualitative questions: What sort of pupils continue to this grade? What sort of pupils fail of promotion in it? What sort of pupils stay to repeat it? The educational life-histories of individual pupils must be studied if these questions are adequately to be answered.

THE FINE AND INDUSTRIAL ARTS IN ELEMENTARY SCHOOLS, GRADE VII

WALTER SARGENT
The University of Chicago

The stimulating sense of increased ability to hand'e materials and implements which comes only when work has been so organized in previous years as to give some degree of mastery along specific lines of manual arts is a strong supplement to the urge of the widening interests apparent in Grade VII.

In representation pupils who have learned to picture the general characteristics of objects, to draw with some degree of care, by thinking out the positions which lines and brush strokes should occupy, before instead of after making them, and who have attempted to portray effects of three dimensions, are now interested in gaining increased ability to make satisfactory drawings. This becomes evident in a desire to represent details with greater accuracy and to picture effects of distance and solidity so the results look like the object. The children appreciate the power to picture a book as lying flat, or a bowl as appearing to be round, or a house as showing its structural features and its apparent size.

In constructive work the pupils are sufficiently mature to undertake some simple individual projects and to appreciate standards of workmanship. Awakening aesthetic appreciation of beauty of proportions and outlines, and of fitness to purpose enables the pupils to use design understandingly in relation to their constructive work and to their school and home surroundings.

The following suggestions are offered regarding the phases which may appropriately receive emphasis in Grade VII.

Representation.—The use of drawing as a means of explanation and description in connection with other school subjects should continue to be an important part of the work. This illustrative drawing offers to the teacher an excellent means of judging the extent to which drawing has become a practical means of expression. It plainly indicates the particular points in which the work is strong and the phases which require more skill and knowledge.

The drawing should be so conducted that there is the maximum of observation and interpretation on the part of the pupil. Ability to draw grows as the pupil compares his drawing with the object or idea and discerns points of likeness and difference so clearly that he knows where his drawing needs alteration and where it does not.

Too often this sort of observation is made by the teacher, who thus unwittingly obtains the practice in comparison of visual images while the pupil receives only the results in verbal terms. The possibilities of observation on the part of the pupils should be utilized to the full. If the lesson is in object-drawing, after the pupils have carried their drawings as far as possible by their own study they may exchange seats and drawings and give to each other the results of the new impressions thus obtained.

Those who persistently make their representations of objects too long and narrow may be seated beside those who have the habit of making drawings which are too short and broad. Those who are representing approximately the same view of an object may place their drawings side by side and compare results.

Some such methods as these will usually give a fresh impetus to observation which has begun to flag, and pupils who are trying to work out a certain pictorial effect will have the value of the impressions and suggestions of others after they have utilized to the full their own powers. One has only to teach drawing classes to find out how great is the temptation for the instructor to do the greater part of the observation which the children should undertake, and to point out the things which they should discover for themselves or for each other.

Experiments seem to show that better progress is made when pupils learn to draw a few things fairly well than when they pass rapidly from one object to another with no gain at each step which relates definitely to that which follows. Thoroughness of mastery at this age is likely to be in inverse ratio to the number of different subjects undertaken.

The cumulative effect of a series of efforts to understand and represent a single object will be evident in some such succession of drawings as the following, where the attention at each step is concentrated upon a single aspect of the thing under consideration, thus defining the problem in the mind of both instructor and pupil, and furnishing a goal for effort and a standard of judgment.

In nature drawing, for example, suppose the topic to be a tulip.

1. Draw with brush and ink to represent with a few lines the growth and general character. Here the whole attention is focused upon the interpretation of the important characteristics. Details are of secondary importance. The movement of the long lines, and the main features of growth are the things to be expressed. The shadow of the plant helps interpret these. Comparison with the shadows of other plants emphasizes the individuality of each and helps to a better appreciation of that of the flower which is being studied (Fig. 1).

2. With a pencil sharp and hard enough to record facts, make careful drawings of details, such as the exact shape of a petal, the construction and outline of a flower and leaf and the fine curvature of a stem. Make blue-prints of the leaves and flowers so as to see a perfect interpretation of these forms. The purpose of these drawings is not primarily an artistic result but an accurate record of such facts as would be used for a science notebook, and which incidentally furnish excellent material for use in design (Fig. 2).

3. Sketch parts of the plant and color them so as to show the exact hue of petals, stem, upper and under side of leaves, etc.

4. Study and represent a flower and a leaf in different positions and turned at different angles (Fig. 3).

5. Make a completed drawing of the plant in pencil and in color.

6. Use the plant forms as elements in design (*a*) in a border

for embroidery, (*b*) in a surface pattern for wall paper, (*c*) in a single unit for a cover for nature-study papers.

A similar opportunity for concentration upon a single topic for a considerable period of time is found in landscape drawing in connection with geography. Suppose the country under consideration is Holland. A large drawing may be begun upon

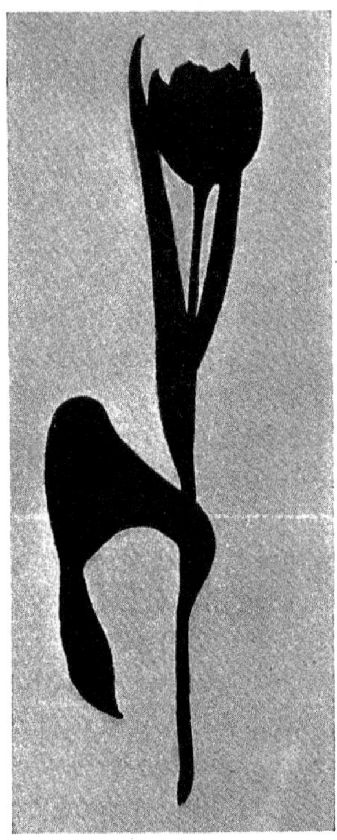

FIG. 1

the board and this may be modified or added to from time to time as the children obtain additional data or more definite knowledge of the subject-matter. Meanwhile each child may start a drawing of his own on a sheet of paper.

At first perhaps the results may be meager and include only a few suggestions of the country, such as a horizontal line to represent its level character and crude suggestions of canals and windmills. Collections of pictures and the hints gathered from descriptions will immediately furnish new material. One group of pupils may be assigned to gather pictures of canals and learn how to represent them so they appear to stretch away into the distance. Another group may collect data regarding the appearance of windmills, and still others may study canal boats, houses, and other items relating to Holland.

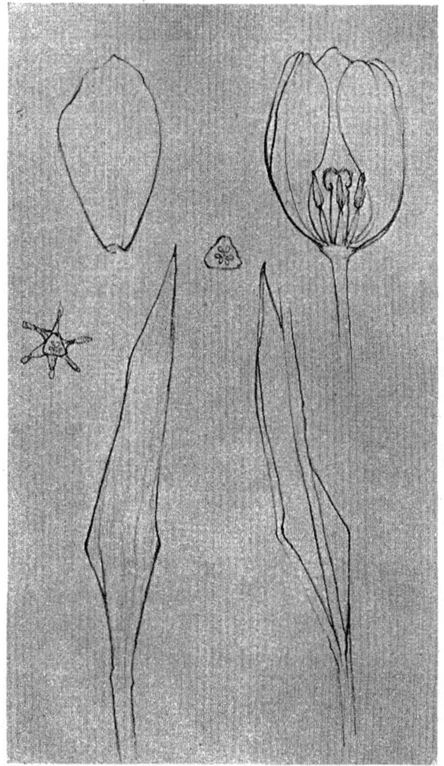

FIG. 2

Day by day the picture on the board will grow and crude drawings be replaced by those which are more adequate because of the continued study. The individual sketches will give opportunity for original compositions. Children will be encouraged to practice on particular objects or effects until they have mastered them. The geography thus furnishes a subject for the drawing, and that in turn is of value to the geography.

The children in Grade VII should develop increased ability to represent three dimensions in terms of only two, so that the solid objects which they draw upon the flat paper shall appear

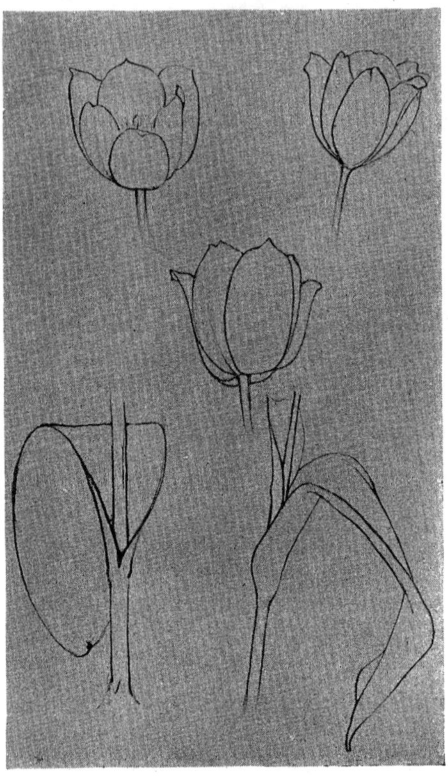

FIG. 3

as solid. This ability is best gained by supplementing the drawing from objects, with much experimental drawing from memory, in which the pupil learns to represent several objects, for example, a tumbler, half-apple, and box, illustrating the more common typical forms of solidity, cylindrical, hemispherical, and rectangular, until he can picture these in any position he chooses without reference to the object.

He should construct such forms on paper with his pencil over and over again, comparing and modifying them till their appearance satisfies his eye. He should do this till he forgets that he is working in two dimensions, and feels that he is shaping these forms in all three. He should not think of his foreshortened circle as an ellipse but as a circle which extends back into the picture and which he shapes until it is a satisfactory picture of a circle lying flat. He should build up his rectangular solids from imagination till his eye can detect any false construction or any shape that does not carry the impression of rectangular solidity. He should play with these figures till he can place them in whatever position he chooses. Modeling similar objects in plastic material is a valuable aid in developing power to draw them.

The old system of drawing type forms by carefully formulated principles of perspective failed partly because it attempted to train the intellect to reason out how objects appear under given conditions, while the important thing at this age is capacity for immediate visual satisfaction with what looks right without the necessity of referring to the intellect for confirmation. Statements of principles are valuable later on but as ordinarily taught do not seem to be of much practical help at this age.

One can seldom draw well an object the general type of which he has not mastered and made his own so he can draw it readily from imagination.

Construction.—The industrial work suggested for Grade VI is still more valuable in Grade VII. Among the projects suited to the abilities of the children are portfolios, letter files, and simple forms of bookbinding required in the making of sketch books, memoranda, and the binding of reference material gathered from magazines, etc., by teachers and pupils. The local needs will usually suggest the best problems.

In woodworking during Grade VI the pupils should have gained a practical acquaintance with the different saws and planes, with the rule, try square, gauge, spokeshave, hammer, nail set and sandpaper. The models attempted should have been such that their usefulness is not greatly impaired by inaccuracies in form and measurements—the pen-tray, for example, may have reached its final stage somewhat narrower or shorter than originally planned, but this result is not so serious as would be the case with a table leg which must correspond exactly with three others.

A wise choice of models at the first enables the teacher to encourage freedom in the use of tools and to give the pupils a sense of achievement. The freedom and relative crudity of some of this work should not be confused with carelessness. The wide difference between the inaccuracy of a first attempt and slovenly work should be recognized.

In Grade VII the pupils should learn to use with some degree of skill the tools with which they have become acquainted during the previous year. The models should be such as make a greater demand for accuracy. The pupils should experience the sense of achievement that comes from producing from raw material well-constructed objects that are of some practical use. The construction work of Grade VII should be such as will bring both boys and girls into increasingly close relation with the occupations of home and community, and should satisfy the desire to be connected with the activities of the world and to do things which have social value. Cooking and serving meals, making garments which are to be worn, planning, as constructive problems in bench work, objects which are of use in school or at home, contribute to this end.

The children should know something of the historical and artistic evolution of industries, particularly those relating to their own constructive work and to local occupations, such as agriculture, building, iron- and woodwork, etc. They should know something of the great amount of thought and effort which have been expended in evolving the forms in which common things now appear. The stories of pottery and furniture and clothing are as full of interpretation of human thought and of the progress of civilization as stories of military campaigns. Such a treatment of history would add something more than a commercial interest to industrial products.

Excellent suggestions for various forms of industrial education for country schools are to be found in the report of the committee of the National Education Association, July, 1905, upon "Industrial Education in Rural Communities."

Design.—In Grades VII and VIII the phases of design which call for judgment regarding the fitness of things and the beauty of proportions and outlines and the suitability of ornament are of increasing importance. The problems of constructive work are also excellent prob'ems in design. The children should be brought up with the idea, impressed by example rather than precept, that the possibilities for beauty lie mostly in the planning and proportioning of essential parts of objects and not in added ornament. The finest beauty of a boat is its shape and not its decoration; of a chair, its proportions and not its carving. No element can add more beauty to the outside appearance of a house than the fine proportioning and spacing of doors and windows. Walter Crane states this principle well when he says,

> Nothing has degraded the form of common things so much as a mistaken love of ornament. . . . . Decoration or ornament we have been too much accustomed to consider as accidental and unrelated addition to an object, not as an essential expression and organic part of it; not as a beauty which may satisfy us in simple line, form, or proportion combined with fitness to purpose, even without any surface ornament at all.[1]

Children are readi'y interested in making designs where the solution lies in the best possible disposition of necessary constructive elements with little or no ornamentation, and soon appear to enjoy such a problem partly because of the definiteness produced by its limitations. The lesson covers in Fig. 4 designed by elementary-school children, illustrate the different results obtained when the possibilities for good design in fine arrangement of parts are rea ized and when they are not. In *B,* (Fig. 4) the child without any foundation of previous training was left free to make his design as he pleased. He has not responded to the vertical and horizontal suggestions of the enclosing space but violates these with his diagonal printing. He finds no pleasure in experimenting with the architectural effects of fine

[1] Walter Crane, *The Bases of Design,* 90.

spacing and well-arranged margins. His primary interest is the barbaric one of collection and display with only secondary regard for arrangement. There is no lasting satisfaction and no clearly defined goal for this interest. It demands ever brighter colors and more profuse ornamentation.

Such designs as *A* in Fig. 4 result from long experience in placing words where they divide the space most pleasingly, and

FIG. 4

in spacing letters in the words till satisfaction is awakened in the harmonious distribution of the words on the page and the letters within the words, rather than the profuse ornamentation.

In such a design as this the exact areas which the printing is to occupy are first chosen and the letters made to conform to these. Children show much interest in working out this problem. They like to experiment by printing the same word in rectangles differing entirely as to proportions, so that in each case the word shall exactly fill the given form (Fig. 5). Such printing should be done freehand and the spaces determined not by measurement but by tentative indications made at first by very light lines and gradually defined as the letters become equably distributed.

For excellent suggestions for teaching lettering see a series of articles by Mr. James Hall in the *School Arts Book,* 1909–10, and an article by Mr. Harold Haven Brown in the *Year Book* of the Council of Supervisors for 1906 entitled, "The Teaching of Lettering."

Design which consists in the best possible arrangement of given elements, so that they fulfil their purpose adequately and gracefully without recourse to sensational or incongruous interests, gives permanent satisfaction in a definite end attained and a single idea perfected. Thus is produced a thing of beauty which is "a joy forever."

FIG. 5

Development of a feeling for beauty of form comes in part by the careful drawing of plant forms suggested for nature drawing, but this should be supplemented by practice in securing a freedom of style, which can be gained by making many free sketches of plant forms with a brush. The plant should be interpreted into as few lines as possible and this convention repeated till, like penmanship, it gains a swing and flow of line that is not labored. The best of the results may be worked over and perfected by the use of tracing paper.

Continued use of water-colors develops ability to match colors more exactly. The children should be expected to distinguish and record relatively subtle differences in color tones, such as the difference between the green of the upper and that of the under sides of leaves. In addition to practice in matching colors, a special study of color intensities will aid discrimination. This may be done by having the children select some color, for example, blue, and paint a spot as intensely blue as the paints will produce, and another spot of gray which is the same value as the blue, that is, neither lighter nor darker, but such a gray as would be obtained by photographing the blue with a plate that rendered the colors in their true relative values.

Have them paint other spots, each time mixing an increasing amount of gray with the blue, so that the spots approach gray without becoming lighter or darker. Let them select from these spots three which make equal steps in intensity between pure blue and gray and cut and mount samples from these to put with the blue and gray so as to form a series of five equally graded steps of intensity. In a similar manner make charts of the other five spectrum colors. Have the children use these charts to show the relative intensity of colors in nature which they are attempting to match.

The study of good pictures, which is of value in all grades, becomes of increasing importance in Grades VII and VIII because of the greater possibility for aesthetic appreciation which becomes evident then. Details of picture study suitable to both these grades will be discussed in the next article.

A reasonable standard of attainment has been reached at the end of the seventh year if the children have developed skill and sureness in the lines in which they are working, so that in drawing, the general character of objects can be shown by a confident rapid sketch and the details truthfully recorded in a careful drawing; in constructive work if the tools can be handled rapidly and with certainty resulting from much practice; and when in the field of design, there appears increasing pleasure in objects well planned and constructed from a utilitarian standpoint and finely proportioned and shaped from the standpoint of formal beauty.

THE DEVELOPMENT OF METHODS IN TEACHING MODERN ELEMENTARY GEOGRAPHY

C. A. PHILLIPS
Warrensburg State Normal School, Warrensburg, Missouri

INTRODUCTION

Since 1600 modern school geography has passed through three distinct periods. First, geography is a study of charts and maps for the purpose of locating land and water forms. These early geographies also included a considerable body of descriptive matter relating to these typical land and water forms, and in addition to these descriptions, some statements are made about the plants, animals and races of men. It is probable that this early geography grew out of the ancient astronomical geography which had been taught in the universities for centuries. At any rate this unorganized, unscientific type of geography prevailed till about 1800.

In the second period, physiography is made the important factor underlying geography. This change occurs after Ritter begins the study and teaching of geography in the University of Berlin. In his theory and teaching, geography is made a science which treats of the earth and its inhabitants, and very soon his theories are adopted in both Europe and America. Moreover, they continue to be dominating ideals till the close of the nineteenth century.

The third period may be called the period of industrial or economic geography. During the last decade we have heard a great deal about this form of geography—this is a perfectly natural tendency in that it is taking some of the emphasis off the physiographical aspects of geography and putting more on the problems growing out of human relations.

The paper will take up in turn these periods, devoting a brief discussion to the early period which will include the deve'opment of methods as they grow out of Pestalozzi's experiments supplemented by those of his disciples. A much larger place will be devoted to the discussion of Ritter's theories and the practice growing out of them. His influence will be traced directly through his own teaching and that of his pupils and followers. Finally a brief discussion will be undertaken of the present situation with regard to the attempts to make industry the basis of geography. The plan is to take up the development of method as it goes on in Europe first, and then trace the development for the United States. In both cases the discussion will follow the periods which have been noted above.

I. THE DEVELOPMENT OF METHODS OF TEACHING GEOGRAPHY IN EUROPE

1. *Place and Book Geography*

To show that this type of geography prevailed during the seventeenth and eighteenth centuries it is only necessary to take up the writings of some of the more important reformers during these centuries. We find all the reformers protesting against the study of such geography, and most of them offer suggestions as to what they think should be taught instead of the material that is being used.

Comenius (1592–1670) was among the first to advocate a change to a more rational method of study and the selection of more valuable material for that study. He suggests that the child should get very early a good knowledge of natural things, such as plants, trees, flowers, sand, clay, the cow, the horse, and the dog. He says, "In the fourth and following years the child should be taken into the fields and along the rivers and should travel to observe plants and animals, running water, and the turning of windmills."[1] Further, he thinks the study of geography should begin at the cradle. At once the child should be taught direction, location, and distance of the parts of the house, such as the nursery, kitchen, bed-chamber. Very early, too, the children should have much outdoor observation in geography, namely, visits to orchards; should be taught to find their way along the streets, and learn where their friends and relations live.

Rousseau (1712–78) thought the geography of his time was practically worthless, for it consisted only in the formal study of globes and maps which inadequately represented the important things needed by Emile. He insisted that Emile should begin the study of geography by getting a correct knowledge of his immediate neighborhood and if any maps were to be used they should be drawn by the child. He thought mere names of places and facts were of no value, but that objects should be studied first-hand, as a matter of experience.[2]

Pestalozzi (1746–1827) was another of the reformers whose indirect influence on the method of teaching geography was very great, though he knew very little about the subject himself. DeGuimps says:

> The first elements of geography were taught us from the land itself. We were first taken to a narrow valley not far from Yverdun, where the river Buron runs. After taking a general view of the valley we were made to examine the details until we had obtained an exact and complete idea of it. We were then told to take some of the clay which lay in beds on one side of the valley and fill the baskets which we had brought along for the purpose. On our return to the castle we took our places at the long tables and reproduced in relief the valley we had just studied, each one doing the part which had been allotted to him. In the course of the next few days more walks and more explorations, each day on higher ground, and each time with a further extension of our work. Only when our relief was finished were we shown the map which by this means we did not see till we were in a position to understand it.[3]

This is home geography, *Heimatskunde,* which according to Monroe was one of the striking Pestalozzian innovations. However, when we read Barnard's account[4] of the methods of instruction advocated by Pestalozzi we are forced to conclude that he was after all not far from place and book geography. For example, Pestalozzi says:

> Thus, for instance, one of the subdivisions of Europe is Germany. Let the child first become acquainted beyond the power of forgetting them with the subdivisions of Germany into ten circles. Now let the names of the cities of Germany be laid before him in alphabetical order to be read; there being at the name of each city a number of the circle in which it lies. As soon as he can read the names of the cities fluently let him be

shown how the numbers annexed to them refer to the heads above and the child will after a few lessons be able to locate all the cities of Germany according to the heads thus set above them. Let there be put before him, for instance, the following German places, with figures: Aachen[8], Aalen[3], Abendburg[4], Acken[10], etc. Then the pupil will read as follows: Aachen is in the Westphalian circle, Abendburg is in the Franconian circle, etc.[4]

Krüsi, in discussing the application of Pestalozzi's methods, says:

In his efforts to systematize geography, Pestalozzi seems to have violated the principles of a sound system of instruction. This resulted from an undue attention on the alphabetical end, and therefore arbitrary arrangement of geographical names, which he wished to impress upon the mind, or rather upon the memories, of the pupils. He evidently had not at that time a correct conception of the true office and purpose of geography.[5]

This confirms the view that Pestalozzi's contribution in the matter of method in teaching geography was indirect, growing out of his principles of education, rather than directly stated or practiced in any of his teaching. His work consisted in giving the point of view and inspiration for such men as Krüsi, Niederer, Plaman, Tobler, Zeller, Fellenberg, von Raumer, and particularly Karl Ritter, the greatest of all German geographers. Ritter himself says:

Pestalozzi knew less of geography than a child in one of our primary schools, yet it was from him that I gained my chief knowledge of this science, for it was in listening to him that I first conceived the idea of the natural method. It was he who opened the way for me and I take pleasure in attributing whatever value my work may possess entirely to him.

It is doubtful whether we should take this statement of Ritter's too seriously. For its parts are contradictory. First he says that Pestalozzi knew very little geography, and then he says that he owes all to him. A fair estimate of the matter would seem to be that Ritter really formed the purpose to make the scientific study and teaching of geography his life-work while under the personal influence and enthusiasm of Pestalozzi, and he felt profoundly grateful to Pestalozzi for helping him to reach this very important decision.

Another reformer, Karl von Raumer (1783–1865), attempted

some experiments in geography-teaching. He was familiar with the theories of Rousseau and wanted to work them out, but he was also directly a follower of Pestalozzi and his method. These experiments of his, then, are tried as the result of his adoption of the theories of both Rousseau and Pestalozzi. Moreover, they represent a direct protest against the kind of geography taught during his time. The inadequacy of place and book geography is pointed out first by means of an imaginary dialogue between two boys, Otto and George, written by von Raumer. Pestalozzi's method of instruction comes into the dialogue, but the gist of it brings out the truth that geography cannot be learned from maps, charts, and merely reading about places. These are wholly inadequate to give correct conceptions of even the primary geographical problems. The only way to learn accurately the type forms in geography is by observation and experience directly connected with the things to be learned. With these theories in mind, von Raumer went to Nuremberg and attempted to put them into practice in his teaching of geography. He says that the experiment was a total failure, due to the fact that the boys did not want to draw the maps, even though the walks around the neighborhood had been very pleasant. He had thought after an accurate observation of the neighborhood the boys would be ready to draw the maps with accuracy and pleasure. Von Raumer concluded that his theory of geographical instruction was wrong, which may have been true in part, but the main cause of the failure is to be found in the fact that the boys were not used to representing their observations by means of drawing. The habit of graphic representation has to be acquired in the same way as other habits, and this habit the boys had not yet acquired. At Erlangen, von Raumer modified his plan somewhat by using the pupils' knowledge of their surroundings as means of introducing them to the study of maps. For example the pupils were handed a large map of the city and told to pick out their own homes, familiar streets, the churches, and other public buildings. This proved a very popular plan. It is easy to see why, for here we have introduced the game element. After the general map was studied the pupils took a detailed map of the city and studied it in the same way. Then the map of the vicinity of Erlangen, Middle Franconia, Germany, finally Europe, and the world. All of this is place geography, but it was an improvement on the kind which was being taught generally in Germany. Von Raumer complained that the arrangement of the material in the textbooks was very poor, in fact, without any system. He makes a quotation from the favorite manual of Stein, which had gone through fourteen editions, and which was considered one of the best geographies of the time. The quotation is about German mountains and lakes, and is as follows:

> The principal mountains are the Harz (Bracken, 3,945 feet high); Schwarzwald (Feldberg, 4,610 feet); the Rocky Alps, the Rhaetian and Noric Alps (Orteles, or Ortles, 14,814 feet; Grossglockner, 11,982 feet; Hochhorn, 10,667 feet; Platey-Kugel, 9,748 feet; Watzman, 9,150 feet; the Carinic and Julian Alps (Terglon, 10,845 feet); the Fichtelgebirge, the Schneeberge, 3,468 feet; the Kahlenberg the Birnbaumerwald, the Sudetic Alps, and Riesengebirge (Riesenkoppe, 4,950 feet); the Moravian Mountains (Spieglitzer, Schneeberg, 4,280 feet); part of the Carpathian, connected by low heights with the Moravian and Sudetic chains, the Thuringian Mountains, the Erzgebirge, the Spessart, the Rhone mountains, the Böhmerwald (Rachel, 3,904 feet, Arber, 4,500 feet); the Wesergebirge, Westerwald, Odenwald, Ardennes, Vosges, Hundsrück, etc. Lakes: Lake of Constance (7 miles long, 3 miles broad, and more than three hundred fathoms deep), Chiemsee, Lake of Cerknitz, the salt and sweet Lake of Mansfeld, the Lakes of Mecklenburg, Brandenburg, and Pomerania, the Drümmersee, the Trinnstätter and Hallstatter in Archducal Austria. The Steinhunder Lake.[7]

It would be impossible to find a better example of complete confusion than the above quotation, and yet, an examination of the textbooks of the time fully warrants von Raumer's criticism. More than that, it verifies the fact that the quotation fully represents material found in the textbooks of his time. He makes another point against them, namely, that it is impossible to tell important facts from relatively unimportant ones, as they are all put together without any regard to value. Indeed, in many cases unimportant facts are mentioned and the more important ones left out entirely. For example, in the description of Cologne reference is made to the perfume manufactured there but no mention is made of the cathedral. This was the state of geography-teaching in Europe as late as 1831 when von Raumer wrote his *Manual of General Geography* in which he tried to remedy some of the deficiencies of the books just mentioned. In the main, this new textbook follows the plan outlined and first used at Erlangen. To complete the reform he adds his second book, *The Description of the Earth's Surface,* etc. This last was a book for beginners. It seems, however, that these new books did not affect practice to any considerable extent. The reason for this is that they overlap the period of Ritter's work and influence.

Our discussion has related mainly to Swiss and German reformers and the practice in these two countries. It is not necessary to discuss the other countries of Europe since they all lag some years behind the progress of Switzerland and Germany in the study and teaching of geography, and it may be added in the whole matter of the development of educational methods. The only proof necessary for the above statement is to cite the fact that practically all the nations of Europe sent students to visit Pestalozzi's school at Yverdun, Fellenburg's school at Hofwyl, and the other experimental schools being conducted in Germany. Krüsi tells us that France, Spain, Russia, England, and even the United States sent students to study in these schools. The theories and methods, to be sure, did not affect France much till after the Franco-Prussian war. Spain and Russia were not affected at all because of the interference of the home governments. In England we find three of Pestalozzi's pupils, namely, Dr. Mayo, Reiner, and Herman Krüsi, Jr., trying to carry out the Pestalozzian methods. They first attempted schools on an independent basis, but later, in 1836, under the patronage of the Home and Colonial Society. A training school was established at Gray's Inn Road and another at Battersea near London. The only thing of note in connection with these schools in the matter of geography-study was the "Lessons on Objects" in which the pupils studied the schoolroom, the school premises and buildings, and, finally, took excursions into the surrounding fields as a means of securing interest. It should be noted, however, that these are only training schools for teachers and the whole number of England's schools was influenced very slightly by them.[8]

It is easy to understand the reason for Germany's great progress in the matter of methods in her schools, for this was just after Fichte's great address to the German nation when she had been crushed by the Napoleonic wars. Fichte urges the government to turn its attention to the schools as a means of redeeming Germany. His advice was accepted, and all the world knows the results both in so far as the schools are concerned and the nation's reconstruction.

2. *Physiographical Geography and Its Human Relations*

This type of geography was brought into scientific form by the world's most eminent geographer, Karl Ritter (1779–1859). Ritter was fortunate both in his teachers and his friends. Among his teachers he had the great Salzman at the famous Schnepfenthal school for eleven years. Both the school and its surroundings on the border of the Thuringian Forest made a profound impression on his character. Here he learned to love all primitive nature-forms. His course of study was in the modern languages rather than in the ancient, being altogether of a practical sort. At the close of his stay with Salzman fortune again favored him, for Herr Hollweg, a rich merchant at Frankfort-on-the-Main, selected him as tutor for his two sons and sent him to the University of Halle for two years. During his stay at the university he had the good fortune to live in the home of Niemeyer, one of the most distinguished professors of the university and also one of the most successful educators of the time. Niemeyer was not only a successful teacher, but was interested in the fundamental principles which underlie education and had published a treatise on the art of teaching. Consequently, young Ritter was daily under the influence of a real teacher and it seems natural that he should adopt the profession of teaching. As soon as he finished his studies at the university, he took up his duties as tutor for Herr Hollweg's two sons at Frankfort. This city was one of the centers of wealth and cu'ture in Germany and his position as tutor in the Hollweg family at once gave him entré into the best society of the city. More than that, he retained the friendship of the Hollweg family throughout his life. One of the sons afterward became a colleague of Ritter in the University of Berlin. While still acting as tutor to the Hollweg children he made a visit to Switzerland, taking the children with him. On this first trip he spent seven days with Pestalozzi at Yverdun. He says these were seven days of supreme enjoyment, and this was the beginning of a friendship which lasted throughout the life of Pestalozzi. Each time Ritter went to Switzerland on one of his excursions he would spend some time with his friend. We have already referred to the influence Ritter attributed to Pestalozzi in the matter of inspiring him to take up the study and teaching of geography. One other friend should be mentioned, Alexander von Humboldt (1769–1859), whom he met for the first time in Frankfort soon after his first visit to Switzerland, which occurred in 1811. It is not possible to estimate the value of this friendship to Ritter, for von Humboldt was the greatest and broadest scientist of his generation. He was interested in science generally but particularly in geology, natural history, and geography. Undoubtedly, Ritter learned much about geography from this great scientist, and it is not too much to say that from von Humboldt came a large share of insight which helped Ritter finally to become the world's first scientific geographer.[9]

Another thing helps to account for the equipment which made possible the career of Ritter. After his first journey to Switzerland in 1811 it was his custom each year to make some journey or journeys to increase his first-hand knowledge about geographical forms and conditions. During these years he made many visits to Switzerland and Italy, also crossed France in all directions; visited Greece, Bulgaria, Hungary, Turkey, Denmark, Austria, Norway, Sweden, England; explored the Pyrenees and visited London, Vienna, and Paris many times. No doubt the reflex influence of these visits upon the countries was very great. However, there is no accurate way to estimate it.

Finally, his opportunity was great, for continental Europe was just beginning to settle down after the Napoleonic wars when he began his career. The conditions in Europe were ripe for the construction of new theories about science, and the study of geography conformed to the spirit of the times.

The real teaching career of Ritter began with his appointment as "*professor extraordinarius*" of geography in the University of Berlin in 1820, which position he continued to occupy till his death. The professorship itself is unique, for it is virtually the first time that geography is put on such a basis in the curriculum of the modern university. Ritter began his work with no hearers at the opening of the course and only a very few at its close. However, before three years, his lecture-room was full and he continued to be one of the most popular lecturers at the university throughout his life. At the very beginning of his teaching he worked out his theories of geography on a thoroughly scientific basis, and so carefully was this done that it won for him the distinction of being called the founder of modern scientific geography. The limits of this paper will allow only a brief statement of his fundamental principles. They may be summarized as follows: (1) Physiography is the real basis of geography; (2) the earth is the arena for the development of human life and history; (3) man and his education are the center of interest in geography and all other factors cluster around his destiny; (4) earth-forms do not come by accident, they are the result of an all-wise plan; (5) the country affects the life of the people; (6) God and his laws are behind the development of the earth as the home for man; (7) geography as a science has for its problems the discovery of these laws of the earth's evolution and the proper appropriation of the earth's resources for the greatest possible development of the human race. [10, 11]

With these principles as a working-basis, geography is no longer a great body of unrelated facts but becomes at once a fund of living material which includes the whole history of the development of the human race, and such was Ritter's thought. Nature and man in interaction—these are with Ritter inseparable. Consequently, he does not try to separate history and geography. This conception no doubt accounts for the fact that in most European countries even to the present time we find the two subjects being taught together.[12] This is particularly true of Germany and Switzerland. By way of parenthesis it might be added that a few of Ritter's followers went entirely over to geology as the controlling factor in man's and nations' destinies. However, this does not represent the real trend of Ritter's thinking.

With reference to method, it is to be noted that Ritter advocated the synthetic, rather than the analytic, type of study. An important device with him was the excursion, which has been adopted by all European countries but is possibly best carried on in Switzerland. Another practice which he advocates is the study of the garden in connection with the school. His theories and the practices growing out of them were adopted by all the states of Europe, not long after the middle of the nineteenth century. France adopted them after the Franco-Prussian War and England somewhat later. It is one of the strange facts of geography-study and -teaching that England, with a'l of her natural facilities, and interest in travel and exploration, lagged so long behind. As late as 1882 Geikie[13] complains that the subject has not received anything like the attention in England which had been given to it in Germany. However, five years later he reports much progress in the methods of teaching geography in England, due in part to his own books and efforts, but no doubt in large measure also to the establishment of chairs of geography in both Oxford and Cambridge. Geikie adopts the theories of Ritter, as he takes the "earth as the dwelling-place of man" as one of the fundamental theses of his discussion.

3. *Industrial or Economic Geography*

Notwithstanding the great industrial progress of Germany in the last few years the course of study for the elementary school has been very little changed, and in fact it seems fair to say that Ritter's geography still prevails. However, some important changes have taken place in the secondary-school curricula.

Especially is this true of the *Realschule* which was established to meet changing industrial conditions. The same lack of progress appears in Switzerland. In France, Klemm reports that the schools of Paris give considerable time to the discussion of commercial geography. He says, "The railroad system of France and Europe is a subject of much study as could be seen from sketch-maps on the blackboard and from work done by the pupils in their journals."[14] The pupils also draw maps on which are shown the places which grow the grape-vine or olive, and they prepare statistical tables showing a comparison of the principal countries of the world in area, population, armies, navies, their productions, values of exports and imports, tonnage of merchant marine, etc.

At the present time there is a very definite movement in England toward economic geography. This is in a large measure due to the interest which the universities have taken in the matter and particularly the publications which come from Oxford. The Herbertson series of geographies,[15] published at Oxford in 1907, and also *Man and his Work,*[16] published by the Herbertsons, are important factors in the movement. It is interesting to note the subtitle of this last book. It is *An Introduction to Human Geography,* and as we look through the book we see that the whole of geography is to be treated from the human and industrial side rather than from the side of ordinary physiographical geography. In this case physiography has been treated only as a valuable auxiliary to the progress of the race. The textbooks abandon the traditional continental divisions and discuss certain natural, industrial regions, for example the region around the Mediterranean Sea. Here the main consideration is given to the broader economic problems growing out of the region. The books were published only in 1907 and it remains to be seen what influence they will exert on the methods of teaching geography in England.

SOURCES OF QUOTATIONS

1. Monroe, W. S. *Comenius and the Beginning of Educational Reform,* 115–16.
2. Payne. *Rousseau's "Emile,"* 136–39.

3. De Guimps. *Pestalozzi and His Life-Work*, 255.
4. Barnard. *Pestalozzi and His Educational System*, 684.
5. Monroe, W. S. *The Pestalozzian Movement in the United States*, 264.
6. Krüsi. *The Life and Works of Pestalozzi*, 177–78.
7. Barnard. *German Pedagogy*, 117.
8. Krüsi. *The Life and Works of Pestalozzi*, chaps. iii, iv.
9. Gage. *Life of Karl Ritter.*
10. Ritter. *Geographical Studies.*
11. ———. *Comparative Geography.*
12. Russell. *German Higher Schools*, chap. xv.
13. Geikie. *The Teaching of Geography.*
14. Klemm. *European Schools*, 362–63.
15. Herbertson, A. J. "Geography Series" (Vol. I, *Preliminary Geography;* Vol. II, *Junior Geography;* Vol. III, *Senior Geography*).
16. Herbertson, A. J. and T. D. *Man and His Work.*

SOME STOCK AND BOND PROBLEMS

GORDON W. THAYER
University of Cincinnati

The problems which follow are an attempt to apply to the field of stocks and bonds the ideas of Professors D. E. Smith and F. M. McMurry in their well-known paper on "Mathematics in Elementary Schools" (*Teachers' College Record*, March, 1903). There the point is made (p. 6) that problems should be concrete, and that they are concrete only when they deal with actual, significant situations. As an instance of what is meant, a series of problems is given relating to the printers' ink industry in this country and based on the actual facts of this industry's development. Because the problems are real, they possess more interest and are more worth working out than those which are more conventional.

Later (pp. 55–56) the same course is urged for the treatment of stocks and bonds, without, however, definite suggestions. This gap it is hoped to fill by the problems below. These are taken from actual transactions, except that the city is not San Francisco, nor are the other names the genuine ones.

The Consolidated Gas Co. of San Francisco, capitalized at $500,000 (What does this mean?), to which sum $500,000 more was later added (Why? What would be the effects?), sold gas at first at 75 cents a thousand feet; after its additional capitalization at 85 cents a thousand feet. (Why?) Soon the Golden Gate Illuminating Co., a competing corporation, was organized, with a capitalization of $350,000; and charged 75 cents a thousand feet for gas. (What effect would this have on the Consolidated Co.?) The Consolidated retaliated with a 70-cent charge, and was in turn undersold by the Golden Gate Co. This continued till both left their rates at 60 cents a thousand feet, at which figure the Golden Gate Co. was able to pay 4 per cent dividends; and its stock sold at 103. (What does this indicate about the capitalization of the Consolidated Co.? Its original capitalization?)

1. Mr. Charles Black, owner of the *San Francisco Evening Times,* and

a stockholder in the Golden Gate Co., owns 2,550 shares, which he bought at 98 4/5. Which would be better for him, to keep them, or sell them at the market price? What would he get by following either policy? What do the above facts indicate about the fair price of gas in San Francisco?

2. Meanwhile the Consolidated Co. finds it necessary, if it is to meet its expenses, and also pay 4 per cent dividends, to draw $38,000 from its accumulated reserve fund of $106,000. (For what purpose was this fund accumulated? How long can the Consolidated Co. continue to do this? Was it good policy to do it at all, and why? What had the company better do?) Had not this step been made necessary, it was the idea of the president to spend $40,000 from the reserve fund for Government 4's at 106½, due in thirty years. How many could the company have bought? What income would they have netted? Why did they not go on with the scheme?

3. Mr. Black, mentioned above, has 25,000 shares in the Consolidated Co., which he bought at 101 and which would now fetch 87 if sold. (Why this drop?) He has also bought 8,000 additional shares in Golden Gate, at par. How much money has he invested in gas stock? If he were to sell it all, how much money would he gain or lose, as compared with his original purchases? What attitude will his *Evening Times* take when people complain about the service or the rates of the two gas companies?

4. He engineers a merger of the two companies into a new company, the United Gas & Electric Co., with a capitalization of $500,000. (Why was this figure not made larger? or smaller?) This company is to take over the business of its two predecessors. Holders of Consolidated stock are entitled to exchange their shares for United common stock at par; Golden Gate stockholders may exchange their shares for common stock at 96; or for preferred, paying 4 per cent per annum, at 106½. (Why this difference in treatment between the two sets of stockholders?) Which would be better for Mr. Black to do? How much would he get in 2½ years' time, from his preferred-stock dividends?

5. The new company raises the price of gas to 80 cents a thousand feet. (Why?) Common stock jumps thereupon to 108, and preferred to 113½. A 9 per cent dividend is declared on the common stock. Mr. Black then exchanges his preferred stock for common. How many shares does this give him? What will be the amount of his annual dividend?

6. A new issue of capital stock, of $500,000, is now voted by the board of directors. (Why?) Mr. Black buys 1,750 of the new shares at 103. To what do his holdings now amount? The city officials now seek to enforce the new state law against "stock watering." (This term will have been explained during the discussion on the previous issues.) (What attitude will Mr. Black's *Evening Times* take toward this? Why? When the officials come up for re-election, will the *Times* support them or not, and why?) As a result of this action of the officials, the stock drops to

99. (Why?) If Mr. Black should now sell all his stock, what would be his loss?

7. On account of the opposition of the *Evening Times*, the officials are defeated for re-election before their attempt to enforce the law has any results. The price of gas is now raised to 85 cents a thousand feet. (Why?) Common stock now rises to 111, and preferred to 115½. To what would Mr. Black's shares now amount, if sold? What would have been their amount if he had retained his preferred stock?

8. A rival gas company is now organized. (Why?) This, at a capitalization of $350,000 (Why not more?), is promptly bought out by the United Co., the shareholders of the new company being entitled to exchange their shares for a corresponding number of shares in the United Co. at 98; a new stock issue being voted by the United Co.'s directors. (Was this whole procedure good policy on the part of the old company, and why?) Common stock drops to 107¾, and preferred to 112. This is now the sixth year since the organization of the United Co., and it has been paying 9 per cent dividends; now the dividend drops to 5 per cent. Why? How much has Mr. Black made since we first noticed his investments in gas?

9. How do his profits from gas stock compare with those from his newspaper corporation, in which he has 75,000 shares and has received 36 per cent in dividends in the same six years? His newspaper stock was secured by him at 104, and is now worth 122. What would it fetch if sold? What would he clear?

10. Next year a candidate for mayor proposes that the city buy out the United Co. for $1,100,000, guaranteeing 4 per cent dividends to the stockholders for a period of ten years, at which time they would be supposed to have transferred their holdings to other lines of business. How about this proposition, from the point of view of the city? From the point of view of the stockholders? How many shares did the company contain? How many did Mr. Black hold? What would he receive if this proposition were carried into effect? Would this, then, be a good bargain, and why?

11. The candidate proposes *as an alternative* that, if the company will not accept this proposition, the city shall issue bonds (What does this mean? What would be the advantages of raising the money in this way instead of by taxes? What the disadvantages?) to build its own gas works, and furnish gas at cost to the consumers of the city. What will be the effect of this proposition on the value of gas stock? What had the company better do? What attitude will Mr. Black's *Evening Times* take toward this candidate for mayor? Why? Mr. Black finds that, if he wants to sell his shares (Why might he want to sell them?) he must sell at 91. What would be his loss? Had he better sell or wait, and why?

12. The candidate is elected (Why, do you suppose?), and makes the first proposition named above to the gas company with this change: since gas stock has fallen to 86 after the election, the dividend proposition is omitted. (Why?) What had Mr. Black and his friends better do? What will sale on these terms bring him? what about waiting for developments?

13. Mr. Black sells out on the city's terms, and invests the proceeds in Artificial Ice Stock at 102½. How many shares can he get? Will the policy of the *Evening Times* on the gas question be affected by his action, and how? The other stockholders sell out, and the city takes over the business. What will be the probable effect in this case on the price of gas to the consumers?

AGRICULTURAL EDUCATION: NATIONAL EDUCATION ASSOCIATION—STATE AND OTHER TEACHERS' ASSOCIATIONS

BENJAMIN MARSHALL DAVIS
Miami University

It is said of the National Education Association that it "has been, and is now the body-guard of public-school instruction in our country." While this statement may not be taken literally, the fact remains that this Association is the one educational organization which is truly national in character, embracing as it does the interests of all parts of the country and all phases of education.

It was organized in Philadelphia on August 26, 1857, under the name of the National Teachers' Association by a group of teachers who met in response to a call sent out the previous year to all the local teachers' associations. The call itself is significant, for it expresses the spirit which has, on the whole, been manifest during the entire existence of the Association: to teachers of the United States "who are willing to unite in a general effort to promote the general welfare of our country by concentrating the wisdom and power of numerous minds, and by distributing among all the accumulated experiences of all" (57).[1]

The name was changed in 1870 to the National Educational Association and in 1907 to the one it now bears. As made to meet the demands of a natural growth but it has never departed from the essential principles on which it was founded. The extent to which the "accumulated experiences of all" have been "distributed among all" may be seen by a reference to the published list of titles of papers and discussions from 1857 to 1907. This list covers over seventy pages and embraces almost

[1] Figures refer to bibliography at end of article or to bibliographies in previous numbers of this series.

every imaginable subject of educational interest (58). Many discussions are of only passing importance; some are but means of exploiting favorite theories; others are real contributions to educational thought.

Beyond the propaganda which is expected of any large educational body the most valuable work of the Association has been through its committees which have been appointed from time to time to investigate and report upon various important questions of general interest.

The Association being a sort of clearing-house for educational ideas, its published *Proceedings* provide a valuable source of information concerning all kinds of tendencies and movements in education. Agricultural education has received a share of attention proportional to the different stages of its development. The interest of the Association in this subject as reflected in the *Proceedings* extends over four periods: the first from 1857 to 1897, the second from 1897 to 1903, the third from 1903 to 1906, and the fourth from 1906 to the present time.

Agriculture was not considered as a separate subject except as referring to agricultural colleges until the latter part of the first period. Industrial education, however, was discussed as early as 1866. In 1875 a Department of Industrial Education was formed. At this meeting the question: "Can Elements of Industrial Education be Introduced into our Common Schools?" was discussed in a paper by John D. Philbrook. He said: "Science and art with reference to their special application to industrial pursuits must be included in the modern school course." Drawing, geometry, natural history, physics, and chemistry were mentioned as the branches which lie at the foundation of industrial education.

At the meeting of the following year (1876) William T. Harris in his report as chairman of committee on "Course of Study from Primary School to University" refers to the difficulty of deciding "the amount of prominence to be given to industrial branches in comparison with those chiefly productive of theoretical culture." He says also: "The primary school has been called upon to fit for life." In the course of study reported by the committee for the district schools, topics relating to nature are suggested as follows: "Inorganic—arithmetic, oral lessons in natural philosophy; organic—geography, oral lessons in natural history."

These two references to the early discussions of industrial education are given to show that the need of such instruction was being considered at this time, and from a somewhat general viewpoint which might include agriculture although it was not specifically mentioned. The Department of Industrial Education, however, gave its attention almost wholly to urban conditions. Drawing and manual training held prominent places in the discussions of all the meetings. In 1890 the name of the Department was very properly changed to Industrial and Manual Training, and in 1899 to Manual Training.

In 1893, at the International Congress of Education held under the auspices of the Association, agriculture had a place on the program (59) but the paper was read by a Russian and not an American. Perhaps his account of the use of agriculture in the rural schools as a school subject had something to do with directing the attention of the Association to the rural-school problem. At any rate, at the meeting of 1895 a committee of twelve was appointed to investigate and report upon rural schools as to maintenance, supervision, supply of teachers, and instruction and discipline.

The report was submitted to the meeting of 1897. It contains a number of suggestions which involve more or less agricultural instruction such as surface features of the earth including soils, weather, plant and animal life, etc. It also emphasizes the need of a course of study "framed with direct reference to actual conditions that prevail in country life and in large measure determine it. Among the most important points to be kept in mind are the following: (1) There is a general lack of appreciation of immediate surroundings; (2) there is an almost total lack of scientific skill in farm work; (3) in the country there is a great dearth of social life." Under (2) certain phases of mechanics, manual training, biology, meteorology and physics of the atmosphere, mineralogy, and chemistry were included. Another portion of the report is devoted to the "farm as the center of interest," and a great many things which we now find in all textbooks on elementary agriculture are mentioned (60).

During the latter part of the second period (1897–1903) agriculture appeared as a topic for discussion at nearly every meeting. At the meeting of 1902 five papers were read as follows: "The Value of a Large Agricultural School in Indian Service"; "Correlation of Schoolroom and Farm Work"; "The Education of the American Farmer"; "The Practical Value of Teaching Agriculture in the Public Schools"; "The Teaching of Agriculture with Reference to Future Employment."

In 1903 a committee on "Industrial Education in Schools for Rural Communities" was appointed. The committee made its report at the meeting of 1905 and represents the most important contribution of the Association to agricultural education in the third period (1903–6). A considerable part of the report deals with agricultural subjects and their adaptation to elementary and secondary rural schools. Among the recommendations of the committee are the following: "A modification of the course of study should be made for the introduction of work, especially in the elements of agriculture and domestic science, and such further lines of industrial education as local conditions make feasible. . . . The establishment of schools distinctly industrial (agricultural high schools) in their character is absolutely necessary for the proper development and organization of the rural-school system."

A detailed course of study for all the grades is submitted. It is an interesting contrast to the course of study reported by the Committee of Twelve of 1897. In the latter the idea that agricultural subjects should receive attention in the rural schools is suggested rather than definitely stated and outlined. In the former this idea is expressed in a definite and concrete outline with illustrative lessons.

The work in agriculture for the secondary schools is particularly well outlined, and illustrated by accounts of work actually carried on in two existing agricultural high schools: one the

Dunn County (Wisconsin) School of Agriculture and Domestic Economy; the other, the Minnesota Agricultural High School connected with the Agricultural College of Minnesota (61).

The fourth period is characterized by a more active interest in agricultural education. Three important steps were taken: (*a*) continuation of Committee on Industrial Education in Schools for Rural Communities; (*b*) formation of National Committee on Agricultural Education; (*c*) organization of a Department of Rural and Agricultural Education.

The Committee on Industrial Education for Schools of Rural Communities made two reports, one at the meeting of the Association in 1907 and the other at the meeting of 1908.

In some preliminary investigation for the supp'ementary report the correspondence showed that "what was most wanted was a definite statement of what was actually being done in different parts of the country in providing facilities for industrial education in rural communities." The supplementary report represents the efforts of the committee to satisfy this demand. It consists of three parts: a discussion of the general problem, including school buildings, school gardens, manual training, nationalizing the work (referring to the Davis bill then before Congress) and in what schools agriculture should be taught; industrial work in New England, New Jersey, Pennsylvania, and New York; experiences and opinions of individual teachers in the preceding territory (62).

The second report (1908) is limited to "a presentation of what is being done in schools representing four types of organization, as showing the possibilities in other schools of these types and the conditions under which these possibilities may become actualities." The schools selected and reported upon are the Waterford High School, at Waterford, Pa., the Cecil County High School, at Calvert, Md., the John Swaney Conso'idated School, in Magnolia Township, Putnam County, Ill., and the congressional district agricultural schools located at Americus and Monroe, Ga. Each type is described in sufficient detail to give a clear understanding of its organization and actual work.

The final conclusions of the Committee are summed up in

nine paragraphs, two of which should be quoted here since they refer to conditions that continue to exist:

> That the supply of properly trained teachers for carrying on this work is totally inadequate to meet even the present demand, and that the increase in the demand for such teachers in the near future requires a very large increase in the facilities for their preparation, and to supply these facilities special training schools should be established throughout the country for the preparation of elementary rural-school teachers; that the normal schools whose graduates find positions in rural schools should broaden and strengthen in every way their courses of instruction along industrial lines adapted to the needs of rural schools; that the agricultural colleges favorably situated for such work should undertake to organize special courses for the purpose of training teachers for the secondary schools, capable of giving instruction in agriculture and related subjects.
>
> That in the growth of public sentiment; in the development of ideals, in the preparation of courses of study, and in the facilities for the training of teachers for industrial work in rural schools, decided progress has been made in recent years; but that much yet remains to be done before the importance and value of this kind of industrial education shall be fully appreciated by all concerned, and before it shall receive its appropriate recognition and find its proper place in our educational system (63).

In 1906 a call was sent out to members of the Association who were interested in agricultural education to be present at the annual meeting of the Department of Superintendence for the purpose of discussing various problems concerning this subject. There was an encouraging response and an interesting meeting was held. At this meeting the National Committee on Agricultural Education was formed. Through the efforts of this committee an application for the privilege of organizing a Department of Rural and Agricultural Education was presented to the Board of Directors of the Association, and favorably acted upon July 8, 1907 (63).

The second conference of this committee was held at the meeting of the Association of 1907. At this session three important papers were read and discussed: "The Work of the National Government in Extending Agricultural Education through the Public Schools"; "What Has Been Done and Is Being Done by Normal Schools and Agricultural Schools for Popular Education in Agriculture" (64); "The Work in Agriculture as Conducted by State and County Organizations of Young People in Club Contests." The third conference of the committee was held at the meeting of the Department of Superintendence held at Washington in 1908. Just at this time the Davis bill (24) and the Burkett bill (24) were being considered as separate measures. Under the direction of the National Committee on Agricultural Education a conference was held with all parties interested in the two measures, resulting in the introduction in Congress of a new bill embodying the essential features of the two separate ones. A subcommittee conferred with the President of the United States, and also with the Senate Committee on Agriculture in behalf of national aid for agricultural instruction.

The fourth and fifth conferences of the committee were held at the meetings of the Department of Superintendence of 1909 and 1910. At the fourth session two committees were appointed, and reports were made at the fifth session. These were on "Credit Value of High-School Agriculture for College Entrance" and "The Course of Study in Agriculture—What Shall It Be?"

Two regular meetings of the Department of Rural and Agricultural Education have been held (in 1908 and 1909). As they are fully reported in the *Proceedings* of the Association no further reference need be made here, except to state that they were well attended and much interest was shown in the discussions. An excellent program has already been prepared for the meeting of 1910. One session promises to be of especial interest, as it is to be held jointly with the departments of Secondary Education and of Science to consider the "Practical Aspects of Science in Secondary Education with Special Reference to Introducing Materials from Agriculture, Household Arts, Technical Industries, Sanitation, etc."

It will be seen from the foregoing account that the National Education Association has been and is an important factor in agricultural education, first in the way of propaganda, by bringing the subject prominently before the teachers of the entire country, and second by real constructive work through its committees and its Department of Rural and Agricu'tural Education.

Through the published *Proceedings* of the Association the

development of the movement for agricultural education can be followed as in no other educational literature excepting that of the National Government through its publications of the Department of Agriculture and of the Bureau of Education.

STATE AND INTERSTATE TEACHERS' ASSOCIATIONS

There are about seventy of these associations. Some were in existence long before the organization of the National Teachers' Association. Most of them publish proceedings of their meetings, but for lack of funds and other causes accounts of these meetings are not always published except in local papers. Enough of these proceedings, however, are available in published form to trace any educational movement as reflected by the discussions of these meetings. One finds that agricultural education began to receive attention from these associations about the same time that the National Education Association became actively interested in it. We find, for example, the Alabama Educational Association in 1905 devoting a considerable part of its program to the subject, and calling W. M. Hays to give an address; the California State Teachers' Association in 1905 holding joint sessions with the State Farmers' Institute, and calling L. D. Harvey and A. C. True to make addresses; the Georgia Teachers' Association in its meetings of 1903, 1906, 1907, and 1908 giving prominence to the subject, in 1908 holding a conference with representative business men from forty-four of the fifty counties of the state concerning the district agricultural high schools. These illustrations are typical of the consideration given agricultural education by most of these associations at their recent meetings. Their contribution consists chiefly in creating an interest in the subject. Sometimes, however, movements are started that result in state legislation.

It is not possible in the limits of this paper to enter into further discussion of the work of these associations, instructive as it might be to follow carefully the development of agricultural education as expressed by these bodies of teachers in various sections of the country.

BIBLIOGRAPHY

The facts of the text have been gathered mainly from the publications of the National Education Association referred to below, and from the published proceedings of various teachers' associations which are in the library of the United States Bureau of Education.

57. *Historical Sketch of the National Educational Association.* Z. RICHARDS. *Proceedings of the National Educational Association* (1891), 118–33.

58. *Bibliography of Topics from 1857–1907. Ibid.* (1906), 659–730.

This is a classified list under fifty-nine heads.

59. "Should Rural Schools Introduce Agriculture, Chemistry, Agricultural Botany, or Arboriculture?" ERGRAFF DE KOVALEVSKY. *Ibid.* (1893), 304–7.

The writer concludes that "instruction in the rural schools can and should have an agricultural bearing."

60. "Report of the Committee of Twelve on Rural Schools." *Ibid.* (1897), pp. 385–582.

This is probably the most complete and important contribution of rural schools in American educational literature up to the date of its publication. Besides a full discussion of the four phases of the subject there are nineteen appendices devoted to such subjects as transportation of pupils, enrichment of the rural-school course, the rural-school problem, the course of study, the farm as a center of interest, etc.

61. *Report of the Committee on Industrial Education in Schools for Rural Communities.* Publications of National Educational Association: Report of Special Committee (1905), 87.

This report contains argument for industrial work, scope of work, statements of what kind of work was being done in the different types of schools in which a beginning in industrial education had been made, and the desirability of a new type of secondary school of distinctively industrial character and adapted to the needs of rural communities.

62. *Ibid.*, "Supplementary Report." *Proceedings of the National Education Association* (1907), 409–46.

63. ——, "Second Report." *Ibid.* (1908), 385–448.

64. "Conference of National Committee on Agricultural Education." *Ibid.* (1907), 1063–84.

EDITORIAL NOTES

The season has arrived when teachers are beginning to arrange their plans for the summer vacation. Fortunately these plans are coming to include in ever-increasing degree some kind of study which shall augment the efficiency of the subsequent year's work. When the first summer schools were opened there were misgivings in the minds of many as to the wisdom of summer study on the part of teachers; there were undoubtedly mistakes of overzealousness which justified some of these misgivings. With the accumulation of experience, however, the most skeptical must be convinced, for in all parts of the country there come together a great number of teachers and they derive benefits of such undoubted advantage that there is a steady increase in the demand for such opportunities.

Summer-School Plans

It is not alone the teachers who derive advantages from summer schools; the institutions which carry on the work profit greatly by contact with the summer constituency. No plan could possibly have been devised which would have operated more successfully than does the summer school to keep universities and schools of all other grades in closest contact. A university teacher of history or science or English working with college students or even with ordinary graduate students may get out of touch with what is actually developing in the surrounding schools; but this same university teacher before his summer class can never lose sight of the school problem. He will be plied with questions fresh from the classroom of the schools; he will be called to book very promptly if he indulges in any unwarranted speculations about the way in which subjects should be presented. On the other side the teacher in the schools does not need to deal at long range through books with the best authorities; the teacher of geography or history or drawing can find some institution which puts him

An Important By-Product

into direct contact with leading authorities. These institutional contacts can be called by-products of the main work of the summer school, which is the training of the individual teacher, but from a larger view they are to be regarded as of prime importance.

The purpose of the present editorial is, however, not mere comment on the value of summer-school courses. There are

Few Courses Well Done rather than Many Courses

certain questions which are constantly being turned over in the minds of prospective summer students on which it may not be out of place to offer the light of institutional experience. Most students want to take more courses than they can pursue with profit. Better a single course well assimilated than many courses hastily skimmed. Better a limit of two or at most three, than an open temptation to get all one can crowd into the day. Someone has described a summer-school student as a person so eager for credits that he cannot stop to get an education. There is another type of student who tries to do too much, namely the student who at great sacrifice has reached the institution for perhaps the only summer that he can afford in a long period of years. With all due regard to the importance of credits and the value of an opportunity when one is on the ground, let the warning be clear and emphatic: take few courses and do them thoroughly.

A second important question is, What kind of courses shall one take?. There are always courses of a so-called professional

Professional Courses and Subject-Matter Courses

character which deal with the theory or philosophy of education or with methods or with educational psychology. On the other side there are courses in subject-matter such as courses in geography, mathematics, manual arts, and reading. Shall one take professional courses or courses in subject-matter? There can be no doubt that the necessity of preparing for examinations of one sort or another has given the professional courses some advantage. On the other hand, there can be no doubt that what most teachers need is subject-matter. Many a teacher is misled by someone's advice into a course in educational psychology when what he or she needs is a good course in plane geometry or elementary geography. There are some students at summer school who will not take anything but advanced courses when what they need is elementary courses. There should be much greater care in the selection of courses. If one's superintendent or principal suggests a summer at this or that institution, let the student canvass the matter carefully before he goes, let him select the courses which he needs, not those which will exhibit the greatest devotion to advanced theory. Summer-school students with their own experience in teaching to guide them ought to be very judicious in the selection of their courses; the fact is that they very often are not at all judicious.

Visiting Courses

A third matter on which comment certainly needs to be made is the matter of visiting courses in which one does not do the reading or written work or take the examination. Such visiting is usually related to the mistake referred to in the paragraph above on undertaking too many courses. The theory of such visiting is that one can pick up without much effort, in a fashion suitable to vacation, some information and some culture. Possibly in some rare cases benefit is derived from visiting. How a teacher of experience can sanction in his or her own person this utterly unpedagogical method of attaching oneself to culture is difficult to understand. There is no such thing as passive reception of knowledge. Any teacher young enough to go to summer school is not too old to acquire bad habits of mind by indulgence in visiting. The cure for visiting is to take one course and do it well. The value of this one course will be not merely the knowledge gained, but also the taste for real acquisition.

Careful Planning before Registering

The purpose of this editorial will be served if it leads its readers to plan in advance the work which many of them will undertake this summer. It is astonishing to see how unformed are the plans of many who come to summer schools. Consultation at home with one's associates, consultation by letter with the university which one is to attend, consideration of one's own need before starting, these are the lines of preparation which these paragraphs are intended to suggest.

BOOK REVIEWS

Methods of Teaching Developed from a Functional Point of View. By W. W. CHARTERS. Chicago: Row, Peterson & Co. Pp. 255. $1.10.

To a considerable extent this book is a formulation of methods of teaching in terms of Dewey's theory of education. This is in striking contrast with the method books based on the Herbartian formula, namely the books of McMurray, DeGarmo, and various English writers. This tendency to adopt some unifying principle, which is lacking in such books as Thorndike's *Principles of Teaching,* is very helpful for some students, and to such Charters' book will appeal. To students of Dewey the following ideas which are prominent in the book will be familiar:

"The aim of education is to assist pupils to appreciate and control the values of life. Subject-matter arises in response to failure or breakdown in old ways of acting; it is invoked to satisfy needs or desires or to solve problems. The intrinsic function of subject-matter is its function in life without reference to its utility in the school. The attention of pupils for the major part of the time should be directed upon these intrinsic functions. Each unit of subject-matter should be definitely organized from the standpoint of its intrinsic function."

This fundamental discussion of subject-matter occupies one-third of the book. Over a third of this part is devoted to concrete examples from composition, literature, arithmetic, history, etc.

"The securing of motives, education's greatest problem," occupies about one-fifth of the book. The central thought is again the Dewey notion of getting the pupil into a situation where he is conscious of a lack or need which he formulates and attacks as a personal problem to be solved. Two-fifths of this discussion is an elaboration of examples from English, arithmetic, and history. The remaining chapters are, "Review of Past Experience," "Control of Values," "Forms of Instruction," "Methods of Development," "Psychological and Logical Organizations," "Methods of Securing Realness," "Drill and Application," "The Assignment," "The Lesson Plan."

The outline of main topics noted in the previous paragraph is admirable. It suggests vividly certain topics which are neglected or subordinated in the Herbartian formula, and it is better for the non-technical student than the psychological terminology used in some method books. But much of the good promise of the chapter-headings is not realized in the text. The Dewey material is spun out at great length with a superabundance of concrete examples and with elaborate analysis and subdivision which puzzle the student. On the other hand such important topics as "The Assignment" and "Drill" are given relatively brief treatment with few concrete examples. In a few cases definitions and distinctions are introduced which give the student unnecessary difficulty, for example, the idea that a unit of subject-matter is a way of acting, and the discussion of explicit, versus implicit, elements in inductive and deductive reasoning.

In general the work represents a valuable departure in textbooks on method and is useful in connection with general-method courses for either elementary- or high-school teachers.

S. Chester Parker

BOOKS RECEIVED

AMERICAN BOOK COMPANY, NEW YORK

Plane Trigonometry. By EDWARD R. ROBBINS. Cloth. Pp. 153+xiii.

Pupil's Notebook and Study Outline in Roman History. By EDNA M. McKINLEY. Paper covers. Pp. 111. $0.25.

Plane Geometry Developed by the Syllabus Method. By EUGENE RANDOLPH SMITH. Cloth. Pp. 192. $0.75.

Easy German Stories. By C. E. RIES. Edited with Notes, Exercises, and Vocabulary by ERNEST H. BIERMANN. Cloth. Pp. 183. $0.35.

German Prose Composition. With Notes and Vocabularies by CARL W. F. OSTHAUS AND ERNEST H. BIERMANN. Cloth. Pp. 191. $0.65.

La petite princesse. By JEANNE MAIRET. Edited for School Use by EDITH HEALY. Cloth. Pp. 154. $0.35.

Select Essays of Elia. By CHARLES LAMB. Edited by JOHN F. GENUNG. Cloth. Pp. 264.

Shirley's Part Songs for Mixed Voices. By JOHN B. SHIRLEY. Cloth. Pp. 272.

Pupil's Notebook and Study Outlines in Oriental and Greek History. By L. B. LEWIS. Paper covers. Pp. 119. $0.25.

Education Through Music. By CHARLES HUBERT FARNSWORTH. Illustrated. Cloth. Pp. 208. $1.00.

Mary of Plymouth. By JAMES OTIS. Cloth. Illustrated. Pp. 156. $0.35.

Ruth of Boston. By JAMES OTIS. Cloth. Illustrated. Pp. 160. $0.35.

Richard of Jamestown. By JAMES OTIS. Cloth. Illustrated. Pp. 165. $0.35.

Germelshausen. Von FRIEDRICH GERSTÄCKER. Edited by A. BUSSE. Cloth. Pp. 121. $0.30.

The Human Body and Health. By ALVIN DAVISON. Cloth. Illustrated. Pp. 191. $0.40.

German Students' Manual. By FRANKLIN J. HOLZWARTH. Cloth. Pp. 243. $1.00.

Selections from Early German Literature. By KLARA HECHTENBERG COLLITZ. Cloth. Pp. 285. $1.00.

Ein Nordischer Held. Von RICHARD ROTH. Edited by HELENE H. BOLL. Cloth. Pp. 175. $0.35.

Speaking and Writing. Book I. By WILLIAM H. MAXWELL, EMMA L. JOHNSTON, AND MADALENE D. BARNUM. Cloth. Pp. 103. $0.20.

D. APPLETON & CO., NEW YORK

Practical Nature-Study and Elementary Agriculture. By JOHN M. COULTER, JOHN G. COULTER, AND ALICE JEAN PATTERSON. Cloth. Pp. 354.

C. W. BARDEEN, SYRACUSE, N. Y.

Cornell Study Bulletins for Teachers, No. 4: Questions in School Hygiene. By GUY MONTROSE WHIPPLE. Edited by CHARLES DEGARMO. Cloth. Pp. 88.

Agriculture and Its Educational Needs. By ANDREW SLOAN DRAPER. Cloth. Pp. 92. $0.50.

THE COMSTOCK PUBLISHING CO., ITHACA, N. Y.

General Biology. By JAMES G. NEEDHAM. Cloth. Illustrated. Pp. 542. $2.00.

GOVERNMENT PRINTING OFFICE, WASHINGTON

Bibliography of Education for 1908–9. Paper covers. Pp. 134.

Report of the Commissioner of Education for the Year Ended June 30, 1909. Vol. I. Cloth. Pp. 598.

Report of the Commissioner of Education for the Year Ended June 30, 1909. Vol. II.

HARPER & BROTHERS, NEW YORK

A Holiday with the Birds. By JEANNETTE MARKS AND JULIA MOODY. Illustrated by CHESTER A. REED. Cloth. Pp. 212. $0.75.

How Americans Are Governed. By CRITTENDEN MARRIOTT. Cloth. Pp. 373. $1.25.

THE MACMILLAN CO., NEW YORK

Attention and Interest. By FELIX ARNOLD. Illustrated. Pp. 272. $1.00.

The "Aeneid" of Virgil Translated into English Prose. By JOHN CONINGTON. Edited with Introduction and Notes by EDGAR S. SHUMWAY. Cloth. Pp. 348. $0.25.

English Humorists. By WILLIAM MAKEPEACE THACKERAY. Edited with an Introduction and Notes by J. C. CASTLEMAN. Cloth. Pp. 337. $0.25.

English Spoken and Written. Book I. By HENRY P. EMERSON AND IDA C. BENDER. Cloth. Illustrated. Pp. 217. $0.35.

The New American Citizen: A Reader for Foreigners. By FRANCES SANKSTONE MINTZ. Illustrated. Cloth. Pp. 206. $0.50.

Games for Playground, Home, School and Gymnasium. By JESSIE H. BANCROFT. Illustrated. Cloth. Pp. 456. $1.50.

The Oregon Trail. By FRANCIS PARKMAN. Edited by CHARLES H. J. DOUGLAS. Cloth. Pp. 362. $0.25.

Walden, or Life in the Woods. By HENRY DAVID THOREAU. Edited with Introduction and Notes by BYRON REES. Cloth. Pp. 388. $0.25.

American Government. By ROSCOE LEWIS ASHLEY. Cloth. Illustrated. Pp. 356+xxxi. $1.00.

The Crown of Wild Olive and *The Queen of the Air.* By JOHN RUSKIN. Edited by WIGHTMAN F. MELTON. Cloth. Pp. 371. $0.25.

CHARLES E. MERRILL CO., NEW YORK

Höher als die Kirche. Von WILHELMINE V. HILLERN. Edited with Notes, Exercises, and Vocabulary by FREDERICK W. J. HEUSER. Cloth. Illustrated. Pp. 184. $0.50.

Essays on Lord Clive and Warren Hastings. By THOMAS BABINGTON MACAULAY. Cloth. Pp. 339. $0.50.

Walden. By HENRY DAVID THOREAU. Edited by J. MILNOR DOREY. Cloth. Pp. 437. $0.50.

SMALL, MAYNARD & CO., BOSTON

Football Grandma: An Auto-Baby-Ography as Told by Tony. Edited by CAROLYN S. CHANNING CABOT. Cloth. Illustrated. Pp. 79.

CHARITIES PUBLICATION COMMITTEE, NEW YORK

How Two Hundred Children Live and Learn. By RUDOLPH R. REEDER. Cloth. Illustrated. Pp. 247. $1.25.

GINN & CO., BOSTON

Manual of Elementary French. By ISIDORE H. B. SPIERS. Cloth. Pp. 58. $0.50.

The Leading Facts of American History. By D. H. MONTGOMERY. Cloth. Illustrated. Pp. 400+xcviii. $1.00.

HOUGHTON MIFFLIN CO., BOSTON

The British Isles. By E. L. TOMLINSON. Cloth. Illustrated. Pp. 283. $0.60.

European Hero Stories. By EVA MARCH TAPPAN. Cloth. Illustrated. Pp. 249. $0.65.

How to Study and Teaching How to Study. By F. M. MCMURRAY. Cloth. Pp. 324. $1.25.

Children's Classics in Dramatic Form. Book II. By AUGUSTA STEVENSON. Cloth. Pp. 128. $0.35.

The Principles of Education. By WILLIAM CARL RUEDIGER. Cloth. Pp. 305.

LAIRD & LEE, CHICAGO

The New Salesmanship. By CHARLES LINDGREN. Half-leather. Pp. 190.

English-Italian, Italian-English Dictionary. Pp. 417. Cloth, $0.50; leather, $0.75.

Rum and Ruin. By EDWARD R. ROE. Cloth. Pp. 251.

THE MANUAL ARTS PRESS, PEORIA, ILL.

Problems in Wood-Turning. By FRED D. CRAWSHAW. Illustrated. Paper. Pp. 35. Illustrative Plates 25.

Simplified Mechanical Perspective. By FRANK FORREST FREDERICK. Illustrated. Cloth. Pp. 56.

RAND, McNALLY & CO., CHICAGO

Elementary Cabinet Work. By FRANK HENRY SELDEN. Illustrated. Cloth. Pp. 278.

SCOTT, FORESMAN & CO., CHICAGO

The Teaching of Geography. By WILLIAM J. SUTHERLAND. Cloth. Illustrated. Pp. 292.

THE UNIVERSITY OF CHICAGO PRESS, CHICAGO

The Story of Paul of Tarsus: A Manual for Teachers. By LOUISE WARREN ATKINSON. Manual. Cloth. Pp. 194. $1.10.
Notebook, Paper Covers, Loose Leaves and Pictures. Pp. 138. $0.59.
Homework Book. Paper and Cloth Covers. Illustrated. Pp. 76. $0.28.

EATON & MAINS, NEW YORK

The Bible, Its Origin and Authority. By W. F. LOFTHOUSE. Cloth. Pp. 151. $0.50.

HENRY ALTEMUS CO., PHILADELPHIA

Elsie and the Arkansaw Bear. By ALBERT BIGELOW PAINE. Illustrated. Cloth. Pp. 253.

THE NATIONAL SOCIETY OF COLLEGE TEACHERS OF EDUCATION

The Aims, Scope, and Methods of a University Course in Public School Administration. By FRANK E. SPAULDING, WILLIAM PAXTON BURRIS, AND EDWARD C. ELLIOTT. Paper Covers. Pp. 94. $0.50.

G. P. PUTNAM'S SONS, NEW YORK

The Education of the Child. By ELLEN KEY. Cloth. Pp. 85.

Exercises in Arithmetic. Nos. 1, 2, 3, 4, and 5. By E. L. THORNDIKE. 5 Numbers. Paper covers. Pp. 48 each.

CURRENT EDUCATIONAL LITERATURE IN THE PERIODICALS[1]

IRENE WARREN

Librarian, School of Education, The University of Chicago

ALDRICH, LOUISE. The British school system. Pop. Educa. 27:397–401. (Ap. '10.)

ASHMUN, MARGARET. Library reading in the high school. School R. 18: 270–73. (Ap. '10.)

BARR, CHARLES J. The John Crerar library. Educa. Bi-mo. 4:301–8. (Ap. '10.)

BENSON, ARTHUR C. Humanistic education without Latin. Liv. Age. 46: 737–42. (Ap. '10.)

BINGHAM, W. VAN DYKE. Educational psychology at the Boston meeting of the American Association for the Advancement of Science. Journ. of Educa. Psychol. 1:159–67. (Mr. '10.)

BROWN, JOHN FRANKLIN. The courses in education in German universities. Journ. of Educa. Psychol. 1:145–58. (Mr. '10.)

CALDWELL, OTIS W. Natural history in the grades. El. School T. 10: 316–25. (Mr. '10.)

CARLTON, W. N. C. The Newberry library. Educa. Bi-mo. 4:296–300. (Ap. '10.)

CHAMBERS, WILL GRANT. Individual differences in grammar-grade children: a comparative study of forty-four seventh and eighth grade pupils. Journ. of Educa. Psychol. 1:61–75. (Fe. '10.)

DAVIS, BENJAMIN MARSHALL. Agricultural education: state normal schools. El. School T. 10:376–87. (Ap. '10.)

DEWING, ARTHUR S. A neglected value in the elective system. Educa. 30:442–47. (Mr. '10.)

DICKEY, HELENE L. The modern library movement. Educa. Bi-mo. 4: 321–23. (Ap. '10.)

[1] Abbreviations.—Atlan. Educa. Journ., Atlantic Educational Journal; Cent., Century; Dial, The Dial; Educa., Education; Educa. Bi-mo., Educational Bimonthly; El. School T., Elementary School Teacher; Harp. W., Harper's Weekly; Hist. Teach. Mag., History Teacher's Magazine; Journ. of Educa. Psychol., Journal of Educational Psychology; Lib. Journ., Library Journal; Liv. Age, Living Age; Pop. Educa., Popular Educator; Pop. Sci. Mo., Popular Science Monthly; Prim. Educa., Primary Education; Pub. Lib., Public Libraries; School R., School Review.

Donnelly, June Richardson. The library school and the library. Lib. Journ. 35:109–11. (Mr. '10.)

Elson, William H. and Bachman, Frank P. Studies and study-values in elementary schools of large cities. El. School T. 10:309–15. (Mr. '10.)

Hadley, Chalmers. American library association. Educa. Bi-mo. 4: 293–95. (Ap. '10.)

Hale, Wm. Gardner. Latin composition in the high school. School. R. 18:225–40. (Ap. '10.)

Hinsdale, Ellen C. The first American students in Germany. Dial. 48: 187–88. (16 Mr. '10.)

Jepson, B. Public school music forty years ago. Educa. Bi-mo. 4:242–46. (Ap. '10.)

Kellerman, Ivy. The denominational college. Pop. Sci. Mo. 77:358–69. (Ap. '10.)

Kilpatrick, Van Eyre. Department of elementary school problems: vocational training in the elementary school. Educa. 30:448–53. (Mr. '10.)

King, Irving. Professor Münsterberg's conception of the problem and content of educational psychology. School R. 18:246–57. (Ap. '10.)

Kirkpatrick, E. A. The point of view of genetic psychology. Journ. of Educa. Psychol. 1:76–82. (Fe. '10.)

Leather, Herbert. England and her retarded children. El. School T. 10:326–33. (Mr. '10.)

Legler, Henry G. The Chicago public library and co-operation with the schools. Educa. Bi-mo. 4:309–20. (Ap. '10.)

Macy, Mary Sutton. The subnormal child in New York city schools. Journ. of Educa. Psychol. 1:132–44. (Mr. '10.)

Manny, Frank A. Pragmatism, pluralism, and the teacher. Atlan. Educa. Journ. 5:5–6. (Ap. '10.)

Nearing, Scott. Child labor and the child. Educa. 30:407–15. (Mr. '10.)

Oberholtzer, Ellis Paxson. Historical pageants. Hist. Teach. Mag. 1: 167–68. (Ap. '10.)

O'Shea, M. V. The influence of dress upon the behavior of pupils. Prim. Educa. 18:185–86. (Ap. '10.)

Pattison, Mrs. F. A. The library and the woman's club. Pub. Lib. 15: 137–42. (Ap. '10.)

Parker, S. Chester. Our inherited practice in elementary schools. El. School T. 10:388–400. (Ap. '10.)

Rex, Frederic. The municipal library. Educa. Bi-mo. 4:286–89. (Ap. '10.)

Richman, I. B. American education and President Eliot's five-foot library. Pub. Lib. 15:142–44.

Riis, Jacob A. The People's Institute of New York. Cent. 79:850–63. (Ap. '10.)

SARGENT, WALTER. The fine and industrial arts in elementary schools, grade VI. El. School T. 10:334–46. (Mr. '10.)

SWETT, HARRY PREBLE. Economic education in the secondary school. Educa. 30:416–20. (Mr. '10.)

TERRY, H. L. Four instruments of confusion in teaching physics. School R. 18:241–45. (Ap. '10.)

THIERGEN, OSKAR. The exchange of assistant teachers between France and Germany. School R. 18:258–63. (Ap. '10.)

TOBEY, EDWARD NELSON. The leading school of tropical medicine. Pop. Sci. Mo. 77:337–43. (Ap. '10.)

(A) universal benefaction. Harp. W. 104:9. (12 Mr. '10.)

VAN HORNE, MARY. The Ryerson Library of the Art Institute. Educa. Bi-mo. 4:290–92. (Ap. '10.)

VAN SICKLE, J. H. Provision for gifted children in public schools. El. School T. 10:357–66. (Ap. '10.)

WINCH, W. H. Some measurements of mental fatigue in adolescent pupils in evening schools. Journ. of Educa. Psychol. 1:83–100. (Fe. '10.)

VOLUME X NUMBER 10

THE ELEMENTARY SCHOOL TEACHER

JUNE, 1910

THE FINE AND INDUSTRIAL ARTS IN ELEMENTARY SCHOOLS, GRADE VIII

WALTER SARGENT
The University of Chicago

The increased maturity of children in Grade VIII should bring ability to sketch rapidly things which they wish to describe, with a surer delineation of the proportions, position, and structure, to select with little hesitation the lines which express individual characteristics, and to appreciate and enjoy representing things that are beautiful in form and color.

In constructive work the previous familiarity with tools and processes should make possible the planning and completion of objects which are of practical value, for example, furniture, clothing, etc. Aesthetic appreciation should show itself in a preference for things which are in good taste, such as well-designed objects, harmonious color, and good examples of pictorial art, not simply because the children have been told what is good, but because that which is good gives the greater pleasure.

The following suggestions relate to phases of the arts which seem especially worth emphasizing in Grade VIII.

Representation.—The common use of drawing as a means of explanation and description should continue to be an important part of the work. Facility in this conversational use of drawing does not come from slowly and carefully finished work. It is gained only by practice in rapid sketching. On the other hand rapid descriptive drawing tends to become superficial unless supplemented by some serious and painstaking representation. Memory and imaginative drawing should also receive consideration as ability in this line is necessary to ready expression of ideas.

Children in this grade should have opportunity for much use of these three modes of representation, especially in connection with subjects which call definitely for one or another of these means of interpretation. For example, incidental blackboard descriptions or sketch notes in connection with arithmetic, geography, or history are often of little value unless they can be made quickly with a few strokes. Children frequently lack power to make such sketches because it is sometimes mistakenly supposed that practice in slowly finished work will give this ability. Facility with this sort of graphic expression should not be left to chance, but should constitute a definite aim. Nature-study, physics, and constructive work, on the other hand, demand truthful representation of form, a clear understanding of details of structure, and accurate records of observation which cannot be hastily sketched or adequately shown by a few strokes of the pencil. The children appreciate the needs of the case in hand and can be led readily to adopt the style of drawing which suits the occasion. Rapid sketching is learned only by sketching rapidly, ability in exact delineation comes only by making exact representations, and facility in expressing ideas out of one's head is developed only through drawing from memory and imagination. The one sort of undifferentiated drawing from objects which so often constitutes the larger part of the special work in drawing will not produce that facility in all three lines which is so valuable an asset.

In any line of graphic expression, whether it be rapid sketching or accurate delineation, the children should learn to draw by selecting the most expressive lines which are usually the long lines, and drawing these in right relation and using them to reckon from in adding details.

The practice suggested for Grades VI and VII of drawing typical solids from imagination till one can build them up by indicating correctly the main constructive lines, and conforming the others to these, develops ability to *construct graphically,* which is indispensable to good drawing.

Children readily learn to discover the few lines which show position and structure and by means of these to determine the directions of others and thus find the solution of an otherwise complex problem. They thus learn to draw objects as if they were building actual things.

For example in drawing a chair, the structural lines suggested in Grade VI for a box give a means of reducing to system and

FIG. 1

representing easily the many lines which if unrelated would prove confusing (Fig. 1). The lines marked 1, 2, and 3 furnish the key to the direction of most of the others. If these are determined in the right proportion and at the right angles, the general structure may easily be completed. All slants extending upward to the left are determined by 1, and all to the right by 2.

The closed book in Fig. 1 represents an outline frequently drawn by children and within this outline the correct appearance arrived at by drawing lines to correspond with the key lines, 1, 2, and 3.

This does not mean that all the slants are parallel to 1 or 2.

The lines converge as they extend away from the observer, but when some facility in representing rectangular objects in different positions has been gained and the eye grows accustomed to interpreting drawings, *it will be found that the attempt to make the shapes look right results in an approximation to the proper convergence.* This method of approach differs from perspective taught by vanishing points and reference to the level of the eye, in that it is based upon an increasing reliance on the testimony of the eye regarding impressions supplied to it directly from the object and not upon an intellectual ability to compute results from external facts. Such computations are valuable as a means of checking up results after the visual perceptions can be depended upon, but it is doubtful if these conditions can be fully attained below the high school.

The same general principles hold regarding the representation of curvilinear objects, such as a glass or a bowl. The question most full of descriptive suggestion is not, "How far below the level of the eye is this glass?" but, "How far can one see into it?" The line answering this question establishes the curve which determines all related circles.

The different phases of nature-drawing suggested for Grade VII are of still greater value in Grade VIII. Silhouette representation with brush, of the growth and character of the plant develops freedom and cultivates appreciation of the style and individuality of the plant. Careful detailed drawings directly aid nature-study and develop a habit of accurate observation. If rightly directed, such drawing as this not only does not hinder aesthetic expression but furnishes some of the most valuable training in that direction. Drawing which never deals at first hand with conscientious study of facts is likely and, except in the case of a genius, almost certain to degenerate into stylistic conventions which soon become tiresome, and although they may be original are seldom worth originating. An occasional close study of the facts of nature often furnishes new poetical suggestions and fresh interpretations.

In this grade children can usually be interested in consecutive work upon a single topic such as horses, houses, boats, vehicles, etc., or a country in connection with geography or an incident in literature or history, or some subject involving poetic interest, such as autumn, spring, morning, etc. Fig. 2 shows cover and pages from a boy's sketch-book.

FIG. 2

When interest in a topic is awakened, the various methods of drawing are all brought into use naturally. The children make rapid notes for general suggestions and careful studies for data. Their sketch-books become valued possessions full of material which contributes to the subject in hand. Usually the children can be led to add to their own sketches a collection of pictures related to the subject under consideration. These may be gathered from magazines and other sources.

This sort of interest in finding pictorial expression for an idea develops a basis for artistic appreciation. When pupils have become interested in trying to interpret their impressions of autumn into lines and colors and have selected from among autumn pictures those which are most in harmony with their own feelings, they are gaining experience which will help them enter into the spirit of a work of art which is an artist's interpretation of this topic with much more sympathy and responsiveness than as if they had made no effort to express it. The search among many sources, in nature, literature, and art for the embodiment of a particular idea or the expression of a mood should be an important element in all picture-study.

In each grade the pictures studied should be such as embody objects and interests which touch somewhere the experiences of the children. The first pleasure which later may develop into aesthetic appreciation may be awakened by well-drawn, vigorously colored pictures made for children as well as by famous masterpieces.

The following description of an experiment in picture-study in upper grades is reprinted by courtesy of *The School Arts Book.*[1]

The topic, "Picture-Study," which occurs in most courses in drawing, deserves all the prominence that is now given to it. The majority of people want to be able to appreciate and enjoy works of art. Intelligent enjoyment of art is seldom gained except through special study definitely planned to accomplish that end. To determine what lines that study should follow has been the purpose of much discussion and experimentation.

One method, perhaps the method of least value in elementary schools, is to analyze pictures in order to discover centers of interest, balance of masses, leading lines, etc. This is helpful to adults as a study of one phase of the painter's way of doing things, but unless presented with clear understanding of its relative value it is likely to fail to develop a sincere enjoyment of pictures.

Another method is to show pictures to the children and encourage them to talk about what they see and enjoy. Incidentally, stories of the artist, the times in which he lived, and the things he chose to paint are presented to add historical interests and associations to the pictures. This way gives

[1] "An Experiment in Picture Study," *The School Arts Book,* October, 1909.

pleasant acquaintance with works of art and awakens oftentimes a sincere liking for them.

If one allowed his judgment to be based upon the written papers which are sometimes asked for after lessons in picture-study, he might be led to doubt some aspects of this method, but perhaps the fault is not in the method but in asking too soon that children make a statement in definite terms of language, regarding matters of feeling.

Perhaps instructors who wish to awaken in their pupils true enjoyment of pictures, an enjoyment that is not a passing preference but an abiding pleasure, might find helpful suggestions from considering carefully the familiar statement that one gets from a picture only what he brings to it. It may follow that preparation for seeing a picture should be made before the picture is presented, in order that the children may have something of value to bring to it, and that the teacher's explanations may be unnecessary at the time. It is possible that such enjoyment of art as we wish our pupils to possess can come only when they have been previously interested in the subject which the artist portrays, so when they come to it they come to something which they themselves have tried to express even though crudely and which they rejoice to see set forth skilfully.

The following experiment was tried with a large number of children in Boston in the sixth, seventh, and eighth years of school, in order to observe the results of giving the children experiences which should prepare them to see the pictures which were to be studied.

Twilight was selected as a topic for special observation. The children were encouraged to gather pictures of twilight from magazine illustrations, photographs, and other sources. They were led to observe twilight effects out of doors. The results of these observations were rendered definite by means of notes made with water-color. The colors of the sky, clouds, trees, and buildings on different evenings were recorded. The children noted whether the buildings seen against the sunset sky appeared in their local color or were flooded with the golden glow, or contrasted with it by appearing to be complimentary in hue. The children were enthusiastic in their descriptions of twilight effects and made many sketches, some of which were crude in color while many were soft and delicate.

The next steps in the experiment were made possible by the cordial co-operation of the Museum of Fine Arts which reproduced in half-tone several of its pictures, some of which represented twilight, and made these reproductions available for the schools at cost. About 1,600 of these were bought by the teachers and distributed to the pupils. Each child made two or three simple copies in pencil of the Museum picture given him, reproducing the effect as well as possible by this means. He then experimented by adding to these pencil sketches the different schemes of twilight color which he had recorded. He thus gained intimate acquaintance with an excellent black and white composition and added to this the color, an element which was the result of his own observation.

After this many of the children wished to visit the Museum in order that they might see the original picture. Those who had opportunity to do so, when they saw for the first time the painting with the composition of which they were already familiar, viewed it with particular attention to see what colors had been used by the artist and how his scheme compared with their own. Usually an art museum appears to a child to be something of a panorama. The previous study of a particular topic, however, served to isolate a few pictures from the mass and make them objects of special attraction. The children felt a fellowship of interest and effort between themselves and the artist.

Even those who did not visit the Museum gained much enjoyment of twilight effects in nature and of descriptions of them in literature.

One principal wrote as follows:

"You will be as pleased as I was myself when I tell you that two of my boys, evidently inspired by our collection of twilight pictures and without any suggestion on my part, brought me two poems bearing upon the theme we were studying in our drawing. One brought in a clipping from a newspaper which told of the ending of the day with the fading of the sunset colors, the night, and the dawning of another day, making application to the closing of a human life in this world and its subsequent awakening in eternity. The other, with the air of a discoverer, laid upon my desk Tennyson's 'Sweet and Low, Wind of the Western Sea.'

"I read these to the class with simply an acknowledgment of the source from which I had obtained them. I was not surprised when boy No. 3 laid Gray's 'Elegy' before me, a day later. I plan to have the class learn this while the strong sidelight of their picture-study is still shining upon it and I see the possibility of other work within the outline for reading, in correlation with drawing."

The possibility of developing other topics in a similar manner is evident. To each great artist some phase of nature has made a particular appeal and it becomes his field for study and interpretation. Perhaps the best way to develop the fullest enjoyment and appreciation of his work is to awaken interests similar to those which inspired his art and to encourage efforts at expression, however crude, of the same thing.

Construction.—Pupils in Grade VIII should have acquired sufficient ability in the use of implements and materials to undertake work, the plans and execution of which involve considerable skill, and which is of such a character that the results are of evident practical value and the workmanship sufficiently excellent to command respect.

Each child who takes woodworking should be able to construct during the year one or two pieces of such articles of furniture as chairs, desks, tables, cabinets, book-racks, etc., which can be put to actual use in the school or at home. If training in previous grades has been thorough and progressive, pupils can undertake individual projects of some importance and enjoy the effort and exercise of skill required to carry them to completion. Such projects undertaken before sufficient command of tools and familiarity with materials and processes have been acquired are generally unsuccessful. While, theoretically, skill may be acquired by means of individual projects from the first, the practical outcome with woodworking classes of reasonable size is that the instructor is unable to give the attention to each pupil which is necessary to the formation of efficient habits. A small proportion of the whole number produce excellent work but the majority make relatively little progress and do not acquire freedom from technical difficulties soon enough to enjoy the results of skill. Figs. 3 and 4 show samples of work by boys of Grade VIII. Objects similar in character were produced by nearly every boy in the school. The time allowed was two hours a week and the classes contained about twenty-four pupils each.

The cooking should develop ability to prepare simple meals and should involve some practice in setting the table in good taste and serving gracefully. Sewing should include making garments which may be worn and some knowledge of design and color as related to dress. Continued attention should be paid to the historical and artistic evolution of whatever industries enter into the school and community life.

Design.—In Grade VIII pupils are sufficiently mature to appreciate to some extent fine forms and harmonious color; to realize the difference between excellence of design which renders an object beautiful and permanently satisfactory, and that sensational or commonplace modification of form and addition of unrelated ornament which contributes nothing toward the perfection of the idea.

The constructive work and domestic science continue to afford some of the most valuable opportunities for design,

Fig. 3

Fig. 4

because they furnish a reason for shapes and materials and an incentive to embody that reason most adequately and gracefully.

Putting into book form the work upon other school topics is a feature of design which is of increasing value each year. It involves the cover design as discussed in the last article, the title-page, margins, arrangement of text, illustrations, tail-pieces, etc. It is not necessary to artistic progress that the children make all their illustrations. The search for and choice of pictures which best embody the idea one wishes illustrated is an excellent means of developing appreciation of art.

One of the most important purposes of design is to develop good aesthetic judgment regarding the things with which one comes into daily contact. Such judgment can be cultivated by choosing the best from among many examples, good and bad, as well as by making original designs. For one who will design a vase or a wall-paper, five thousand will buy the article. It is therefore important to know how to choose well, and designing is not always the surest way of developing discrimination.

This choosing should be from such collections as the pupil will be obliged to make his choice from when he comes to buy for himself, as well as from examples which will always be beyond his reach. For instance if one wishes to cultivate good taste regarding vases, it is well worth while to study those in fine collections, but such study will lose nothing of practical value if it is supplemented by a choice, from among the material available in a local store, of the vase best suited to show the beauty of a particular style of bouquet, such as a few sprays of tall, slender flowers or a round bunch of short-stemmed blossoms.

Lamps are an interesting subject for study, historically and artistically, but added to knowledge of, and interest in, the finest known examples should be some exercise of judgment in choosing the best possible from available sources and this necessitates some concrete acquaintance with these sources. The present generation can thus be led to patronize the best at hand and create a demand for what is still better.

Children should also make or have access to collections of pictures of well-designed dwellings of all classes, public buildings for towns similar in size and means to their own locality, and be led to choose wisely among these. They should be encouraged to report on the most beautiful scenes in town. Where cameras are owned by pupils, a collection of local views should be made. A study of one place under various aspects gives results full of interest and artistic suggestion—as, for example, a street scene, or a landscape, at various hours of day and night, and in different seasons. This encourages the sort of study which the artist gives to his chosen subject.

An example of sensible teaching of design is that of a country teacher who found her one-room schoolhouse ill furnished, with no pictures, papers in the windows instead of curtains, an unpleasant wall-color, and poor furniture.

She undertook to change one item after another. The children discussed the best color for the wall. A tone was decided upon and presented to the committee who agreed to retint the room. Curtains were then considered. Samples were obtained and the best color and material decided upon. The children not only were allowed to have a part in the selection but were represented at the purchasing. Chairs, pictures, and frames were later discussed and choices made with the aid of catalogues and visits to stores. The making of the changes occupied two or three years and the money was obtained in part from entertainments given by the children. The artistic training was such that it developed much practical acquaintance with ways of selecting furnishings and incidentally the children developed a sense of ownership in the school. They sometimes inquired of the teacher, after a visitor had gone, whether any remarks had been made regarding the excellent appearance of the room.

Continued use of water-colors should develop increased discernment and enjoyment of colors as they occur in nature. Children in this grade should also become familiar with simple color-harmonies, partly by acquaintance with good examples and partly by experimenting with colors to render them more pleasing in combination.

One can usually secure excellent color-harmonies by choosing with some care among color-prints, particularly those from the

Orient, from fabrics, and often from nature. The groups of colors occurring in lichens, faded leaves, etc., sometimes furnish good material. The children should match these colors and use them in designs.

Simple experiments in harmonizing colors may be tried by introducing a common element into each of a group of two or three colors to bring them into closer relation. For example, two colors like red and blue, which in full intensity are not usually pleasing, can be made more agreeable in combination by mixing a little of each with the other. The red still counts as red and the blue as blue, but the common element has made them less antagonistic. A little gray or some of a third color mixed with each produces a similar result. Children should try such experiments with a number of colors and choose for use in their designs the tones where the proportion of mixture gives the best effect.

By the end of the eighth year children should have gained ability to use drawing as a common means of expression, and to make rapid descriptive sketches, careful, well-constructed drawings, or truthful records of observations, as occasion may require. They should be able to undertake common constructive problems with knowledge of tools and processes, and some ability to convert raw materials into a finished product according to a predetermined idea. They should have taste in choosing what is good among things relating to the home and community and should enjoy beauty of form and harmony of color in nature and in art.

They should have enough acquaintance with what artists have produced to lead them to find some favorites among objects of fine art as they have among books, so that they will desire to possess reproductions of these.

They should also have gained an interest in productive labor sufficient to interpret things to them in terms of the effort and skill required to produce them and should have developed a healthful enjoyment in the exercise of their abilities which will demand for its satisfaction an occupation which adds to the well-being of the community.

RETARDATION STATISTICS OF THREE CHICAGO SCHOOLS

CLARA SCHMITT
Fellow in Education, The University of Chicago

Ayres's *Laggards in Our Schools* has been the means of directing the attention of the educational world to the problem of the progress of pupils through the schools. Ayres's statistics go to show that many children do not advance through the grades at the rate expected of the normal child, that they are then retarded and many of the retarded ones are eliminated before they reach the eighth grade. He defines retardation as "referring to the pupil who is above the normal age for his grade; elimination is the dropping out of pupils upon reaching the age of compulsory attendance without having reached the eighth grade."[1] He gives a table defining the normal ages for the eight grades of the elementary school. "These ages," he says, "have been accepted by common consent as the 'normal ages' for these grades by nearly all schoolmen who have interested themselves in the problem."

Normal Ages of Children in the Grades[2]

First Grade	6 to 8 years
Second Grade	7 to 9 years
Third Grade	8 to 10 years
Fourth Grade	9 to 11 years
Fifth Grade	10 to 12 years
Sixth Grade	11 to 13 years
Seventh Grade	12 to 14 years
Eighth Grade	13 to 15 years

On the basis of this assumption of normal ages there is compiled a table showing the age and grade distribution in Memphis, Tenn., in June, 1908, and the number and percentage of retarded pupils.[3] After the same method he computes the retardation in

[1] P. 8,

[2] P. 38.

[3] P. 37.

31 cities with resulting percentages ranging from 7.5 per cent for Medford, Mass., to 75.8 per cent for Memphis, Tenn. (colored) and an average of 33.7 per cent children above normal age for their grade.[4]

TABLE SHOWING AGE AND GRADE DISTRIBUTION FOR MEMPHIS, TENN.*

Age	Grade								Total
	1	2	3	4	5	6	7	8	
6	782	11							793
7	609	177	50						932
8	368	403	131	5					907
9	120	349	333	104	8				914
10	44	191	335	264	67	6	1		908
11	21	81	230	302	219	83	9		945
12	12	45	109	229	201	203	77	6	882
13	1	13	43	126	182	245	178	63	851
14	4	6	25	44	85	158	175	130	627
15	1	2	6	10	26	69	92	110	316
16			1	3	8	25	43	73	153
17	1			2	1	1	3	10	18
18					1		1		2
Total	2,053	1,278	1,269	1,089	798	790	579	392	8,248
Above normal age	572	687	749	716	504	498	314	193	4,233
Percentage above normal age	27.8	53.7	59.0	65.7	63.1	63.0	54.2	49.2	51.3

* Ayres, *op cit.*, p. 37.

The next problem which Ayres attacks is how to determine the number of beginners in a given year. The number in the first grade is composed of the beginners for that year plus the retarded ones who have entered one, two, three, or more years before. Upon making an age distribution of the children in the schools of Medford, Mass., on September 30, 1907, there was found to be little variation between the numbers between the various age groups from seven to twelve inclusive. He concludes, then, that all the children are in school between those ages and an average of the numbers in the six groups will closely approximate the number of beginners.

[4] P. 45.

Rates of progress through the grades is the interesting problem taken up on p. 73. A comparison of slow and rapid pupils in 5 cities shows that the children making slow progress are from six to fourteen times as numerous as those making rapid progress save in one exceptional case where the slow ones are one hundred and twenty-four times as numerous. Of 9,489 pupils of New York City, 5 per cent reached their present grades in 86 per cent of the normal time; 55 per cent in 100 per cent of the normal time, and 40 per cent in 128 per cent of the normal time. From a set of data showing the time required to do the work of four grades in each of 29 cities, Ayres computes the time required by the average child to do the work of eight grades.[5] The average of the items of the data just mentioned gives 4.67 years for the completion of the work of the first four grades. Doubling this figure gives 9.34 years for the time necessary to complete eight grades. To this is added 0.8, the computed difference between the ages of the beginners and of the first grade, making ten years the time necessary to complete eight grades.

In order to test the validity of Mr. Ayres's conclusions and to find out something of the actual situation I made an investigation of 3 schools of Chicago. The conclusions quoted above are only those from Mr. Ayres's book which are comparable with the findings of my own work. I went to each school and made from the principal's register two tables, one showing the age and grade distribution as does the one for Medford, Mass., quoted above, and the other showing the number of weeks spent in each grade by the pupils in that grade. These represent conditions as existing upon the entrance of the child in school on September 1, 1909. In the age columns of each register the age of the child in years and months is recorded at the time of his entrance. In my table the months have been disregarded and the age in years is recorded. A child was counted as six years old if he had passed his sixth and not yet reached his seventh birthday upon entering school in September. Thus the six-year-old group in-

[5] These figures were found by taking the difference between the average ages of the first- and fifth-grade pupils. The normal difference would be four years.

cludes all children between six and seven, the seven-year-old group includes all between seven and eight, etc. The same thing is not true for the five-year-old group. The school law of Illinois allows children to be admitted to school after the sixth birthday, but it is the practice of principals to admit five-year-old children if they will reach the sixth birthday early in the term in which they are admitted. Thus the five-year-old group includes those whose ages are between five years and seven months and six years.

A third mass of data was obtained in the following manner. The 1903 registers for two schools and the 1902 register for the third school were brought out. The names of the children in the first grade of each register were copied and the progress of each child as portrayed by the registers of each succeeding year up to and including that for September, 1909, was traced through. Out of an original total of 511 names only 135 were found still upon the register of the school in which they were found as first graders. This 135, however, forms a beginning of the authentic individual school histories which Thorndike has so often pointed out as necessary before conclusions upon school progress can be reached with accuracy. A second method of getting the same kind of information which will be described later was followed in one of the schools.

One of these schools, which I shall call School A, is situated in the district most highly favored intellectually and financially, short of great wealth, in Chicago. It is attended by the children of teachers and other professional men. School B is situated in a contiguous district inhabited largely by working people of the higher classes, skilled workers and others receiving trade-union wages. So far as the normal physical standard of food, housing, and clothing are concerned there is no difference between the districts. The same may in general be said of the district of School C, except that it contains a large percentage of Negroes. This race constitutes between one-fourth and one-third of the school membership.[6]

[6] Estimated as the lines marched out of the building as the register did not show nationality or race.

Table I shows the age-grade distribution for School A. According to Ayres's definition the numbers above and to the right of the heavy line are retarded. Thus there would be two in the first grade, thirteen in the second, seventeen in the third, and so on. But upon comparing Table I with Table II it will be seen that the number of beginners in September is exactly equal to the number of five- and six-year-old children in the school at that time. One is led to believe, then, that children enter the school before the age of seven. The assumption is further borne out by the statement made by the principal of this

TABLE I

Age and Grade Distribution for School A

Grade	Age															Total	Percentage of Retardation *	Percentage of Retardation †
	5	6	7	8	9	10	11	12	13	14	15	16	17	18	?			
I	13	100	37	2												152	1.3	25.6
II ..		14	75	40	6	7										142	9.1	37.3
III ..			8	57	39	13	4									121	14.0	49.5
IV...				12	48	47	16	8	5		1					137	21.1	56.2
V....				2	9	31	31	27	19	6	4					129	43.4	67.4
VI ..						11	37	30	23	7	5					113	30.9	57.5
VII..						2	6	29	28	13	9	3	1			91	28.5	59.3
VIII.								6	31	30	16	2	1	1		87	22.9	57.4
Total	13	114	120	115	102	111	94	100	106	56	35	5	2	1		980		

* According to Ayres's age standard.

† According to the more probable standard.

school. He has for several years averaged the ages of the beginners and of the graduates. These averages have always been six plus a small fraction and fifteen plus a small fraction respectively. We must then set six years for the standard for the normal age of the first grade instead of seven as Ayres has done. The double rule of Table I shows the division between the normal and retarded pupils according to this now more probable standard. The first column to the right of the column headed *total* gives the percentage of retardation according to Ayres's standard, the second column gives the retardation according to the more probable standard. The percentages according to the two standards run as follows:

	Grade							
	I	II	III	IV	V	VI	VII	VIII
Ayres's standard	1.3	9.1	14.0	21.1	43.4	30.9	28.5	22.9
Newer standard	25.6	37.3	49.5	56.4	67.4	57.5	59.3	57.4

The age and grade tables for the schools B and C are not essentially different except that the retardation for the first three grades are higher. The three schools are combined in Table III. In School B the actual number of beginners is 88 and the number of five- and six-year-old children is 79. In School C the actual number of beginners is 125, of five- and six-year-old children, 104. The combined tables, III and IV, show 326 beginners and 296 five- and six-year-old children, making a total discrepancy of 30. This discrepancy is accounted for to some extent by the gaps in the information columns of the registers. Occasionally the age column or the weeks-in-grade column was not filled in. Were it not for this the various corresponding totals of the two sets of tables would be identical. However, a few children do enter school later than six years of age.

TABLE II

Showing Time Spent in Each Grade upon Entering School September 1, 1909, School A. Figures below Double Rule Show Number Certainly Repeating Grade

Weeks in Grade September, 1909	Grade 1	Grade 2	Grade 3	Grade 4	Grade 5	Grade 6	Grade 7	Grade 8	
0 (beginners)	113	75	69	76	67	73	47	45	Possibly normal
0–10	14	20	13	0	1	2	3	0	" "
11–20	11	40	45	55	49	51	40	33	" "
21–30	5	6	1	3	3	0	1	0	" "
31–40	9	12	2	15	16	4	6	6	Repeating grade
41–50	...	2	...	...	...	...	0	...	" "
51–60	...	1	...	...	...	...	4	...	" "
61–70	...	...	...	...	...	...	...	...	" "
71–80	...	...	...	...	2	...	...	...	" "
Total	152	156	130	149	137	130	97	84	
Percentage of repeaters	5.9	9.0	1.5	10.0	13.1	3.0	10.0	7.1	

TABLE III

AGES AND GRADE TABLE FOR THE THREE SCHOOLS COMBINED

GRADE	AGE 5	6	7	8	9	10	11	12	13	14	15	16	17	18	TOTAL	PERCENTAGE OF RETARDATION *	PERCENTAGE OF RETARDATION †
I....	39	257	163	25	13	3	1			1		1			533	8.2	40.7
II ...		30	172	103	32	15	9	1							362	15.7	44.1
III ..			29	135	120	48	20	8	2		1				363	24.2	54.8
IV ..				37	116	132	63	30	26	4	3			1	412	30.8	62.8
V ...				3	23	93	98	70	55	16	6				364	40.3	67.3
VI...					2	47	90	81	66	43	16	1	1		347	36.0	59.9
VII..					1	6	29	74	77	46	32	6	2		273	31.5	59.7
VIII.							4	29	84	83	53	9	2		264	24.2	55.6
Total	39	287	364	303	407	344	314	293	310	192	111	17	5	1	2,918		

* According to Ayres's standard.
† More probable standard.

TABLE IV

SHOWING LENGTH OF TIME IN GRADE (ENTERING SEPTEMBER, 1909) FOR THE THREE SCHOOLS COMBINED. THOSE BELOW DOUBLE RULE ARE CERTAINLY REPEATING GRADES

WEEKS IN GRADE SEPTEMBER, 1909	GRADE I	II	III	IV	V	VI	VII	VIII	
0 (beginners)....	326	172	203	247	168	217	124	133	Possibly normal
0–10...........	28	57	17	23	4	6	3	...	" "
11–20..........	43	81	104	92	148	110	98	105	" "
21–30..........	33	11	10	7	15	1	5	1	" "
31–40..........	53	38	41	37	37	15	15	20	Repeating grade
41–50..........	6	10	2	3	...	...	1	...	" "
51–60..........	4	2	1	...	1	...	4	...	" "
61–70..........	3	...	...	...	...	...	...	...	" "
71–80..........	1	...	...	...	...	1	...	...	" "
81–90..........	2	...	...	...	...	...	...	...	" "
91–100.........	1	...	...	...	...	...	...	...	" "
151–160........	1	...	...	...	...	...	...	...	" "
Total	501	371	378	409	373	350	250*	259	
Percentage of repeaters......	14.1	13.4	11.6	9.7	10.1	4.5	8.0	7.7	

* In School B in the seventh grade were 41 pupils whose record as to length of time in grade could not be found. These added to the 250 on record makes a total of 291 in the seventh grade. Had the record of each pupil been full the various totals of the corresponding tables would be the same. All percentages are calculated upon the known figures.

Tables II and IV are made out from the column of the register showing the number of weeks each child had already spent in the grade in which he entered in September, 1909. Table II shows the situation for School A alone, Table IV for the three schools. The registers show in which grade a child is enrolled upon entering school—as Grade 1, 2, 3, etc.—and the number of weeks he has already spent in that grade upon enrolment. They do not show in which half of the grade the pupil is enrolled. Thus if it is shown that a certain individual is in Grade 3 and has spent 20 weeks in that grade upon his enrolment in September, one does not know whether he is beginning the second half of Grade 3 or repeating the first half. If, however, an individual is enrolled in September in a grade in which he has already spent 30 weeks it is almost certain that before he can leave that grade, assuming that he is in the second half, he will have spent 50 weeks in the grade. So far as time in that particular grade is concerned, he is retarded ten weeks, and some time during the 20-week period necessary to complete a half-grade he is a repeater. According to this standard, then, those below the double rule in Tables II and IV are certainly repeaters. It is as certain that some above that line are repeaters. Those in the column marked "0 to 10" are most probably repeating that half of the grade in which they have spent more than 0 weeks and less than 10. Some of those in the column marked "11 to 20" are repeating that half of the grade in which they have spent the time indicated, etc. Therefore the percentage of repeaters shown in the last column of the table is too low. The percentage of known repeaters for the three schools is as follows:

	Grade							
	I	II	III	IV	V	VI	VII	VIII
School A	5.9	9.0	1.5	10.0	13.1	3.0	10.0	7.1
School B	27.0	31.9	19.6	5.1	8.1	8.6	11.3	7.9
School C	8.0	5.3	15.0	11.4	10.0	1.9	4.4	8.0
Combined	14.1	13.4	11.6	9.7	10.1	4.5	8.0	7.7

The register of School A for 1902 contained the names of 120 first-grade children. Of these 23 were still in the school in

September, 1909. In the registers of this school, with the help of the principal, it was possible to find in which half of a grade a child was enrolled upon entering school in any year. The school careers of these 23 children are shown in Table V. The first column indicates the individual pupil in Grade I in 1902, the second column his age in 1902, and the third column the term

TABLE V

SHOWING PROGRESS OF 23 PUPILS WHOSE RECORDS WERE TRACED FROM 1902 TO SEPTEMBER, 1909

Pupils in Grade 1 in 1902	Age 1902	Term Entered	Grade 1903	Grade 1904	Grade 1905	Grade 1906	Grade 1907	Grade 1908	Grade 1909
5^2.....	6	1st, 1902	2^2	3^1	3^1	4^1	5^1	6^1	7^1
6^2.....	7	1st, 1902	2^2	3^1	4^1	4^2	5^2	6^1	6^2
7^2.....	8	1st, 1899	2^2	3^1	4^1	4^2	5^2	6^2	7^1
17^1.....	6	1st, 1902	1^2	2^2	3^1	3^1	4^1	5^1	6^1
25^1.....	6	1st, 1902	2^2	3^2	4^1	5^1	6^1	7^2	8^1
37^2.....	7	1st, 1902	3^1	4^1	..	..	..	7^1	8^1
47^1.....	6	1st, 1902	1^1	2^2	3^1	4^2	5^2	6^2	7^2
51^2.....	7	1st, 1902	2^1	3^1	4^2	5^2	6^1	7^2	8^1
54^1.....	6	1st, 1902	2^2	3^1	4^2	5^2	6^2	7^2	8^1
56^1.....	6	1st, 1901	1^1	..	..	4^2	5^2	6^2	7^2
68^1.....	6	1st, 1902	2^1	2^2	3^1	4^1	5^1	6^1	7^1
70^2.....	6	1st, 1902	2^2	3^2	4^1	5^1	6^1	7^1	7^2
71^2.....	7	Before 1st, 1900	2^2	2^2	3^1	4^1	4^1	4^2	5^2
81^1.....	6	1st, 1902	..	2^1	2^2	..	..	4^2	5^2
87^2.....	6	Before 1st, 1901	2^2	3^2	3^1	4^1	5^1	6^1	7^1
91^1.....	6	1st, 1902	2^1	2^2	3^1	4^1	5^1	6^2	7^2
96^1.....	6	1st, 1902	..	3^2	4^1	..	..	7^1	8^2
100^2.....	6	1st, 1902	2^1	2^1	3^2	..	4^1	4^2	5^2
101^2.....	7	1st, 1902	2^2	3^2	4^1	5^1	5^2	6^2	7^1
105^1.....	6	2d, 1901	2^2	3^1	4^2	5^1	6^1	7^2	8^1
110^1.....	6	1st, 1902	2^1	2^2	3^1	4^2	5^1	6^2	7^2
113^1.....	6	1st, 1902	2^1	2^2	3^2	4^1	5^1	6^1	7^1
116^1.....	6	2d, 1901	2^1	3^1	4^2	5^2	6^2	7^2	8^1

in which he entered school. If *before* is written in this column his standing in school indicated that he had entered school before the time of the earliest record found which is marked in the column. The superior figures 1 and 2 with the pupil's and the grade number indicate in which half he was enrolled upon entering school in any year: 1 means the first half or low fifth, low sixth, etc.; 2 means the second half or high fifth, high sixth, etc. The table, then, is to be interpreted thus: Pupil No. 105 was enrolled in grade low one in 1902, was then six years of age, had entered school the second term of 1901, enrolled in grade high two in September, 1903, in low three in 1904, in high four in 1905, in low five in 1906, in low six in 1907, in high seven in 1908, and in low eight in 1909. Considering only the time between 1902 and 1909, he has progressed somewhat irregularly but has accomplished the normal amount of work for that time and attained grade low eight. If all the children had progressed normally all would have been registered in grade low eight in September, 1909. They are, however, seen to be registered as follows:

Number in high eight	(8^2) is	1	(accelerated)
Number in low eight	(8^1) is	6	(normal)
Number in high seven	(7^2) is	5	(retarded)
Number in low seven	(7^1) is	6	
Number in high six	(6^2) is	1	
Number in low six	(6^1) is	1	
Number in high five	(5^2) is	3	
Total............		23	

Percentage of 23 accelerated is 4
Percentage of 23 normal is 26
Percentage of 23 retarded is 69*

* A close examination of the individual records discloses a larger percentage of retardation. Individuals 116 and 105 were retarded in 1902 but were counted normal in the table. No. 51, being in grade 1^2 in September, 1902, should normally be in grade 8^2 in September, 1909.

As the records of the first-grade children of 1903 of Schools B and C were traced and half-grades could not be distinguished, they should all normally be in the seventh grade in September, 1909. Of 180 names from School B, 65, and of 211 names from School C, 47 are still found upon the registers of the respective schools. These 112 are distributed as follows:

Number in Grade Eight is	10	(accelerated)
Number in Grade Seven is	26	(normal)
Number in Grade Six is	42	(retarded)
Number in Grade Five is	23	
Number in Grade Four is	9	
Number in Grade Three is	2	
Total..........	112	

For the three schools combined:

Number accelerated is	11	or	8.1 per cent
Number normal is	32	or	23.7 per cent
Number retarded is	92	or	68.1 per cent
Total.......	135		

With these figures and those for the same items obtained from Table III may be compared the figures from the report for 1907 of the Cincinnati public schools. On p. 79 of this report is an age-grade table for all the pupils in the schools in June, 1907. This table upon its face appears to be upon the same basis as Ayres's table as regards normal ages for grades. But we are told upon p. 78, "The age of all pupils is given at the birthday occurring between November 1, 1906, and November 1, 1907, so that most of the pupils will appear one year older upon this table than they were upon entering school in September." Thus seven appears upon the table as the normal age for the first grade, while in reality most of the children were six when entering it for the first time in September. The table shows that there were 4,992 six years of age or less upon entering in September, and 4,403 who were seven years of age at that time. As no other age group in the table is as large as the six-year group we must conclude that children are in school in Cincinnati at six years of age. The number of accelerated, normal, and retarded children shown by the table and compiled on p. 80 is as follows:

Accelerated	3,697
Normal	12,269
Retarded	22,433
Total	38,399

A comparison of percentages shows:

	Cincinnati	Chicago (3 schools)	Chicago (135 school biographies)
Accelerated	9.6	9.5	8.1
Normal	31.9	34.9	23.7
Retarded	58.4	55.6	68.1

These figures show considerable similarity. Less than one-tenth do the work of the school faster than the expected normal time, about one-third do it in the time expected, and over one-half require one or more years more than the expected time to do it.

At the suggestion of Professor Dearborn a questionnaire, as reproduced below, was given to the children of School B. It was filled out by all of Grades Eight, Seven, Six, and Five present upon one day and by a section of Grade Four. The object of the experiment was to test the credibility of the method in the way that it would have to be used by an investigator collecting a large mass of statistics. The blank was filled out by 374 children.

Name..

Age.................................. Grade..................................

At what age did you enter school?..

How long have you been in each of the following grades?

Low 1st.............................. High 1st..............................

Low 2d.............................. High 2d..............................

Low 3d.............................. High 3d..............................

Low 4th.............................. High 4th..............................

Low 5th.............................. High 5th..............................

Low 6th.............................. High 6th..............................

Low 7th.............................. High 7th..............................

Low 8th.............................. High 8th..............................

What grades, if any, have you skipped?..

What grades, if any, have you repeated?..

The blanks were given to the principal with the simple request that they be filled. His method of getting it done is not known. They were returned filled in every conceivable way, and it was found that if any results were to be obtained from them it would be necessary to evaluate them at some other than their face value. Of the 374 blanks returned 132 were answered fully and without contradictions. The remainder were studied carefully and given the most probable evaluation. Often portions of the blank were left unfilled. This may have been mere carelessness on the part of the child or he may have forgotten how much time he had spent in a certain half-grade and so omitted filling that space. These omissions were filled in, in their evaluation, in such a way as would account for the time reported as having been spent in school, i.e., the difference between the age at entering and the present age. Many other small considerations entered in in evaluating the individual blanks which it would be too tedious to discuss and which might not apply to any other similar set.

The blanks were divided into four groups according to the character of school progress shown, the normal group, composed of those who had completed one grade per year of school life;

what I have called the pure accelerated group, those who have skipped one or more half-grades and repeated none; the pure repeaters who have repeated one or more half-grades and skipped none; and the mixed group who have skipped one or more half-grades and repeated one or more half-grades. This grouping is shown in Table VI. Under the head of an interrogation point are those so imperfectly filled that to determine any grouping for them was impossible.

TABLE VI

Grade	Normal	Pure Accelerated	Pure Repeaters	Mixed	?	Total
VIII	7	21	11	31	6	76
VII	27	12	12	21	18	90
VI	27	13	14	25	16	93
V	8	16	9	23	27	83
IV	12	3	6	9	2	32

This shows the number of pupils in each half-grade who have progressed normally, are accelerated without having repeated (pure accelerated), have repeated without skipping (pure repeaters), have both repeated and skipped (mixed).

The most significant item of this table is the column headed *mixed* which shows the large number of irregular careers through the grades, and the comparatively small number in the normal column. The number of half-grades skipped and repeated is shown by grades in Table VII.

TABLE VII

	Skipped	Repeated	Gained	Lost	Number Pupils
Grade VIII	103	68	35	..	70
Grade VII	64	79	..	15	72
Grade VI	75	109	..	34	77
Grade V	62	93	..	31	56
Grade IV	15	38	..	23	30

Our table shows that the eighth grade gained on an average of one-half of a half-grade or one-fourth of a year per pupil: the seventh grade has lost nearly one-tenth of a year; the sixth grade has lost more than one-fourth of a year; the fifth grade has lost nearly one-fourth of a year; and the fourth grade has lost nearly one-half of a year.[7]

Table VIII shows the number of times each half-grade was repeated by the 305 children whose blanks were evaluated. Table IX shows how many half-grades were skipped by the same children. These show that the grades most repeated are those between the second and the fifth inclusive, those skipped the most are high first, high second, low and high third, and high fourth. The third and the fourth grades appear in both groups, indicating that it is in those grades that the most readjustment takes place.

TABLE VIII

SHOWING NUMBER OF TIMES EACH HALF-GRADE WAS REPEATED BY 305 CHILDREN

Low First	17	High First	15
Low Second	24	High Second	25
Low Third	30	High Third	32
Low Fourth	47	High Fourth	34
Low Fifth	38	High Fifth	36
Low Sixth	19	High Sixth	26
Low Seventh	11	High Seventh	12
Low Eighth	5	High Eighth	4

TABLE IX

SHOWING NUMBER OF TIMES EACH HALF-GRADE WAS SKIPPED BY 305 CHILDREN

Low First	24	High First	39
Low Second	20	High Second	31
Low Third	30	High Third	35
Low Fourth	11	High Fourth	29
Low Fifth	19	High Fifth	19
Low Sixth	18	High Sixth	21
Low Seventh	14	High Seventh	8
Low Eighth	0		

[7] There is an apparent discrepancy between the eighth-grade data of this table and of Table III, which shows 55 per cent. retardation. It is accounted for in the following way: 11 of the 31 mixed pupils repeated more than they skipped and are therefore retarded; 11 from Table VI are pure repeaters, and 8 others of the *mixed* pupils started late and did not skip enough to reach the eighth grade at the normal age. This gives a retardation percentage of 42.8 on 70 pupils; the retardation percentage on the age-grade table for this school is 49.4 on 91 pupils half of whom have graduated and left the school in the interval between the securing of the two sets of data.

From these blanks was obtained an additional item of information as to the time at which children enter school. Of those who answered the question, "At what age did you enter school?" 238 entered at six years of age or less, 50 at seven years, 8 at eight years, and 4 at nine years of age. A number who answered that they had entered at seven years of age or more were adjudged not real beginners, as their blanks showed in each case that less than two weeks of time was spent in the first half of the first grade. These children had most certainly received private instruction and could not be classed as beginners. Superintendent Greenwood of Kansas City, in a criticism of Mr. Ayres's methods, made the statement that children often entered school at seven years of age or more and progressed more rapidly than those entering at six.[8] This may be true for Kansas City where children are not permitted to enter the kindergarten before six. The information gained from our blanks does not indicate that the same may be true for Chicago. These show that the number of half-grades skipped by those entering at seven and now below the eighth grade is 24, half-grades repeated 39, leaving a net loss of 15 half-grades for 50 pupils. Since a large majority of children enter school at six years of age that must be considered the normal age for the first grade, or we are reduced to the alternative of allowing to this majority two years instead of one for the completion of the grade.

The results of this study show that the retardation of our schools is probably much greater than Mr. Ayres's figures show, a thing which Mr. Ayres himself suspected. They also indicate that what we have been calling retardation is not retardation but a course of study unsuited to the powers of the children who pursue it. To say that more than half of our children are backward is certainly to make an anomalous statement. Though there are enough really backward children in our schools for whom special teaching and care are necessary, it would seem that the thing now most important is such study as will result in subject-matter properly adapted to the child's abilities and age.

[8] *Education*, May, 1908.

NATURAL HISTORY IN THE GRADES

OTIS W. CALDWELL
The University of Chicago

V. FIFTH GRADE

In presenting this statement of the work done in the fifth grade, especial recognition should be made of the assistance given by Miss Myrta McClellan, who has taught the nature-study in the Fifth Grade for the greater part of the school year, and to Miss Ada Milam, who is completing the year's work. The lesson outlines that are appended are those used by Miss McClellan, and the pupils' papers are the uncorrected written discussions prepared under Miss Milam's direction.

The nature materials used in this grade are chiefly plants and animals, these being centered largely about the work of the garden. A study is made of the processes involved, the habits of life, and conditions affecting the successful development of plants and animals and control of these conditions. Although the topics included in the grade are here listed under three headings, they are considered in their relations to one another.

1. *Animal life.*—In the preceding grades opportunity has been given for general acquaintance with a few common insects. Using this acquaintance as a basis, the attitude of investigation may be developed by a somewhat detailed study of a stand of bees, their communal life, their structure, the uses made of the parts of the body as in flying, walking, feeding, carrying food, and in protecting themselves against enemies; the honeycomb, its structures and uses, rate at which nectar is made into honey and deposited in honey cells, the kinds of flowers upon which bees are working, in what seasons and on what kinds of days do bees work most; the queen bee, care of eggs, larvae, and the young bees; swarming; enemies of honey-bees. Brief study of bumble bees and reading assignments upon habits of bees. During the two years preceding this year bees were kept in the

University Elementary School and studied by the Fifth Grade. An observation hive, especially well adapted for class or individual study (sold by A. I. Root Co., Medina, Ohio), was kept in the schoolroom for a part of the time. It was so placed that the bees passed in and out through a window, but were always observable from within. The sides and top of the box could be removed and the interior of the hive readily studied.

FIG. 1.—The children are preparing the bees for winter by closing the hive and carrying it into a cool room where it will remain until spring. Some of the children who are afraid of being stung by the bees have covered their heads and hands with cheese cloth.

One or two lessons upon wasps as relatives of the bees are interesting at this point. Include the homes and habits of the "mud-dauber" wasps; the way in which they store food in the cells for the use of their larvae, the lint-cutting habits of some wasps and hornets, a comparison of this lint with wood pulp from which paper is manufactured.

A study is made of the industrial significance of domesticated plants and animals, including corn, cotton, wheat, horses, cows, cattle, and sheep. The history and improvement of these things are left for the Seventh Grade. In preceding grades considerable work has been done with identification of birds. In this grade a study is made of birds as factors in the life of the community, and of state regulations for bird protection. There are many excellent helps for the teacher upon this topic, among which are: *Useful Birds and Their Protection,* by E. H. Forbush, published by the Massachusetts Board of Agriculture, Boston, Mass.; "The Economic Values of Some Common Illinois Birds," by Alfred O. Gross and Stephen A. Forbes, published in the *Arbor and Bird Day Annual of 1909,* by the Superintendent of Public Instruction, Springfield, Ill.; and chaps. xviii, xix, xx, and xxi in Hodge's *Nature-Study and Life,* published by Ginn & Co.

2. *Plant life.*—In the schoolroom plants are grown in aquaria and pots, and propagation is studied by use of slips and cuttings of geranium, coleus, begonia, wandering-jew, willow, etc. The pupils are instructed in the proper methods of making cuttings. The reasons for retaining two or three leaves, two or three inches of the stem, and the terminal buds are discussed. The relative advantage of pruning away parts of the leaves may be shown by planting some with and some without this pruning and noting the later growth. The cuttings are planted at such a depth that the terminal bud and leaves stand immediately above the sand. They should then be covered by a square of glass so that constant moisture and temperature may be maintained, care being taken to ventilate the plants frequently. In ten days or two weeks the glass may be kept propped up, and a few days thereafter it may be removed permanently. Throughout, frequent examination of one or two plants should be made to study the origin and development of roots. When well rooted, plants should be potted in two-inch pots in rich soil. If properly watered and lighted they may be grown in these pots until the outdoor gardens are ready for planting, when the potted plants furnish excellent material with which to get early results in the garden.

Rusts and insects that are injurious to plants, methods of

prevention, insect galls, and a few observations upon the life-cycle of some insect-producing galls are topics of great interest. Weeds were studied chiefly in connection with seed distribution and the garden. As shown in the appended lesson plans there was an autumn field trip for the collection of seeds of many kinds. Weed seeds were planted and germinated in the school-

Fig. 2

room, and the characteristics noted so that in future garden work this knowledge may be used in proper care of the garden. Structures and agencies of seed distribution were studied in detail, a small inexpensive hand lens proving of much assistance and interest in this connection. The advantage of wide seed distribution, and the relative probability of all seeds developing into mature plants are included. A brief review of the work of the lower grades upon plant structures and how a plant works, serves as the basis for a study of the plant life-cycle which is completed by a study of the flower as a means of seed formation. The parts of a flower and the function of each part in seed formation, omitting all technical details, are studied. Pollination in different common plants and agencies for securing it are fascinating topics. Reproduction of seed plants furnishes an addition to the series which began in the Second Grade, in which series a study has been made of methods of establishing new living things. This is a most important aspect of nature-study, and the whole series,

FIG. 3.—Fifth-grade children working in their gardens. Their plans were made before outdoor work began and they are now planting according to these plans. Note also the grape arbor at the left end of the toolhouse. The lattice-work was put on by the fifth-grade pupils.

together with the studies of how individual plants and animals live, should make a good basis for the study of hygiene in the Sixth Grade.

3. *Garden work.*—In the late autumn this grade is assigned to the work of building a "cold frame" in which it is expected that early vegetables and flowering plants will be produced. In spring and summer each pupil has his own garden, makes his own plan subject to the approval of his teacher, does his own planting and cultivation, and owns the results of his work.

Individual ownership and responsibility are essential to pupils of this age. The work is chiefly elementary agriculture and horticulture in continuation of previous garden work and of the indoor studies outlined above.

Use is made of common plants of the home and vegetable garden; also of important plants which are relatively unknown to the pupils, as sugar beets, peanuts, broom-corn, etc. Constant effort is given to secure from each pupil a genuine interest in the habits and needs of the particular plants he is growing, the soil, watering, lighting, and the injurious insects that attack them. A fine quality and quantity of result in flowers, vegetables, or fruit is an appreciable end to the pupil. This is not likely to be secured without care, industry, and study.

The work has proven full of interest and value. It furnishes concrete experience which makes significant the indoor experiments and study upon the structure, water content and water-lifting power of soils, soil replenishment and the relation of leguminous plants to soils. The work of this grade supplies a first-hand basis of interpretation for later work in elementary science, as well as for other subjects of the curriculum.

The following are skeleton outlines of Fifth Grade lesson plans as used by Miss Myrta McClellan of the University Elementary School.

The work of the first two weeks deals with seed distribution. The subject is introduced by a discussion of how in the home the children are cared for until mature, when they go to homes of their own. From this the question is raised as to how plants care for their seeds and how seeds get into new homes. The short time that a mature seed remains with the parent plant is a point for emphasis. There follow discussion and listing the agencies of seed distribution; a field trip for collection of all available kinds of seeds and fruits; this is a Saturday trip and much of the day is given to it; structure of the seeds and fruits studied, experiments with them, and a classification under headings indicating how the pupils think they are distributed; collection of collateral evidence (books and experiences of others) to test correctness of conclusions; learn to recognize different kinds of seeds by sight; plant seeds in pots, see what ones will germinate at this time of year, note characteristics, record in notes and drawings for future use in garden and outdoor work.

Reproduction of plants by means of cuttings is next considered. Discuss manner in which the children think cuttings must be made. There must be stem, bud, and leaf. Discuss kind of soil for planting; clean sand is best until roots need nourishment. Have each child make a cutting and plant it. Discuss watering, lighting, and covering. Have children develop reasons so far as possible. Working in close quarters in schoolroom will require great care and neatness. Label all work done. Write a story of the cuttings and their treatment. Summarize in one lesson all work done up to date.

During the winter should come a series of lessons upon cattle, beginning with the uses of cattle, milk, cream, butter, cheese, draft animals, plowing, road animals, to propel machinery, for threshing grain, for riding. Use pictures and reading-matter as basis of work. Uses of cattle for beef; parts used, parts most valuable, best types of beef cattle, of dairy cattle; visit stock-yards. Needs of cattle for best growth, regions of largest production of cattle, relation of climate to production of cattle. Disappearance of former cattle ranches as permanent agriculture develops.

Cattle ranges of steppes of Russia, the plains of Australia, the Llanos of the Orinoco, and the pampas of Argentina. Milk cattle and dairy cattle the next topic. Dairy cattle of the U.S., Holland, Canada, Norway, Switzerland, Denmark. Value of their products. Zebu of India as a type of cattle not usually seen in this country. The value of each in the nation to which it is native.

Before leaving the subject of cattle, a brief review. Add a discussion of the tsetse fly as a deadly enemy of cattle and the fact that parts of Africa have no cattle probably because of this.

The horse as a factor in man's work and development of the country the next topic of study. This covered in two lessons as the children are able to use the work on the cow and compare the work on the horse with it in such a way that little additional time is needed. The horse is more useful to a man merely because of his greater speed.

As a means of ascertaining what the children are getting from the study of birds, Miss Milam, at present fifth-grade teacher in the University Elementary School, asked the children to write a brief paper upon a common bird of economic value. This exercise was unannounced until the time of beginning it, and but a few minutes were allowed for it. Two sample papers are here presented. The papers are exactly as handed in by the children, and while faulty in some ways show some definite results.

MAY 4, 1910. GRADE 5

The robin is a bird of economic value. It is quite a tame bird and is a friend of everyone. The robin was first known in Massachusetts but was brought further south and is now mostly all over the United States. It's appearance is gray and orange. The back is gray and the breast is orange. It is nine inches from the tip of the bill to the tip of the tail. It feeds mostly on angle worms but partly on fruit and grain.

MAY 4, 1910. GRADE 5

One of the birds of economic value is the Robin. He is a friendly bird and does good by eating the harmful insects that eat the vegetables. He goes south every year and returns in the spring builds his nest and lays pretty blue egg and then the little birds hatch out of the eggs learns to fly and it is then time to go home. He has a red breast and a brown back.

The sparrow is another bird but he is not of economic value. He drives the other birds away and takes their food away. He has onley one friend and that is the truck gardner. He stayes here all winter. His breast is grey and his back is brown.

THE DEVELOPMENT OF METHODS IN TEACHING MODERN ELEMENTARY GEOGRAPHY

C. A. PHILLIPS
Warrensburg State Normal School, Warrensburg, Missouri

II. THE DEVELOPMENT OF METHODS IN THE TEACHING OF GEOGRAPHY IN THE UNITED STATES

This discussion will be carried on under the same general heads as those used in connection with European geography. It is to be noted that the progress in the development of method in the United States is slightly behind, in point of time, that in Switzerland and Germany except in industrial and economic geography. In these latter phases of the study the United States has gone on as rapidly as any of the European countries. This of course is due to the intense commercial development of the last few years which has been increasing in intensity throughout the United States.

1. *Place and Book Geography*

Mrs. Earle says:

> Geography was an *accomplishment* rather than a necessary study and was spoken of as a diversion for a winter's evening. Many objections were made that it took the scholar's attention away from ciphering. It was not taught in the elementary schools till this century. Morse's *Geography* was not written till after the Revolution. It had a mean little map of the United States, only a few inches square. On it all the land west of the Mississippi River was called Louisiana and nearly all north of the Ohio River, the Northwest Territory.[17]

We now regard these early geographies as rare curiosities both in matter and form. They were usually 12mo and sometimes as small as 32mo. The information they purport to give is also very often very remarkable. The early ones, up to 1820, were usually bound in full leather; in a few cases wood was used. At first there were only a few maps and illustrations. The divisions of the earth were made by the use of the globe.[18] All these early geographies were fine examples of the place and book geography. Among the more important ones may be mentioned Morse's *American* first published in 1789, but later in 1793 the work was enlarged to 1,250 pages and published in two volumes under the title, *American Universal Geography*. The third edition was published in 1796 and contained about 1,500 pages. The fourth edition appeared in 1801 and 1802 and was thoroughly revised and contained a good many maps. The fifth edition was published in 1805. In this edition Vol. I has only three maps, the world, North America, and South America. Vol. II has three maps also, Europe, Asia, and Africa. But the preface of this edition says that this defect is to be remedied as it is to be accompanied by a good general atlas drawn by Arrowsmith and Lewis.[19]

The earliest rival of Morse's books was a small volume published by Nathaniel Dwight in 1795 at Hartford. This was a book of questions and answers, from which many interesting bits of information may be obtained; for example:

> Q. What curiosities are there in Portugal?
>
> A. There are lakes into which a stone being cast causes a rumbling noise like the noise of an earthquake.
>
> Q. What are the customs and diversions of the Irish?
>
> A. There are a few customs existing in Ireland peculiar to this country. These are their funeral howlings and presenting their corpses in the streets to excite the charity of strangers, their convivial meetings on Sunday and dancing to bagpipes which are usually attended with quarreling.
>
> Q. What curiosities are there in France?
>
> A. A fountain near Grenoble emits a flame which will burn paper, straw, etc., but will not burn gunpowder. Within about eight leagues of the same place is an inaccessible mountain in the form of a pyramid reversed.
>
> Q. What are the characteristics of the Hottentots?
>
> A. They are the most abject of the human race. They besmear their bodies with soot and grease, live upon carrion, old leather shoes, and everything of the most loathsome kind; dress themselves in sheepskins untanned, turning the wool to their flesh in the winter and the other side in the summer. Their dress serves them for their bed at night, for a covering by day, and for a winding-sheet when they die.[18]

The Montor's *Instructor* published in 1804 was another interesting geography. It presents much of the material in verse form. This is a good example:

One river of enormous size,
To west of Mississippi lies,
The river this called Missouri,
And toward southwest its course lies.
This river, from what I can see,
Can't less than the Ohio be.[18]

The prose part is also fully as interesting, for much of it is written in the form of paradoxes of which the following is a good example:

Three men went on a journey in which, though their heads traveled twelve yards farther than their feet, all returned alive with their heads on."

Among the other early American geographies may be mentioned the Davis *Geography* published in 1813 and the Cummings, in 1814. The Adams *Geography* published in 1818 was divided into three parts: (1) "Geography of Orthography"; (2) "Grammar of Geography"; (3) "Description of the Earth." The first four excerpts below are from Part II, the others from Part III.

"A mountain is a vast protuberance of the earth." "Europe is distinguished for its learning, politeness, government, and laws; for the industry of its inhabitants and the temperature of its climate." "The White Mountains are the highest, not only in New Hampshire, but in the United States." "Switzerland is a small romantic country lying upon the Alps and is the highest spot in Europe. St. Gothard is the highest mountain." "Several mineral springs break forth in different parts of the United States. The most celebrated are those of Saratoga and Balls Town in the State of New York. The latter place is much frequented by gay and fashionable people as well as by invalids." "Beer is the common drink of the inhabitants of New York State. The forests abound with bears, wolves, deer and elks." "Many of the towns and plantations in Maine are destitute of any settled minister. Missionaries sent among them have been very affectionately received."[18]

Peter Parley's *Method of Telling about Geography* was published in 1829 at first, and several editions were issued at different times. He also published his *Natural Geography* in 1845. This is thought to be the first American geography to take the flat quarto shape. One rhyme is of peculiar interest and may be found both in his *Method of Telling about Geography* and in *Natural Geography*. The rhyme is as follows:

The world is round and like a ball
Seems swinging in the air;
A sky extends around it all
And stars are shining there.

Water and land upon the face
Of this round world we see;
The land is man's safe dwelling place
But ships sail on the sea.

Two mighty continents there are
And many islands too
And mountains hills and valleys there
With level plains we view.

The ocean, like the broad blue sky,
Extends around the sphere;
While seas and lakes and rivers lie
Unfolded bright and clear.

Around the earth, on every side
Where hills and plains are spread.
The various tribes of men abide,
White, black, and copper-red.

And animals and plants there be
Of various name and form,
And in the bosom of the sea
All sorts of fishes swarm.

Geography goes high and low
To set them forth and show them;
The more attention you bestow
The better will you know them.[20]

The Woodbridge and Willard *Universal Geography* was published in 1824. This is only for advanced students and the most peculiar thing about the volume is the last part by Willard which connects geography and ancient history.[21]

These are all good examples of place and book geographies, and in general they are designed for the higher schools rather than the elementary school. One of the first attempts to put geography in elementary form was made by Morse when he wrote his *Geography Made Easy* in 1800. This was an abridgment of the *American Universal Geography* and ran through many editions. In fact, it seems that it may be fairly claimed that this was the most popular elementary geography of the first half of the nineteenth century. It is a small, leather-bound, 12mo of about four hundred pages. From this little volume many interesting quotations might be made, but a few will have to suffice here. We read as follows:

The Wakon Bird, which probably is of the same species as the Bird of Paradise, received its name from the ideas the Indians have of its superior excellence; the Wakon Bird being in their language, the Bird of the Great Spirit. Its tail is composed of four or five feathers which are three times as long as its body, and which are beautifully shaded with green and purple. It carries this fine length of plumage in the same manner as the peacock does his, but it is not known whether, like him, it ever raises it to an erect position. . . . .

Among reptiles the American crocodile is described as follows:

The alligator or American crocodile is a terrible creature of prodigious strength, activity, and swiftness in the water. They are from six to twenty-four feet in length; their bodies as large as that of a horse, covered with horny plates or scales, said to be impenetrable to a rifle-ball except about the head and four legs. They make a frightful appearance and at certain seasons a most hideous roar, resembling distant thunder. They are oviparous and lay from one to two hundred eggs in a nest. Their principal food is fish, but they devour dogs and hogs. The old feed on the young alligators till they get so large that they cannot make a prey of them. . . . .

The Coach-Whip, Glass and Joint Snakes are great curiosities, the latter, when struck, breaks like a pipe-stem without producing a tincture of blood. . . . .

Columbia College, in the City of New York, is in a flourishing state and has more than one hundred scholars besides medical students. The officers of instruction and immediate government are a President, a Professor of Logic and Geography, a Professor of Languages and a Professor of Mathematics and Natural Philosophy. A complete medical school is annexed to the college and able professors appointed in every branch of that important science, who regularly teach their respective branches with reputation.

In writing about Louisiana, St. Louis is described as

a village of two hundred houses, beautifully situated on the Mississippi, fourteen miles below the Missouri, in latitude 38° 18′ north. Considerable settlements are made on the banks of the latter river for several hundred miles. This town and its districts contain 5,667 inhabitants.[22]

W. C. Woodbridge, 1794–1845, was mentioned above, but some further detail should be given his work. The *System of Modern Geography* was first published in 1833. Later he revised this in 1853 in collaboration with Mrs. Willard. In the introduction of the first edition he tells about the very bad conditions of geography-teaching in the United States and particularly of the poor textbooks. He had just returned from a visit to Europe where he had visited Pestalozzi in Switzerland and also studied a number of the Pestalozzian schools of Switzerland. During this visit he also spent considerable time with Ritter and Humboldt talking about the problems of geography and finally he had been a teacher in Fellenburg's School at Hofwyl. His thought was to make geography into a science and to this end he published the books mentioned. However, he was not equal to the task as can be readily seen from examination of his textbooks, though it must be confessed that his books represent considerable progress when compared with those of Morse. It is of interest to note some of his directions in the matter of method which may be found under the heading "Remarks to Inexperienced Teachers" in both editions of his textbooks. They are as follows:

1. Let the instructor first ascertain that a student has observed the country around him and is familiar with the points of the compass and the application of common geographical terms.

2. Let the student next draw simple maps beginning with a plan of his table or the room in which he is, proceeding to delineate successively a plan of the house, garden, neighborhood, and town until he has represented with tolerable correctness the relative situations and outlines of the principal objects within his view.

3. When he is prepared to understand the lines and points of a map, require him to become familiar with the definitions of geography and the outlines of continents and oceans as presented by the descriptions and questions of this work (pp. 10 to 19) in connection with the atlas and by the questions which follow the table of contents on the map of the world and the grand divisions. The questions should of course be varied and multiplied by the instructor until each lesson is understood and remembered.

4. At first the questions may be answered with the aid and guidance of the instructor, but the student should endeavor as soon as possible to fix the image of the map in his mind and answer from his recollection of it.

5. Nothing will assist so much in this as drawing maps by the eye. Let him draw on the slate the outline of one country at a time; then insert the rivers and mountains and then the cities; first using the map and finally drawing from memory.

6. As soon as the exercise is familiar let a whole class recite in this manner according to such directions as the following:

Draw the outlines of England.

Write the names of the seas, etc., around it.

Draw the mountains. The rivers. Thames, etc.

Let the instructor inspect the slates. He will thus keep all employed and ascertain the knowledge of each pupil without mistake. This plan has been practiced with great success in many schools. The author has published a set of outlines and skeleton maps under the title of *Geographical Copy Books.* In these the pupil begins by inserting only the cities on the outline map; he then copies the outlines on the skeleton map; and is thus easily led on until he can draw the maps from memory alone.[23]

Among other topics discussed in this same connection with directions are these: "Structure," "Physical Geography," "Civil Geography," "Analysis of the Continents," "Topography," etc.

In general it seems fair to say that the place and book geography was the type which prevailed throughout the United States till after the Civil War, and it is quite probable that it is still much used in some of the remote parts of the country.

2. *Physiographical Geography and Its Human Relations*

We have classified Woodbridge as belonging to the place and book period; however it seems fair to say that he does not represent merely that phase of geography. His textbooks are the best evidences of his broader view, especially in those parts in which he gives the directions quoted above. He was fully aware of the inadequacy of the Morse *Geography* and consciously strove to make his works more valuable, but he was unable to find new principles on which to base his discussions.

Another forerunner of the new geography was Horace Mann, 1796–1859. Mann went to Europe in 1843 to study school systems. His *Seventh Annual Report* gives an account of his travels and his impressions of the schools he visited. During this visit he went to Berlin to see Ritter who was then in the zenith of his teaching-power and influence in Germany.

In describing the geography-teaching Mann says in his report that discrimination must be used, for in some respects he thought the work was imperfect, while in others the teaching was pre-eminently well done. The following quotation indicates in part his attitude.

> The practice seemed to be uniform of beginning with objects perfectly familiar to the child—the schoolhouse with the grounds around it, the home with its yards, or gardens, and the streets leading from the one to the other. First of all, the children were initiated into the ideas of space, without which we can know no more of geography than we can of history without the ideas of time. Mr. Karl Ritter, of Berlin—probably the greatest geographer now living, expressed a decided opinion to me, that this was the true mode of beginning.[24]

The above quotation is important because it tells directly about the practice in geography-teaching in Germany, and it is especially valuable for it serves to connect Mann definitely with the geography of Ritter. It seems quite certain that Mann accepted the theories of Ritter but there is no possible way to estimate the influence of Mann on geography-teaching in the United States.

One other thing reported by Mann is worth some attention, namely, the use of maps in the study of geography.

A large map was suspended on the wall, or sometimes the blackboard was used; if the map was used, the teacher told about the country, tracing the important places on the map, or if the blackboard was used, the teacher drew the map showing the important cities, rivers, mountains, etc. In either case the pupils were required on the following day to reproduce the lesson. Mr. Mann thought this was excellent, in fact, the best geography-teaching he had ever seen. He makes a specific comment that such teaching is vastly superior to the study of a few names of places from some lifeless atlas.

The only adverse criticism is that the Germans study only national geography, but give little attention to universal geography.

We have noted briefly the work of Woodbridge and Mann. In spite of the suggestion of these two writers, physiographical geography in the United States really gets its first great impetus from Arnold Guyot, 1807–1884, who came to this country in 1848 and settled in Cambridge, Massachusetts. He was thoroughly familiar with the schools of Germany and Switzerland, having taught in them, and was one of Ritter's best students. He had spent four years as a student in the University of Berlin. From 1848 to 1854 he was in the employ of the Massachusetts Board of Education as an inspector and institute lecturer. In 1854 he went to Princeton as professor of geology and physical geography.

His coming marks the beginning of a definite movement away from the old place and book geography to that of the physiographical geography. He was to the United States what Ritter had been to Europe. His theories were those of Ritter, only slightly re-constructed to suit the conditions in the United States. An examination of his first publication, *The Earth and Man* (1849), shows how thoroughly he had adopted the theories of Ritter. His first chapter in this book may be summarized as follows:

1. The forms, the arrangement, and the distribution of the terrestrial masses on the surface of the globe, accidental in appearance, yet reveal a plan which we are enabled to understand by the evolution of history.

2. The continents are made for human societies as the body was made for the soul.

3. Each of the northern or historical continents is peculiarly adapted by its nature to perform a special part corresponding to the wants of humanity in one of the great phases of its history. Thus nature and history, the earth and man stand in the closest relations to each other and form only one grand harmony.[25]

These are all statements of Ritter's *Geography* and one could almost forget that he is reading Guyot and believe these are some statements from Ritter's *Comparative Geography,* so closely does the language follow the statement of Ritter's fundamental principles. This whole book is hardly more than an elaboration of the important teachings of Ritter. In 1868 Guyot published his *Geographical Teaching.* This is a book of methods to put into practice the theories outlined in the *Earth and Man.* Some type lessons are given which are fundamental in their form and content. For example there is a series of "Lessons about Home."

The first of this series is an illustrative lesson on "Physical Forms"; this is a lesson on a neighborhood in western New York. It is in the form of a regular recitation. The pupils are the children of the farmers of the vicinity and the time is summer. A brief section of the lesson is quoted as follows:

TEACHER. I would like all of you to think carefully a moment, and try to remember everything you saw on your way to school. (The pupils are then called upon to tell what they saw).

JOHN. I saw some men mowing in Mr. B's meadow.

CHARLES. I saw a red squirrel running along the fence by the woods.

MARY. I saw some cows and a colt, and two calves and some sheep and lambs, in Mr. G's pasture.

FANNY. I saw some cherries that are turning red in the orchard across the road.

TEACHER. You have remembered several things, and I have no doubt if you should think a little longer you could name many more; but we have as many as we can talk about in one morning. We are going to have a lesson on some of the things you have seen in coming to school. Mary spoke of something she saw in a *pasture*. How many passed pastures in coming to school? (Hands are raised.) Mary, can you tell me what a pasture is?

MARY. It is a field where the cattle, horses, and sheep stay.

TEACHER. Why are they in the pasture?

MARY. We drive them there to eat grass.

TEACHER. Do they need anything but food during the day?

CHILDREN. They want drink, too.

TEACHER. Very well. Where do they find drink?

JAMES. There is a creek in our pasture.

SARAH. There is a spring in ours; etc.[26]

At this point the teacher directs the attention of the class to water forms, and they discuss in some detail, the spring, the creek, the brook, a mill-pond, a river, and a lake. After this the teacher takes up land forms, taking the pasture as the point of departure. They talk about rough land, hills, level land, plains, mountains, and a swamp. At the close a brief summary is made by the pupils, telling the topics brought out in the lesson. The plan suggests that each one of these topics mentioned shall be made the subject for other lessons later on. More than that, the woods, animals, and the relations of the kind of land to the industries of the people are to be made subjects for study.

There can be no question but that this type of lesson represents the best method of study as we have found it in Europe, and furthermore it comes to be the prevailing plan for a larger part of the United States, during the last part of the nineteenth century. Indeed, we do not know anything better yet. It takes up problems within the range of the experience of the child and makes them the starting-point for all geographical knowledge.

It puts the larger emphasis on thinking rather than remembering, in fact, it presents all the best values of the developing method.

A second lesson treats of the "Industries of the Locality." The theory here is that the industries should be studied after the physical geography has been presented. The same conversational plan is used and the homes of the people are first brought up for consideration. This is followed by a discussion of the house, furniture, food, clothing, and the occupations of various men of the community. A good many are farmers, but there is one man who has a sawmill, another a gristmill, one is a blacksmith, one a cabinet-maker, and one keeps a store, etc. The most interesting thing about the lesson is the fact that it is conducted in such a way as to show the interdependence of all these various workers, and at the same time the material of the lesson is kept within the experience of the children. No better plan for the study of the industrial phases of geography has been discovered. Indeed, this is practically the scheme of the teachers who would make the industry the important thing in geography-study. They would start with the industry first, however, and then go to the other problems which are related to the industry in some way.

After a thorough study of the type forms mentioned then Guyot would have the children go on with a study of direction and distance, the globe, continents, and the world.

Guyot published also a series of textbooks which practically failed because there were no teachers to use them, and partly because he as a university professor was not quite familiar enough with elementary-school conditions to bring his material down to the level of the children.

Next to the influence of Guyot, probably should be mentioned that of Colonel Francis W. Parker, 1837–1902. Perhaps it would be better to say that they were interested in different aspects of geography than to compare them at all. Guyot, was a university professor, profoundly interested in the scientific aspects of geography, while Colonel Parker was the city superintendent and president of a normal school, trying to find suitable material and methods for putting his theories into practice. However, Colonel Parker was no less a follower of Ritter than was Guyot. He had spent three years in Berlin, 1872–75, where the influence of Ritter was still all-powerful under the teaching of his distinguished pupil, Kiepert, who had succeeded him as professor of geography in the university. There seems to be no doubt whatever that Colonel Parker fully accepted the theories of Ritter and Kiepert. More than that, he frequently refers to Guyot and quotes from his works. Some of the students of Colonel Parker who were graduated from the old Cook County Normal, and have distinguished themselves both as students and teachers of geography, report that the first books they had to master when they came to study geography with Colonel Parker were Ritter's *Comparative Geography* and *Geographical Studies.* Another bit of good evidence as to how thoroughly he adopted the principles of Ritter may be found by reading the introduction to *How to Study Geography.*[27] Here we have again the statement of the doctrine that the "earth is the home of man," and all the remainder of the book is taken up in an effort to bring this great truth into realization for the children of the elementary school. This is done by taking up some of the typical problems of geography grade by grade.

Farnham, in his book telling of the Oswego methods in geography, quotes both Ritter and Humboldt and is undoubtedly influenced by Guyot's writing. Professedly, the Oswego movement is under Pestalozzian ideals and in general no doubt this is true. But in the matter of geography the ideals of Ritter are much more predominant than those of Pestalozzi. The reasons assigned for teaching geography give full confirmation of this statement. For example, they are said to be:

(1) To explain the development of man by imparting knowledge of continental structure and climate and their influence upon man mediate and immediate. (3) To explain and illumine history. History is a record of the deeds of the human race. The civilization and progress of a people depend very largely upon the structure and climate of their country. (7) To develop man's reverence for human progress. Study the geography of Holland and the development of agriculture and commerce.[28]

These principles are all clearly related to those we have been discussing of Ritter and Guyot. More than that, it may be fairly said that the whole book treats of the earth as the "home of man," and starts the children into the study of geography with the school, its surrounding, the town, the state, the continent, etc.

The Frye Geography is one of the influential factors of this movement. Alexander Frye was one of Colonel Parker's pupils; in fact, he graduated from the Cook County Normal. His training and no doubt much of his inspiration in the matter of geography came from Colonel Parker. His *Elementary Geography* in particular may be said to follow the subject-matter and method which could be called Ritter and Parker geography.[29]

The McMurray *Special Methods in Geography* also follows in the same general trend, the only difference being a slight leaning toward industrial and economic geography. For example, such topics as these are there emphasized:

(1) Food products and occupations connected with them; (2) building material and trades related; (3) clothing materials used in manufacture; (4) local commerce, roads, bridges, and railroads.[30]

The second chapter takes up synthetic geography, going from the home outward with twenty important topics or types. Chapter iii makes a detailed study of these twenty types. Of course we know that McMurray was a graduate of Jena, and that, in part, may account for his method, for it is very much the German plan with the exception, possibly, of the industrial element.

One has only to glance over the elementary geographies of the Rand McNally series, the Dodge series, the Frye series, Natural series, etc., to see how thoroughly they have all appropriated the principles and methods of Ritter, Guyot, and Parker.

It may be observed, too, that these are the books which in the main represent current practice.

One general observation should be made in discussing American geography as related to European; that is, that the movement in the United States differs from that in Europe in that the historical element does not receive so much emphasis in the United States as it does abroad. The historical element is recognized by both Guyot and Parker but present-day practice virtually recognizes a separate course in history and geography for the elementary school. It seems possible to account for this difference in the fact that while we have all the typical geographical forms they cannot be connected with the great historical movements of the race as they are in Europe. Home geography with us does not include the regions which were the scenes of so many of the world's great historical problems as does home geography in Europe. We connect up only fairly well, too, the historical problems of our national development with the geography involved in them.

3. *Industrial and Economic Geography*

In the foregoing discussion we have called attention to the fact that Guyot, Parker, and McMurray have brought in some of the industrial phases of geography, and several other names might be mentioned in the same connection, but on the whole it is about fair to say that this type of geography is in the theoretical stage, except for a few city systems, normal training schools, and university laboratory schools. The establishment of schools of commerce and chairs of geography in a few American universities has brought out the necessity of doing something to come to a better understanding of our industrial and economic problems. This movement is beginning to reach down into the secondary and elementary schools. And, further, the tremendous commercial tension in the business world is demanding more trained workers to carry on its work. For this reason society is turning to the school and asking it to help solve the problems of industry and commerce.

One of the advanced statements of the idea involved in industrial and economic geography has been made by Dewey, where he says:

I should say that geography has to do with all those aspects of social life which are concerned with the interaction of the life of man and nature; or, that it has to do with the world considered as the scene of social interaction. . . . . [And again he says] The four stages of geography referred to above, namely, mathematical, physical, political, and commercial, represent then four increasing stages of abstraction in discussing the mutual relation of human life and nature. The beginning must be the commercial geography. I mean by this, that the essence of any geographical fact is the consciousness of two persons, or two groups of persons who are at once separated and connected by the physical environment and that the interest is in seeing how these people are at once kept apart and brought together in their actions by the instrumentality of this physical environment. The ultimate significance of lake, river, mountain, and plain is not physical but social. It is the part which it plays in modifying and functioning human relationship. This evidently involves an extension of the term commercial.[31]

SOURCES OF QUOTATIONS

17. EARLE, MRS. ALICE MORSE. *Child Life in Old Colonial Days,* 147–48.
18. JOHNSON, CLIFTON. "Geography of Our Forefathers," *New Eng. Mag.,* XXIX, 61–72.
19. MORSE. *Universal American Geography.* Fifth Edition, Preface.
20. PARLEY. *Grammar of Geography,* 15–16.
21. WOODBRIDGE AND WILLARD. *Universal Geography.*
22. MORSE. *Geography Made Easy* (1813), 93-94; 111–113; 153; 294.
23. WOODBRIDGE. *System of Modern Geography with Atlas* (1853), Introduction.
24. MANN. "Seventh Annual Report," *Common School Journal,* VI, 135–144.
25. GUYOT. *Earth and Man,* 16.
26. GUYOT. *Geographical Teaching,* 9–18.
27. PARKER. *How to Study Geography,* 1–19.
28. FARNHAM. *Oswego Methods in Geography,* 11–12.
29. FRYE. *Elementary Geography.*
30. MCMURRAY. *Special Method in Geography,* 1–29.
31. DEWEY. *Ethical Principles Underlying Education,* 20.

EDITORIAL NOTES

With this issue the tenth volume of the *Elementary School Teacher* closes. There are three series of articles which will be continued in the next volume, namely the series on natural history by Professor Caldwell, the series on agricultural education by Professor Davis, and the series on history of education by Professor Parker. The series by Professor Sargent is completed in this number and will, after some revision and enlargement, appear in the form of a book.

It will not be out of place for us to comment editorially on these series. Professor Sargent has shown with great detail the importance of systematic sequent work in a sphere of school activity which has suffered because of lack of careful organization. Professor Parker has struck out in a line of historical studies which will contribute new life to the history of education. This history has too often been abstract, dealing only with educational theory. Here is the practical side of school method brought to light in a most suggestive way. The articles on geography by Mr. Phillips may very properly be regarded as part of this series. Mr. Phillips' work grew out of one of Professor Parker's courses. When all of our school subjects are understood in the light of their history, we shall be very much more intelligent in estimating the value of our current reforms.

Professor Davis has brought together a body of information which makes it possible to follow the development of interest in agricultural education in all directions. Those who are introducing courses in agriculture and those who wish to secure material to guide them in the discussion of this subject will find in Professor Davis' papers a summary of the whole movement not available elsewhere. In subsequent papers Professor Davis will focus all these studies of current activities on the problems of the organization of courses for various types of schools.

Professor Caldwell will contribute further numbers to the

series on natural history showing how this subject can be made increasingly systematic in the upper grades. The problem of organizing school studies of nature broadly and at the same time in a fashion to satisfy the demand of preparation for maturer science is one of the most urgent current problems in elementary education. The solution of this problem is rendered the more difficult because the material is so varied in different environments. Professor Caldwell is giving concrete examples and a broad range of suggestions for the use of other special specimens.

This year's issues have emphasized the importance of scientific studies of educational problems. The papers on elimination are among the notable contributions of the journal to the educational literature of the year. Professor Dearborn shows that our schools lose the high-grade students as well as the low, thereby making it clear that mental deficiency is not the cause which explains the withdrawal of children from these schools. Mr. Staples showed that far-reaching social and economic results follow elimination; that later success in life is intimately related to the period of schooling. Miss Schmitt and Professor Thorndike contribute the detail studies of schools which alone will show the exact extent of retardation.

Several of the papers, notably the papers by Mr. Courtis, show the value of minute comparisons of classes and methods. Such papers ought to increase in number, for it is only through such studies that teachers can criticize school work on impersonal, objective grounds.

Doubtless readers of this journal have availed themselves of the guidance of Miss Warren's list of educational articles which appears in every number. If not, special attention should be given to this unique current bibliography of educational discussions. It is hoped that in time this may be expanded so as to indicate briefly what is in the more significant articles. As the list stands now, however, it is worth posting in every principal's office as a means to progress. No teacher can keep alive without reading broadly. Here is a librarian's contribution to the teachers' continued professional study. It is valuable in its immediate function and it is also valuable as an example to those who for any purpose are interested in the preparation of series of educational readings.

Space does not permit reference to each of the articles. Two general facts must be obvious to every reader. First, the papers all contain facts. We need more explicit accounts of what is going on everywhere in educational institutions. Experience goes to waste in limitless quantities. Anyone who will send facts about his or her work will find here an open forum. Secondly, this journal is not the exponent of any single school. All that is best in the practice and experience of the Elementary School of the University of Chicago will sooner or later find its way into the pages of this journal, but contributions from other schools are earnestly solicited provided only that these contributions set forth in clear perspective actual practices and sifted results. The time for mere inspirational reading in education is over. Facts are what we need. This journal stands for empiricism in education, for clear statement of practices and very little speculation; for systematic, detailed expositions of course of study rather than pious hopes for educational reform.

BOOK REVIEWS

Attention and Interest. A Study in Psychology and Education. By FELIX ARNOLD, PH.D. MacMillan, 1910. Pp. 272.

This book discusses attention from its objective and psychological aspects, interest from the ideal point of view, and education from the standpoint of attention and interest in the schoolroom. The author does not uphold any special theory or school but "attempts to clarify and arrange the many facts that have been brought to light by numerous experiments in the psychological laboratories." A bibliography accompanies the topics treated.

From a methodological viewpoint the exposition of the subject-matter of each chapter is treated under the categories of description, illustration, development, explanation, and definition.

After briefly outlining in general a point of view in psychology the writer discusses the real, the ideal, and the possible. Illustrations are given to show the development of these aspects of experience and an explanation of the "subject-object relationship" is offered. This furnishes the material for discussion in the first chapter.

Attention is defined as "a process of sensori-motor control which tends to increase the clearness and distinctness of the given field." The second chapter treats of the characteristic changes found in (1) clearness and distinctness, (2) persistence, (3) fluctuation, (4) unity, and (5) facilitation and arrest which are conditioned by simplicity or complexity, pleasure-pain, quality of impressions, time, age, preadjustment, reinforcement, practice, fatigue, pause, hunger, obstructed breathing, weak-mindedness, and extraneous stimulation.

All of these topics are treated with brevity and in a few instances upon meager experimental evidence, as, for example, the conclusions on "weak-mindedness" rest entirely upon Reis's experiments on six paralytics, eight hebephreniacs, and two normal subjects. The many interesting and conflicting experiments which have been made on *intensity* in the field of attention are simply dismissed on the basis of being "discussions of a hair-splitting variety."

Under the heading "illustrations" simple tests are given to accompany each of the above-listed phases of the general problem. In "development" there is a gradual change in the field under fixation from indistinctness and obscurity to distinctness and clearness; from childhood and adolescence to adult life there is a gradual increase in sustained attention. The biological and psychological "explanation" of these phenomena is to be found in the effort the organism puts forth "to further the production of distinctness in the essential aspect of any background."

Chap. iii discusses the psychological and chap. iv the physiological phases of attention in more detail. In the former it is assumed that ideas exist as psychic dispositions, since "the impression is lifted into the focus of consciousness and held there by ideal traces and dispositions." There may be fusion, assimilation, and complication, free ideas or deliberate revival which may or may not be accompanied by intense feelings of strain and effort. Illustrations and simple tests are appended to this chapter and it contains a brief discussion of the development of voluntary attention.

From a physiological standpoint it is noted that there are organic changes in respiration, vasoconstriction, and circulation, while the sensory changes involve accommodation, fixation, and motor diffusion, innervation, control, and fatigue. For an explanation of attention we must study the organic changes which are probably necessary whenever effort becomes localized; the sensory adjustment, which gives fixation and clearness; and the motor attitude, which gives meaning.

Chaps. vi and vii are devoted to interest and chap. viii to a recapitulation. We are urged to look at interest as "an attitude taken toward a situation, and characterized (1) by motor tendencies and feelings of expectation, anticipation, and strain, (2) by meaning implicit in the situation or by free images and ideas, and (3) by a reference of attitude and ideal content to some future condition of the self." The impelling aspect is always due to interest, the controlling to attention.

Part III consists of the final chapters, ix and x, on attention and interest in the schoolroom. These chapters, which contain suggestive material, are least satisfactory on account of the brevity of treatment, the occasional lack of direct correlation with the previous chapters, and the somewhat hortatory manner in which the material is presented. The teacher is too often told what he *should* do without a knowledge of the rational and experimental basis on which the advice is given.

Some of the keynotes of the advice in these chapters are: Each child should be permitted to react toward a situation in a sensori-motor manner. For example, in the primary work in arithmetic the child should be busy measuring desks, books, etc., under the teacher's guidance. Other suggestions for work in arithmetic are given, as well as for teaching spelling, reading, geography, history, nature-study, and grammar.

The instruction and discipline should be arranged in such a manner that whatever the pupil does ends in pleasure. Instinctive tendencies are to be developed into definite interests. The teacher must use positive interests, show signs of approval and disapproval of the child's work, emphasize self-activity, offer opportunities for imitation, make appeals through various senses.

From the teacher's standpoint value would have been added to this book if the author had given more suggestions on how children's interests vary at different stages of growth, how dormant interests may be awakened, and how sustained attention may be developed.

Bird T. Baldwin

The University of Chicago

CURRENT EDUCATIONAL LITERATURE IN THE PERIODICALS[1]

IRENE WARREN
Librarian, School of Education, The University of Chicago

Alan, John S. Law in school and state. Educa. 30:509–11. (Ap. '10.)

Bailey, Henry Turner. Elementary schools as a factor in industrial education. Man. Train. Mag. 11:297–301. (Ap. '10.)

Balliet, Thomas M. Interest as related to education. Amer. Educa. 13: 355–56. (Ap. '10.)

———. Undergraduate instruction in pedagogy. Pedgog. Sem. 17:63–69. (Mr. '10.)

Barber, W. T. A. John Wesley's ideas on education. Journ. of Educa. (Lond.) 41:277–78. (Ap. '10.)

Bennett, Charles A. Visiting manual training schools in Europe—IV. Man. Train. Mag. 11:345–65. (Ap. '10.)

Bullard, R. L. Education in Cuba. Educa. R. 39:378–84. (Ap. '10.)

Burgerstein, Leo. Co-education and hygiene with special reference to European experience and views. Pedagog. Sem. 17:1–15. (Mr. '10.)

———. The main problems of schoolroom sanitation and school work. Pedagog. Sem. 17:16–28. (Mr. '10.)

———. Some remarks on the relations of body and mind. Pedagog. Sem. 17:29–39. (Mr. '10.)

Clippenger, Walter G. Some vitalizing aspects of modern education. Relig. Educa. 5:67–78. (Ap. '10.)

Cooper, Clayton Sedgwick. College men and the Bible. A great awakening among the students of America. Cent. 80:145–51. (My. '10.)

Crafts, H. A. A railway school for farmers. Sci. Amer. 102:356–57. (30 Ap. '10.)

[1] Abbreviations.—Amer. Educa., American Education; Cent., Century Magazine; Educa., Education; Educa. R., Educational Review; El. School T., Elementary School Teacher; Good Housekeep., Good Housekeeping; Journ. of Educa. (Bost.), Journal of Education (Boston); Journ. of Educa. (Lond.), Journal of Education (London); Journ. of Geog., Journal of Geography; Kind-Prim. Mag., The Kindergarten-Primary Magazine; Kind. R., Kindergarten Review; Lib. Journ., Library Journal; Man. Train. Mag., Manual Training Magazine; New Eng. Mag., New England Magazine; Out., Outlook; Pedagog. Sem., Pedagogical Seminary; Pop. Educa., Popular Educator; Relig. Educa., Religious Education; School W., School World; Sci. Amer., Scientific American; Teach. Coll. Rec., Teachers College Record; West. Journ. of Educa., Western Journal of Education.

DEAN, ARTHUR D. Industrial education. Amer. Educa. 13:348–50. (Ap. '10.)

DEWEY, JOHN. Science as subject-matter and as method.—(I.) Journ. of Educa. (Bost.) 71:395–96. (14 Ap. '10.)

———. Science as subject-matter and as method.—(II.) Journ. of Educa. (Bost.) 71:427–28. (21 Ap. '10.)

DODGE, RICHARD ELWOOD. Report of committee on geography for secondary schools. Journ. of Geog. 8:159–65. (Mr. '10.)

DRAPER, MIRIAM S. The children's museum in Brooklyn. Lib. Journ. 35: 149–54. (Ap. '10.)

EARLE, E. LYELL. The international congress at Brussels. Kind. Prim. Mag. 22:265–67. (My. '10.)

ELSON, WILLIAM H., AND BACHMAN, FRANK P. Different courses for elementary schools. Educa. R. 39:357–64. (Ap. '10.)

FLEMING, D. J. Education through social helpfulness. Relig. Educa. 5: 79–82. (Ap. '10.)

(The) French schools debate. Journ. of Educa. (Lond.) 51:239–40. (Ap. '10.)

GODDARD, HENRY H. Research in school hygiene in the light of experiences in an institution for the feeble minded. Pedagog. Sem. 17:51–53. Mr. '10.)

GYMER, ROSINA C. Juvenile court and Cleveland Public Library. Lib. Journ. 35:159–60. (Ap. '10.)

HARDING, B. F. Secondary education. Educa. 30:500–508. (Ap. '10.)

HARRIS, RACHEL D. Work with children at the colored branch of the Louisville Free Public Library. Lib. Journ. 35:160–61. (Ap. '10.)

HERBERT, CLARA W. Juvenile court library in Washington, D.C. Lib. Journ. 35:159. (Ap. '10.)

HILLIS, ANNIE P. The serious note in the education of women. Out. 94: 851–55. (Ap. '10.)

HOLMES, JESSE H. The public school and the church. Relig. Educa. 5: 37–45. (Ap. '10.)

JONES, LEWIS H. Education as growth. West. Journ. of Educa. 3:119–29. (Mr. '10.)

KINMAN, G. W. Superannuation and pensions in small schools. Journ. of Educa. (Lond.) 41:237–38. (Ap. '10.)

KIRKWOOD, EDITH BROWN. Home science in Illinois. Good Housekeep. 50: 602–9. (My. '10.)

LAUTNER, JOHN E. State industrial education in Massachusetts. West. Journ. of Educa. 3:97–118. (Mr. '10.)

LINDSEY, BEN B. Childhood and morality. Address delivered at the general session of the N.E.A., Denver, Colo., July 8. Kind. R. 20:129–42. (N. '09.)

LODGE, THORNTON H. Vocational subjects in the secondary school. Educa. R. 39:333-41. (Ap. '10.)

MANNY, FRANK A. The kindergarten and after. Kind. R. 20:525-30. (My. '10.)

MAPLES, E. W. The rating of schools. School W. 12:121-23. (Ap. '10.)

MARKS, JEANNETTE. The crowded hours of the college girl. New Eng. Mag. 42:204-7. (Ap. '10.)

MASON, DANIEL GREGORY. The college man and music. Out. 94:808-10. (9 Ap. '10.)

MEAD, EDWIN D. Proposed removal of the Academy of Geneva to America in 1794. Educa. R. 39:365-77. (Ap. '10.)

MOFFATT, JAMES D. Debt of the nation to the denominational college. Relig. Educa. 5:46-51. (Ap. '10.)

MONROE, PAUL. Opportunity and need for research work in the history of education. Pedagog. Sem. 17:54-62. (Mr. '10.)

MOORE, ANNIE CARROLL. Work with children from institutions for the deaf and dumb. Lib. Journ. 35:158-59. (Ap. '10.)

NEARING, SCOTT. Child labor and the child. Educa. 30:494-99. (Ap. '10.)

ORMROD, H. NORA. The humanities for children of eight to nine years. Journ. of Educa. (Lond.) 41:275-77. (Ap. '10.)

O'SHEA, M. V. Waste in memory work. Pop. Educa. 27:449-51. (My. '10.)

PHILLIPS, C. A. The development of methods in teaching modern elementary geography. El. School T. 10:427-39. (My. '10.)

REESE, CARA. Cincinnati schools. Good Housekeep. 50:610-15. (My. '10.)

SARGENT, WALTER. The fine and industrial arts in elementary schools, grade VII. El. School T. 10:415-26. (My. '10.)

SCHOFIELD, J. Holiday camps for secondary schools. School W. 12:123-27. (Ap. '10.)

SHERWOOD, HERBERT FRANCIS. Children of the land. Out. 94:891-901. (23 Ap. '10.)

SNEDDEN, DAVID. The movement for vocational education and its probable effects on liberal education—II. Amer. Educa. 13:300-304. (Mr. '10.)

STEVENS, W. F. Use of the library by foreigners as shown by the Carnegie Library of Homestead, Pa. Lib. Journ. 35:161-62. (Ap. '10.)

STOREY, THOMAS A. The responsibilities of the training school for teachers in matters of hygiene. Pedagog. Sem. 17:40-43. (Mr. '10.)

STRAUS, ESTHER. Critical moments in the children's room. Lib. Journ. 35:147-49. (Ap. '10.)

THORNDIKE, EDWARD L. Handwriting. Teach. Coll. Rec. 11:1-93. (Mr. '10.)

———. Repeaters in the upper grammar grades. El. School T. 10:409-14. (My. '10.)

Underhill, Ethel P. Crumbs of comfort to the children's librarian. Lib. Journ. 35:155–57. (Ap. '10.)

Whipple, Guy Montrose. The instruction of teachers in school hygiene. Pedagog. Sem. 17:44–50. (Mr. '10.)

Winship, A. E. Teachers College, Columbia University. Journ. of Educa. (Bost.) 71:425–27. (21 Ap. '10.)

Wood, Dr. Thomas D. Rural school sanitation. Amer. Educa. 13:351–54. (Ap. '10.)

The Elementary School Teacher

June, 1910

Vol. X, No. 10

THE UNIVERSITY OF CHICAGO PRESS
CHICAGO AND NEW YORK
OTTO HARRASSOWITZ, LEIPZIG

The Elementary School Teacher

PUBLISHED MONTHLY EXCEPT IN JULY AND AUGUST

EDITED BY

THE FACULTY OF THE SCHOOL OF EDUCATION

WITH THE CO-OPERATION OF

THE FACULTY OF THE FRANCIS W. PARKER SCHOOL

Vol. X CONTENTS FOR JUNE, 1910 No. 10

The Elementary School Teacher is published monthly from September to June. ¶The subscription price is $1.50 per year; the price of single copies is 20 cents. ¶Postage is prepaid by the publishers on all orders from the United States, Mexico, Cuba, Porto Rico, Panama Canal Zone, Republic of Panama, Hawaiian Islands, Philippine Islands, Guam, Tutuila (Samoa), Shanghai. ¶Postage is charged extra as follows: For Canada, 30 cents on annual subscriptions (total $1.80), on single copies, 3 cents (total 23 cents); for all other countries in the Postal Union, 46 cents on annual subscriptions (total $1.96), on single copies, 6 cents (total 26 cents). ¶Remittances should be made payable to The University of Chicago Press, and should be in Chicago or New York exchange, postal or express money order. If local check is used, 10 cents must be added for collection.

Otto Harrassowitz, Querstrasse 14, Leipzig, Germany, has been appointed agent for the European continent and is authorized to quote the following prices: Yearly subscriptions, including postage, M.8.25 each; single copies, including postage, M.1.10 each.

Claims for missing numbers should be made within the month following the regular month of publication. The publishers expect to supply missing numbers free only when they have been lost in transit.

Business correspondence should be addressed to The University of Chicago Press, Chicago, Ill.

Communications for the editors should be addressed to them at The University of Chicago, Chicago, Ill.

Entered October 12, 1903, at the Post-Office at Chicago, Ill., as second-class matter, under Act of Congress March 3, 1879

EDUCATION WITH REFERENCE TO SEX

EIGHTH YEARBOOK OF THE NATIONAL SOCIETY FOR THE SCIENTIFIC STUDY OF EDUCATION
By CHARLES RICHMOND HENDERSON

THIS study, which was made at the request of the Executive Committee of the Society, and published after their critical examination, and upon the approval of three medical advisers who have read it, is divided into two parts. The first part is chiefly medical and economic, and seeks to prove the necessity for social control of some kind.

This argument demonstrates the necessity for education with reference to sex—the theme of the second part of the work. In this part is found a careful discussion of educational aims, the scope of educational activities, the co-operating agencies in education, the care of infancy, personal hygiene and training, the influence of ideal interests, the principles of formal instruction in relation to sex—its necessity, difficulties and methods.

Part I, 75 pages, 8vo, paper; net 75c, postpaid 78c
Part II, 100 pages; net 75c, postpaid 80c : : :

Address Dept. P.
The University of Chicago Press
CHICAGO NEW YORK

Before Deciding Where to Attend School
SEND FOR CATALOG OF
Valparaiso University
(Accredited) Valparaiso, Indiana
One of the Largest Universities and Training Schools in the United States

25 Departments **Excellent Equipments**
187 Instructors **School the Entire Year**

Students may enter at any time and select their studies from any, or from many, of the following departments:

Preparatory, Teacher's, Kindergarten, Primary, Pedagogy, Manual Training, Scientific, Classical, Higher English, Civil Engineering, German, French, Spanish, Italian, Law, Pharmacy, Medical, Dental, Elocution and Oratory, Music, Fine Art, Commercial, Penmanship, Phonography and Typewriting, Review.

The Expenses Are Made So Low that anyone can meet them. **Tuition, $18 per quarter of 12 weeks.** Board and furnished room, **$1.70 to $2.75 per week.**
Catalog giving full particulars mailed free. Address,
H. B. BROWN, President, or O. P. KINSEY, Vice-President.
CALENDAR for 1910-11:—*Thirty-Eighth Year will open September 20, 1910; Second Term, December 13, 1910; Third Term, March 7, 1911; Fourth Term, May 30, 1911.* 5

If you do not receive our advertising matter regularly, ask to be put on our mailing list.
THE UNIVERSITY OF CHICAGO PRESS

NEW METHODS. **Methods of Sunday-school instruction are undergoing a rapid transformation.**
CONSTRUCTIVE BIBLE STUDIES.
A set of textbooks for those who wish to do systematic work in the Sunday school. Write today for circulars and specimen pages.
ADDRESS DEPT. P
THE UNIVERSITY OF CHICAGO PRESS
CHICAGO AND NEW YORK

The Clark Teachers' Agency

Has among its clients the VERY FIRST educational institutions. September vacancies at salaries up to $3,000 in Colleges and Public and Private Schools. **21st Year. B. F. Clark, Prop. Chicago,** Steinway Hall. **Spokane, Wash.,** 225 Peyton Blk.

The James F. McCullough Teachers' Agency

A Successful School and College Bureau

All calls for teachers direct from school authorities. Positive personal recommendations. Competent teachers in demand. Registration fee $1.00. WRITE US. 9 JACKSON BOULEVARD, CHICAGO

Prof. Genung
English

HOME STUDY COURSES
Over one hundred Home Study Courses under professors in Harvard, Brown, Cornell, and leading colleges.
Academic and Preparatory, Agricultural, Commercial, Normal and Civil Service Departments.
Preparation for College, Teachers' and Civil Service Examinations.
250 page catalogue free. Write to-day.
The Home Correspondence School
Dept. 250. SPRINGFIELD, MASS. 12

THE H. R. HUNTTING CO.
SPRINGFIELD, MASS.
MAKE A SPECIALTY OF
SECOND-HAND, OUT OF PRINT AND RARE BOOKS
CATALOGUES ISSUED CORRESPONDENCE SOLICITED

PRINCIPLES AND IDEALS FOR THE SUNDAY SCHOOL

By Ernest D. Burton and Shailer Mathews
208 pp., 8vo., cloth, *net*, $1.00; postpaid, $1.11

THE authors point out how the Sunday School may be made a religious school in which shall prevail the same pedagogical principles that obtain in the day schools. The *Philadelphia Press* said: "Undoubtedly this is the most thoughtful and best considered book of Sunday-School methods that has yet been published." *You* should have a copy.

AT ALL BOOKSELLERS OR DIRECT FROM
THE UNIVERSITY OF CHICAGO PRESS
CHICAGO and NEW YORK

NORMAL COLLEGE OF THE NORTH AMERICAN GYMNASTIC UNION

415-419 E. MICHIGAN ST. :: INDIANAPOLIS, IND.

Offers high school graduates two-year and four-year courses leading to certification as teacher of physical training and to academic title and degree. Summer session 1910 held at Madison, Wis., during summer session of University of Wisconsin. College year 1910–1911 begins Sept. 19. Write for illustrated catalogue.

The Normal College conducts a Physical Training Teachers' Bureau; registration restricted to graduates (1866–1910). 5

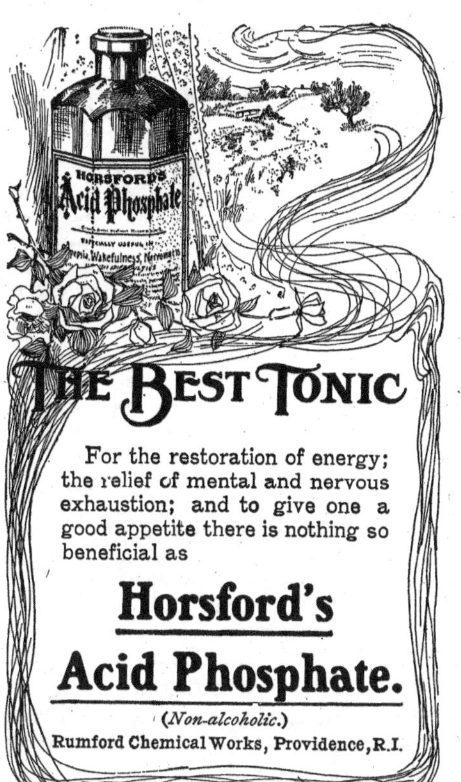
HORSFORD'S
Acid Phosphate

No 2
L. C. SMITH & BROS. TYPEWRITER CO.
No 2

In the
wake
of MENNEN'S

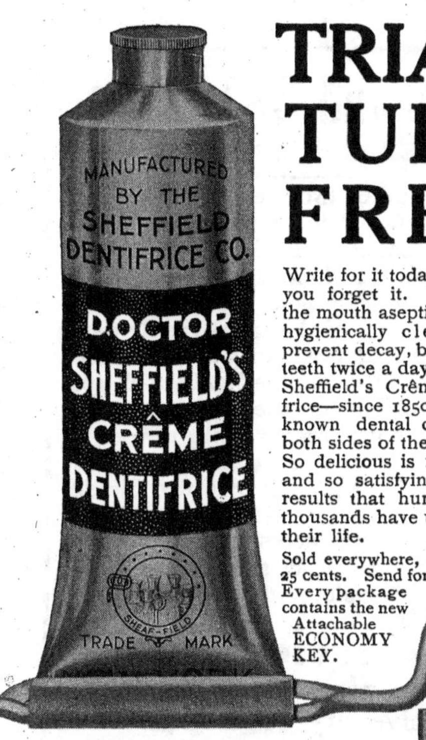

TRIAL TUBE FREE

Write for it today—before you forget it. To keep the mouth aseptically and hygienically clean and prevent decay, brush your teeth twice a day with Dr. Sheffield's Crême Dentifrice—since 1850 the best known dental cream on both sides of the Atlantic. So delicious is its flavor, and so satisfying are its results that hundreds of thousands have used it all their life.

Sold everywhere, or by mail 25 cents. Send for trial tube. Every package contains the new Attachable ECONOMY KEY.

The Sheffield Dentifrice Co.
Box 12 New London, Conn. U. S. A.

Modern Constitutions

By WALTER FAIRLEIGH DODD, Ph.D.

Two vols., 750 pages, 8vo, cloth; net, $5.00; postpaid, $5.42

THIS volume contains the texts, in English translation where English is not the original language, of the constitutions or fundamental laws of the Argentine nation, Australia, Austria-Hungary, Belgium, Brazil, Canada, Chile, Denmark, France, Germany, Italy, Japan, Mexico, Netherlands, Norway, Portugal, Russia, Spain, Sweden, Switzerland, and the United States. These constitutions have not heretofore been available in any one English collection, and a number of them have not before appeared in English translation.

Each constitution is preceded by a brief historical introduction, and is followed by a select list of the most important books dealing with the government of the country under consideration.

Address Dept. P.

The University of Chicago Press
CHICAGO NEW YORK

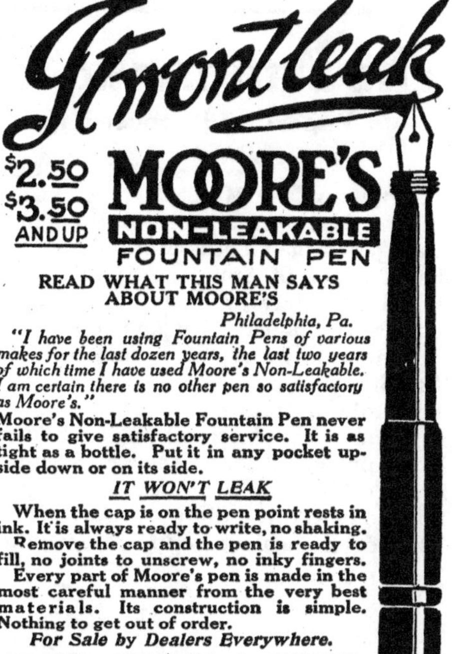

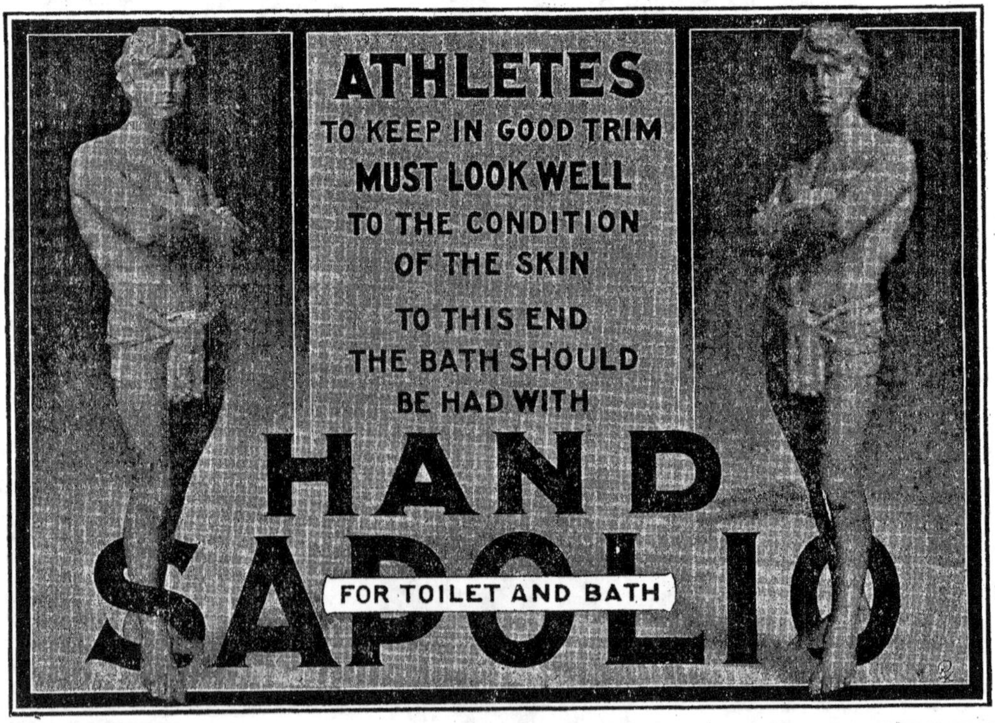

www.ingramcontent.com/pod-product-compliance
Lightning Source LLC
LaVergne TN
LVHW010522100826
845148LV00001B/71

* 9 7 8 1 4 2 5 5 7 3 7 6 8 *